GOLDEN KAMUY

Story and Art by Satoru Noda

26

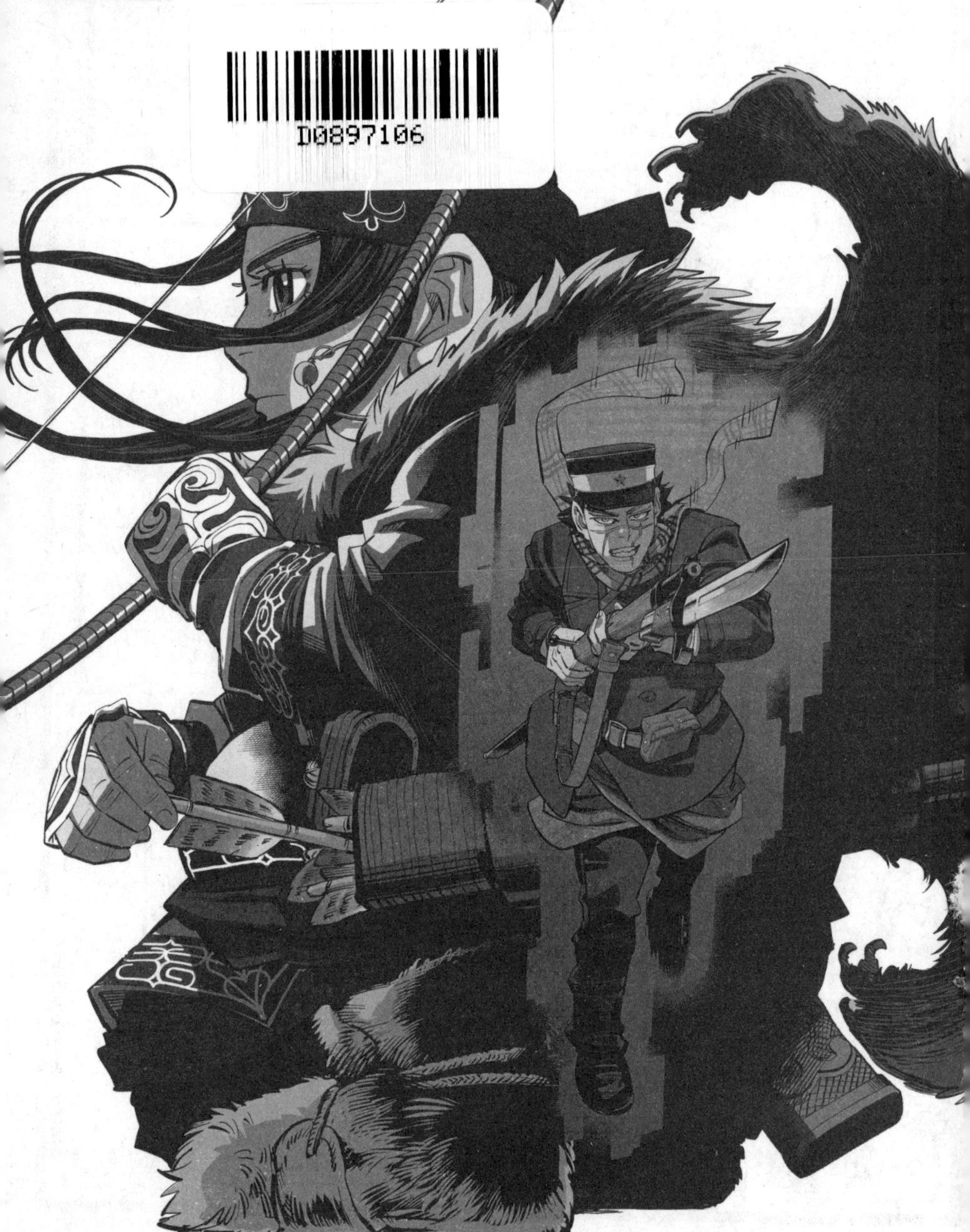

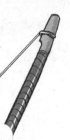

The Story So Far

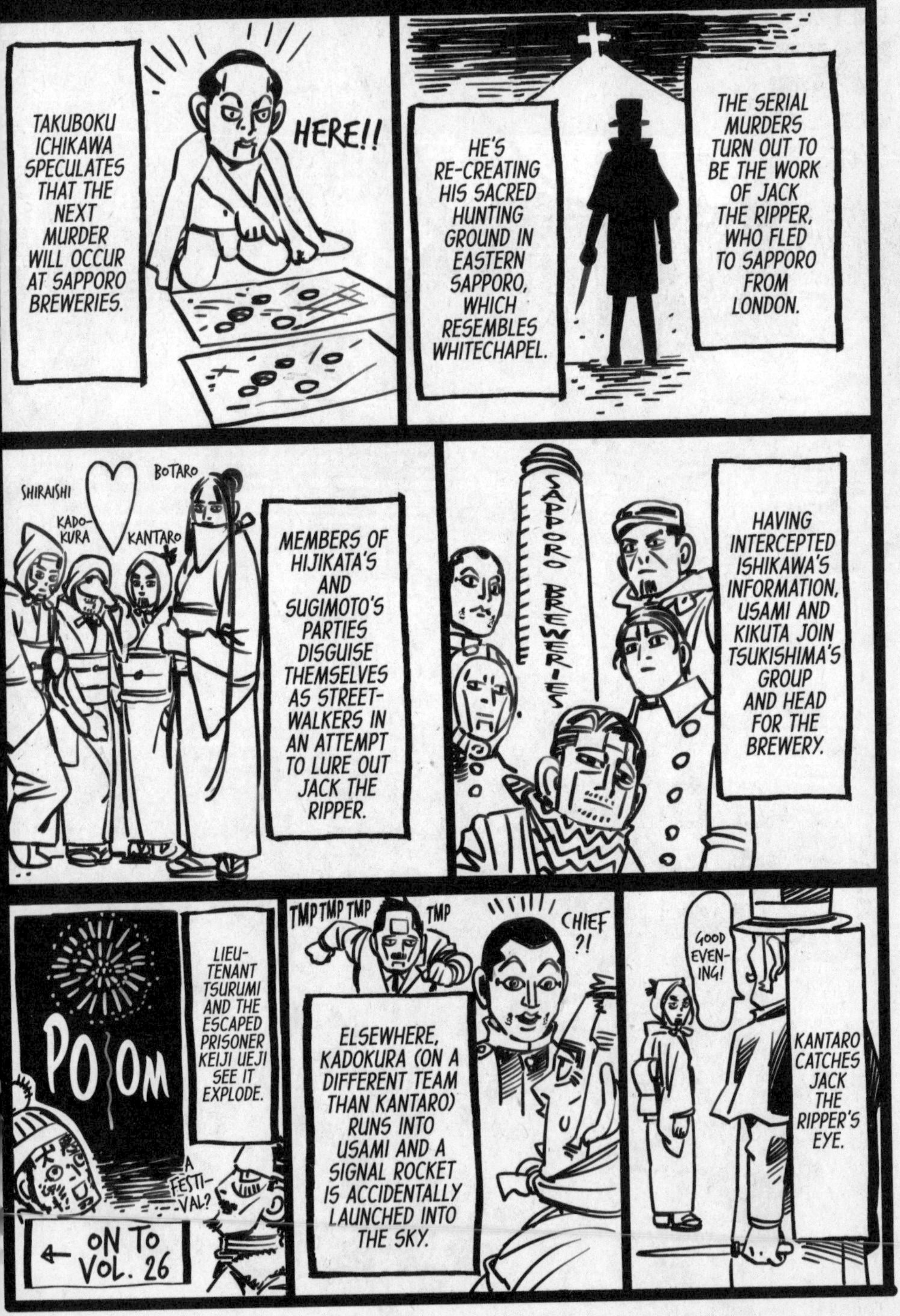
THE SERIAL MURDERS TURN OUT TO BE THE WORK OF JACK THE RIPPER, WHO FLED TO SAPPORO FROM LONDON.
HE'S RE-CREATING HIS SACRED HUNTING GROUND IN EASTERN SAPPORO, WHICH RESEMBLES WHITECHAPEL.
TAKUBOKU ICHIKAWA SPECULATES THAT THE NEXT MURDER WILL OCCUR AT SAPPORO BREWERIES.
HERE!!
HAVING INTERCEPTED ISHIKAWA'S INFORMATION, USAMI AND KIKUTA JOIN TSUKISHIMA'S GROUP AND HEAD FOR THE BREWERY.
SAPPORO BREWERIES
MEMBERS OF HIJIKATA'S AND SUGIMOTO'S PARTIES DISGUISE THEMSELVES AS STREET-WALKERS IN AN ATTEMPT TO LURE OUT JACK THE RIPPER.
BOTARO
KANTARO
KADO-KURA
SHIRAISHI
KANTARO CATCHES JACK THE RIPPER'S EYE.
GOOD EVEN-ING!
CHIEF ?!
TMP
TMP TMP TMP
ELSEWHERE, KADOKURA (ON A DIFFERENT TEAM THAN KANTARO) RUNS INTO USAMI AND A SIGNAL ROCKET IS ACCIDENTALLY LAUNCHED INTO THE SKY.
LIEU-TENANT TSURUMI AND THE ESCAPED PRISONER KEIJI UEJI SEE IT EXPLODE.
POOM
A FESTI-VAL?
ON TO VOL. 26

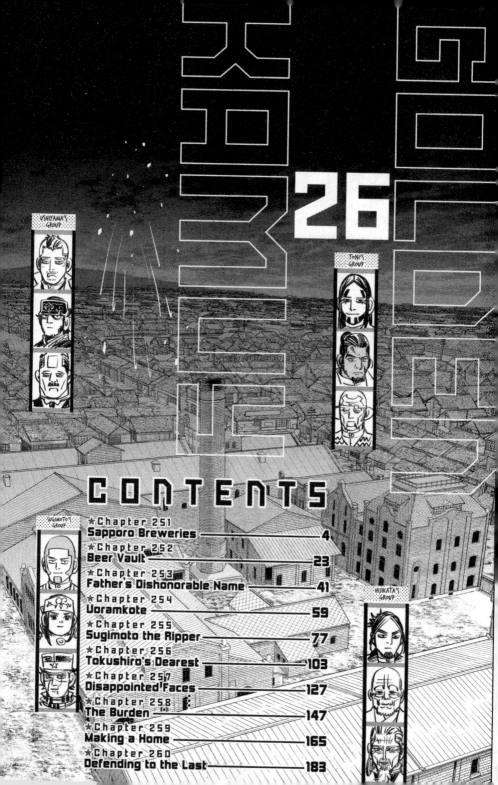

GOLDEN KAMUY

26

USHIYAMA'S GROUP

TONI'S GROUP

SUGIMOTO'S GROUP

HIJIKATA'S GROUP

CONTENTS

★Chapter 251
Sapporo Breweries ———————— 4

★Chapter 252
Beer Vault ———————————— 23

★Chapter 253
Father's Dishonorable Name ———— 41

★Chapter 254
Uoramkote ——————————— 59

★Chapter 255
Sugimoto the Ripper ——————— 77

★Chapter 256
Tokushiro's Dearest ——————— 103

★Chapter 257
Disappointed Faces ——————— 127

★Chapter 258
The Burden —————————— 147

★Chapter 259
Making a Home ———————— 165

★Chapter 260
Defending to the Last —————— 183

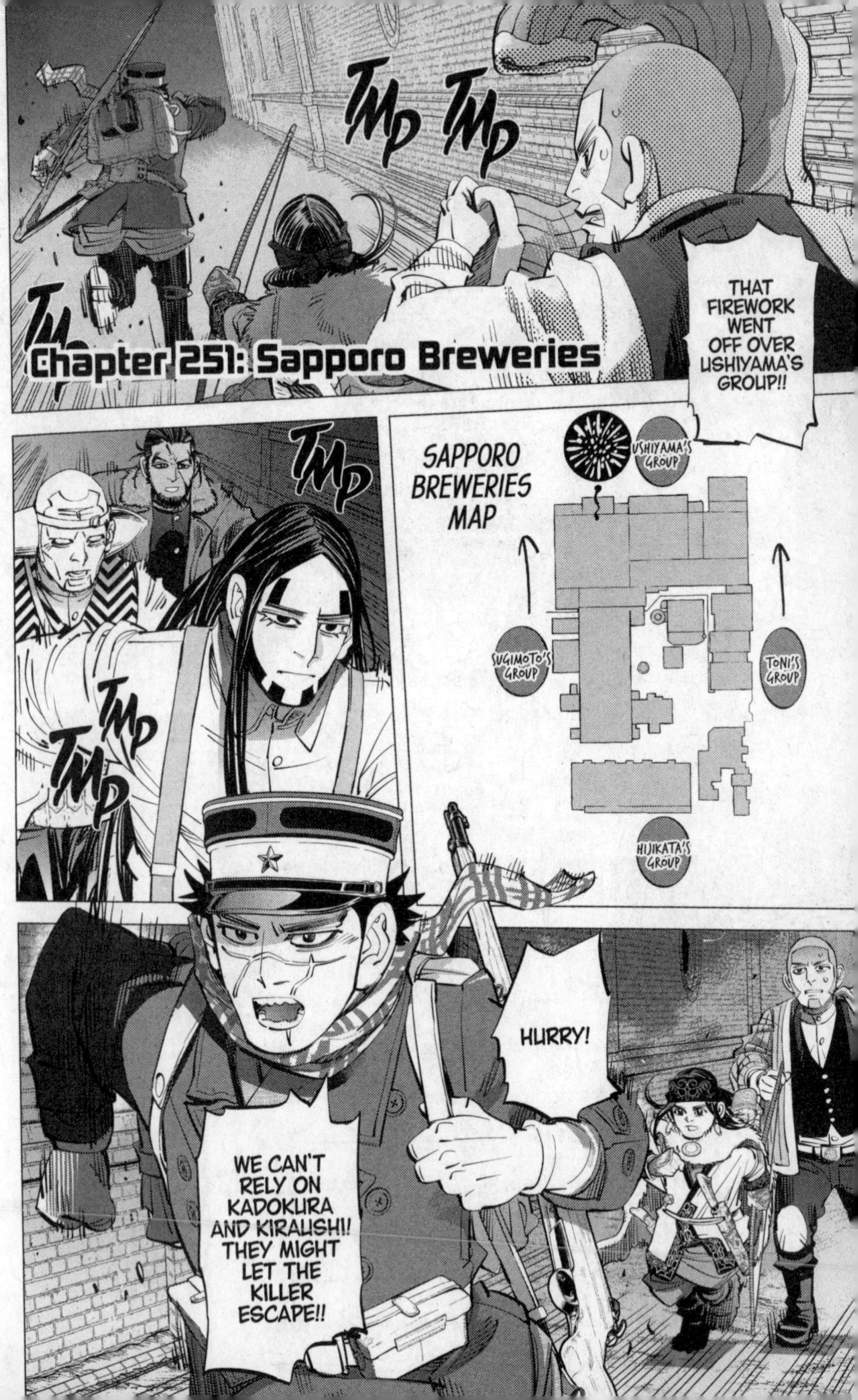
TMP TMP
THAT FIREWORK WENT OFF OVER USHIYAMA'S GROUP!!
Chapter 251: Sapporo Breweries
SAPPORO BREWERIES MAP
USHIYAMA'S GROUP
TONI'S GROUP
SUGIMOTO'S GROUP
HIJIKATA'S GROUP
TMP
TMP
TMP
HURRY!
WE CAN'T RELY ON KADOKURA AND KIRAUSHI!! THEY MIGHT LET THE KILLER ESCAPE!!

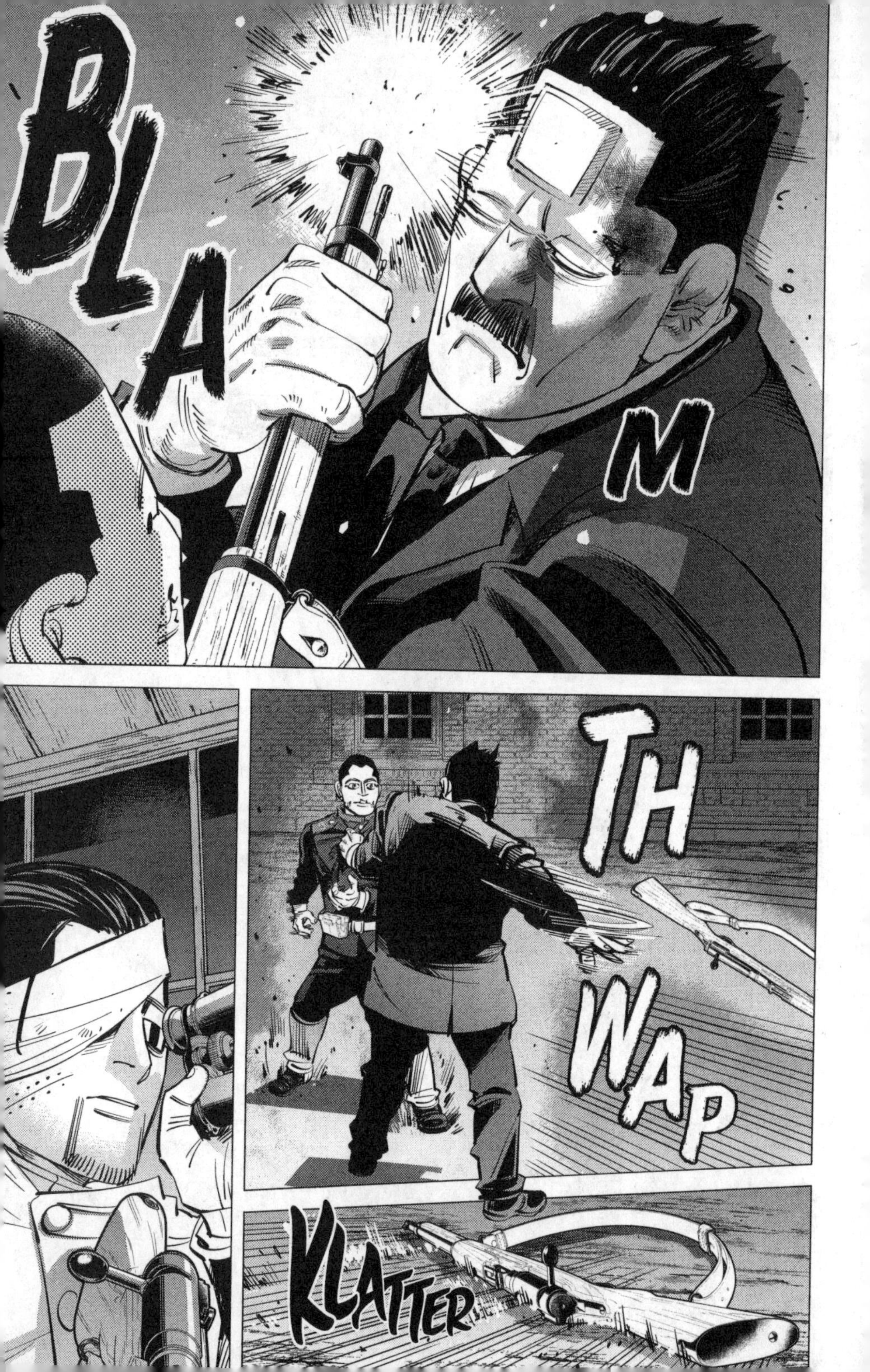
BLAM
THWAP
KLATTER

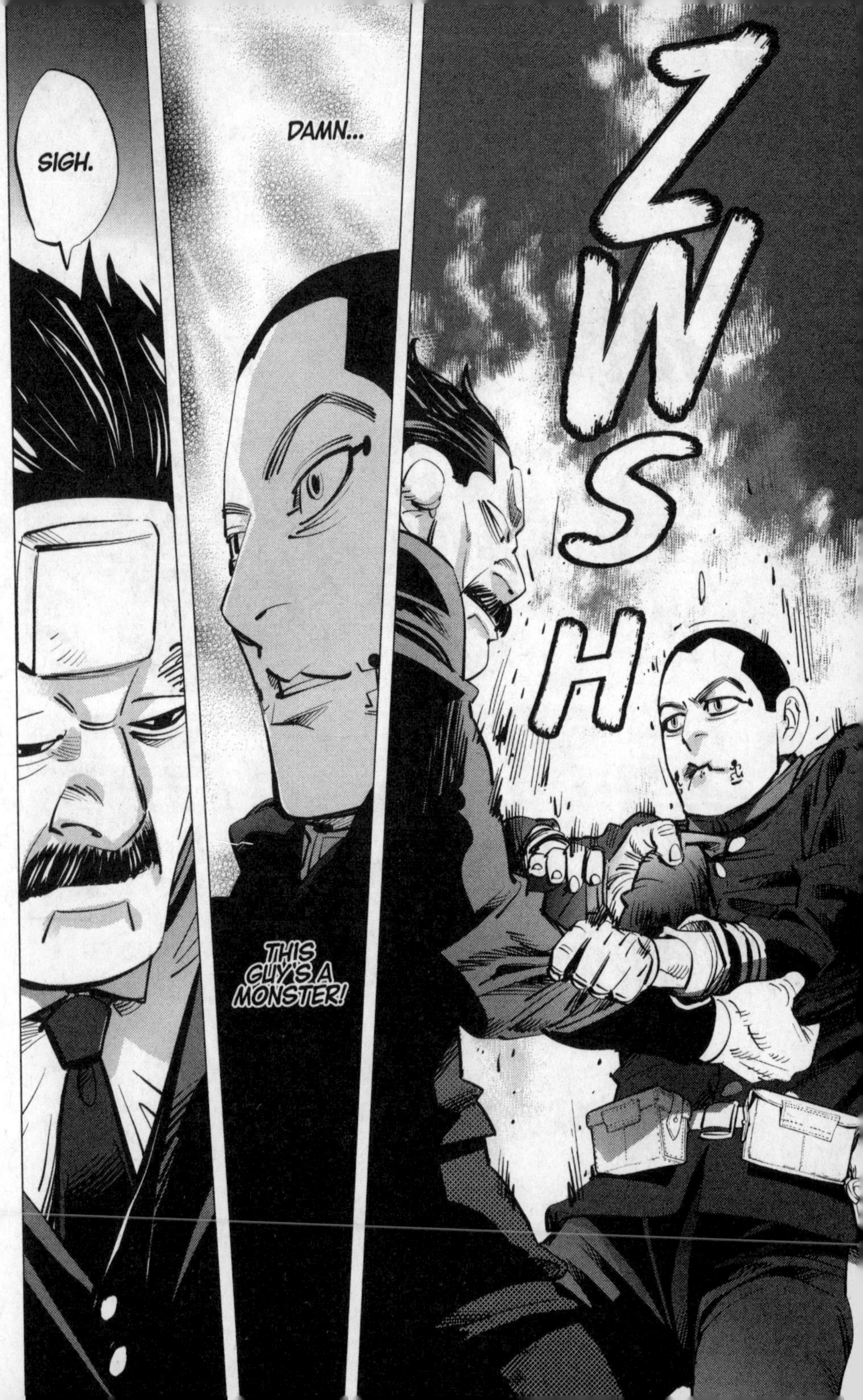
ZWSH
DAMN...
THIS GUY'S A MONSTER!
SIGH.

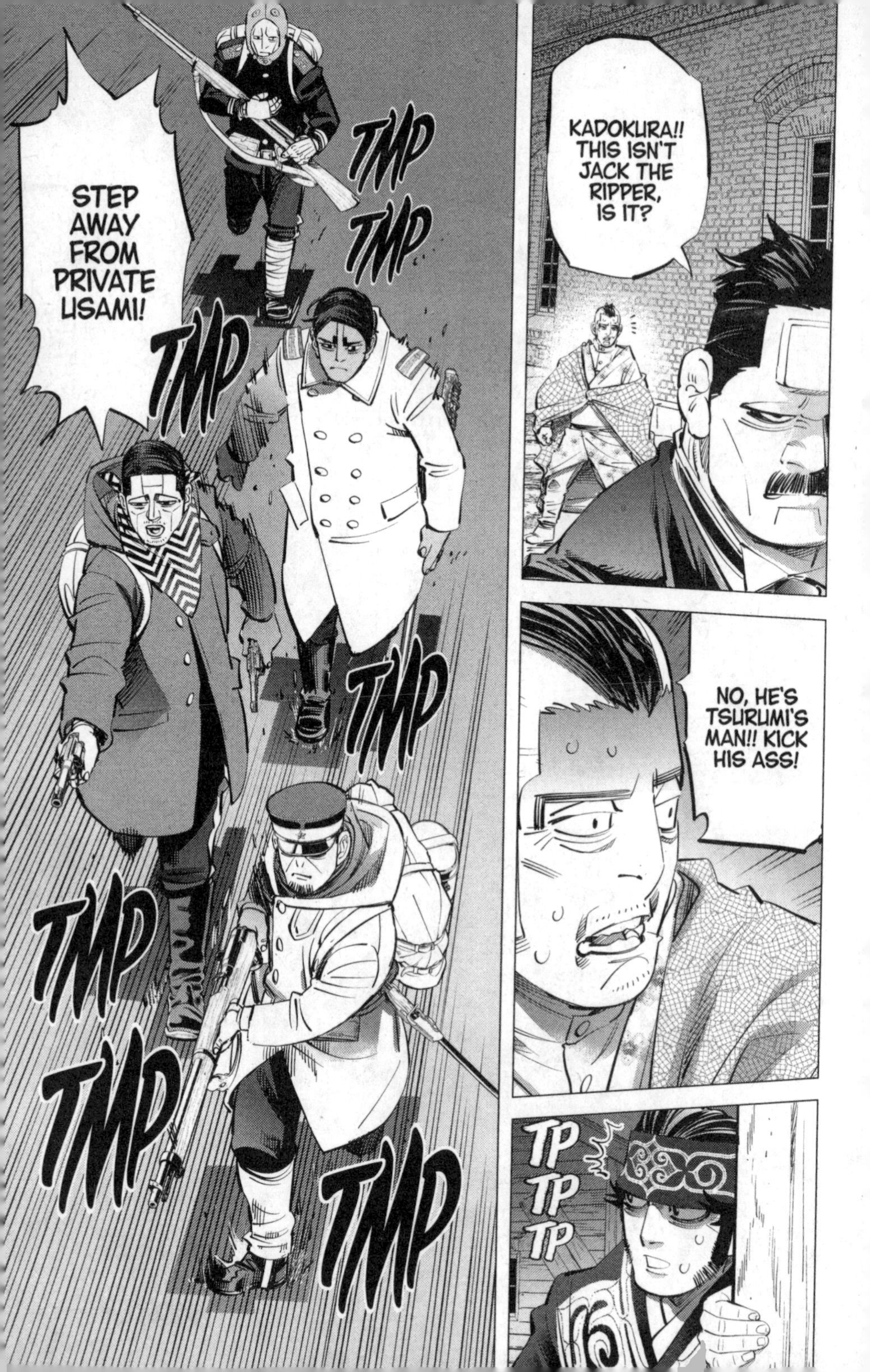
KADOKURA!! THIS ISN'T JACK THE RIPPER, IS IT?
NO, HE'S TSURUMI'S MAN!! KICK HIS ASS!
TP TP TP
STEP AWAY FROM PRIVATE USAMI!
TMP TMP
TMP
TMP
TMP
TMP
TMP

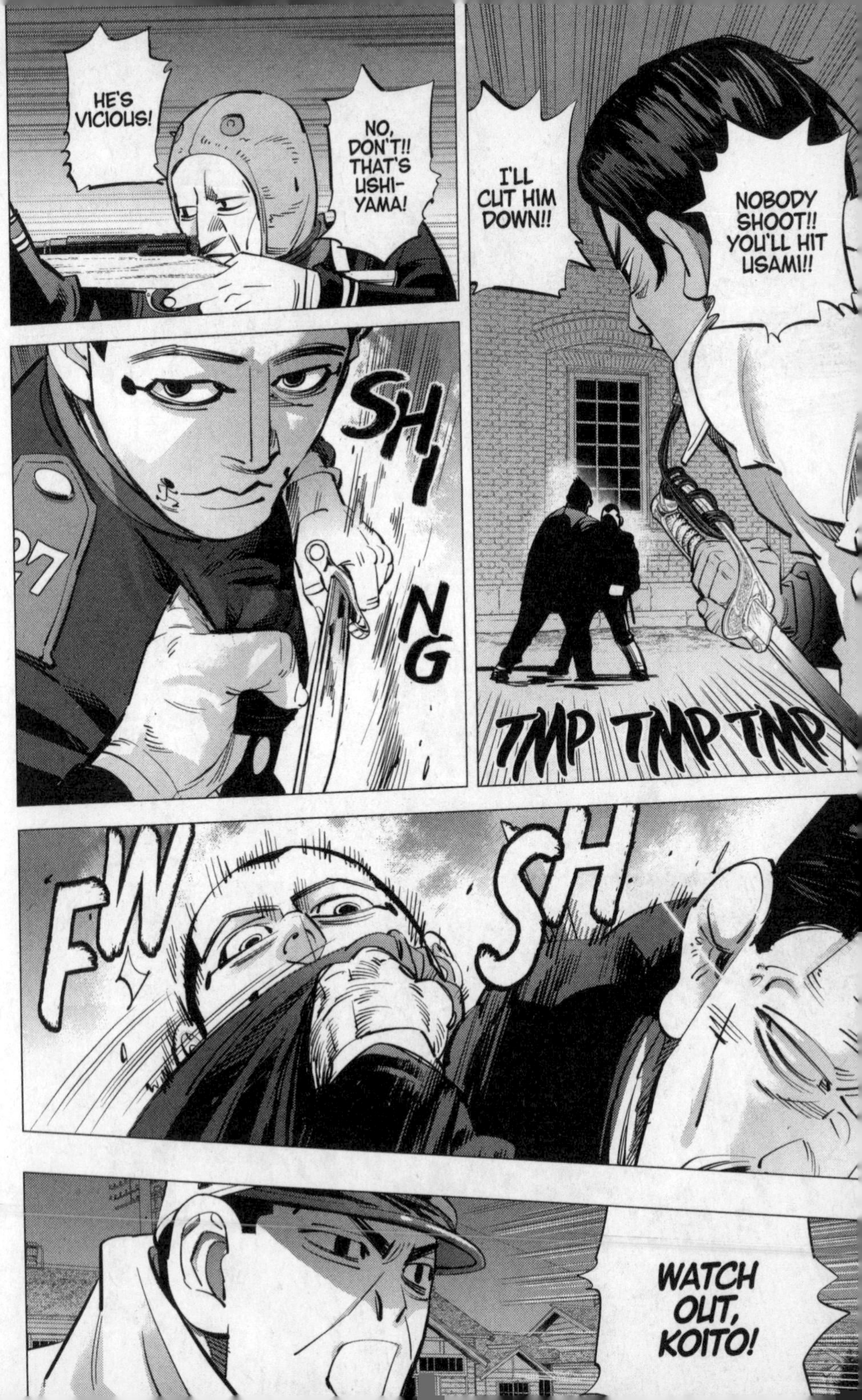
NOBODY SHOOT!! YOU'LL HIT USAMI!!
I'LL CUT HIM DOWN!!
NO, DON'T!! THAT'S USHI-YAMA!
HE'S VICIOUS!
TMP TMP TMP
SHING
FWSH
WATCH OUT, KOITO!

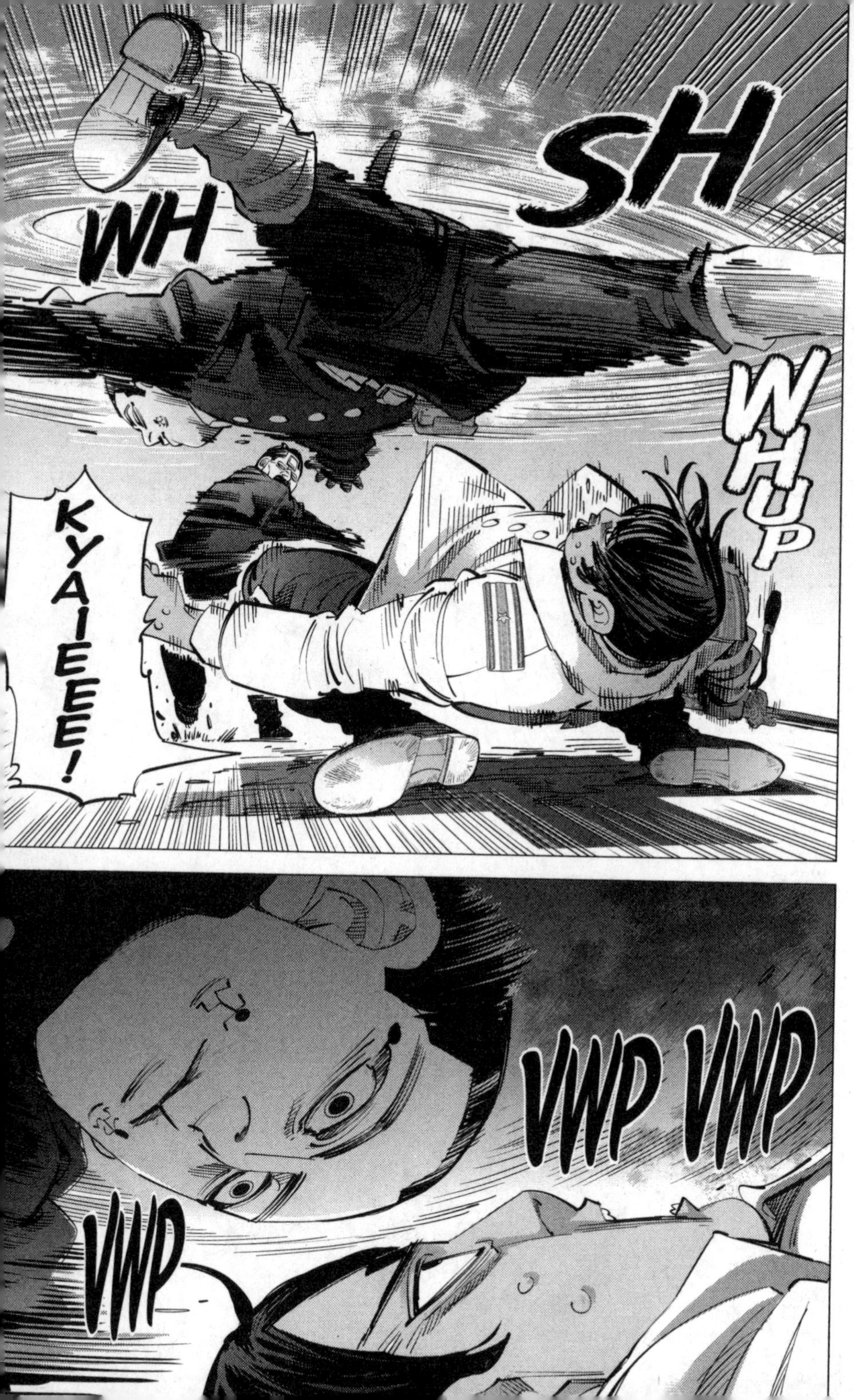
SH
WHUP
WH
KYAIEEE!
VWP VWP
VWP

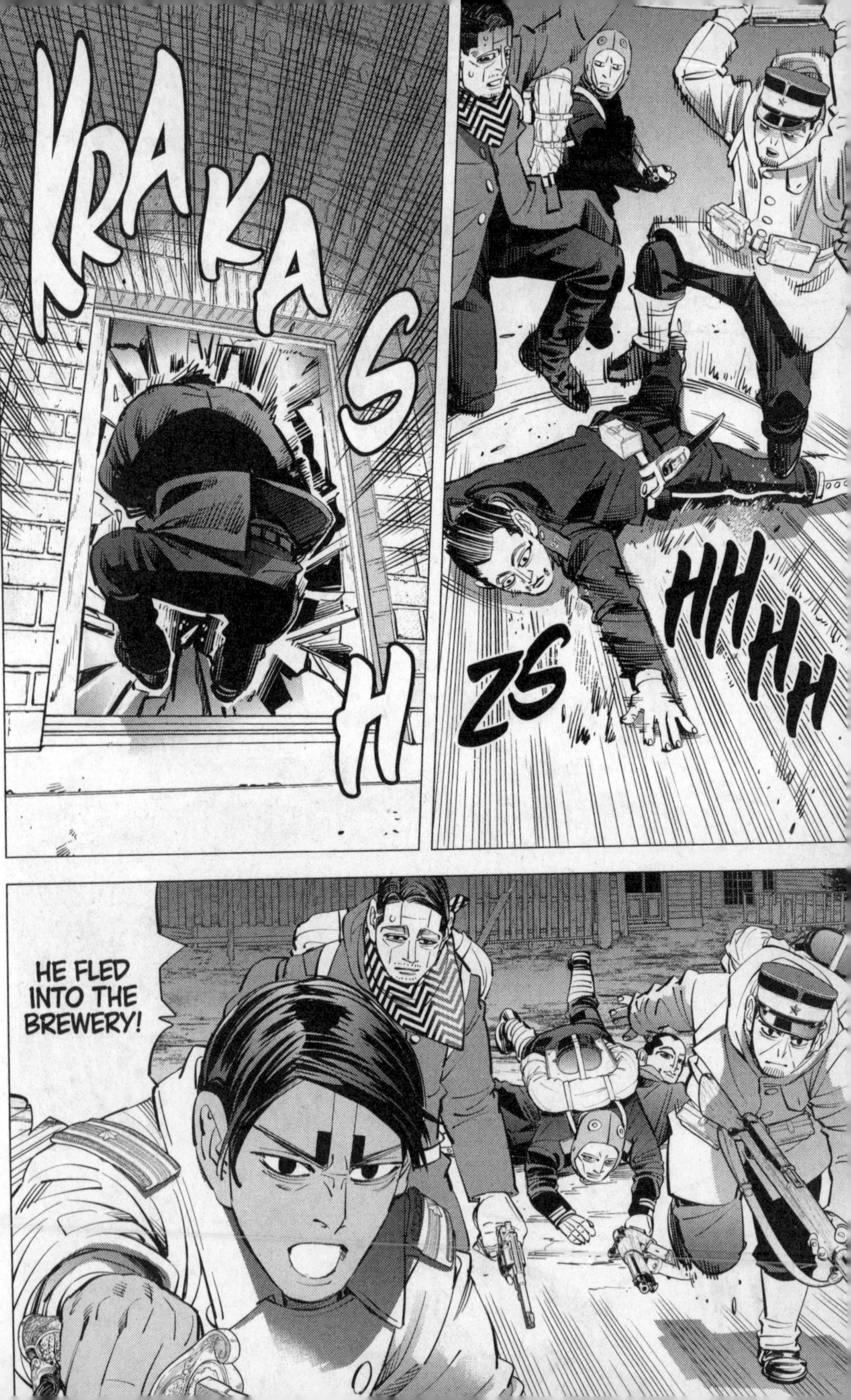
ZS
HHHHH
KRAKASH
HE FLED INTO THE BREWERY!

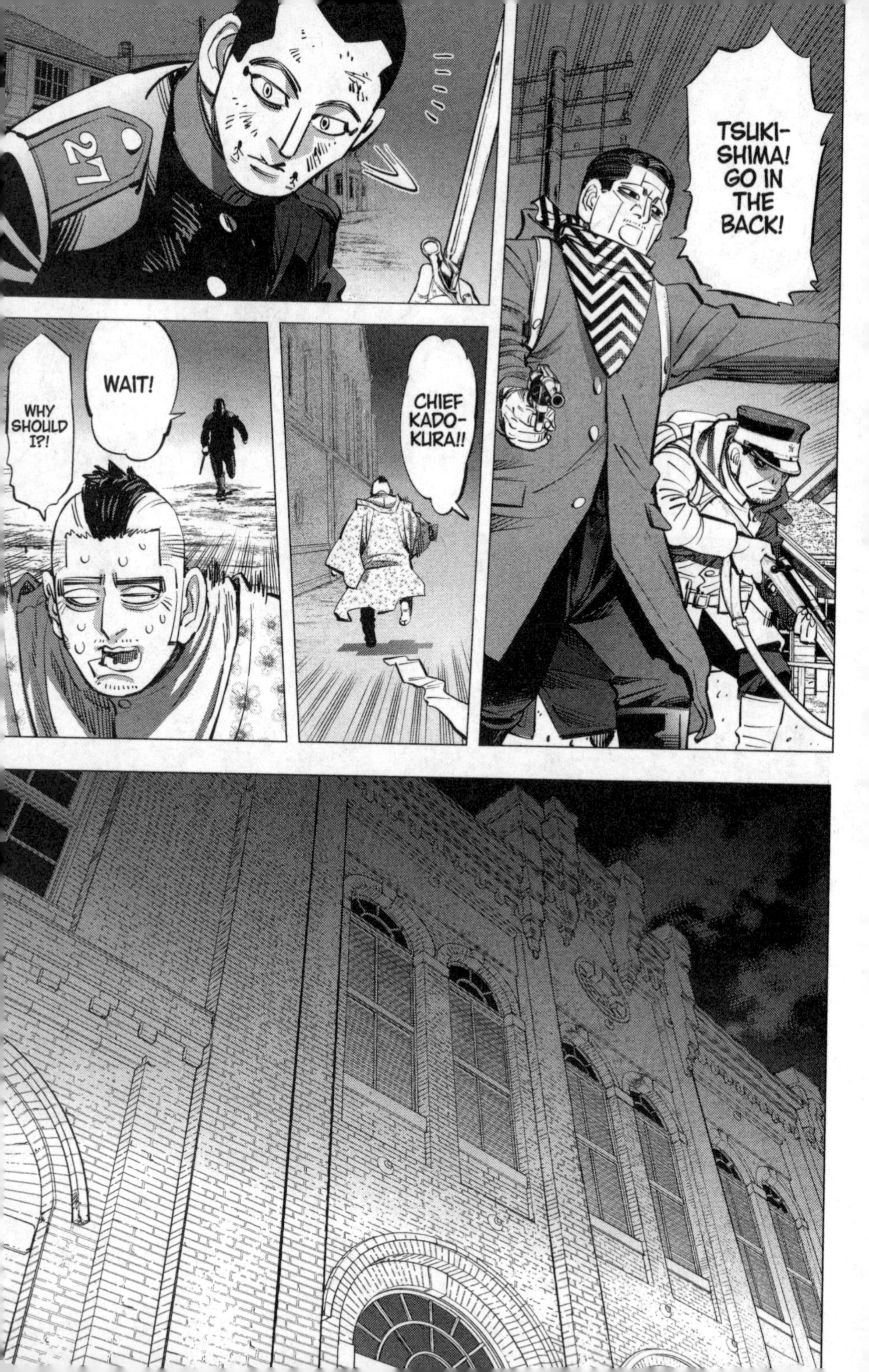
TSUKI-SHIMA! GO IN THE BACK!
CHIEF KADO-KURA!!
WAIT!
WHY SHOULD I?!

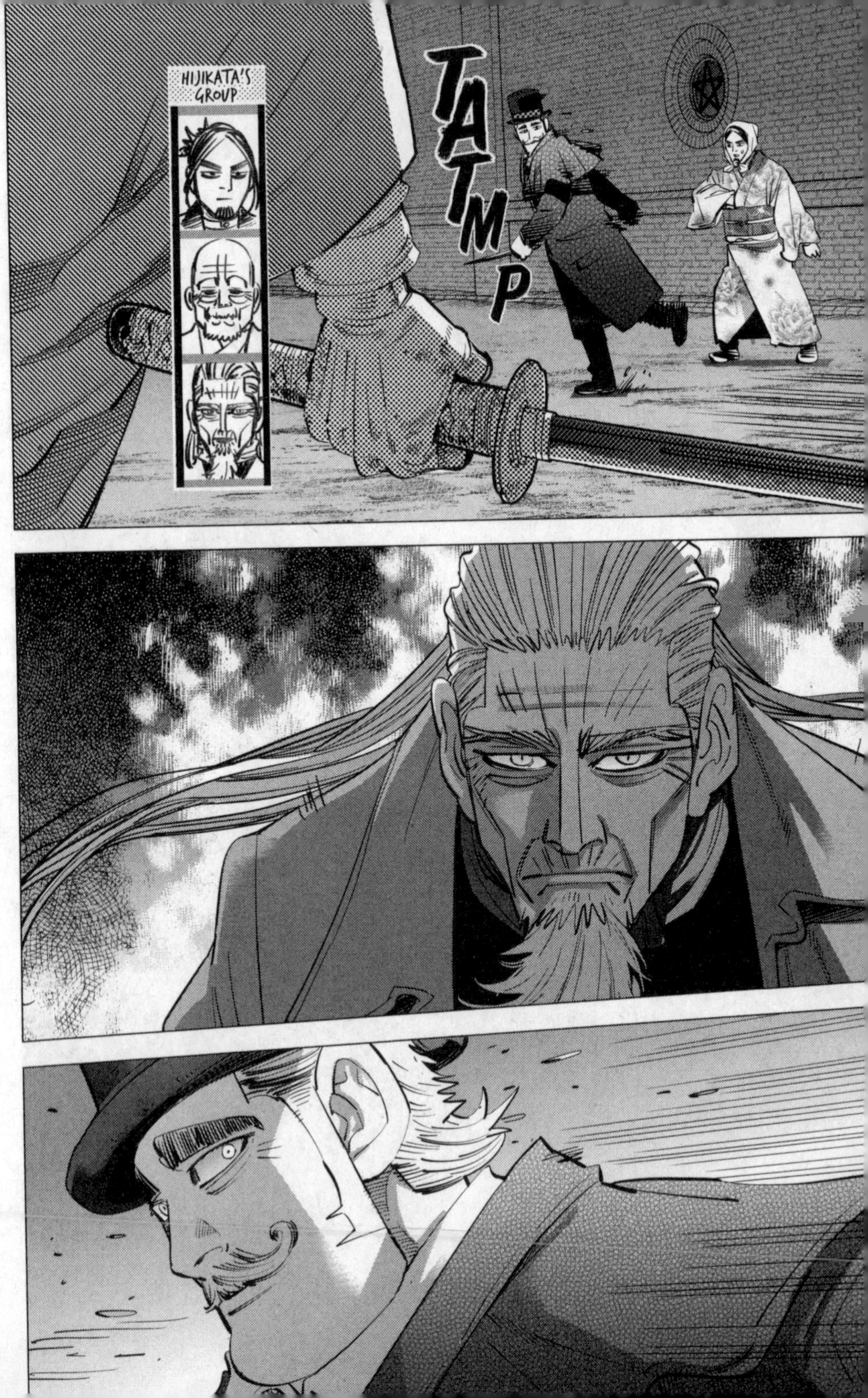
TATMP
HIJIKATA'S GROUP

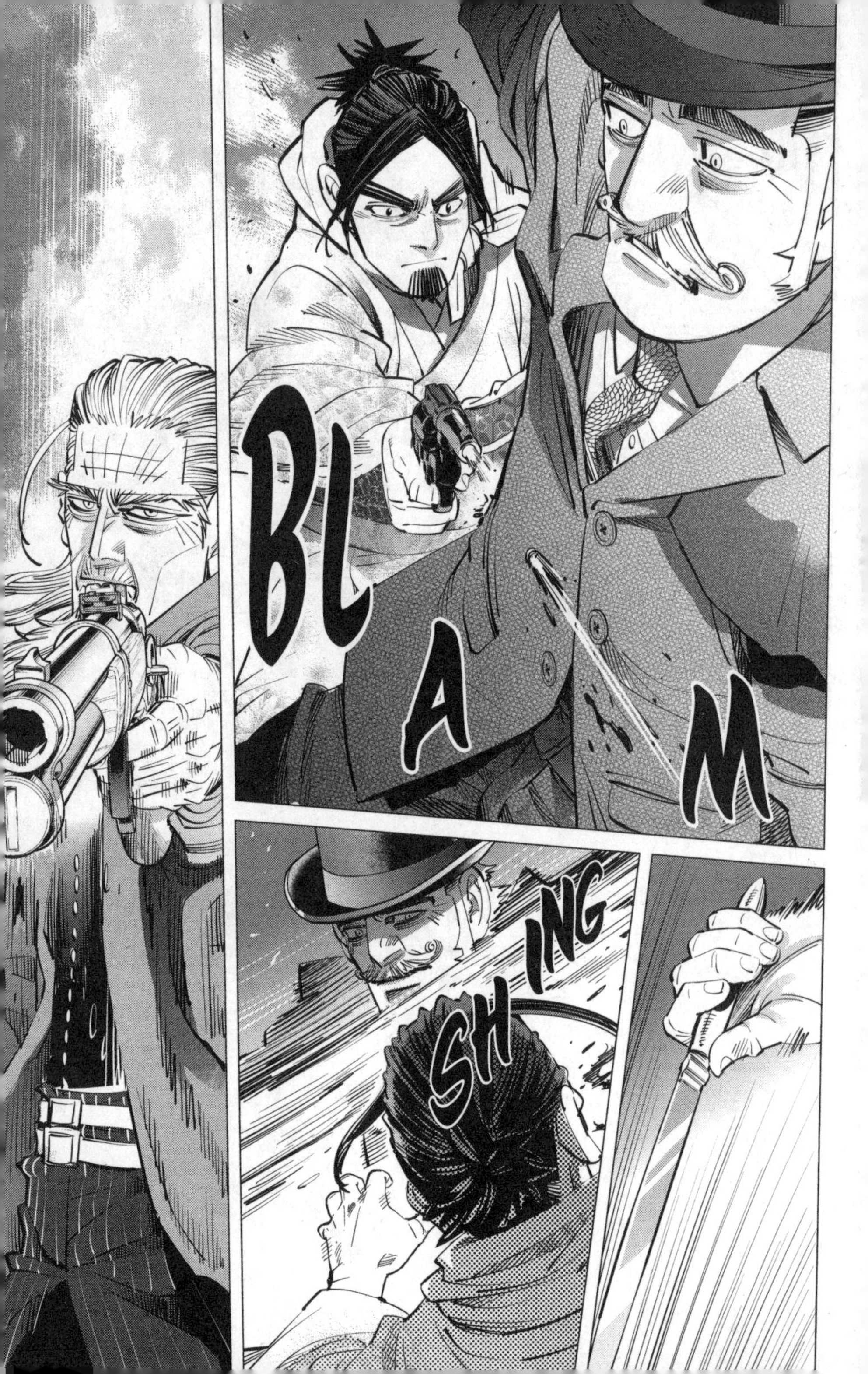
BLAM
SHING

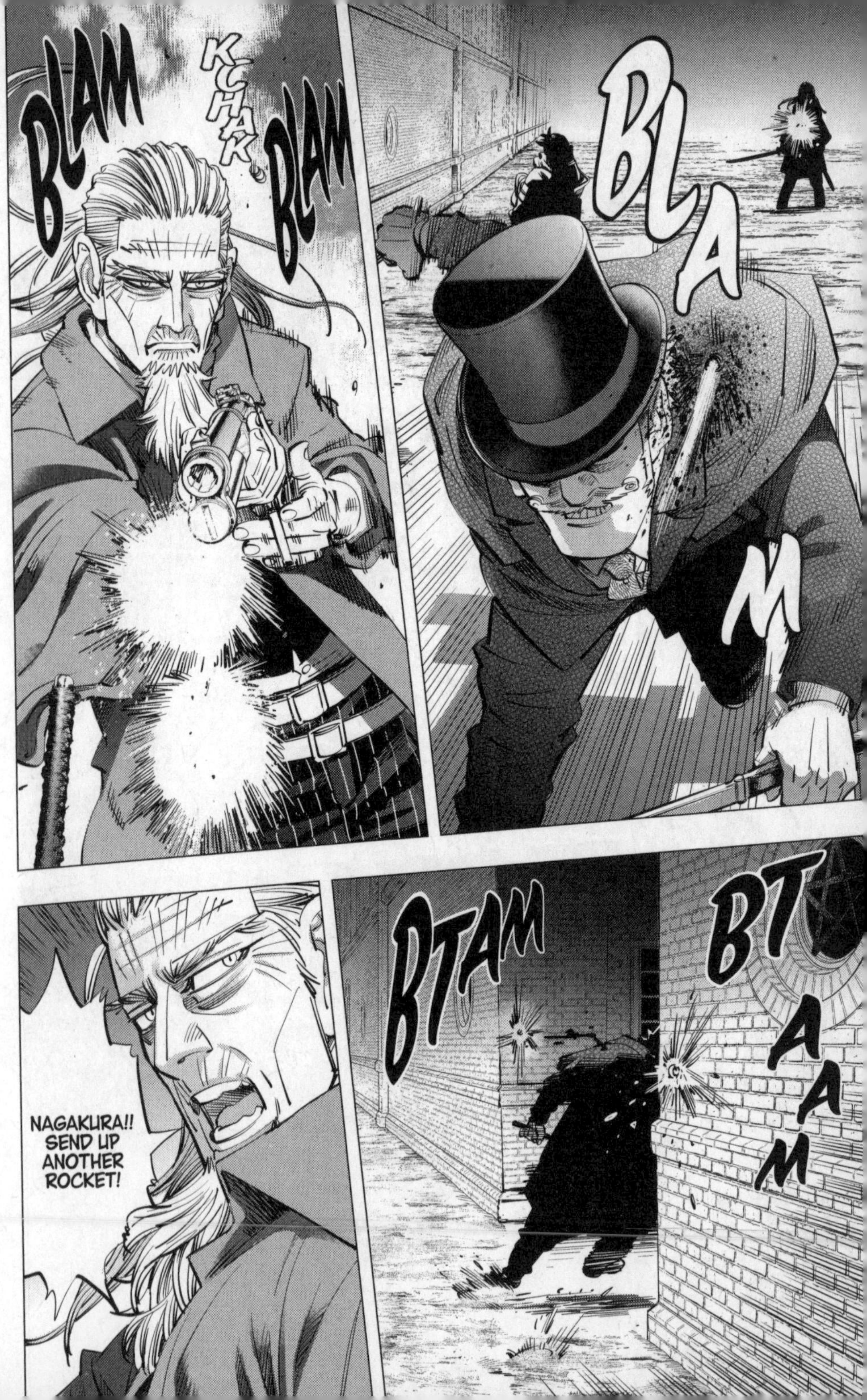
BLAM
BLAM
KCHAK
BLAM
BTAAM
BTAM
NAGAKURA!! SEND UP ANOTHER ROCKET!

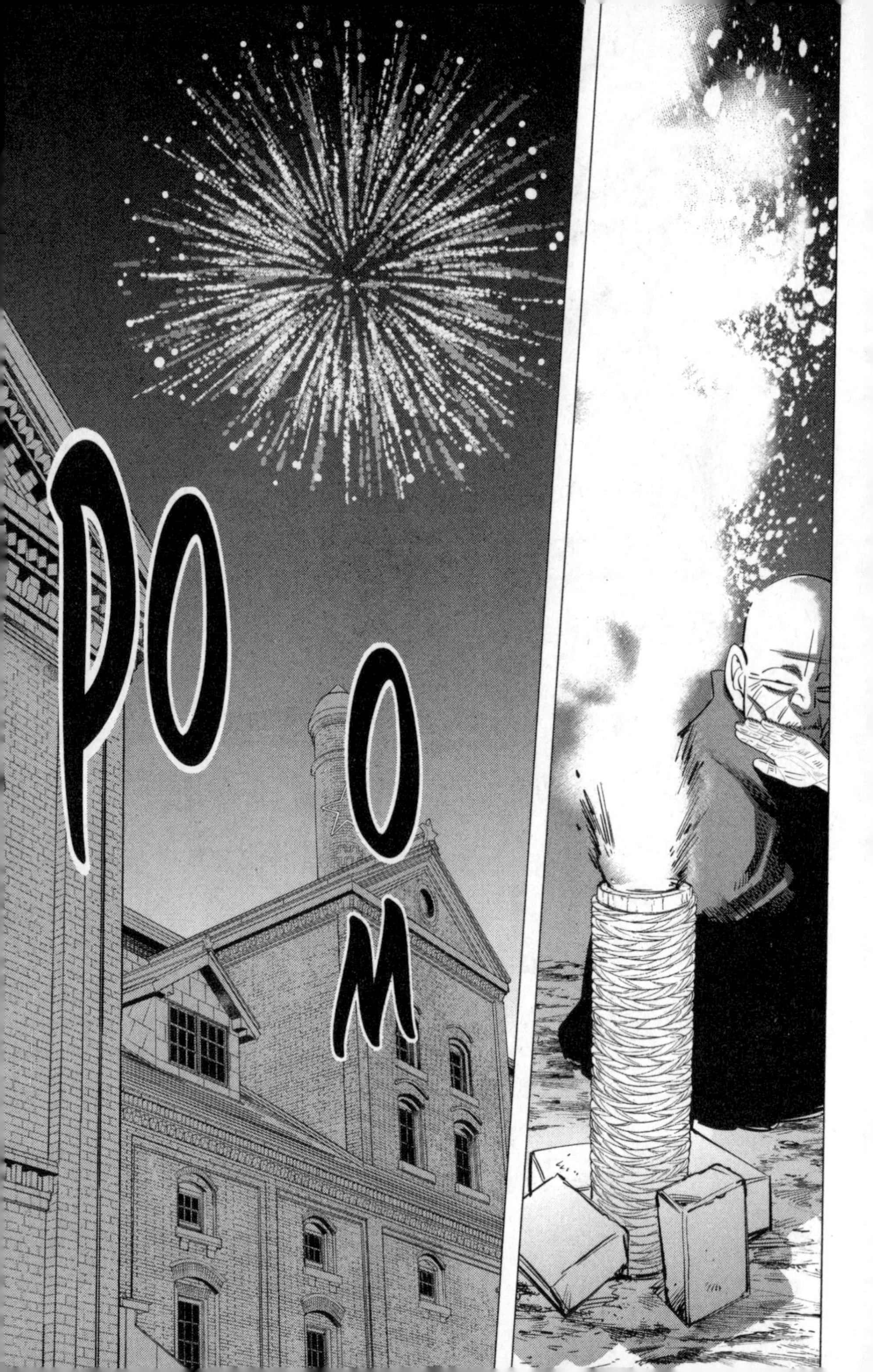
POOM

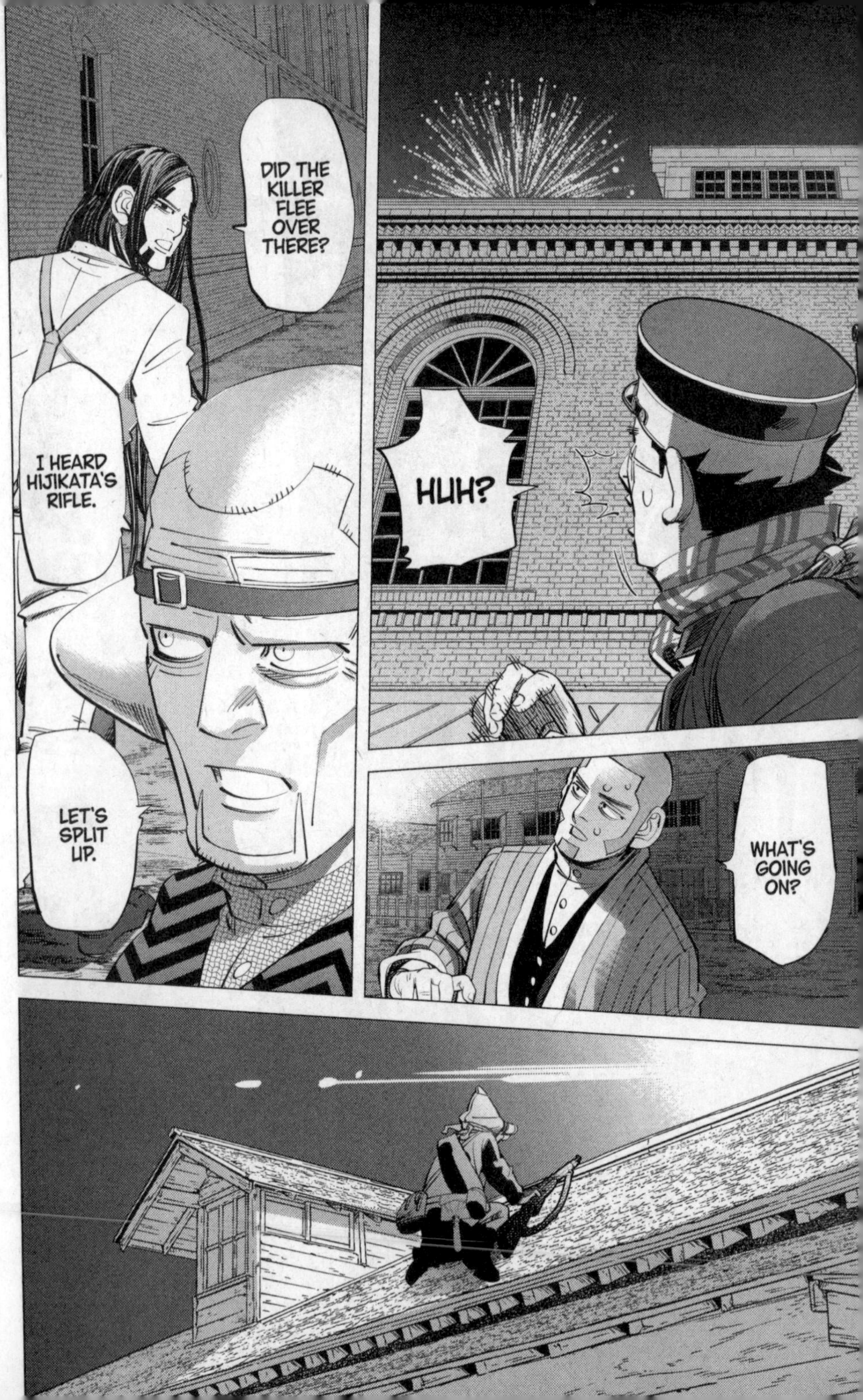
HUH?
WHAT'S GOING ON?
DID THE KILLER FLEE OVER THERE?
I HEARD HIJIKATA'S RIFLE.
LET'S SPLIT UP.

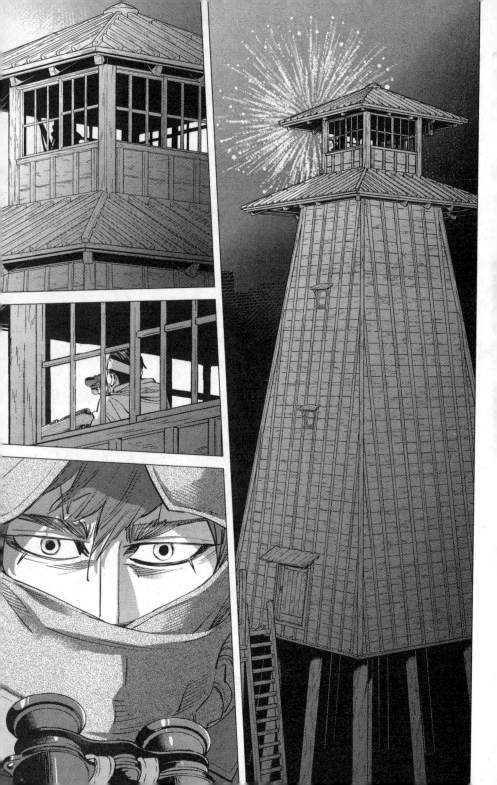

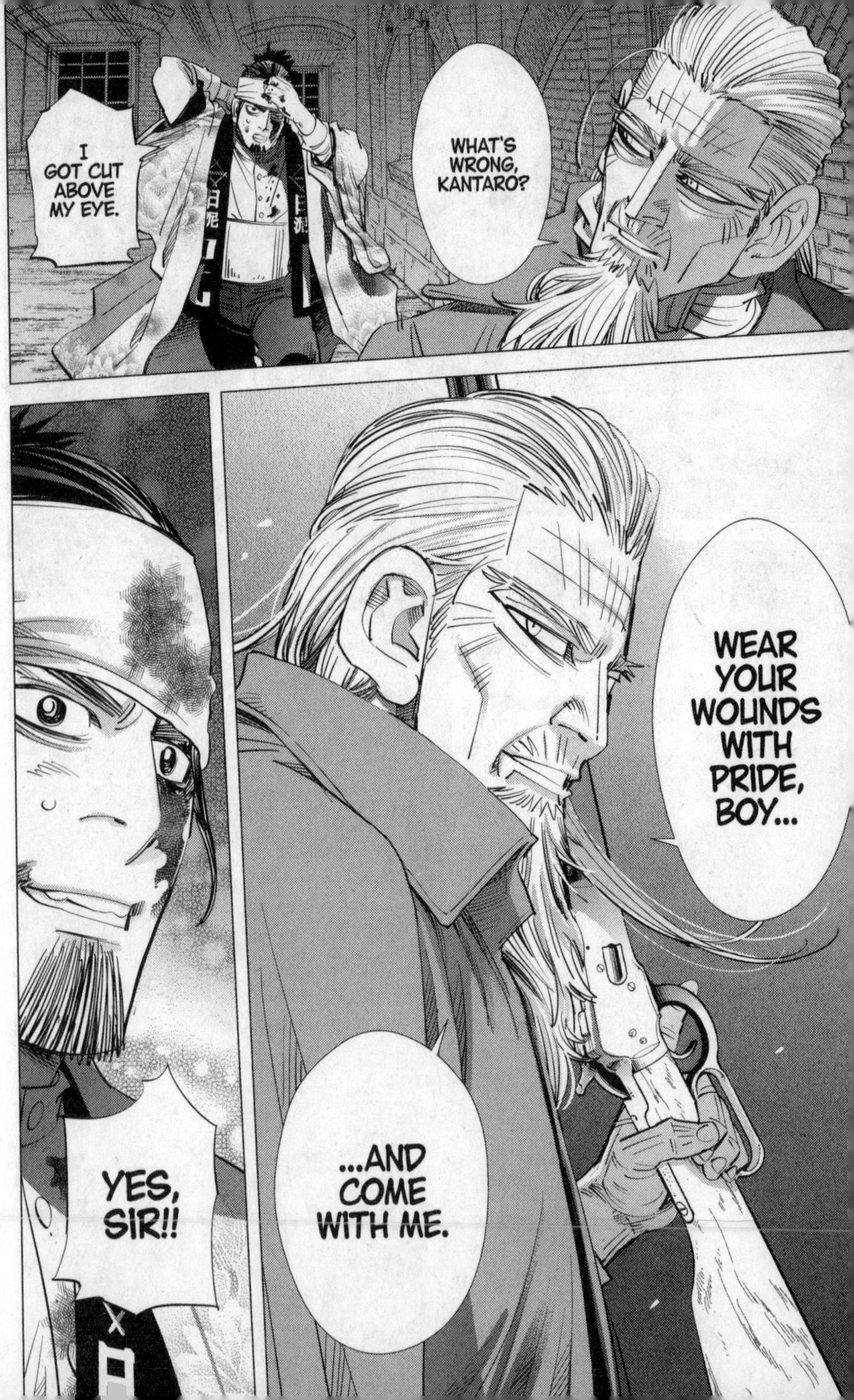
WHAT'S WRONG, KANTARO?
I GOT CUT ABOVE MY EYE.
WEAR YOUR WOUNDS WITH PRIDE, BOY...
...AND COME WITH ME.
YES, SIR!!

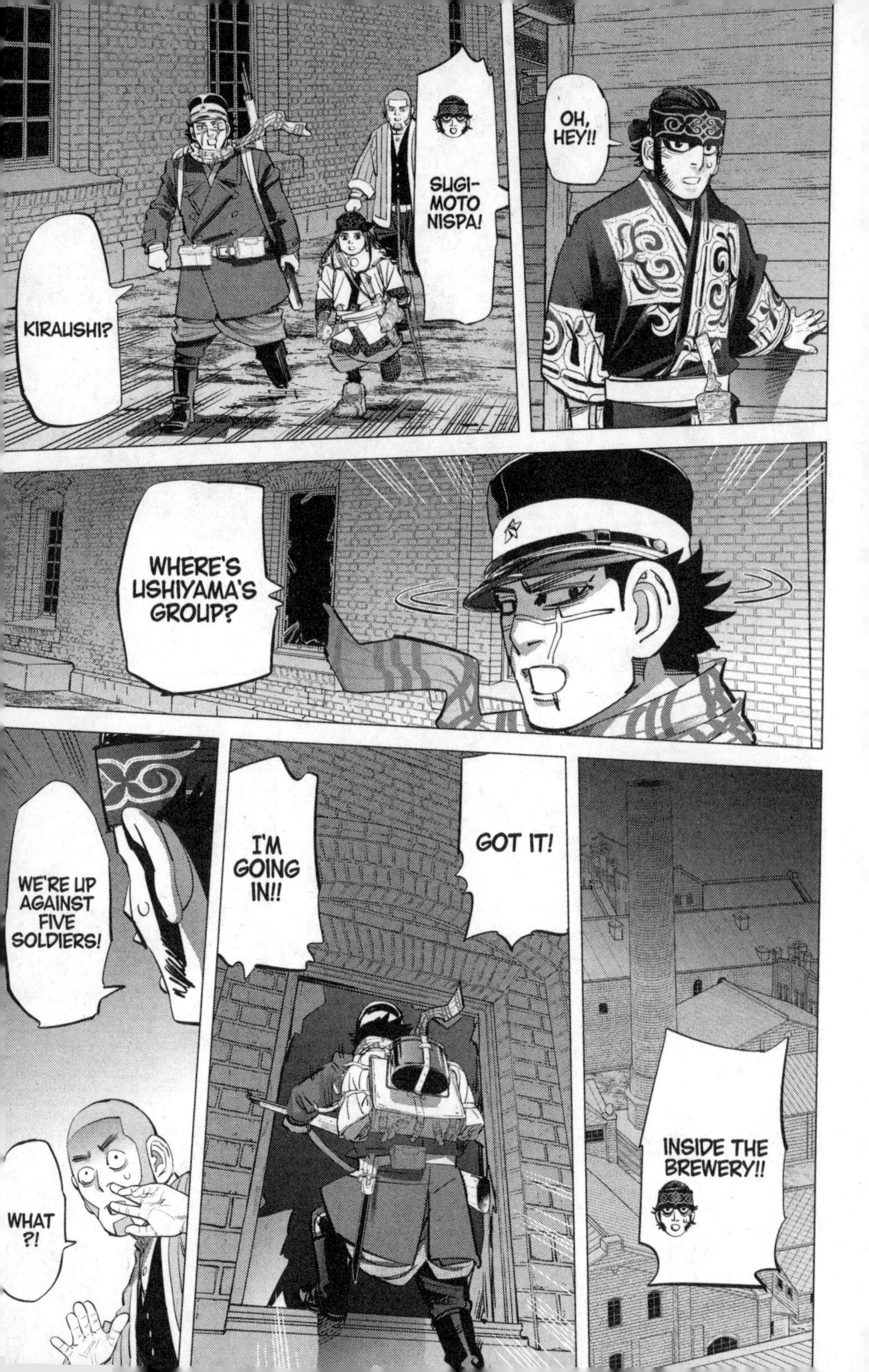
OH, HEY!!
SUGI-MOTO NISPA!
KIRAUSHI?
WHERE'S USHIYAMA'S GROUP?
INSIDE THE BREWERY!!
GOT IT!
I'M GOING IN!!
WE'RE UP AGAINST FIVE SOLDIERS!
WHAT ?!

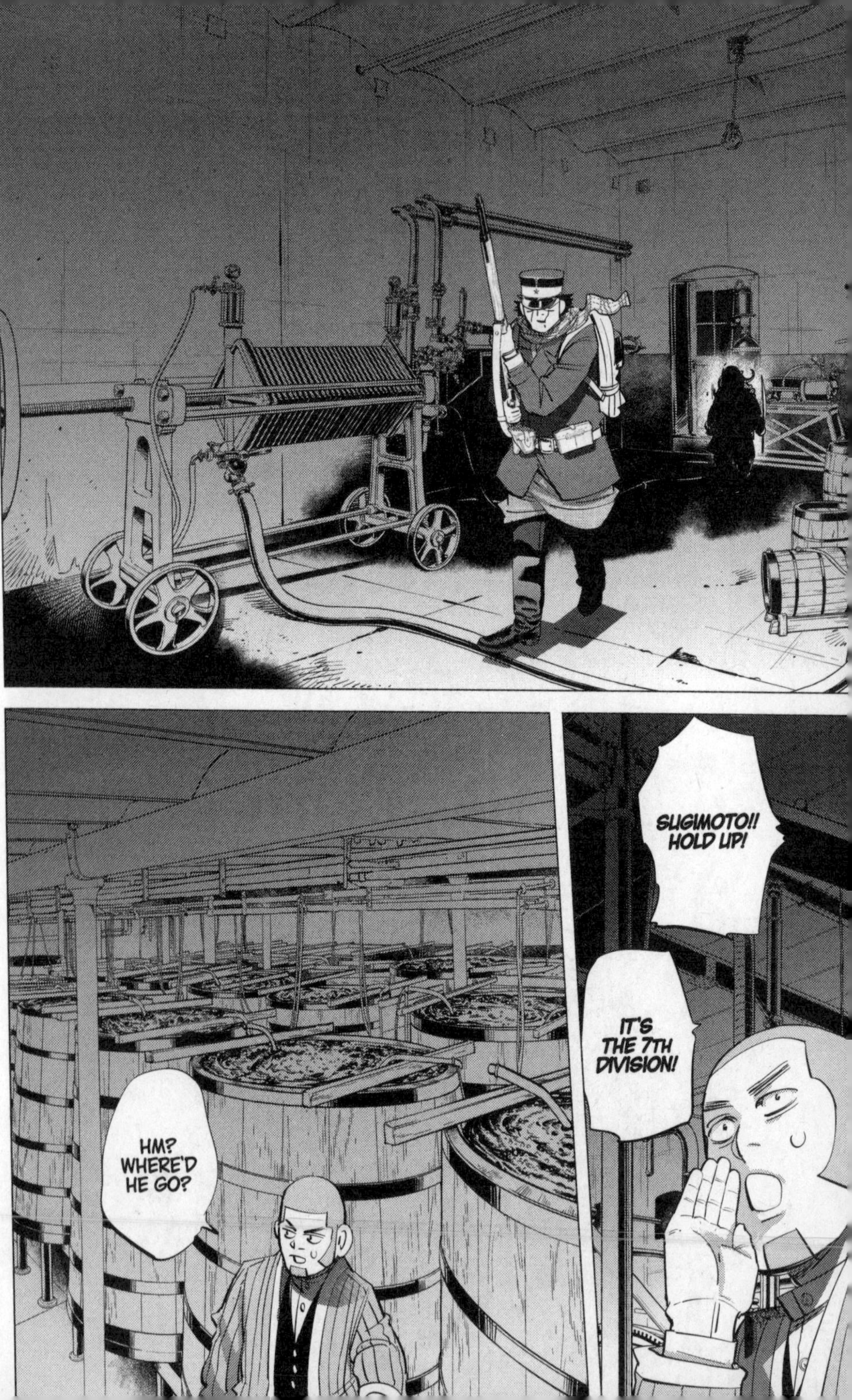
SUGIMOTO!! HOLD UP!
IT'S THE 7TH DIVISION!
HM? WHERE'D HE GO?

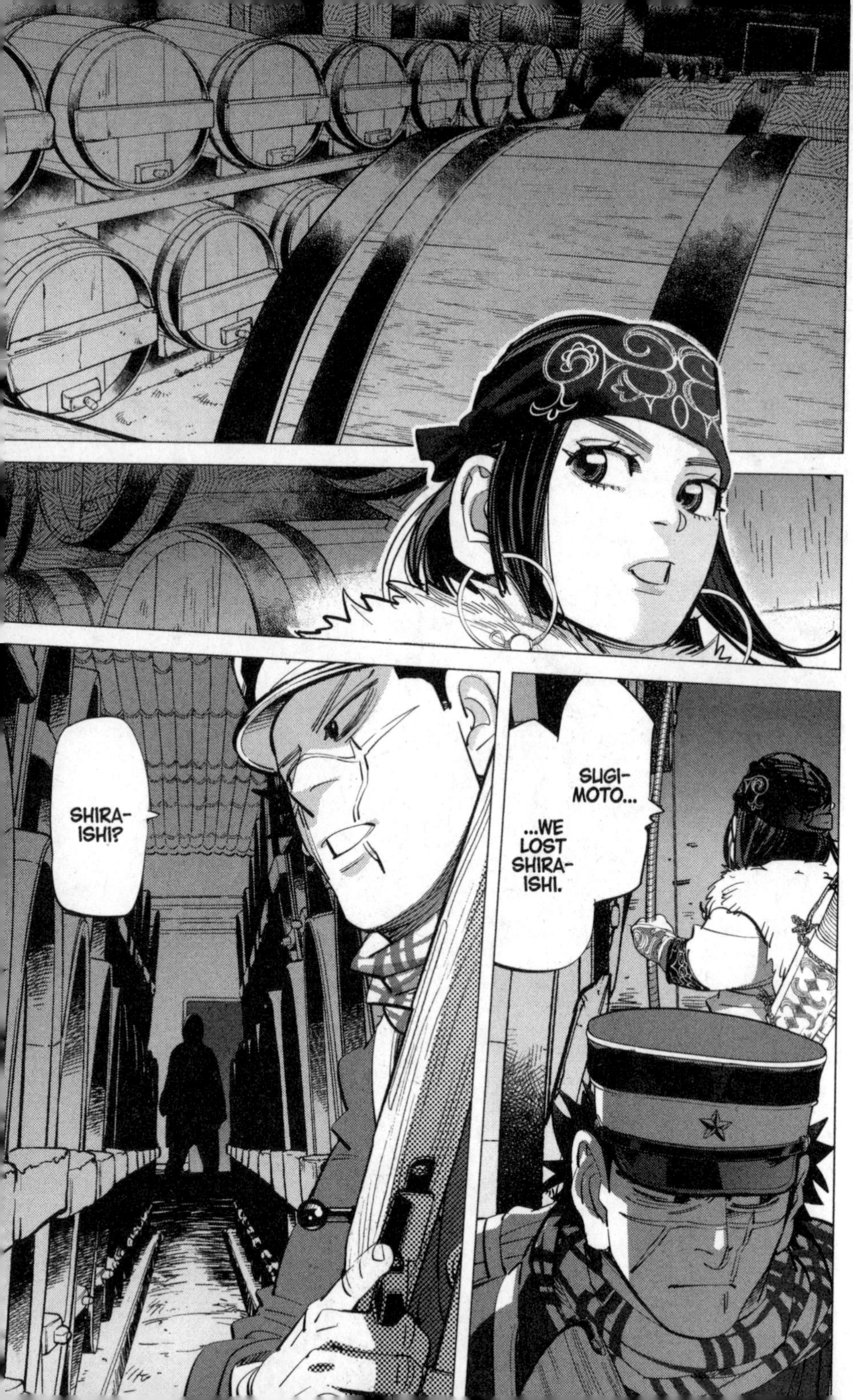
SUGI-
MOTO...
...WE
LOST
SHIRA-
ISHI.
SHIRA-
ISHI?

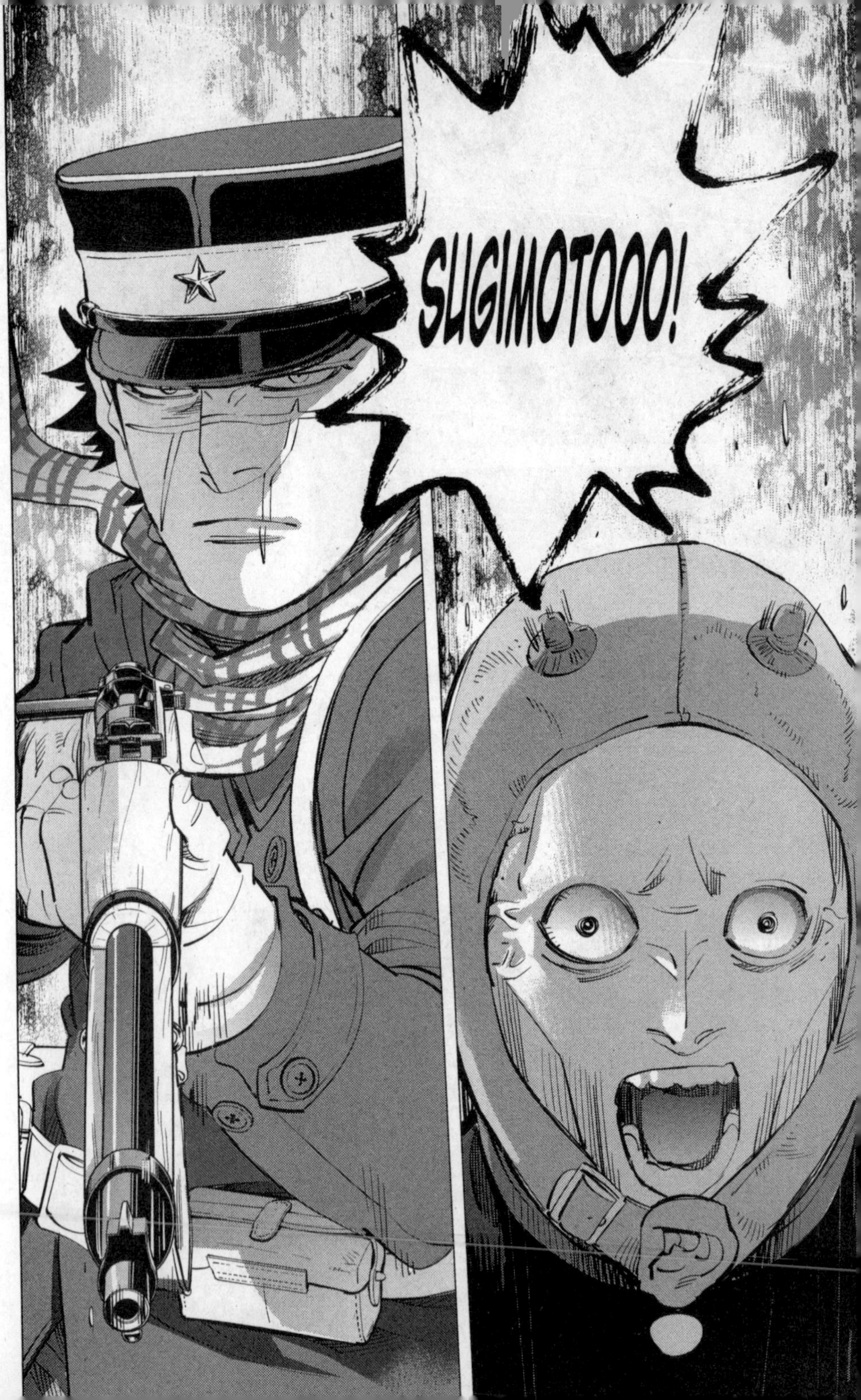
SUGIMOTOOO!

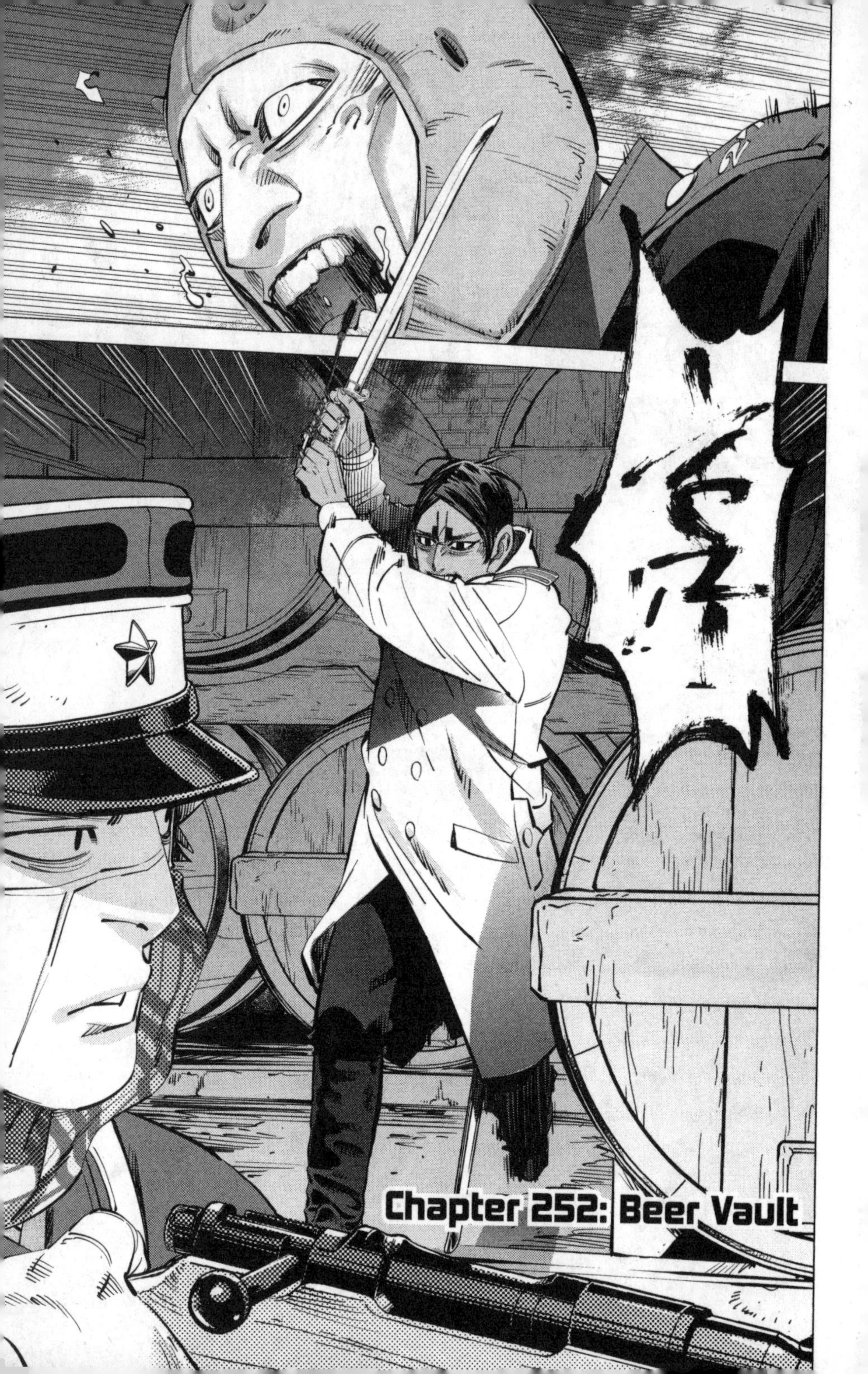
Chapter 252: Beer Vault

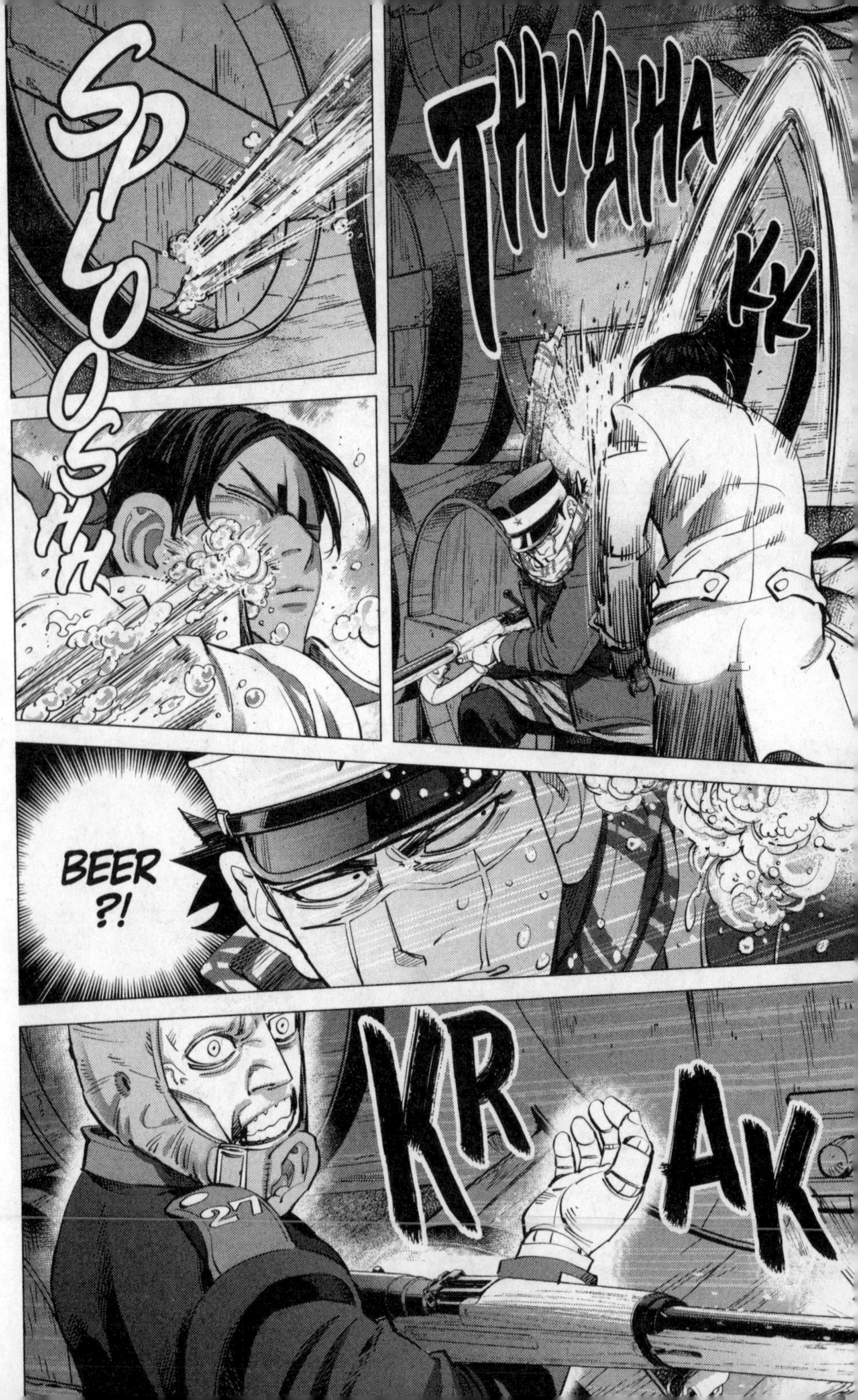
THWAHAKK
SPLOOSHH
BEER?!
KRAK

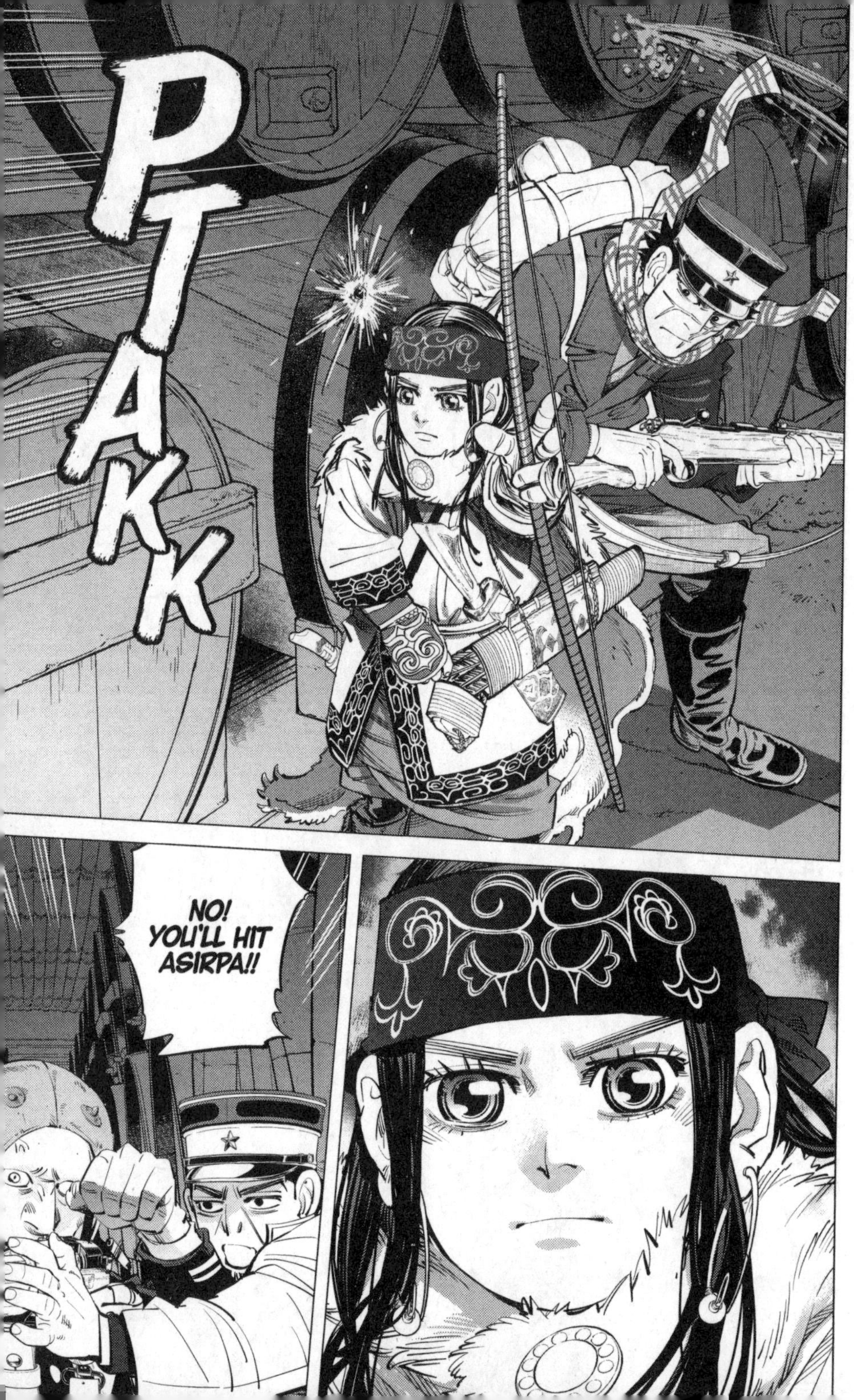
PTAKK
NO! YOU'LL HIT ASIRPA!!

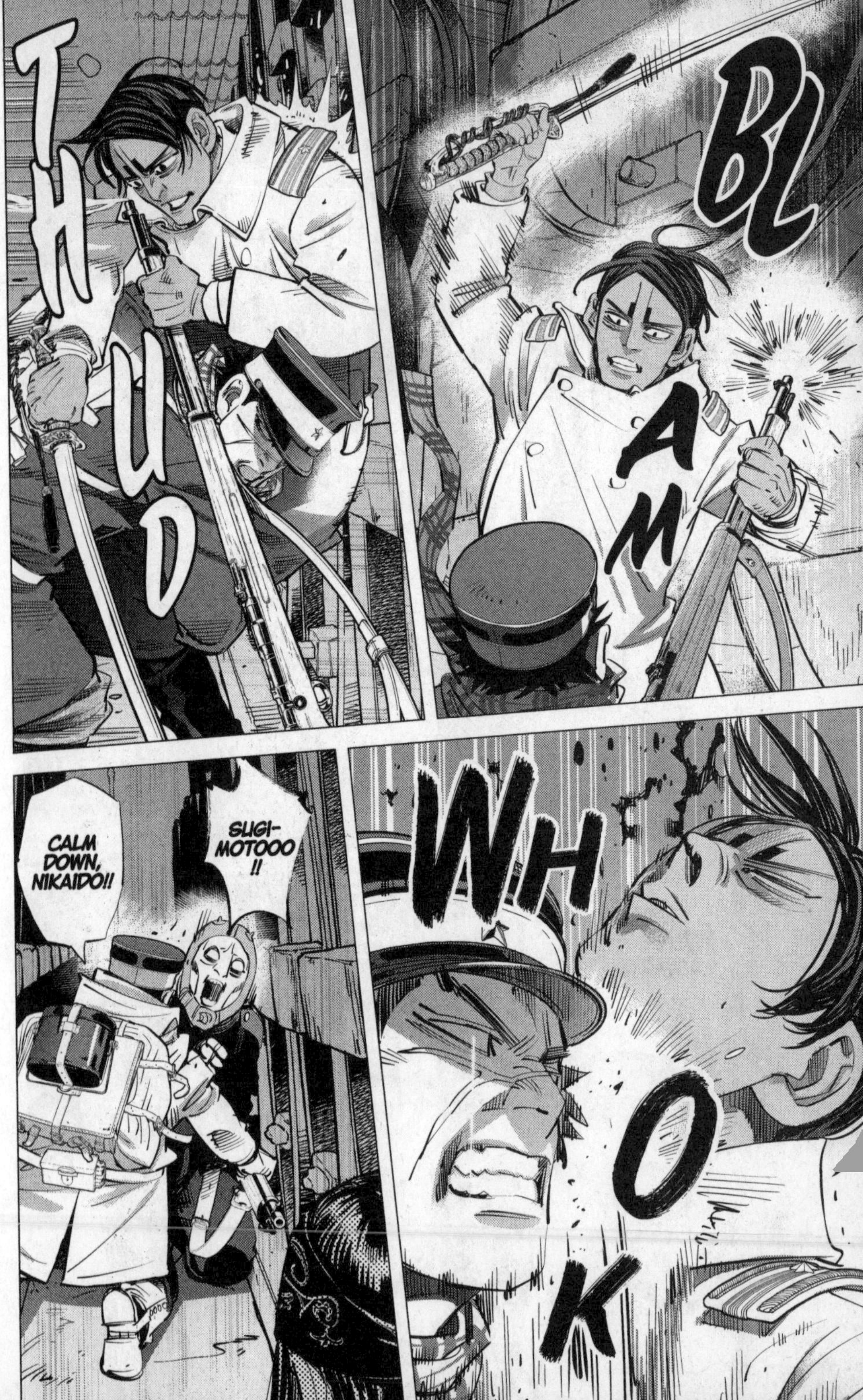
BLAM
THUD
WHOK
SUGI-MOTOOO!!
CALM DOWN, NIKAIDO!!

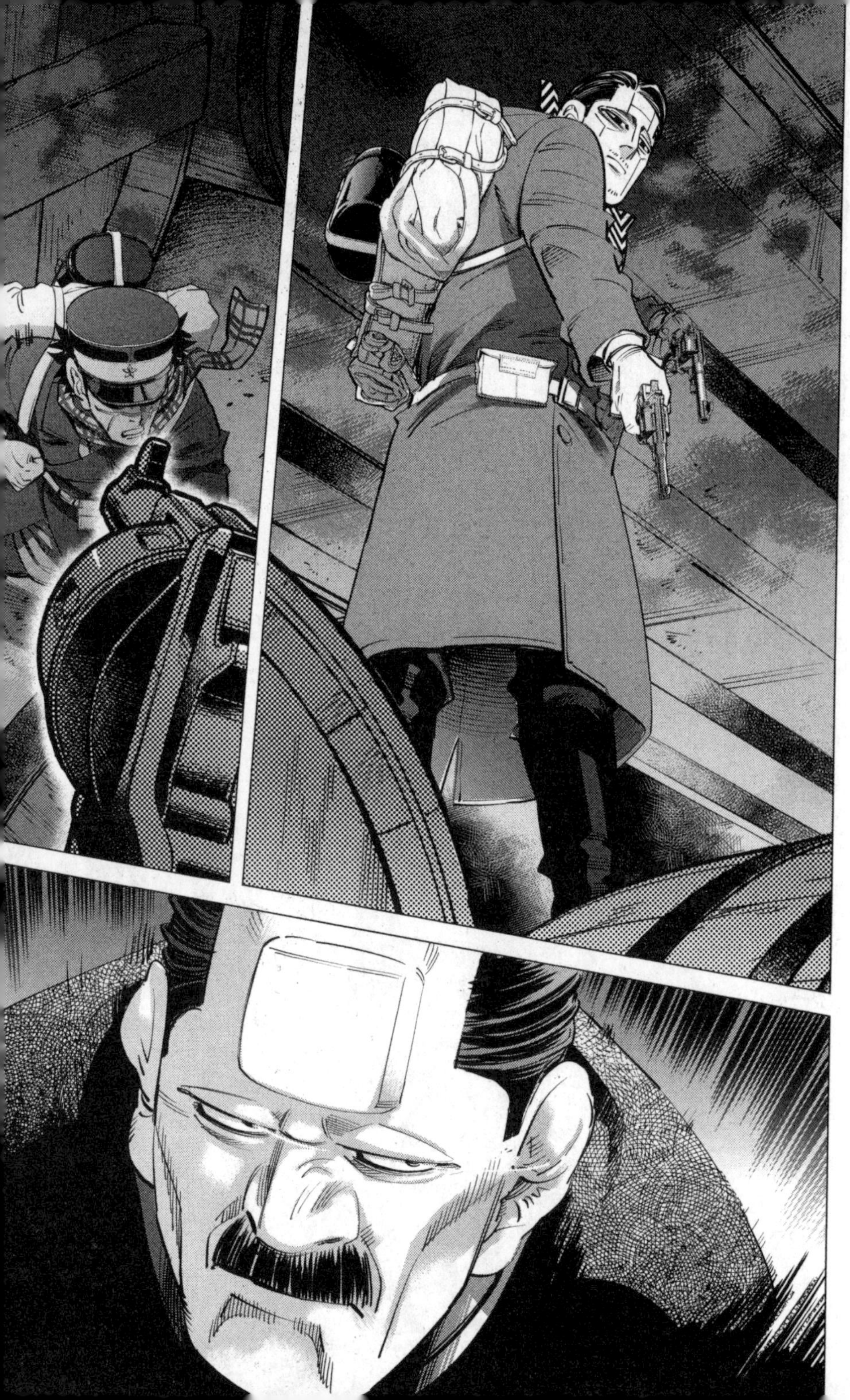

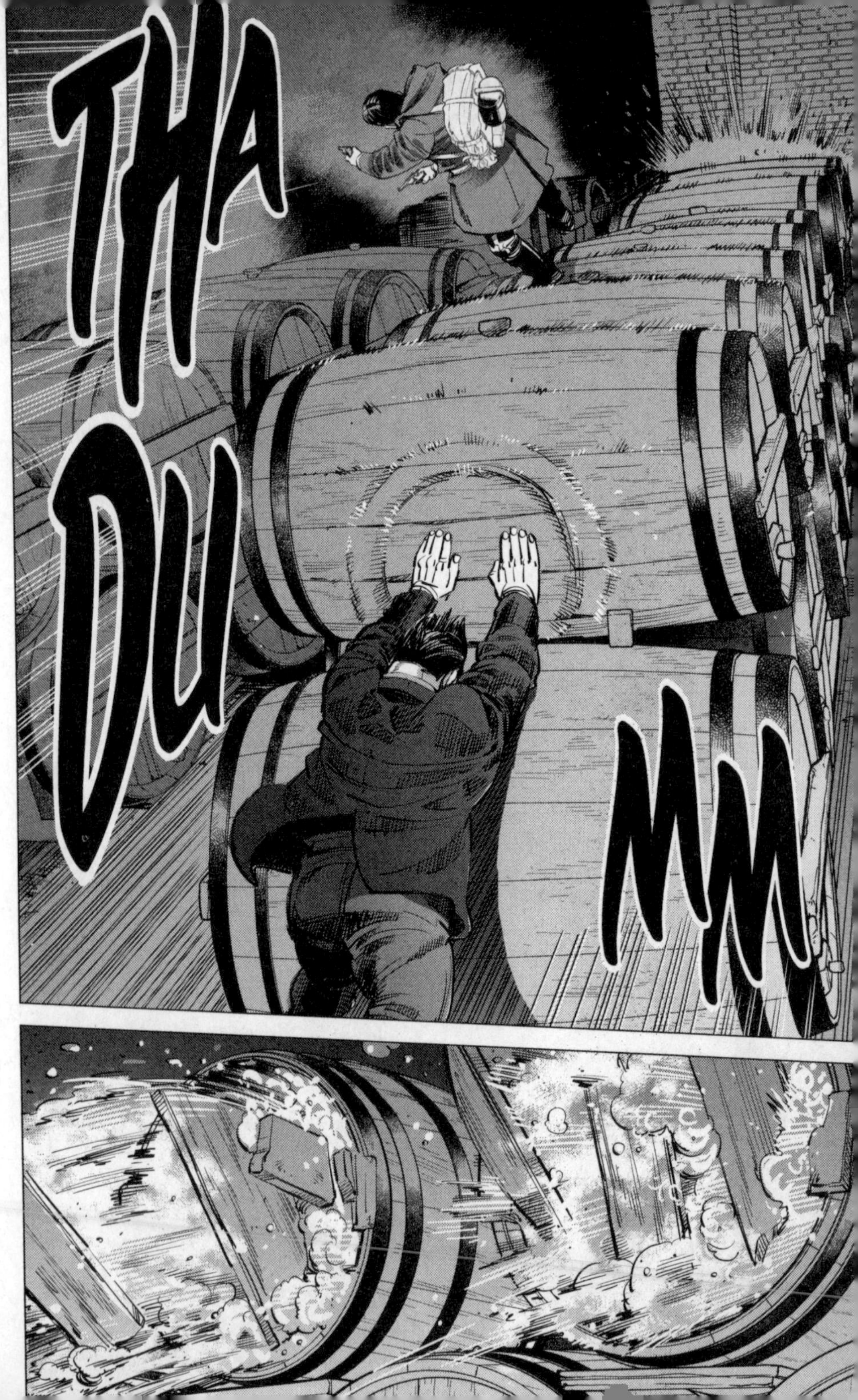
THADUMM

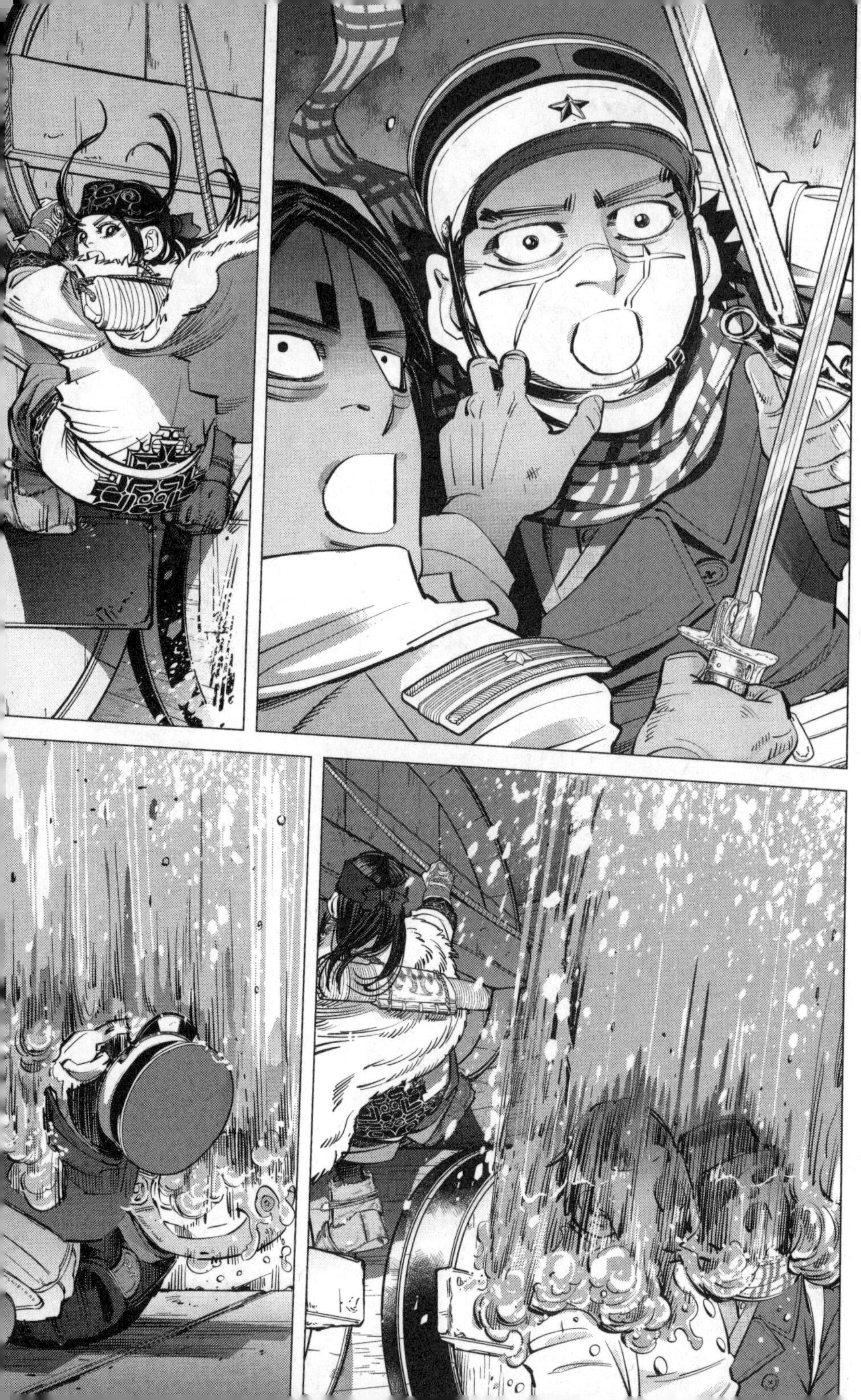

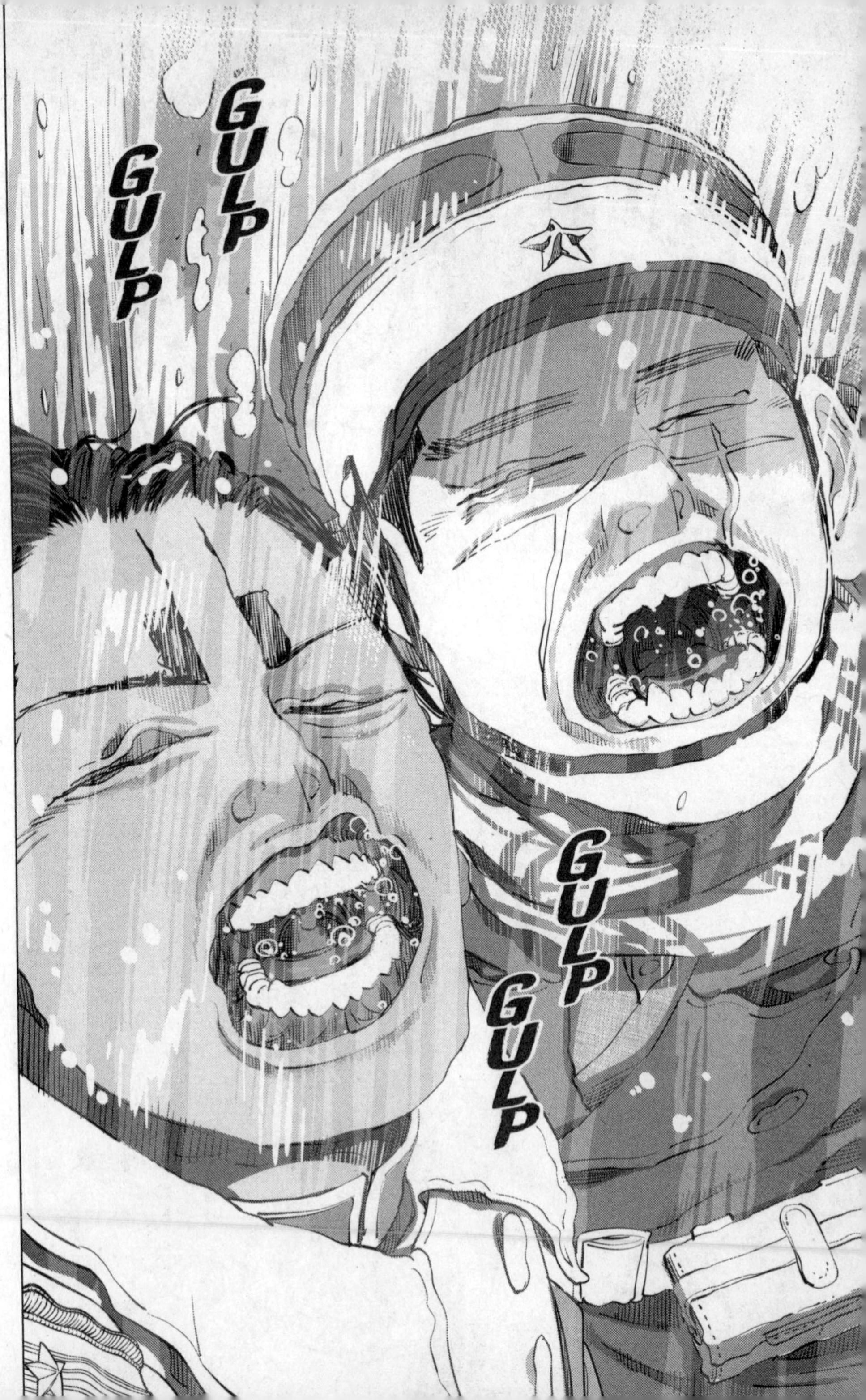
GULP GULP GULP
GULP GULP GULP

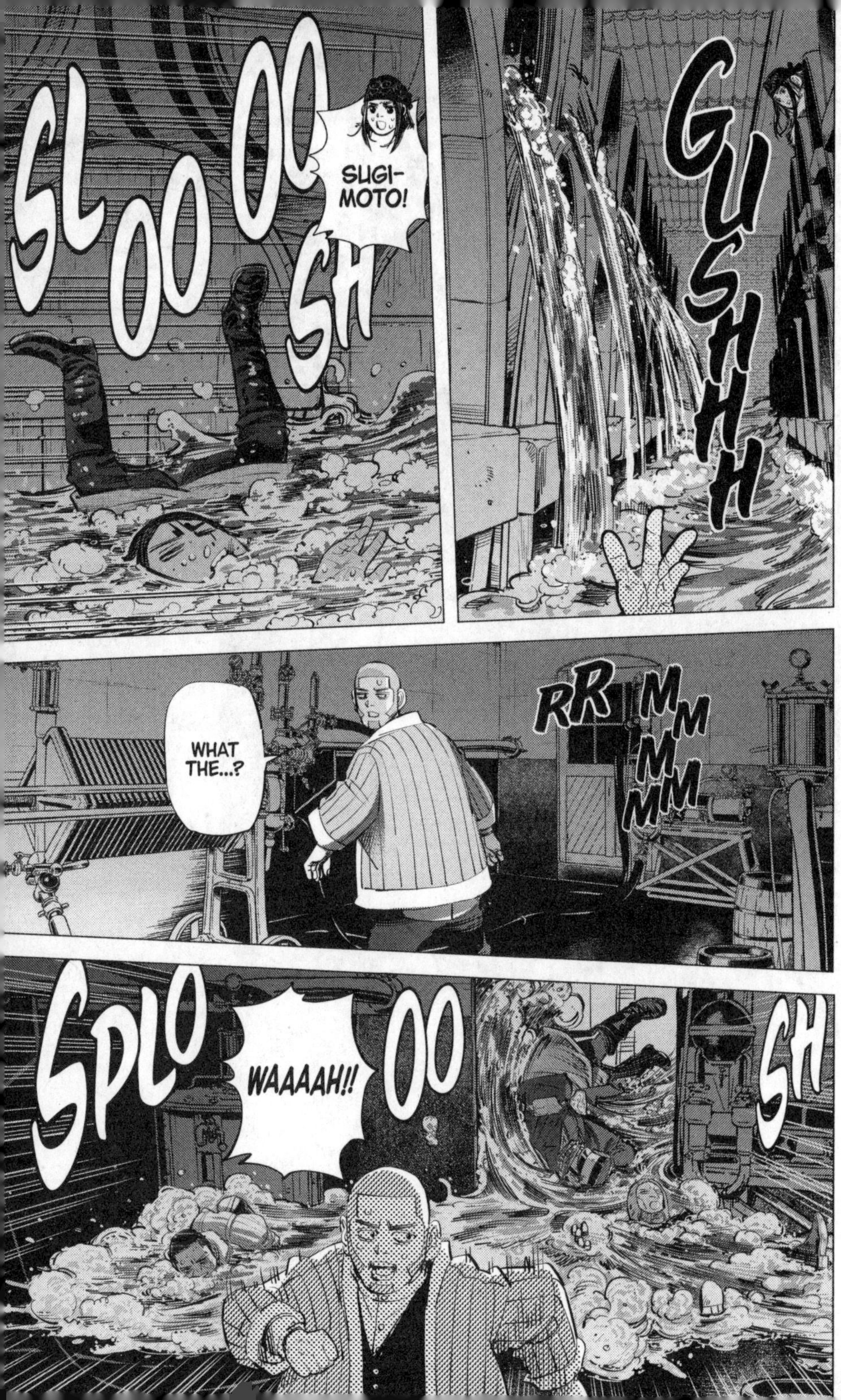
GUSHHH
SUGI-
MOTO!
SLOOOOSH
RRMMMMMM
WHAT THE...?
SPLOOOOSH
WAAAAH!!

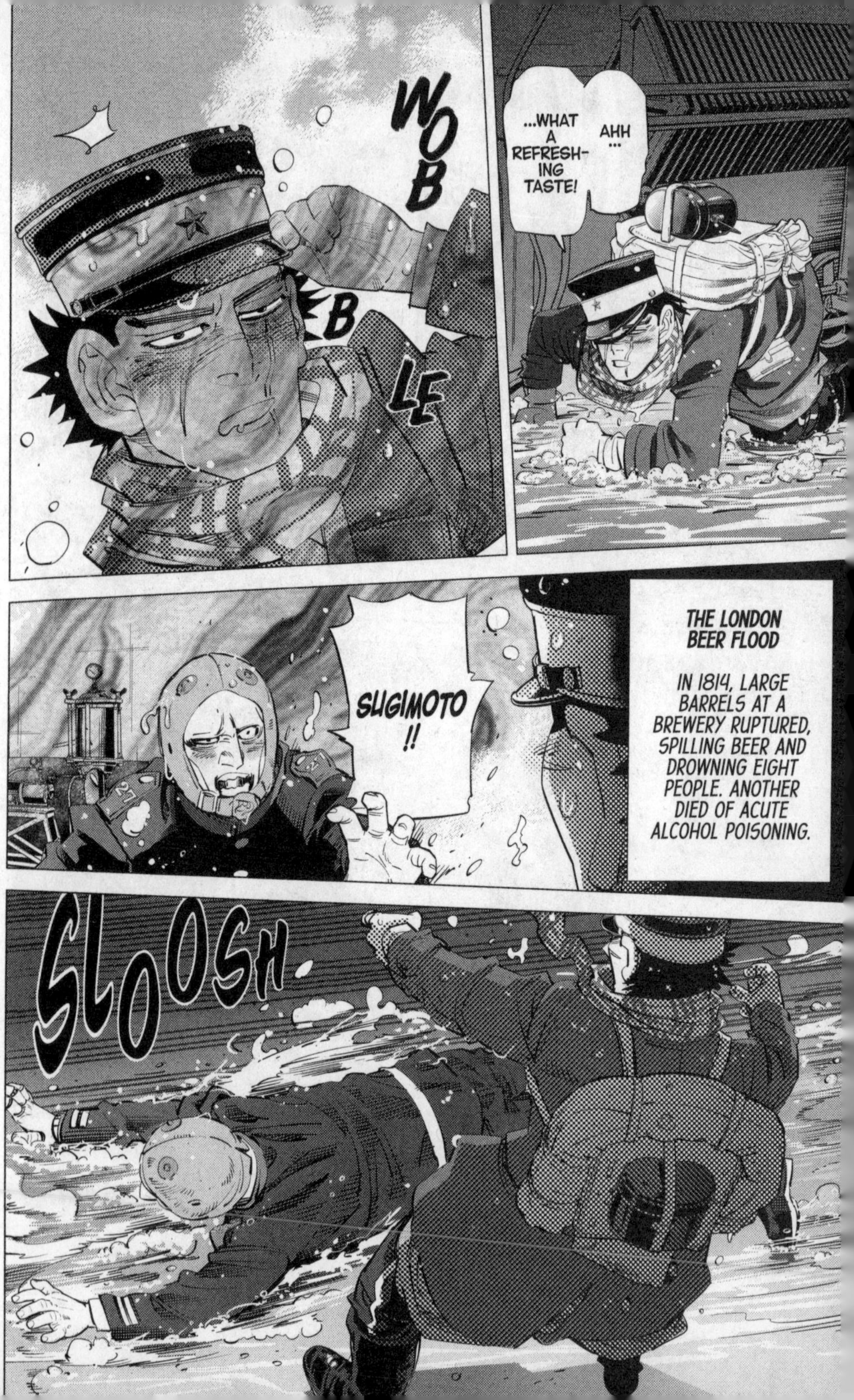
AHH...
...WHAT A REFRESHING TASTE!
WOBBLE
THE LONDON BEER FLOOD
IN 1814, LARGE BARRELS AT A BREWERY RUPTURED, SPILLING BEER AND DROWNING EIGHT PEOPLE. ANOTHER DIED OF ACUTE ALCOHOL POISONING.
SUGIMOTO!!
SLOOSH

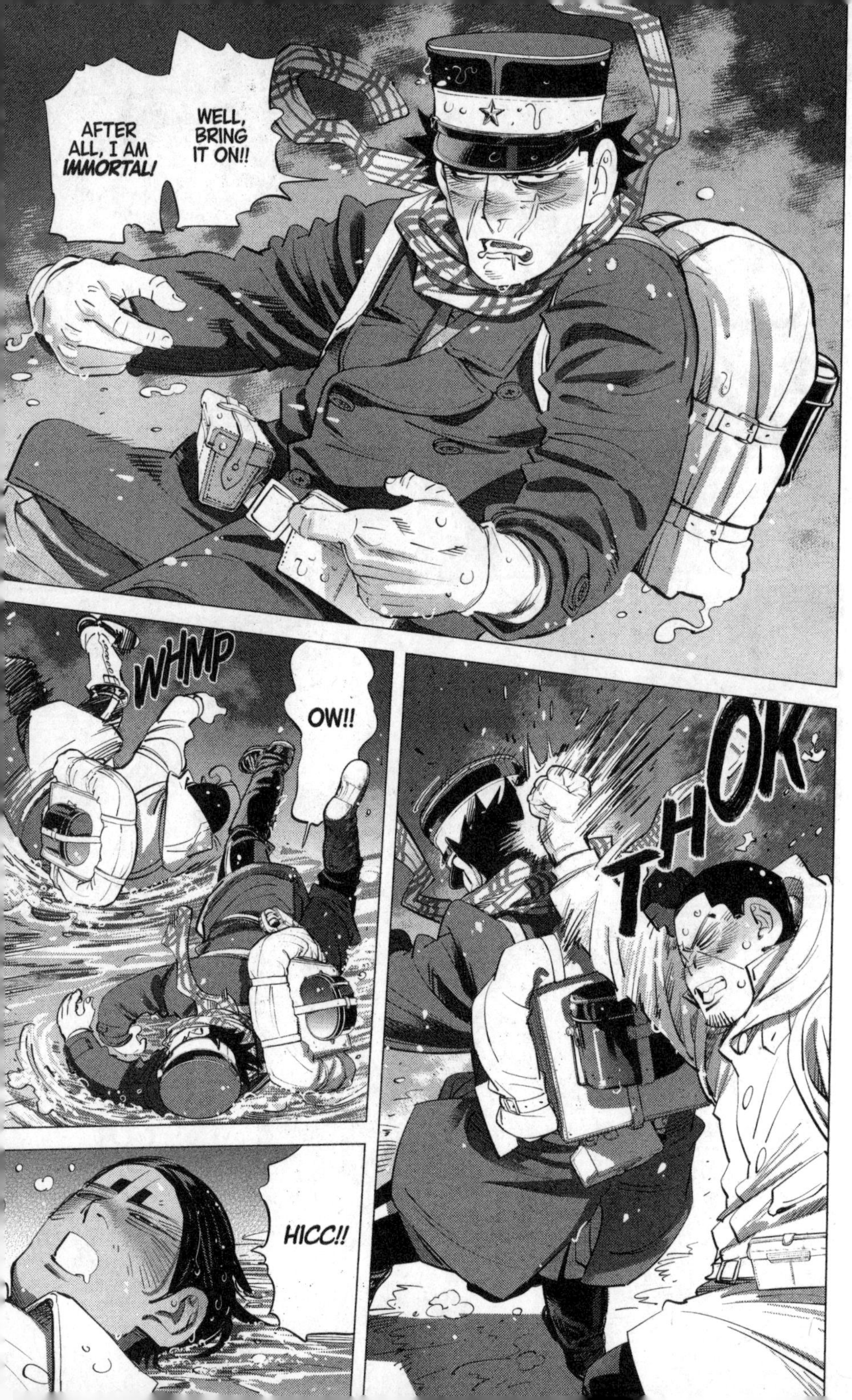
WELL, BRING IT ON!!
AFTER ALL, I AM **IMMORTAL!**
THOK
OW!!
WHMP
HICC!!

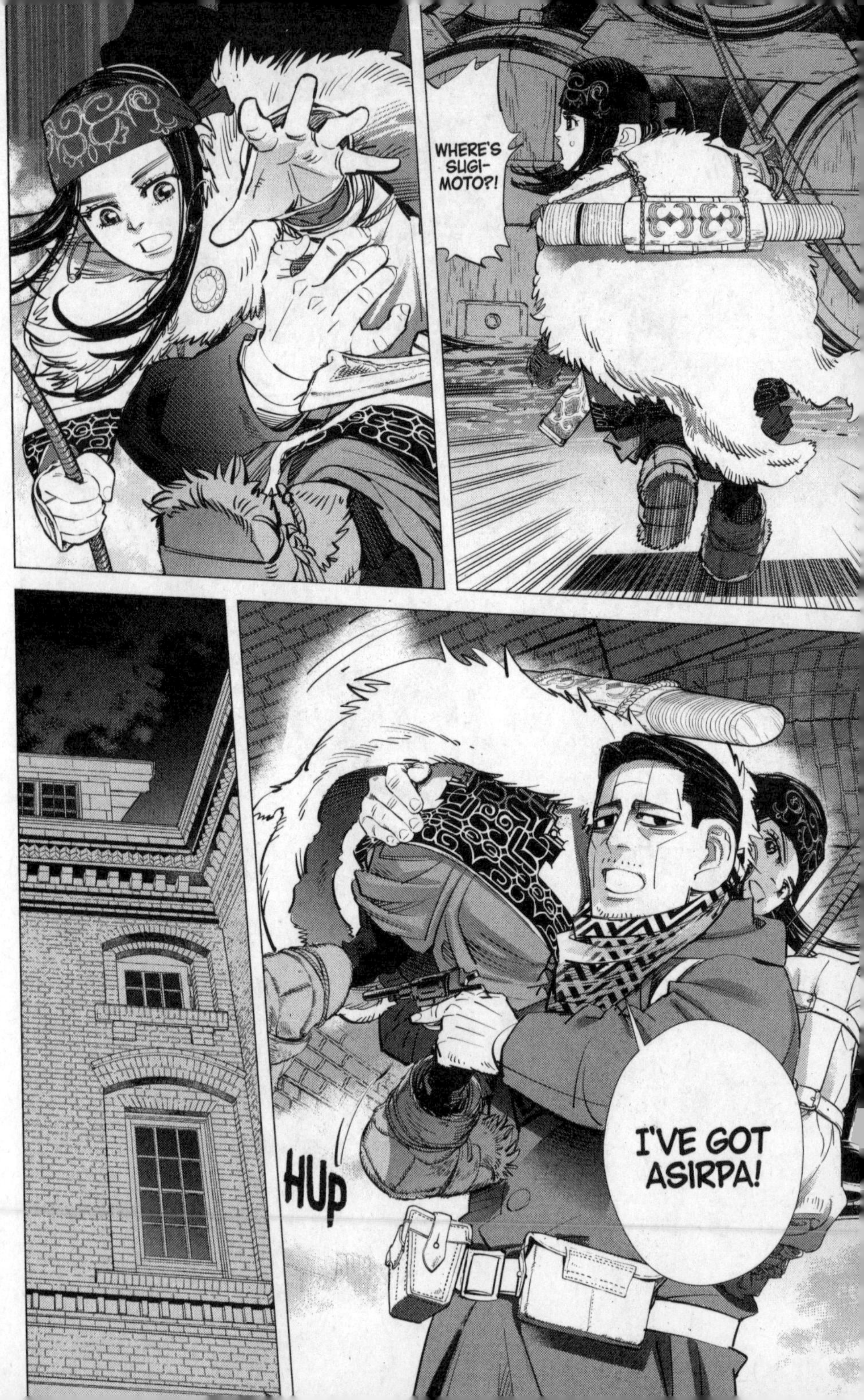
WHERE'S SUGI-MOTO?!
I'VE GOT ASIRPA!
HUP

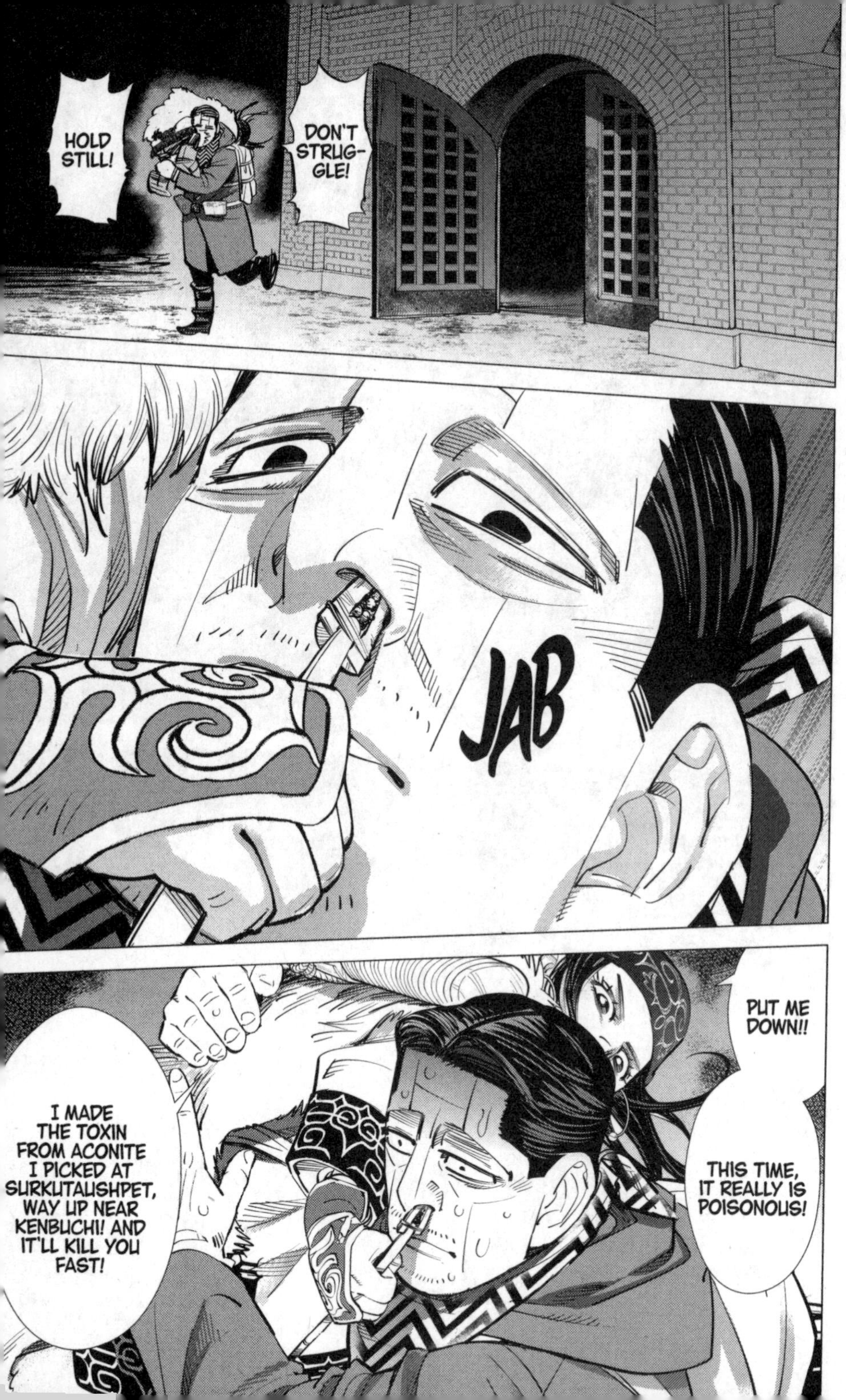
DON'T STRUG-GLE!
HOLD STILL!
JAB
PUT ME DOWN!!
THIS TIME, IT REALLY IS POISONOUS!
I MADE THE TOXIN FROM ACONITE I PICKED AT SURKUTAUSHPET, WAY UP NEAR KENBUCHI! AND IT'LL KILL YOU FAST!

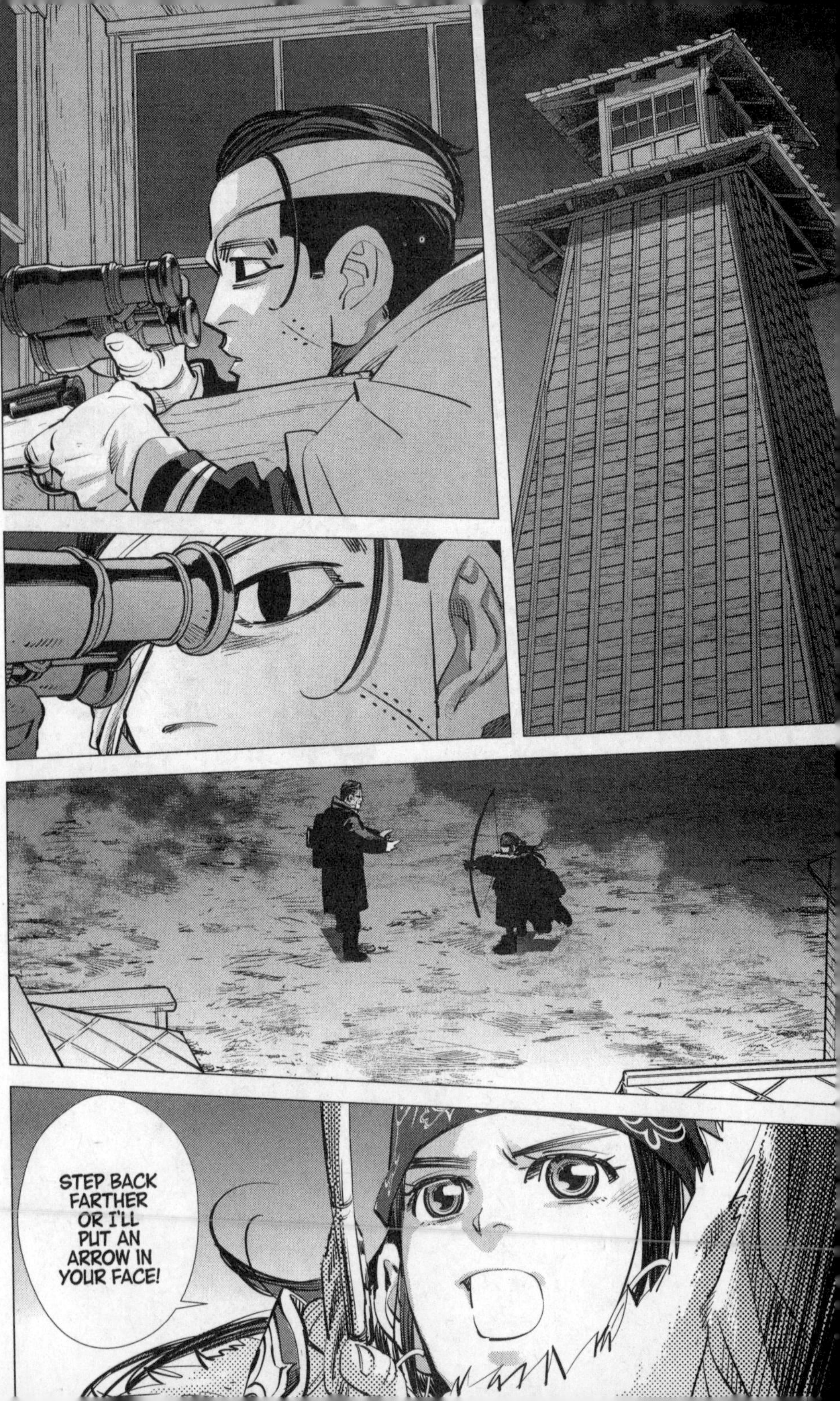
STEP BACK FARTHER OR I'LL PUT AN ARROW IN YOUR FACE!

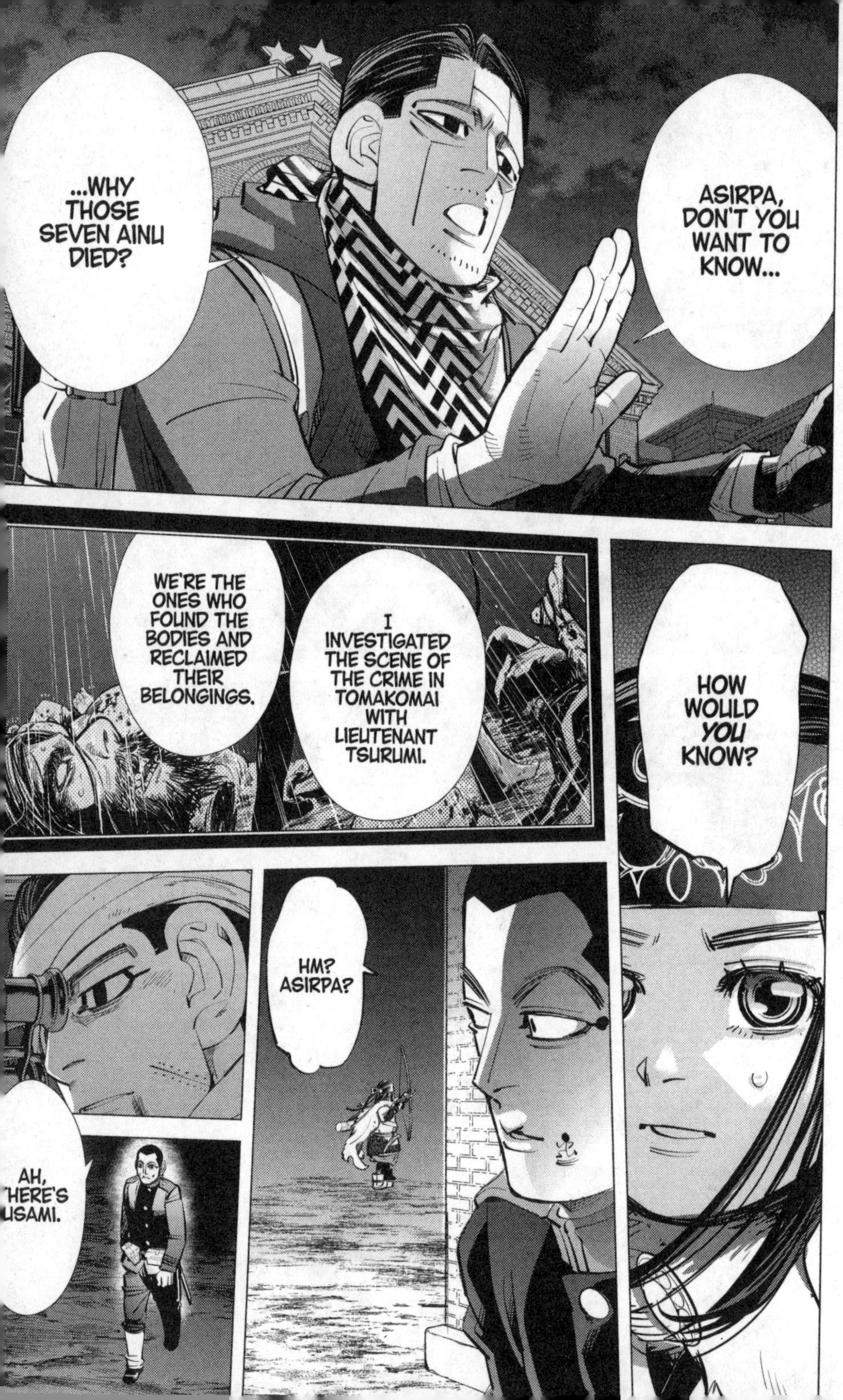
ASIRPA, DON'T YOU WANT TO KNOW...
...WHY THOSE SEVEN AINU DIED?
HOW WOULD *YOU* KNOW?
I INVESTIGATED THE SCENE OF THE CRIME IN TOMAKOMAI WITH LIEUTENANT TSURUMI.
WE'RE THE ONES WHO FOUND THE BODIES AND RECLAIMED THEIR BELONGINGS.
HM? ASIRPA?
AH, THERE'S USAMI.

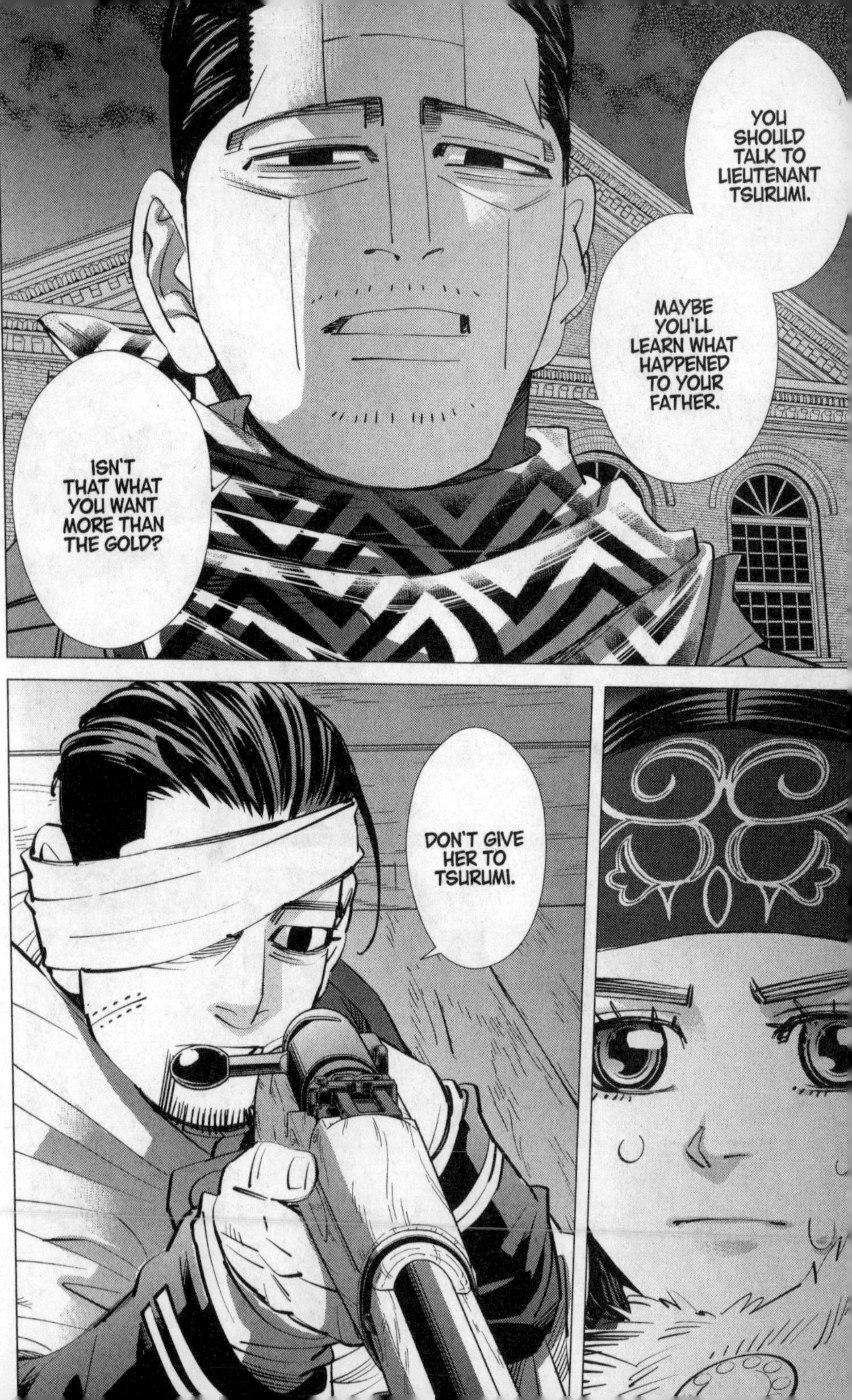
YOU SHOULD TALK TO LIEUTENANT TSURUMI.
MAYBE YOU'LL LEARN WHAT HAPPENED TO YOUR FATHER.
ISN'T THAT WHAT YOU WANT MORE THAN THE GOLD?
DON'T GIVE HER TO TSURUMI.

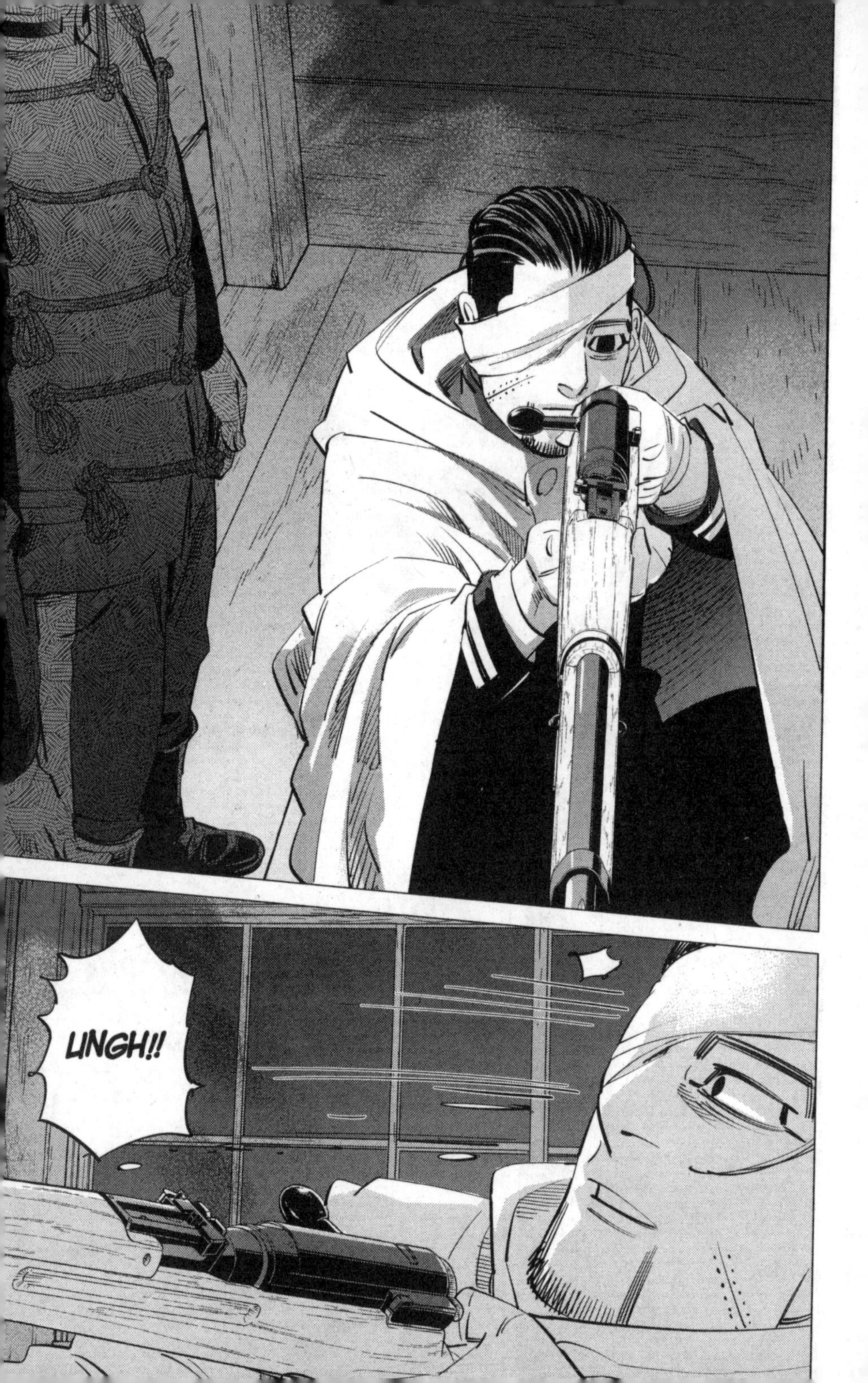
UNGH!!

THAT CAME FROM A SKILLED SHARP-SHOOTER.

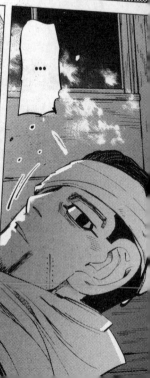

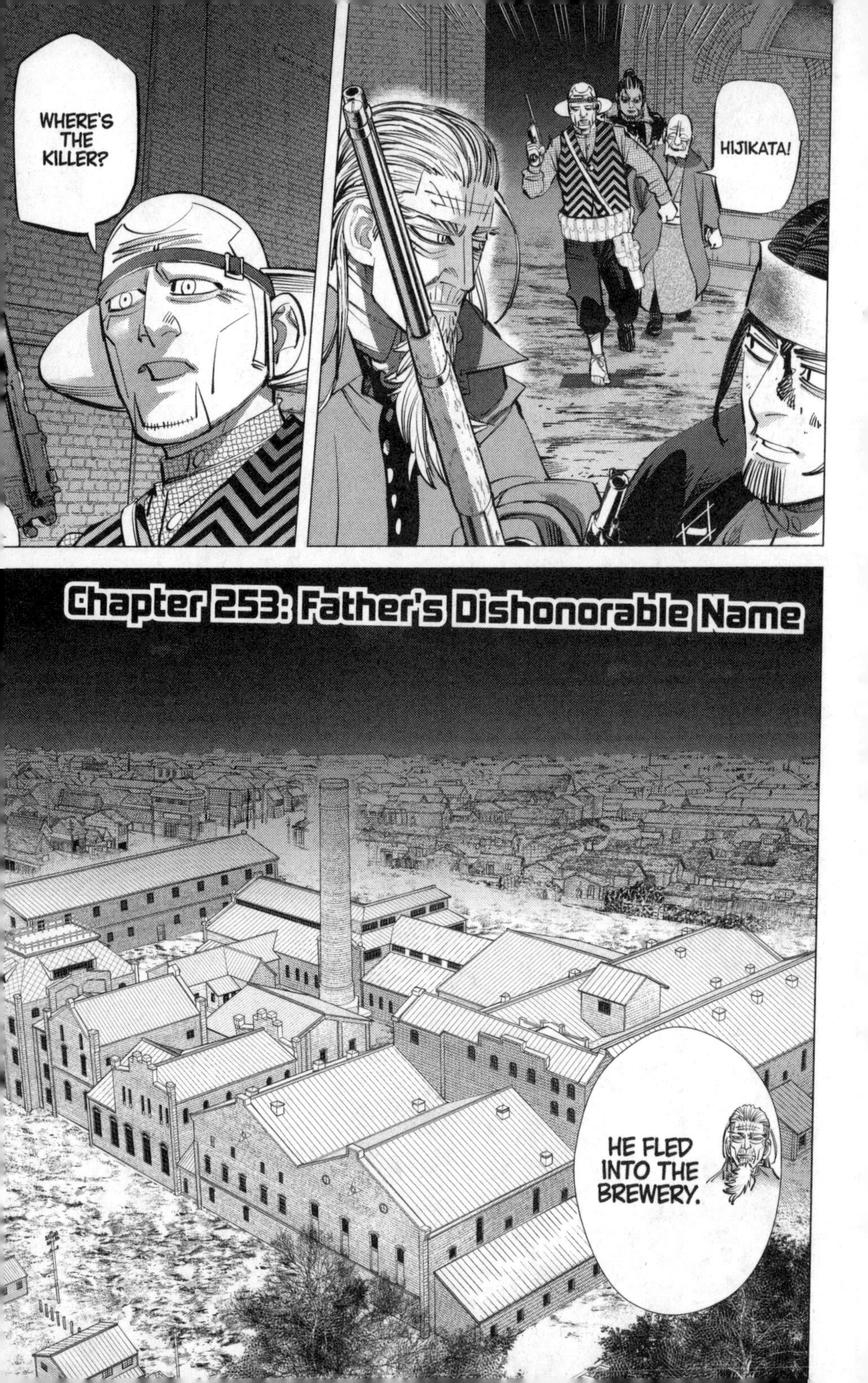
HIJIKATA!
WHERE'S THE KILLER?
Chapter 253: Father's Dishonorable Name
HE FLED INTO THE BREWERY.

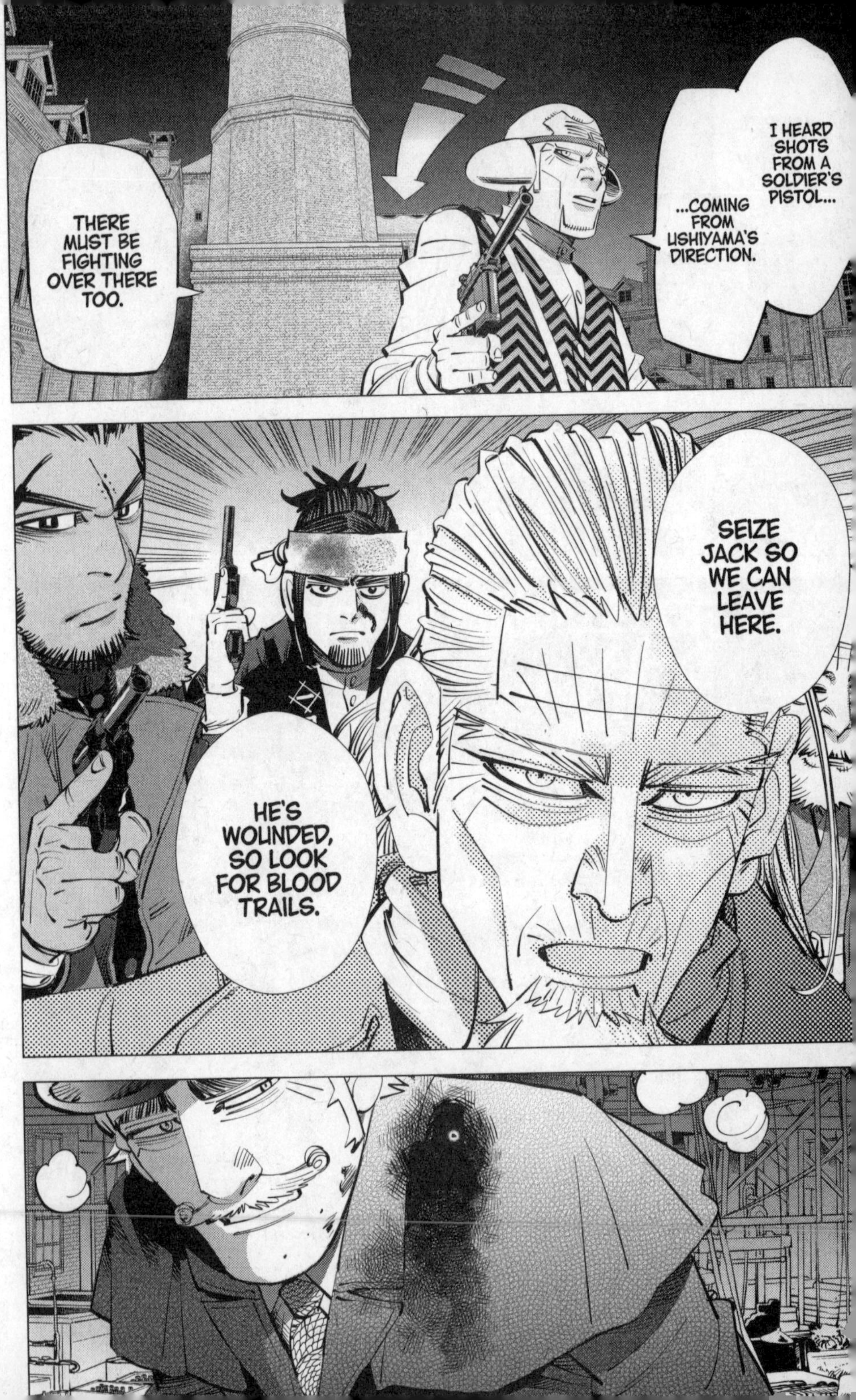
I HEARD SHOTS FROM A SOLDIER'S PISTOL...
...COMING FROM USHIYAMA'S DIRECTION.
THERE MUST BE FIGHTING OVER THERE TOO.
SEIZE JACK SO WE CAN LEAVE HERE.
HE'S WOUNDED, SO LOOK FOR BLOOD TRAILS.

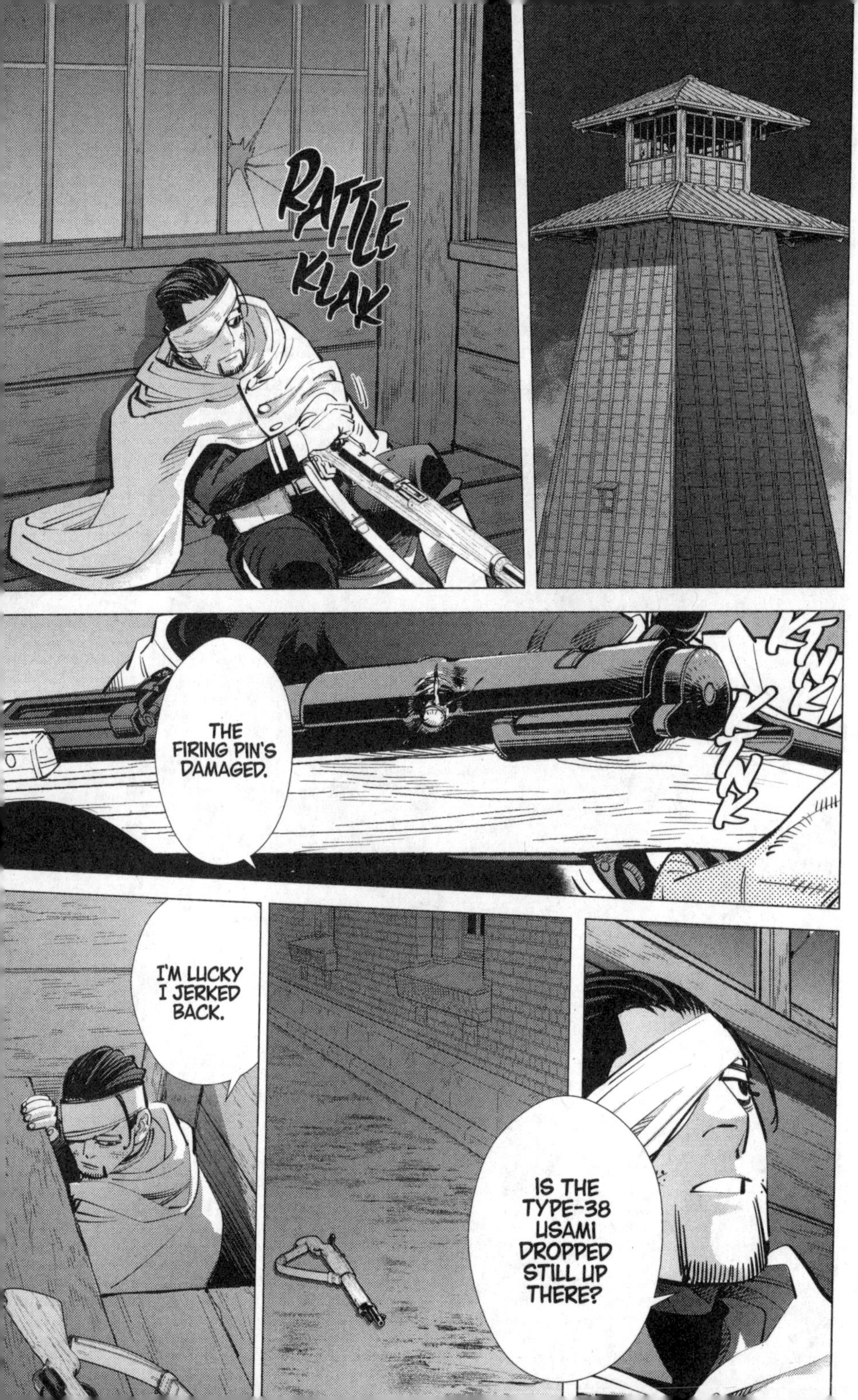
RATTLE
KLAK
KTNK
KTNK
THE FIRING PIN'S DAMAGED.
IS THE TYPE-38 USAMI DROPPED STILL UP THERE?
I'M LUCKY I JERKED BACK.

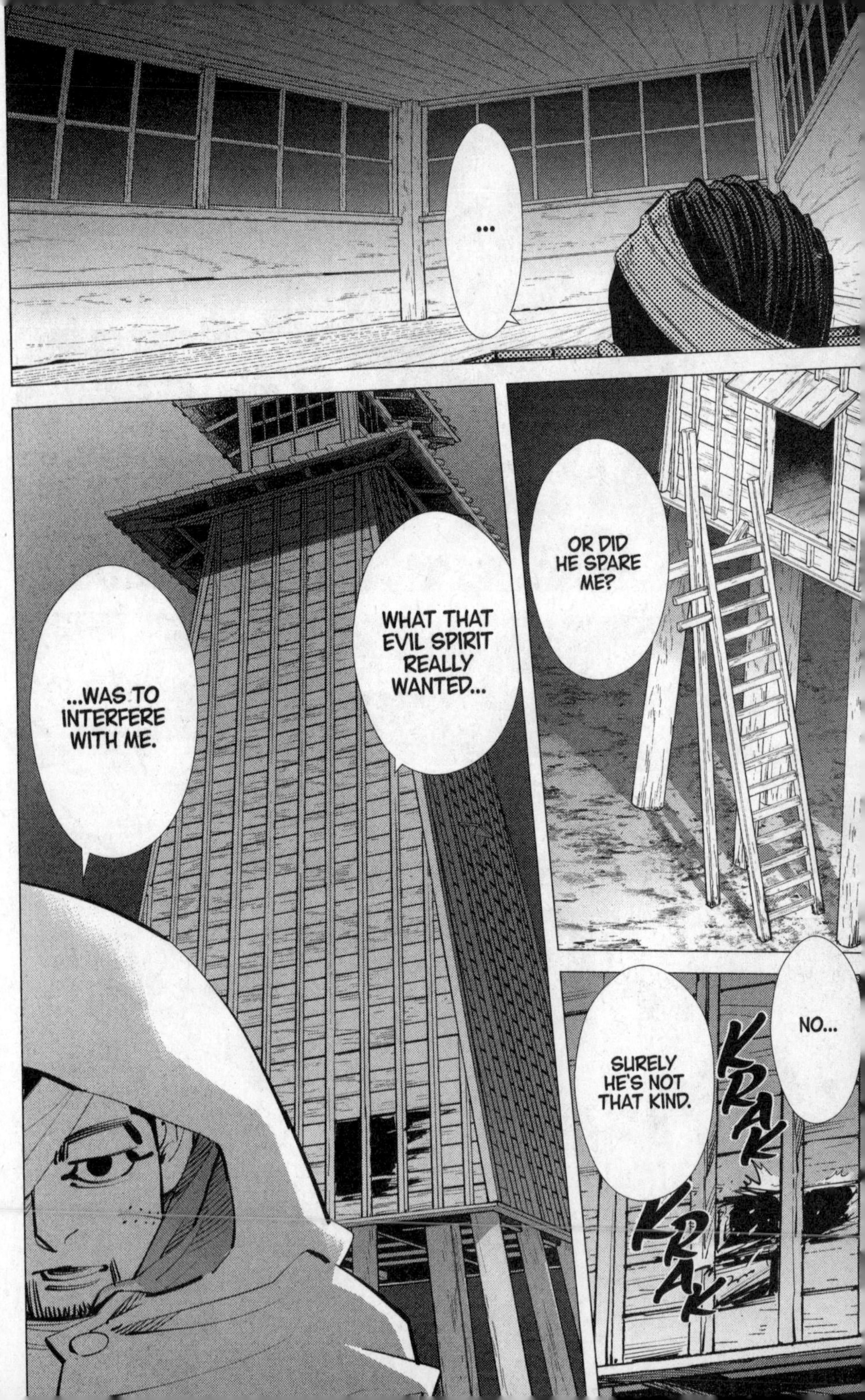
...
OR DID HE SPARE ME?
NO...
SURELY HE'S NOT THAT KIND.
KRAK
KRAK
WHAT THAT EVIL SPIRIT REALLY WANTED...
...WAS TO INTERFERE WITH ME.

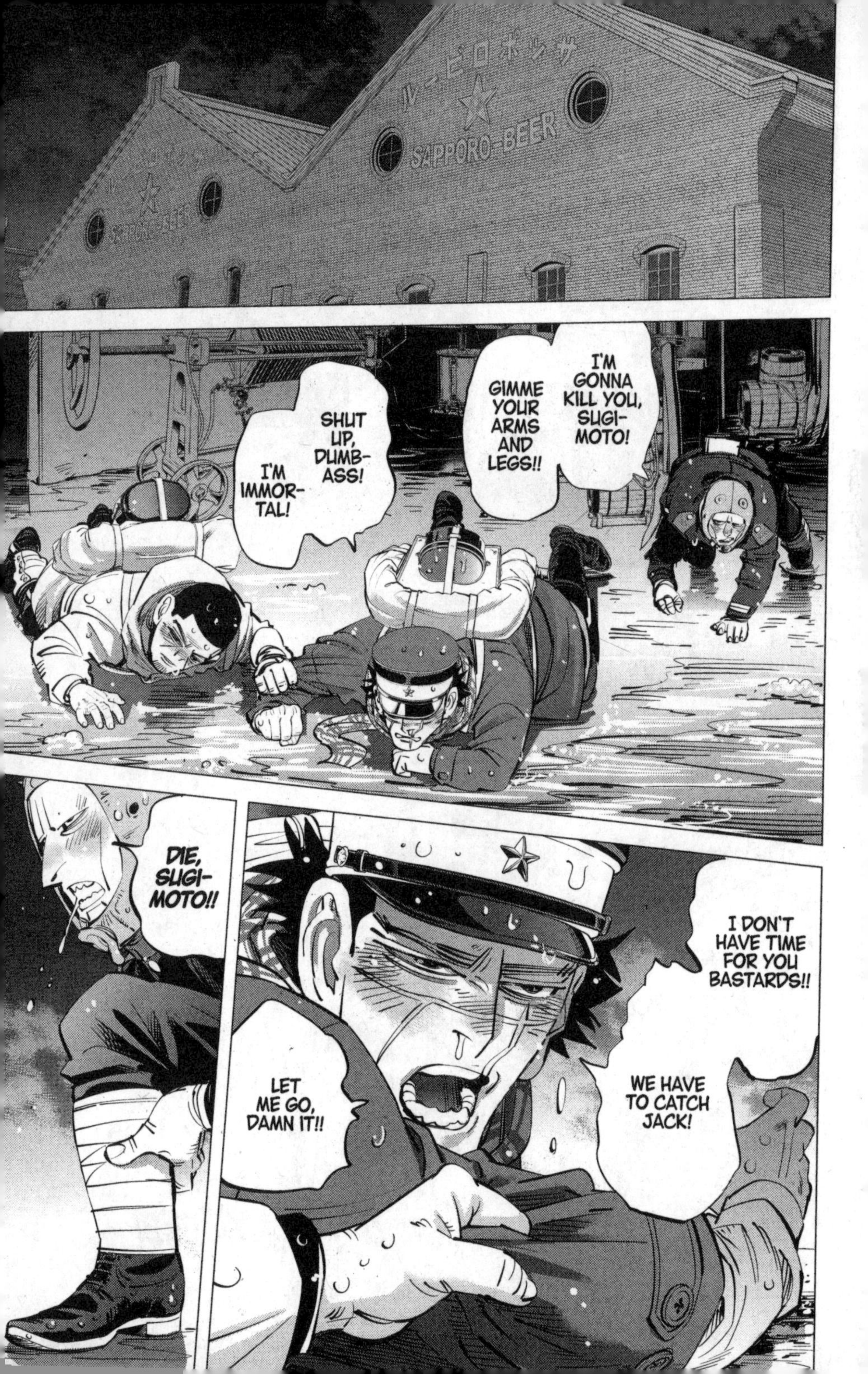
サッポロビール
SAPPORO-BEER
I'M GONNA KILL YOU, SUGI-MOTO!
GIMME YOUR ARMS AND LEGS!!
SHUT UP, DUMB-ASS!
I'M IMMOR-TAL!
I DON'T HAVE TIME FOR YOU BASTARDS!!
WE HAVE TO CATCH JACK!
LET ME GO, DAMN IT!!
DIE, SUGI-MOTO!!

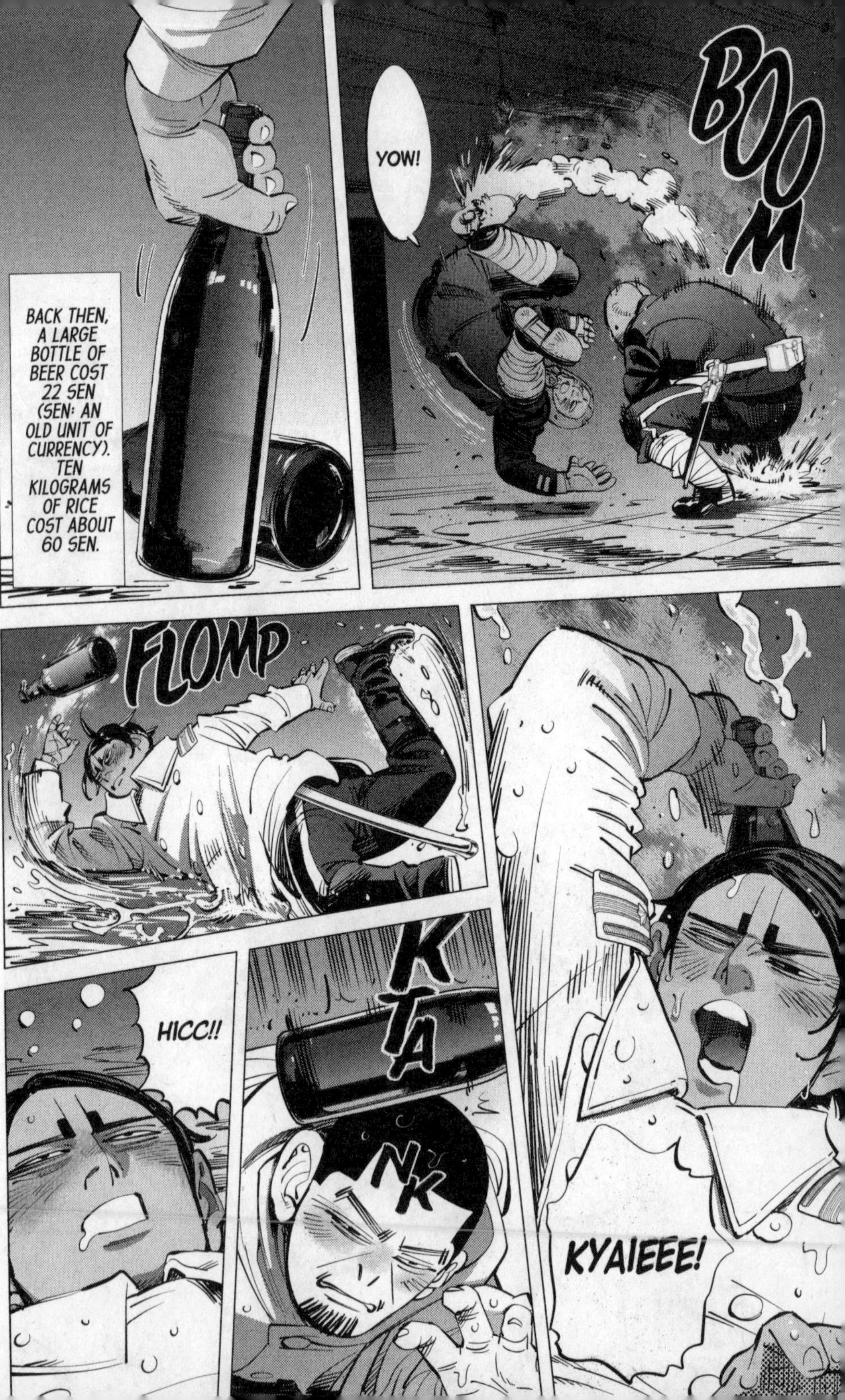
YOW!
BOOM
BACK THEN, A LARGE BOTTLE OF BEER COST 22 SEN (SEN: AN OLD UNIT OF CURRENCY). TEN KILOGRAMS OF RICE COST ABOUT 60 SEN.
KYAIEEE!
FLOMP
KTANK
HICC!!

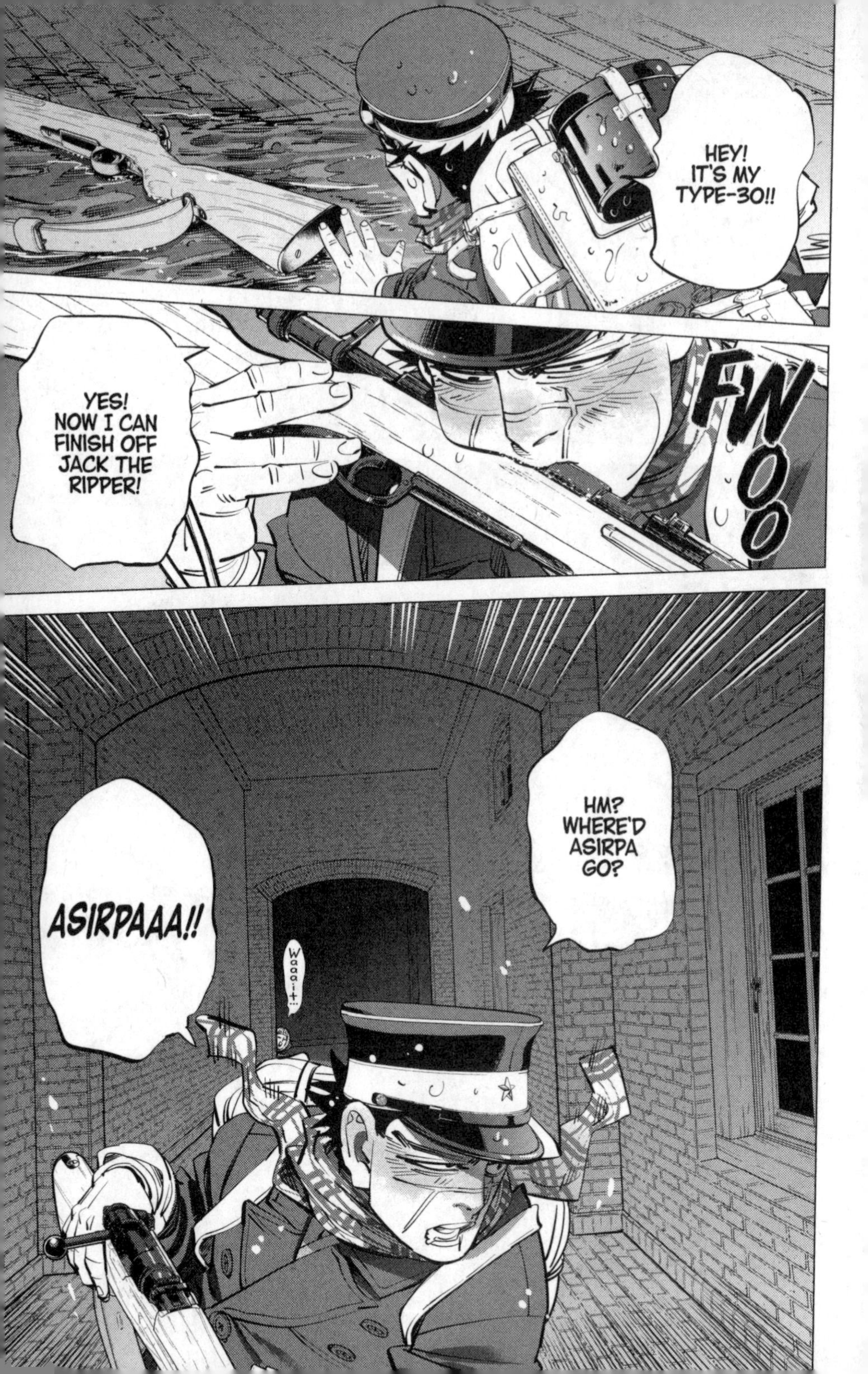
HEY! IT'S MY TYPE-30!!
FWOO
YES! NOW I CAN FINISH OFF JACK THE RIPPER!
HM? WHERE'D ASIRPA GO?
ASIRPAAA!!
Waaait...

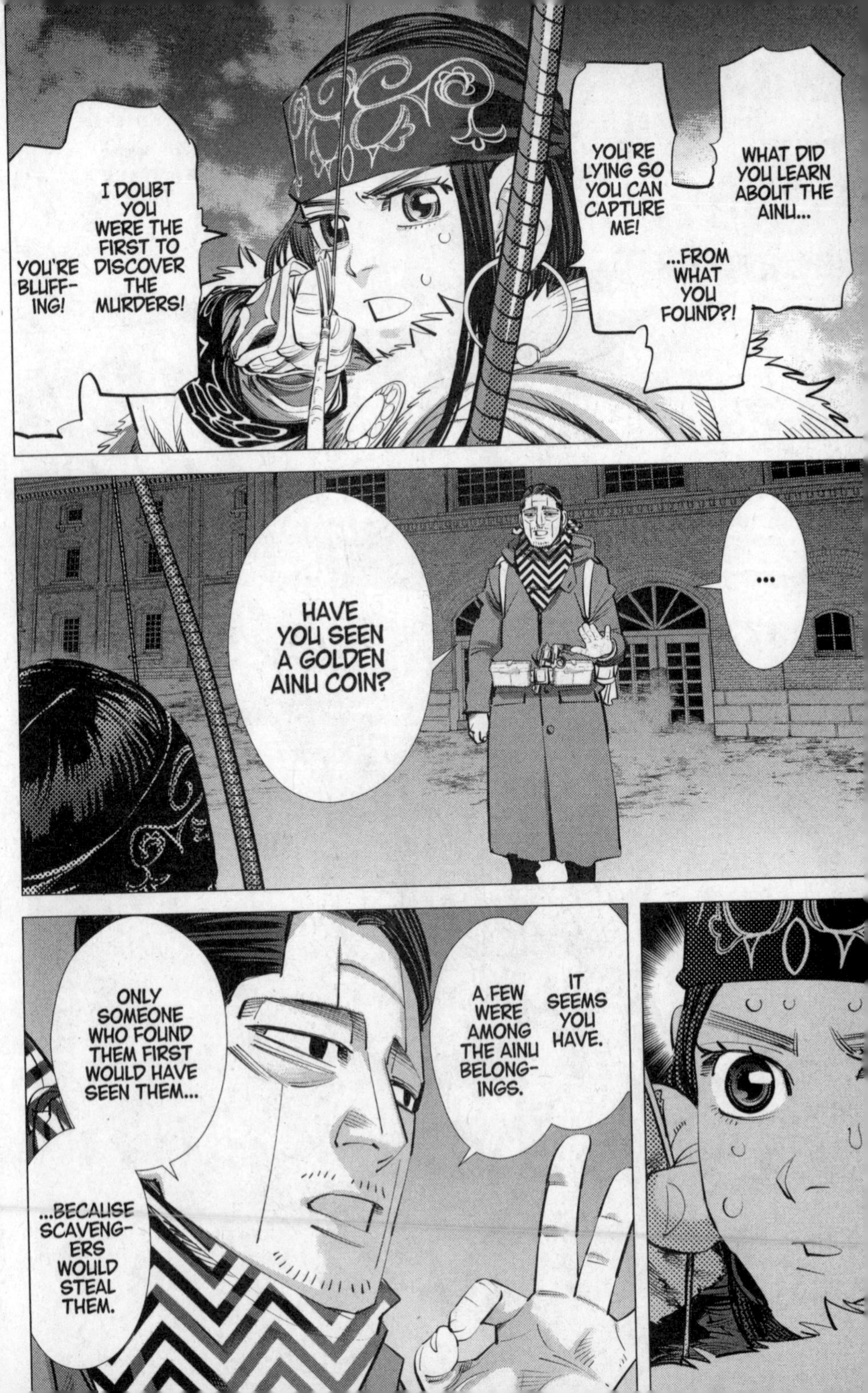
WHAT DID YOU LEARN ABOUT THE AINU...
...FROM WHAT YOU FOUND?!
YOU'RE LYING SO YOU CAN CAPTURE ME!
I DOUBT YOU WERE THE FIRST TO DISCOVER THE MURDERS!
YOU'RE BLUFF-ING!
...
HAVE YOU SEEN A GOLDEN AINU COIN?
IT SEEMS YOU HAVE.
A FEW WERE AMONG THE AINU BELONG-INGS.
ONLY SOMEONE WHO FOUND THEM FIRST WOULD HAVE SEEN THEM...
...BECAUSE SCAVENG-ERS WOULD STEAL THEM.

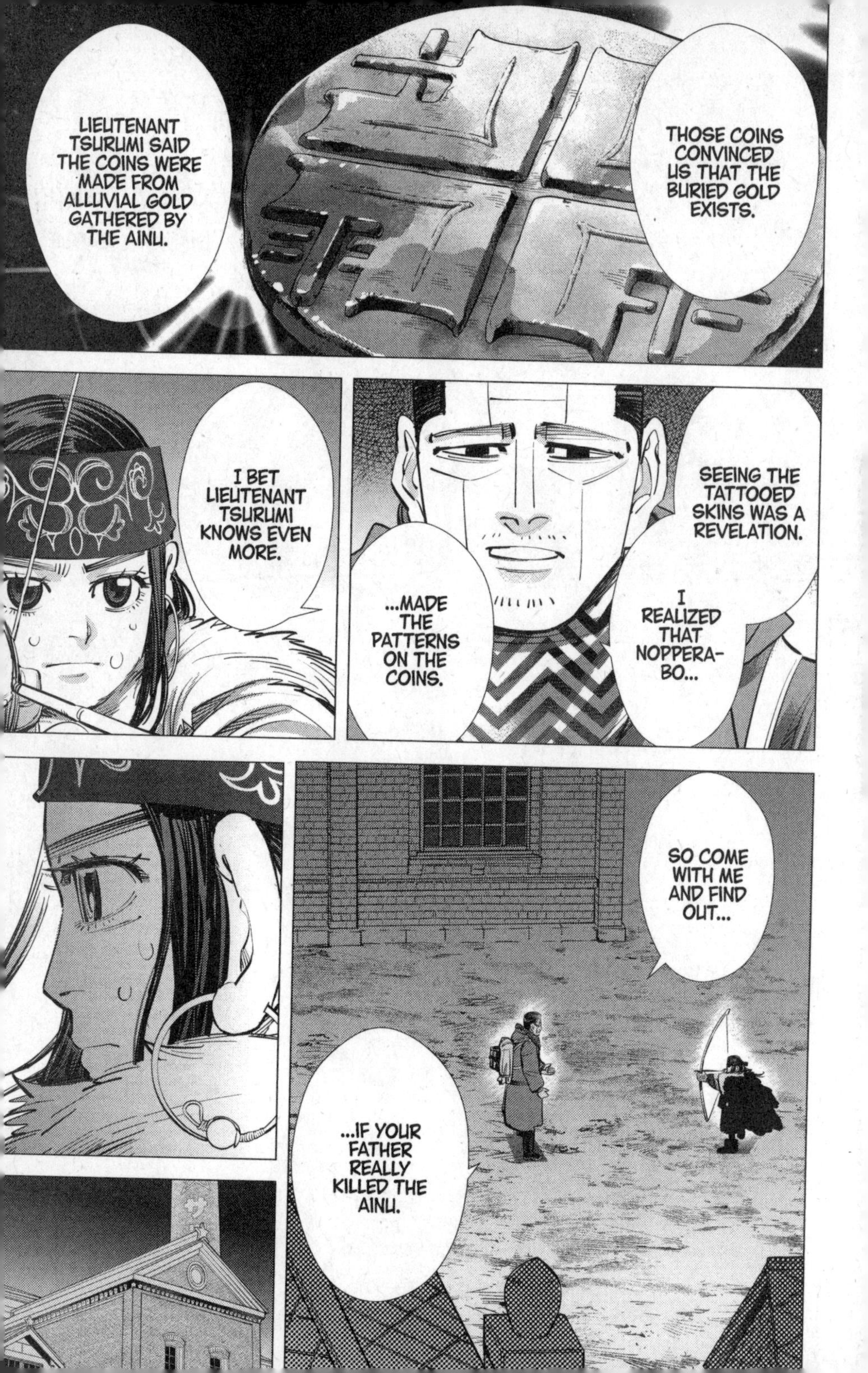
THOSE COINS CONVINCED US THAT THE BURIED GOLD EXISTS.
LIEUTENANT TSURUMI SAID THE COINS WERE MADE FROM ALLUVIAL GOLD GATHERED BY THE AINU.
SEEING THE TATTOOED SKINS WAS A REVELATION.
I REALIZED THAT NOPPERA-BO...
...MADE THE PATTERNS ON THE COINS.
I BET LIEUTENANT TSURUMI KNOWS EVEN MORE.
SO COME WITH ME AND FIND OUT...
...IF YOUR FATHER REALLY KILLED THE AINU.

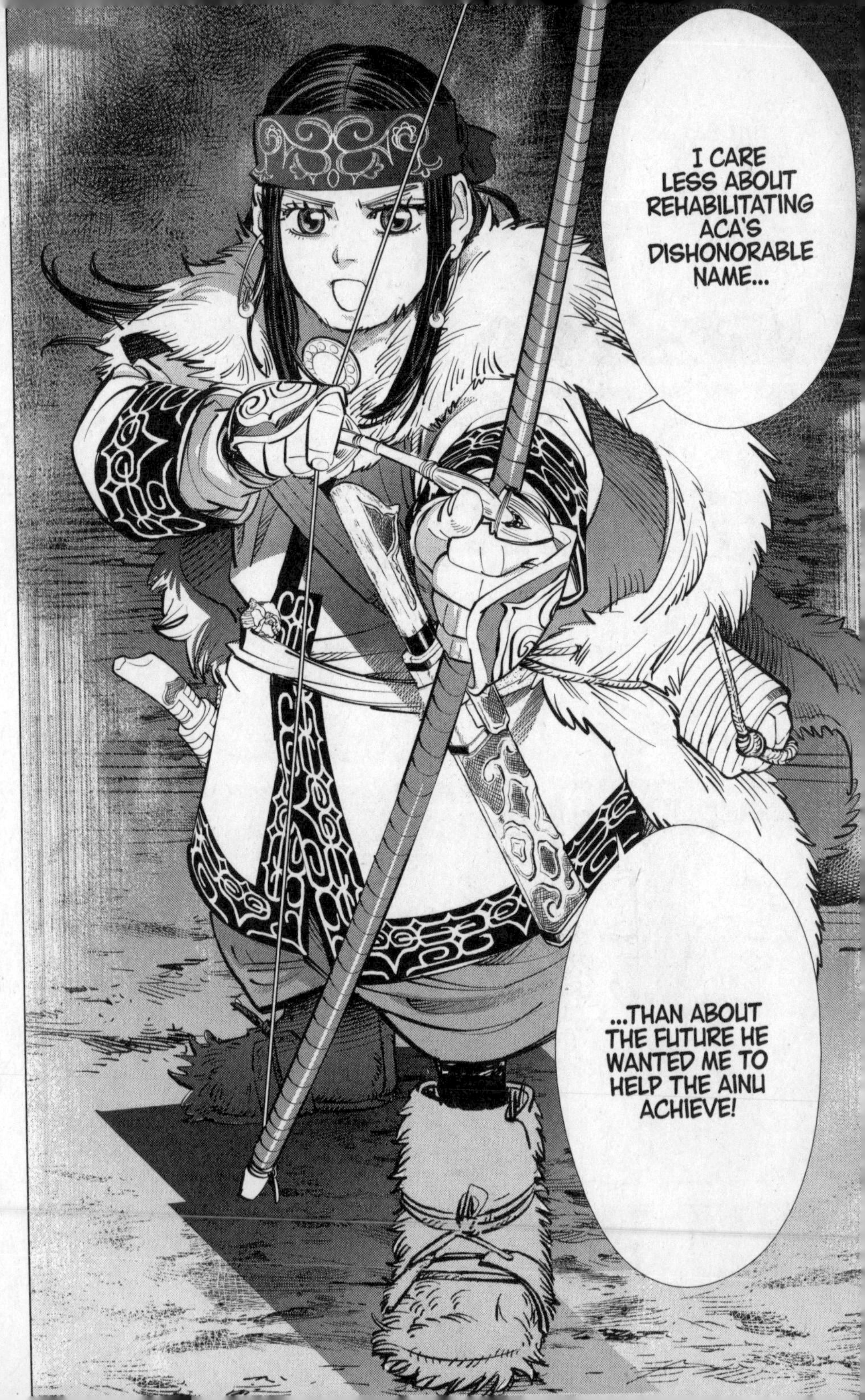
I CARE LESS ABOUT REHABILITATING ACA'S DISHONORABLE NAME...
...THAN ABOUT THE FUTURE HE WANTED ME TO HELP THE AINU ACHIEVE!

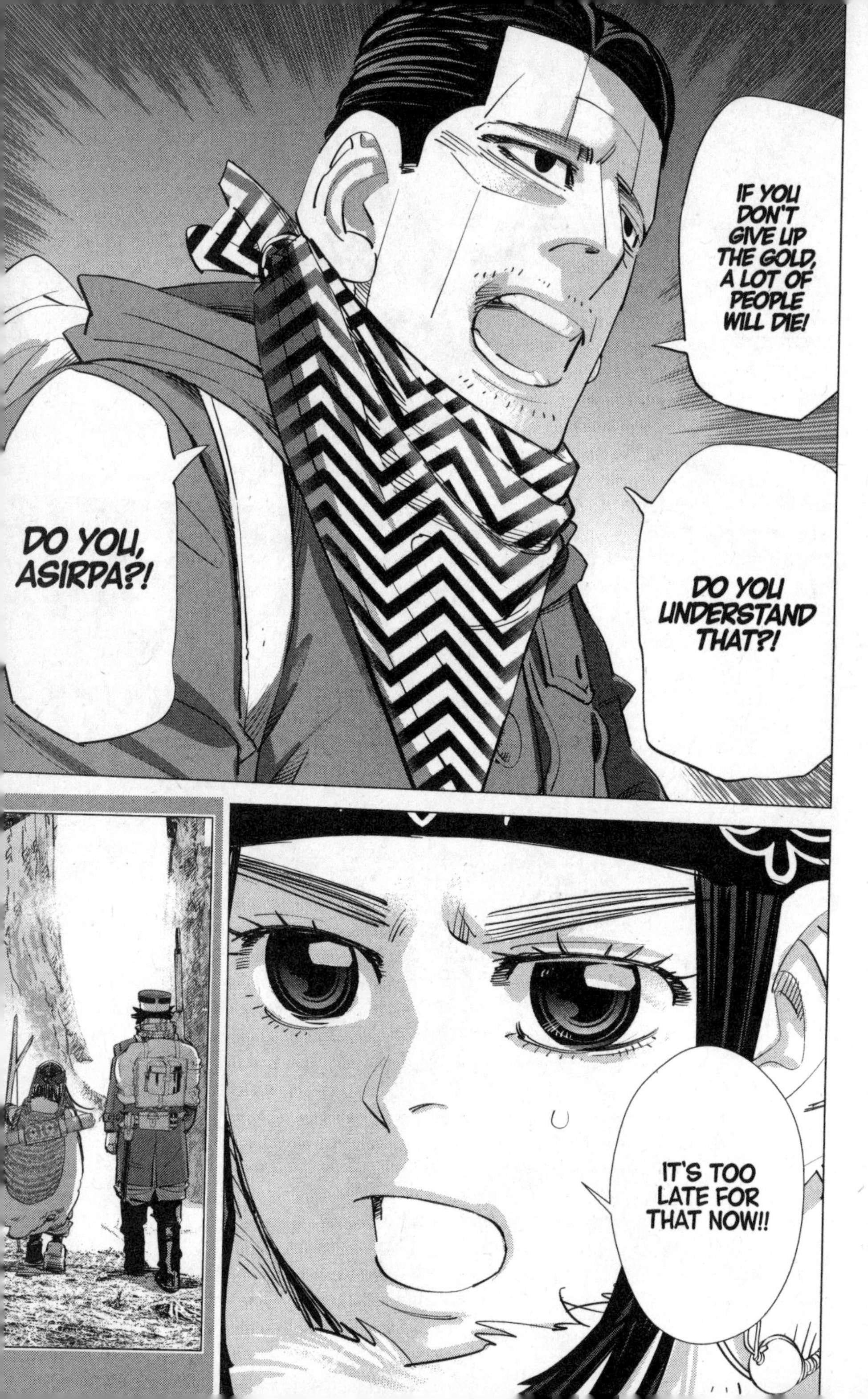
IF YOU DON'T GIVE UP THE GOLD, A LOT OF PEOPLE WILL DIE!
DO YOU UNDERSTAND THAT?!
DO YOU, ASIRPA?!
IT'S TOO LATE FOR THAT NOW!!

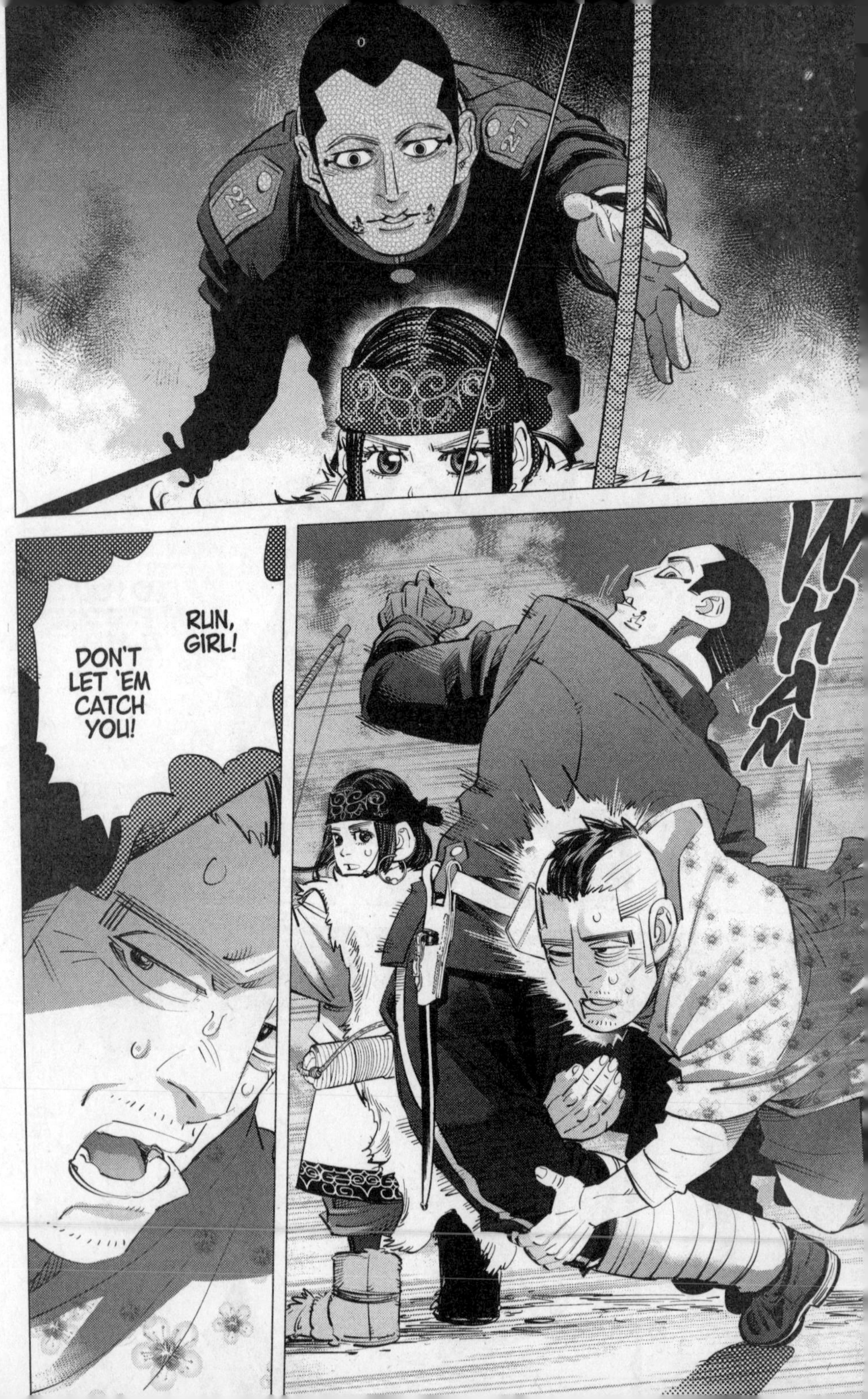
WHAM
RUN, GIRL!
DON'T LET 'EM CATCH YOU!

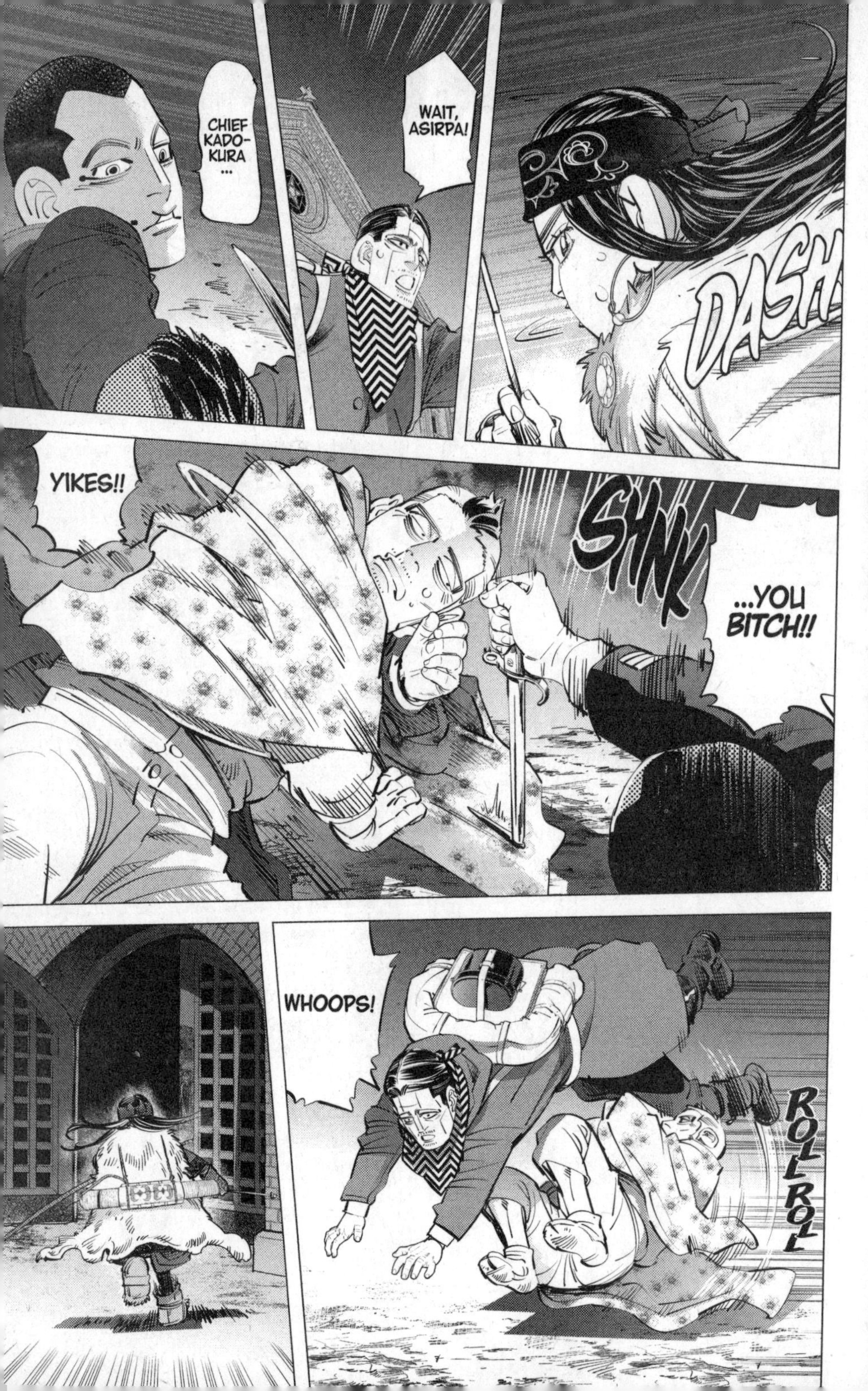
DASH
WAIT, ASIRPA!
CHIEF KADO-KURA ...
SHNK
...YOU BITCH!!
YIKES!!
ROLL ROLL
WHOOPS!

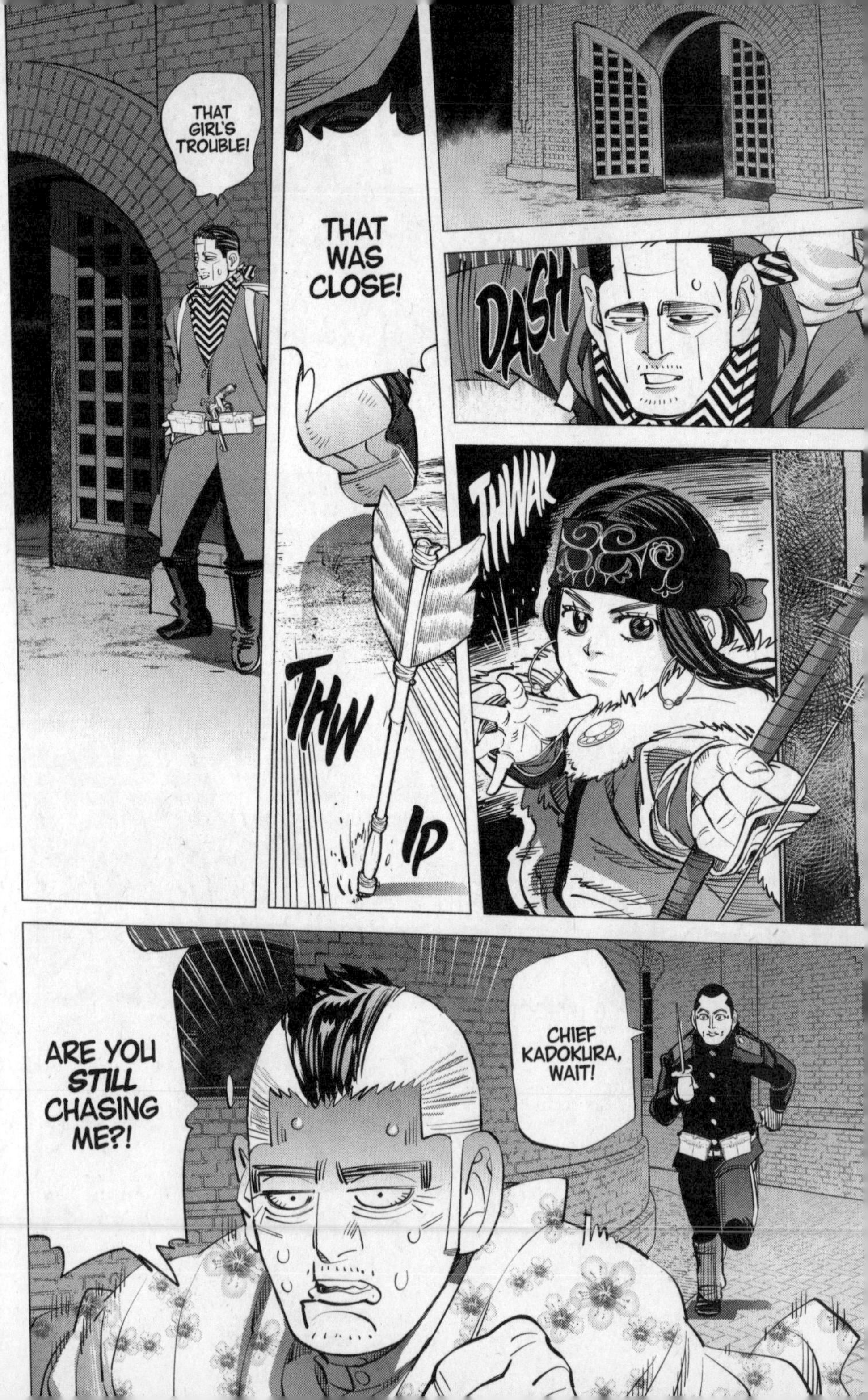
DASH
THWAK
THAT WAS CLOSE!
THWIP
THAT GIRL'S TROUBLE!
CHIEF KADOKURA, WAIT!
ARE YOU STILL CHASING ME?!

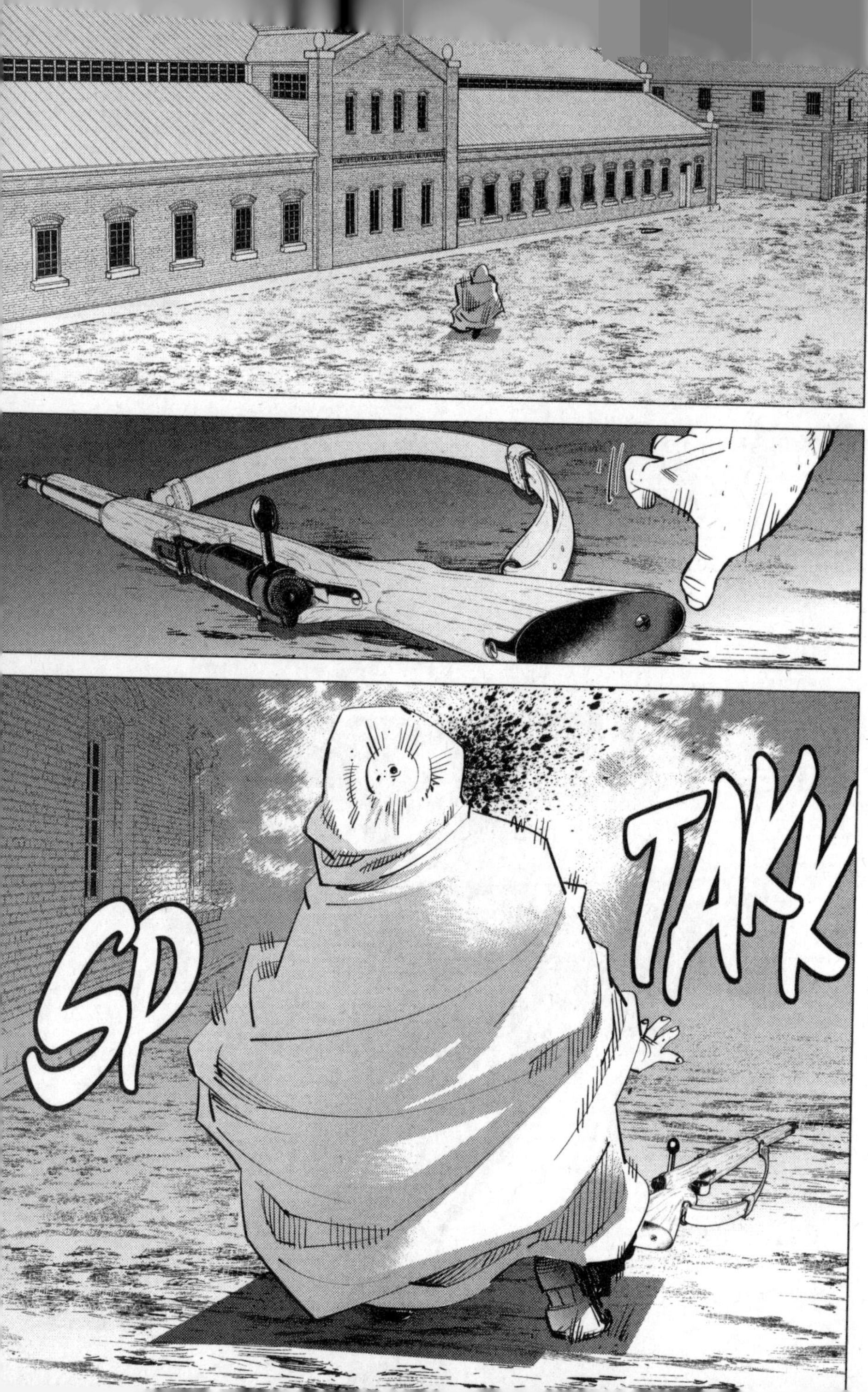
TAKK
SP

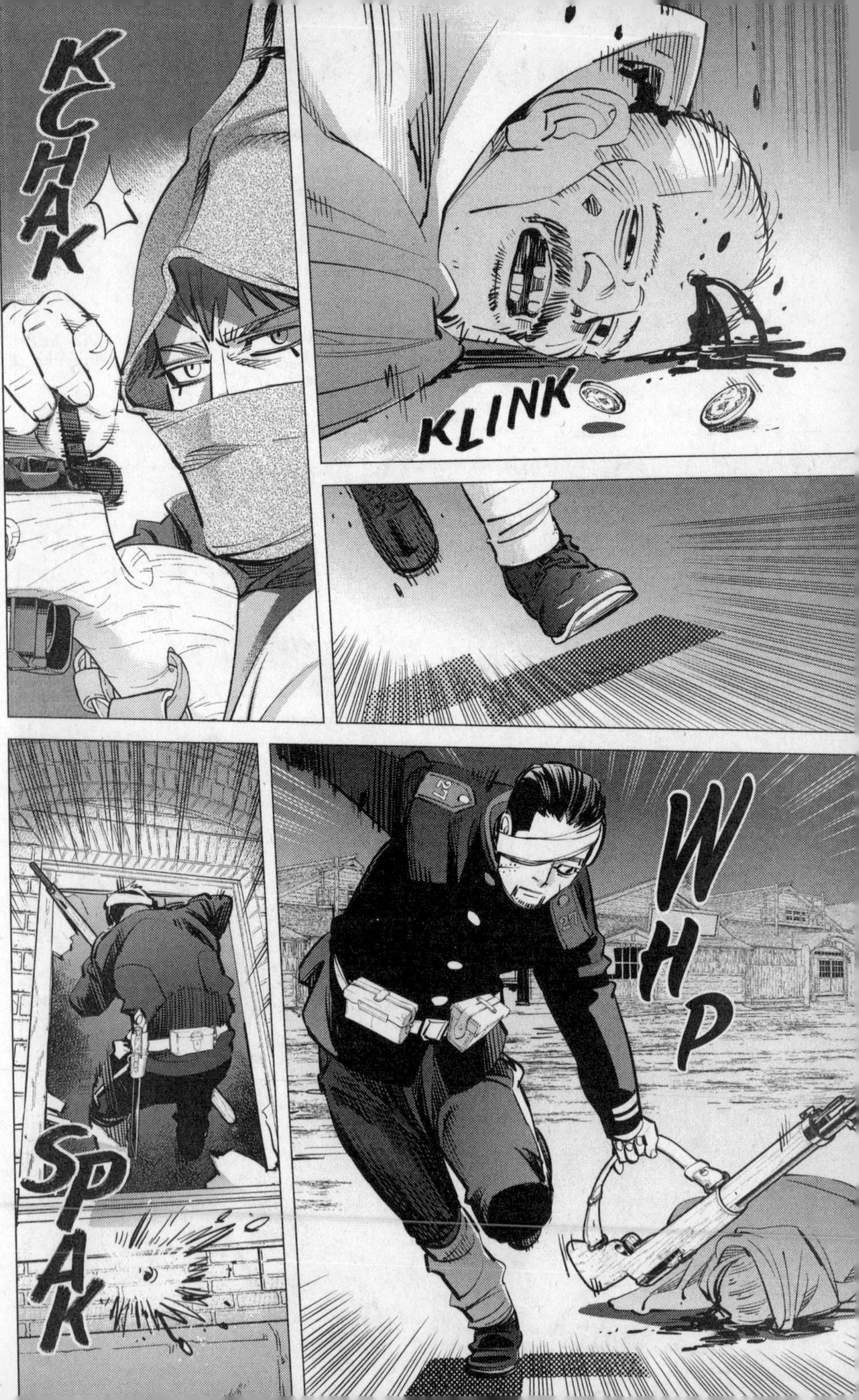
KLINK
KCHAK
WHP
SPAK

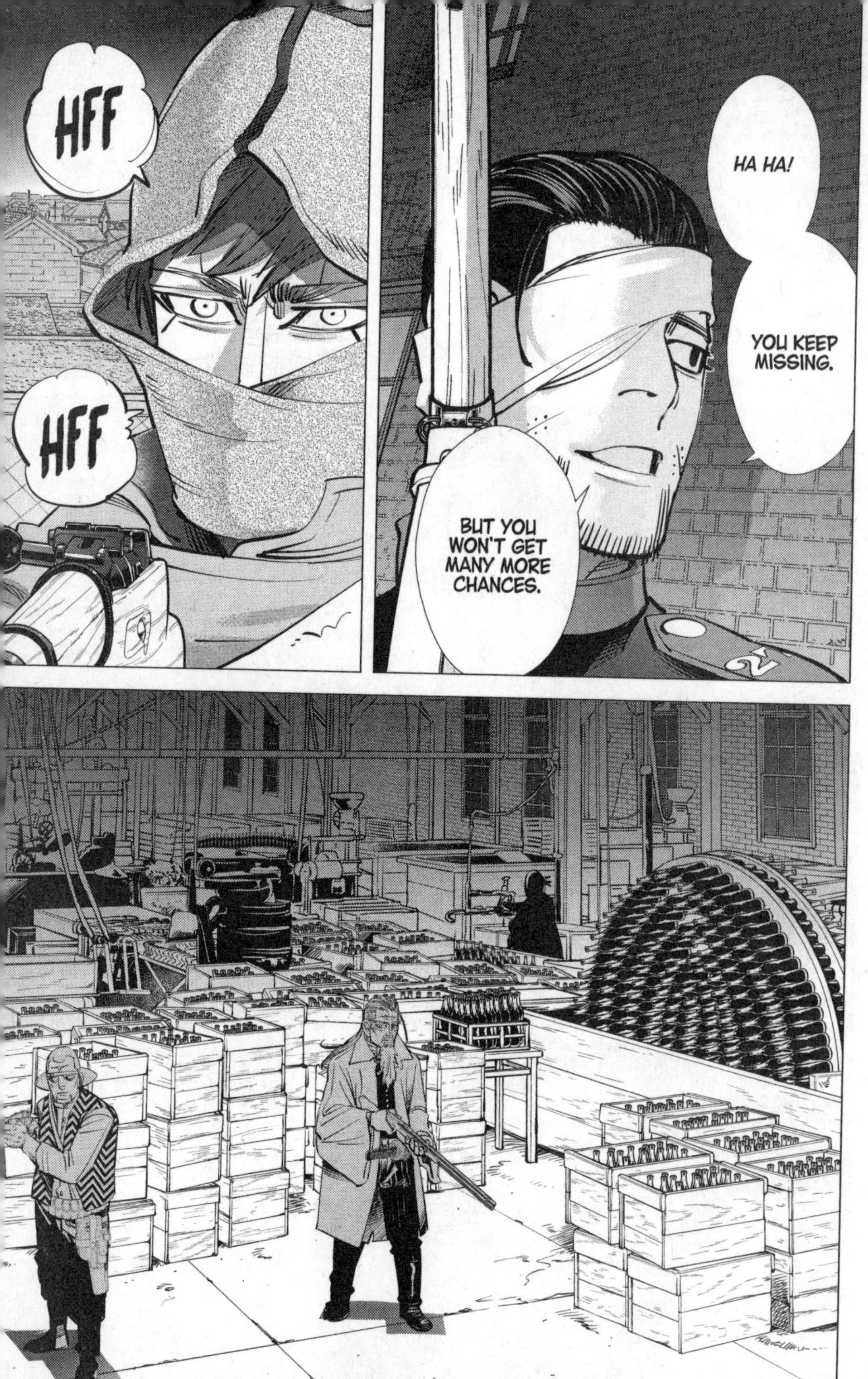
HA HA!
YOU KEEP MISSING.
BUT YOU WON'T GET MANY MORE CHANCES.
HFF
HFF

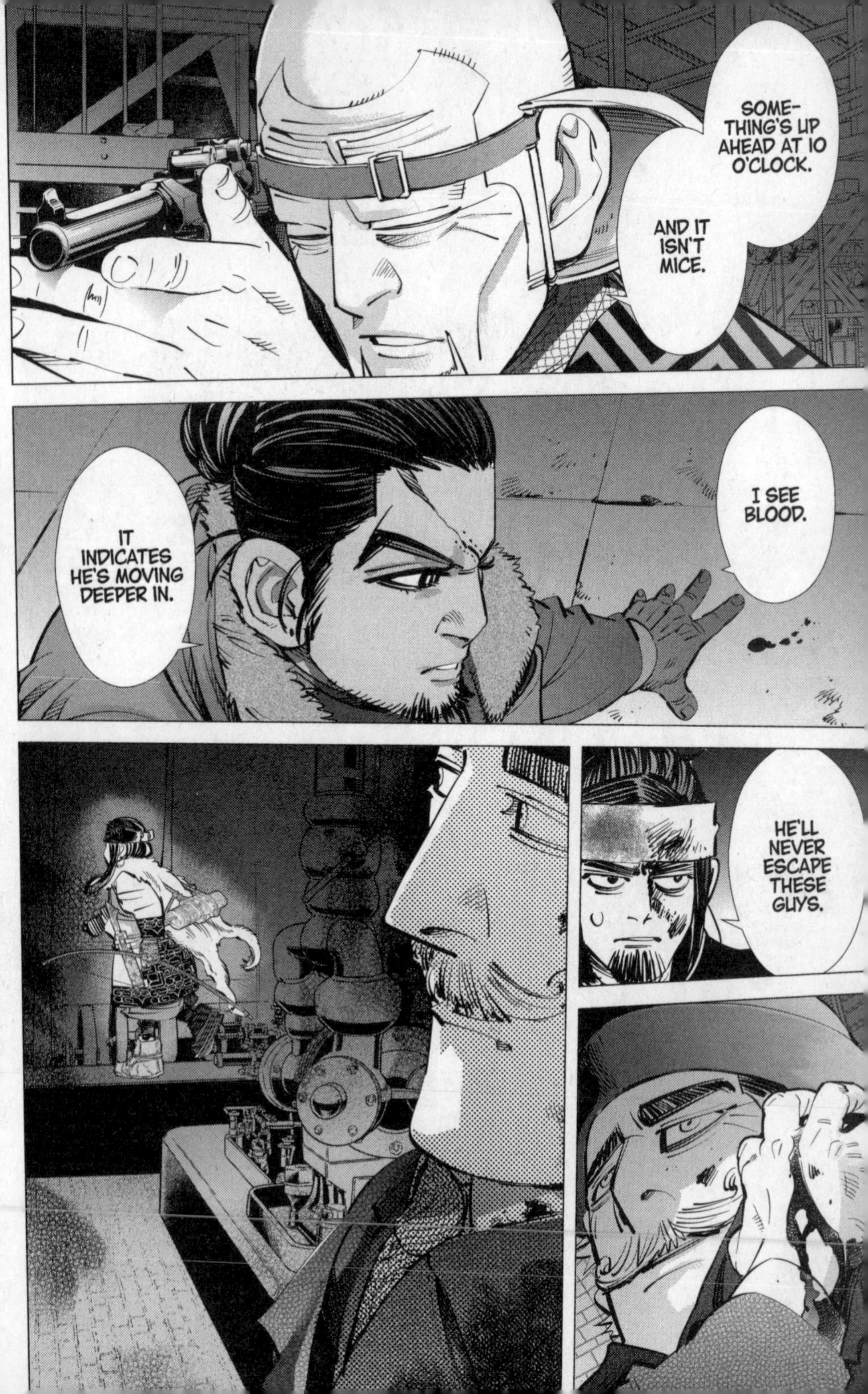
SOME-THING'S UP AHEAD AT 10 O'CLOCK.
AND IT ISN'T MICE.
I SEE BLOOD.
IT INDICATES HE'S MOVING DEEPER IN.
HE'LL NEVER ESCAPE THESE GUYS.

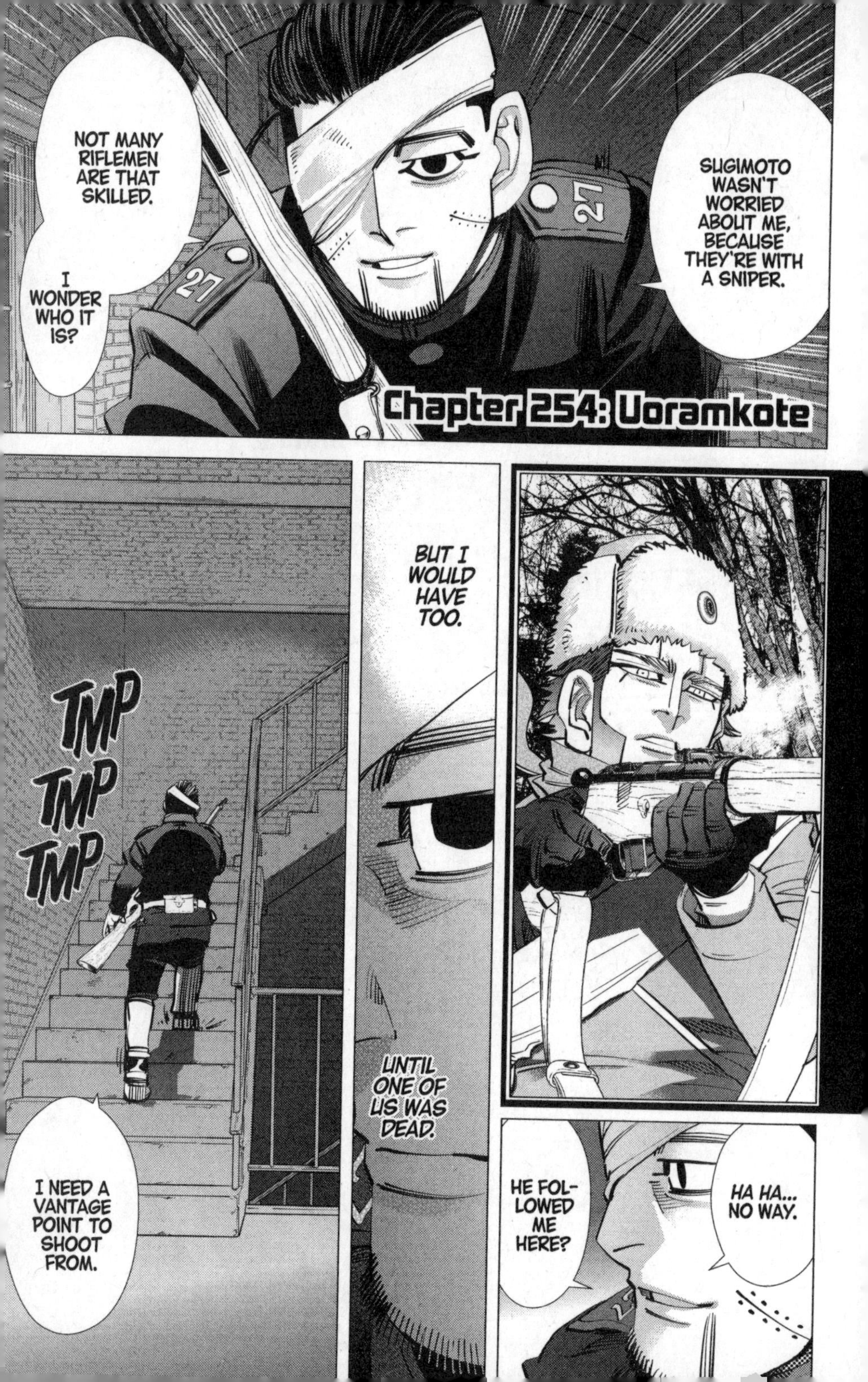
SUGIMOTO WASN'T WORRIED ABOUT ME, BECAUSE THEY'RE WITH A SNIPER.
NOT MANY RIFLEMEN ARE THAT SKILLED.
I WONDER WHO IT IS?
Chapter 254: Uoramkote
HA HA... NO WAY.
HE FOL-LOWED ME HERE?
BUT I WOULD HAVE TOO.
UNTIL ONE OF US WAS DEAD.
TMP TMP TMP
I NEED A VANTAGE POINT TO SHOOT FROM.

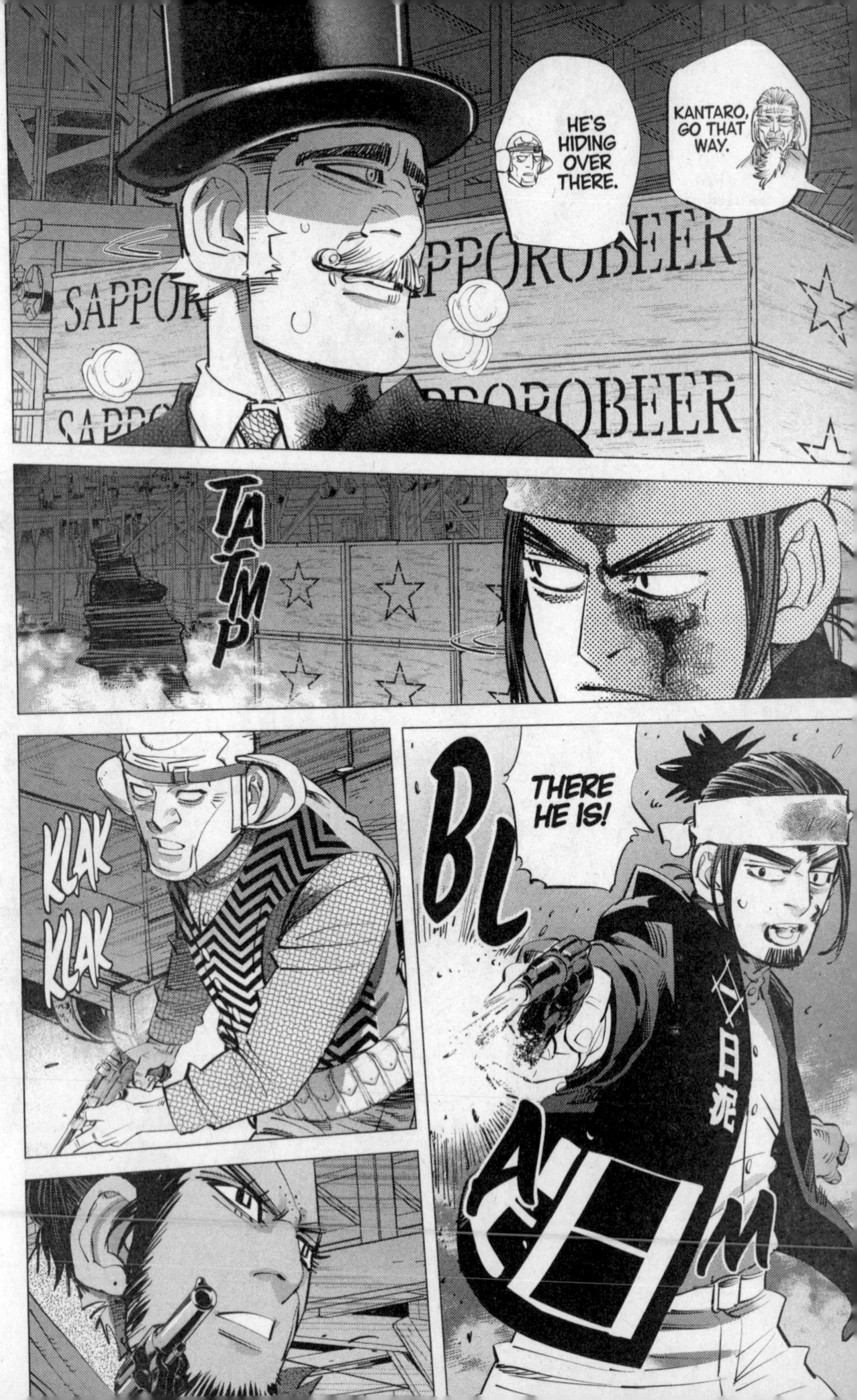
KANTARO, GO THAT WAY.
HE'S HIDING OVER THERE.
SAPPOROBEER
SAPPOROBEER
TATMP
THERE HE IS!
BLAM
KLAK KLAK

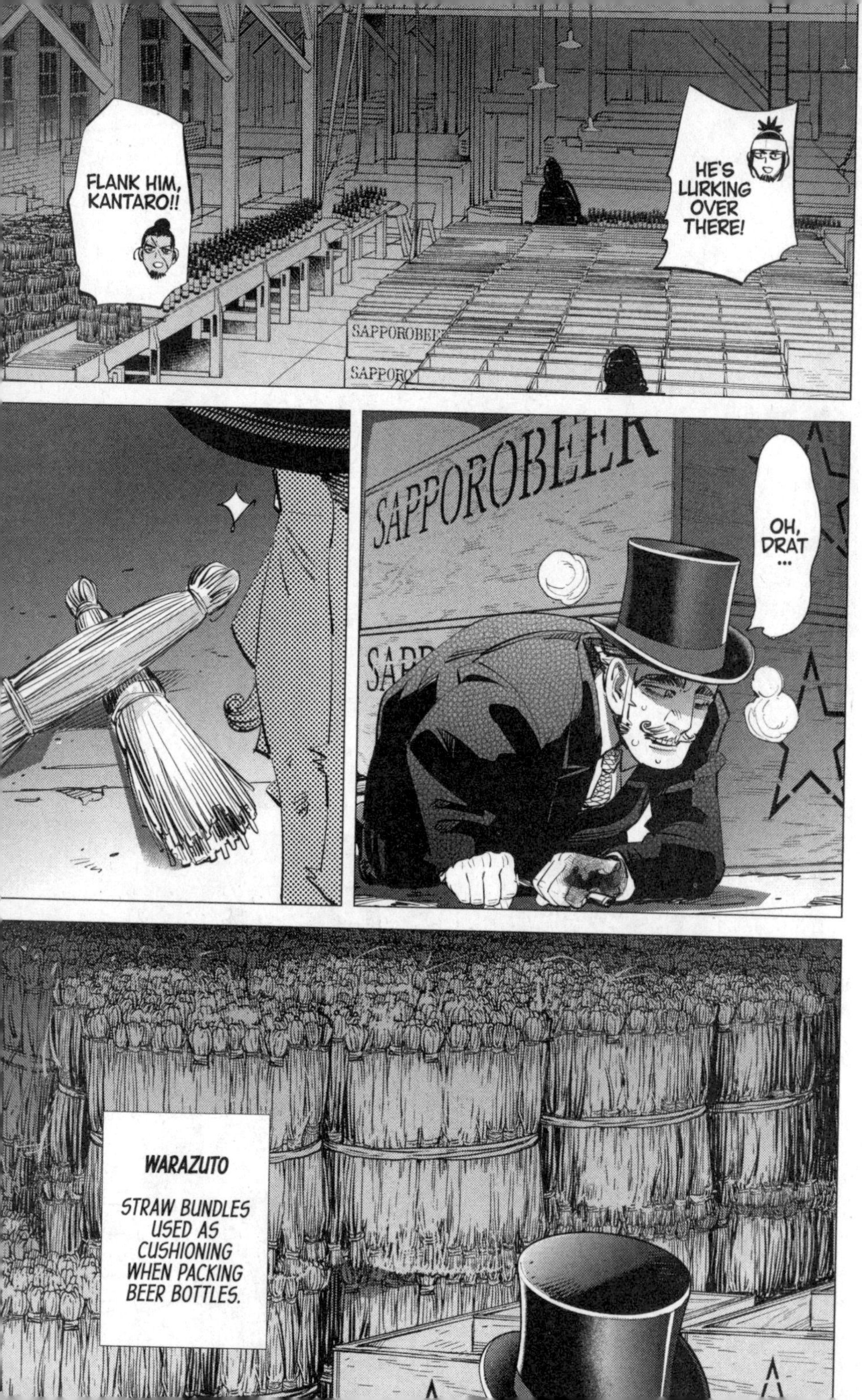
HE'S LURKING OVER THERE!
FLANK HIM, KANTARO!!
SAPPOROBEER
OH, DRAT ...
WARAZUTO
STRAW BUNDLES USED AS CUSHIONING WHEN PACKING BEER BOTTLES.

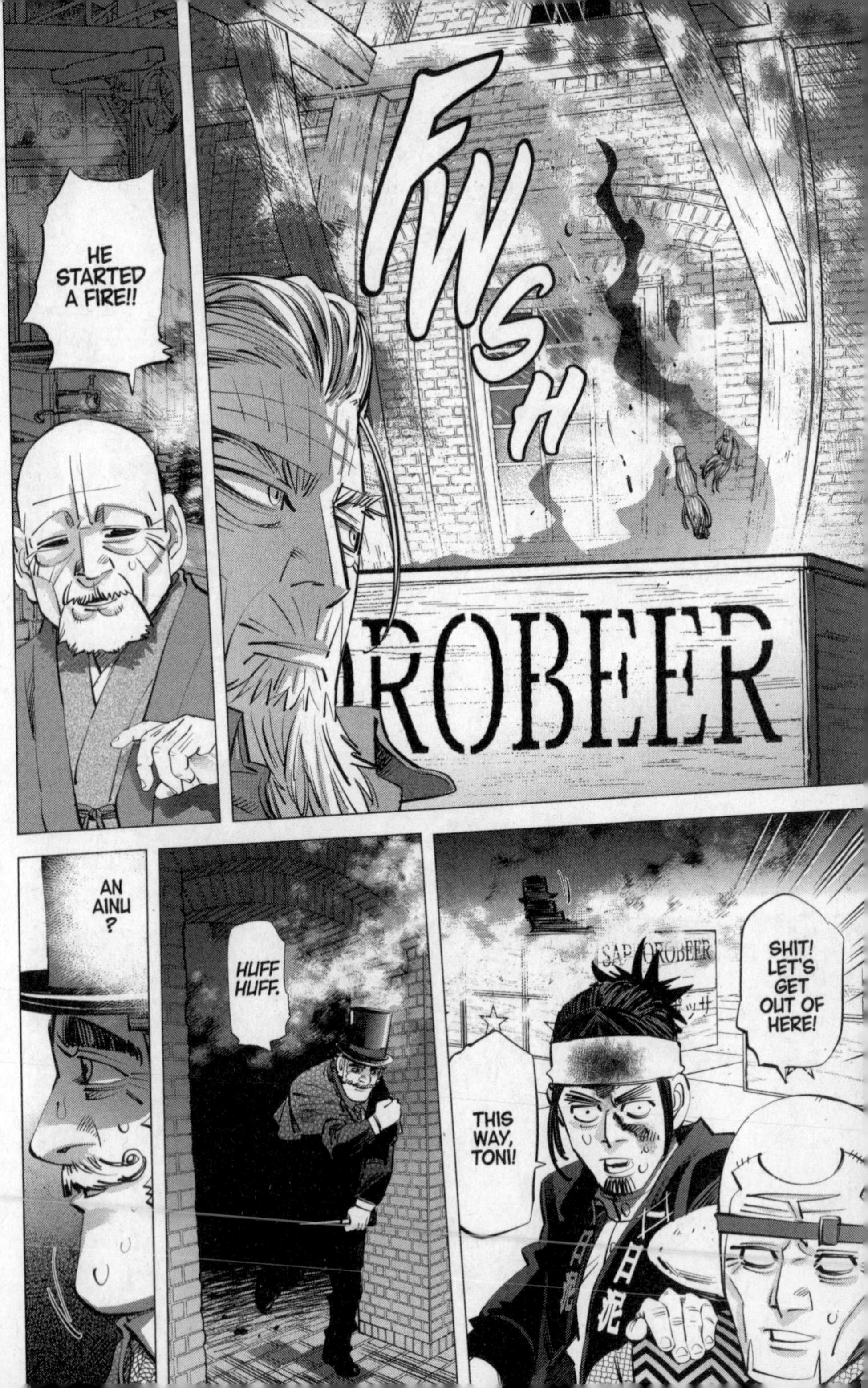
FWSH
ROBEER
HE STARTED A FIRE!!
SHIT! LET'S GET OUT OF HERE!
THIS WAY, TONI!
HUFF HUFF.
AN AINU?

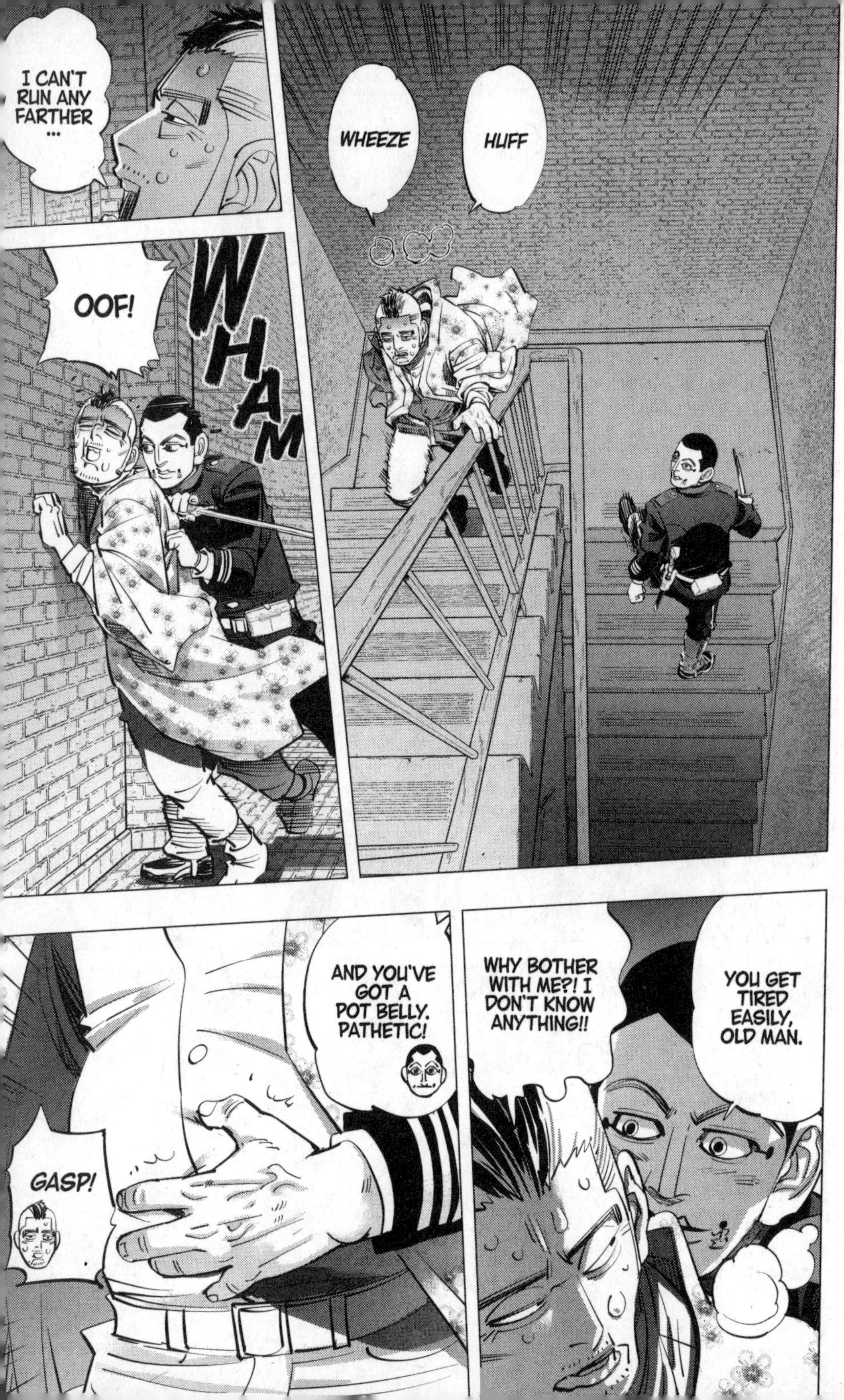
HUFF
WHEEZE
I CAN'T RUN ANY FARTHER ...
WHAM
OOF!
YOU GET TIRED EASILY, OLD MAN.
WHY BOTHER WITH ME?! I DON'T KNOW ANYTHING!!
AND YOU'VE GOT A POT BELLY. PATHETIC!
GASP!

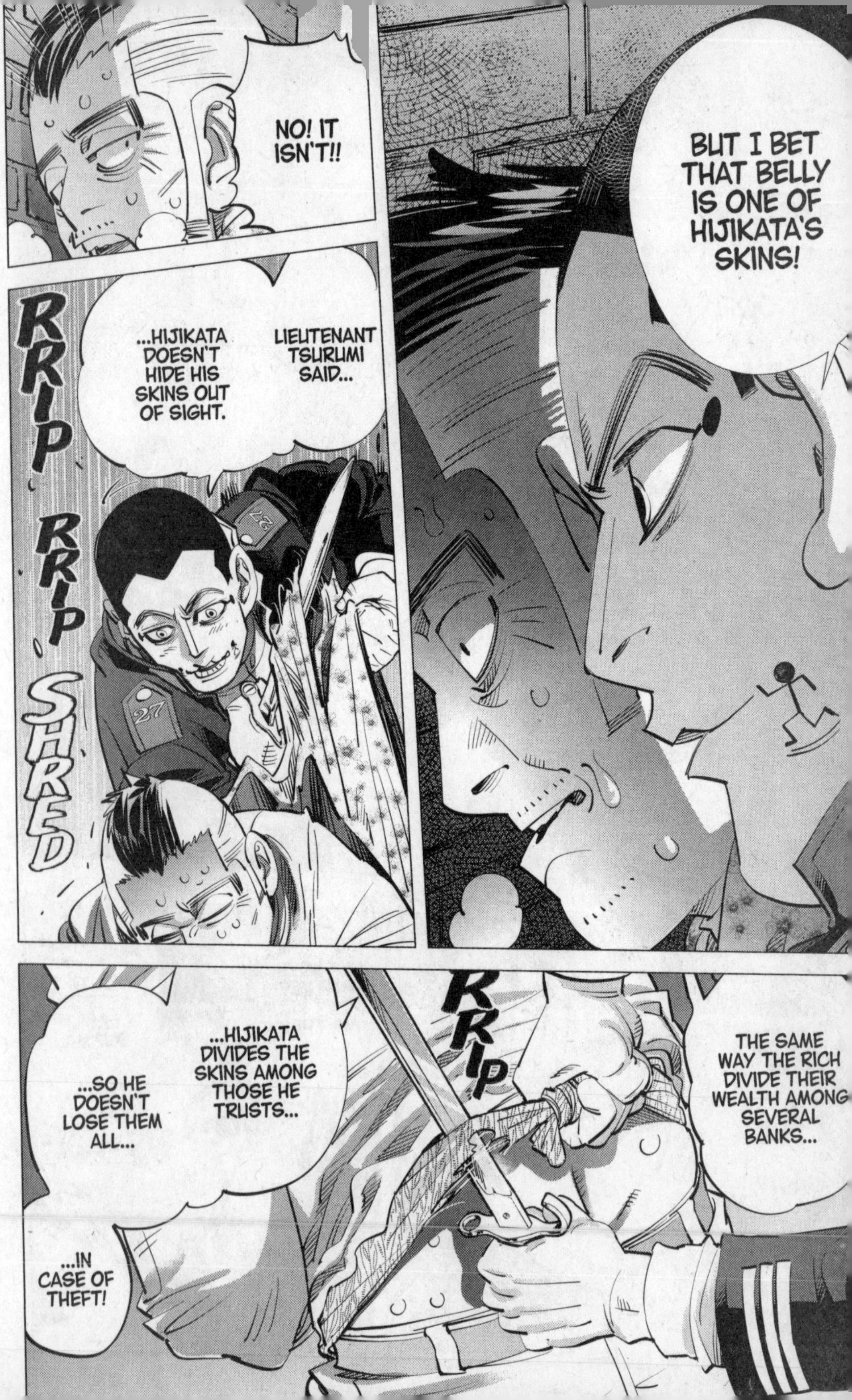
BUT I BET THAT BELLY IS ONE OF HIJIKATA'S SKINS!
NO! IT ISN'T!!
LIEUTENANT TSURUMI SAID...
...HIJIKATA DOESN'T HIDE HIS SKINS OUT OF SIGHT.
RRIP
RRIP
SHRED
THE SAME WAY THE RICH DIVIDE THEIR WEALTH AMONG SEVERAL BANKS...
RRIP
...HIJIKATA DIVIDES THE SKINS AMONG THOSE HE TRUSTS...
...SO HE DOESN'T LOSE THEM ALL...
...IN CASE OF THEFT!

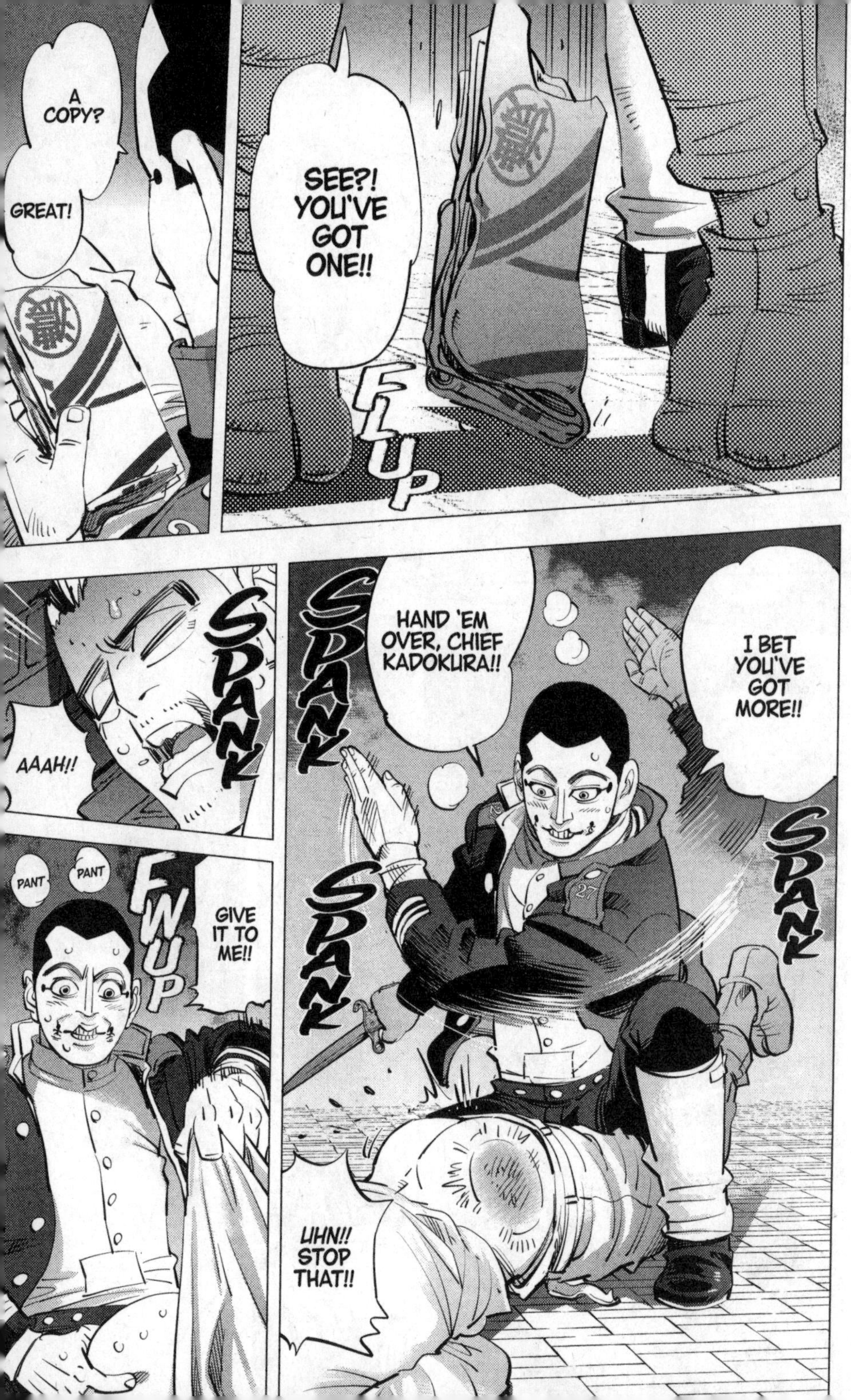
SEE?! YOU'VE GOT ONE!!
FLUP
A COPY?
GREAT!
I BET YOU'VE GOT MORE!!
HAND 'EM OVER, CHIEF KADOKURA!!
SPANK
SPANK
SPANK
SPANK
UHN!! STOP THAT!!
SPANK
AAAH!!
PANT
PANT
FWUP
GIVE IT TO ME!!

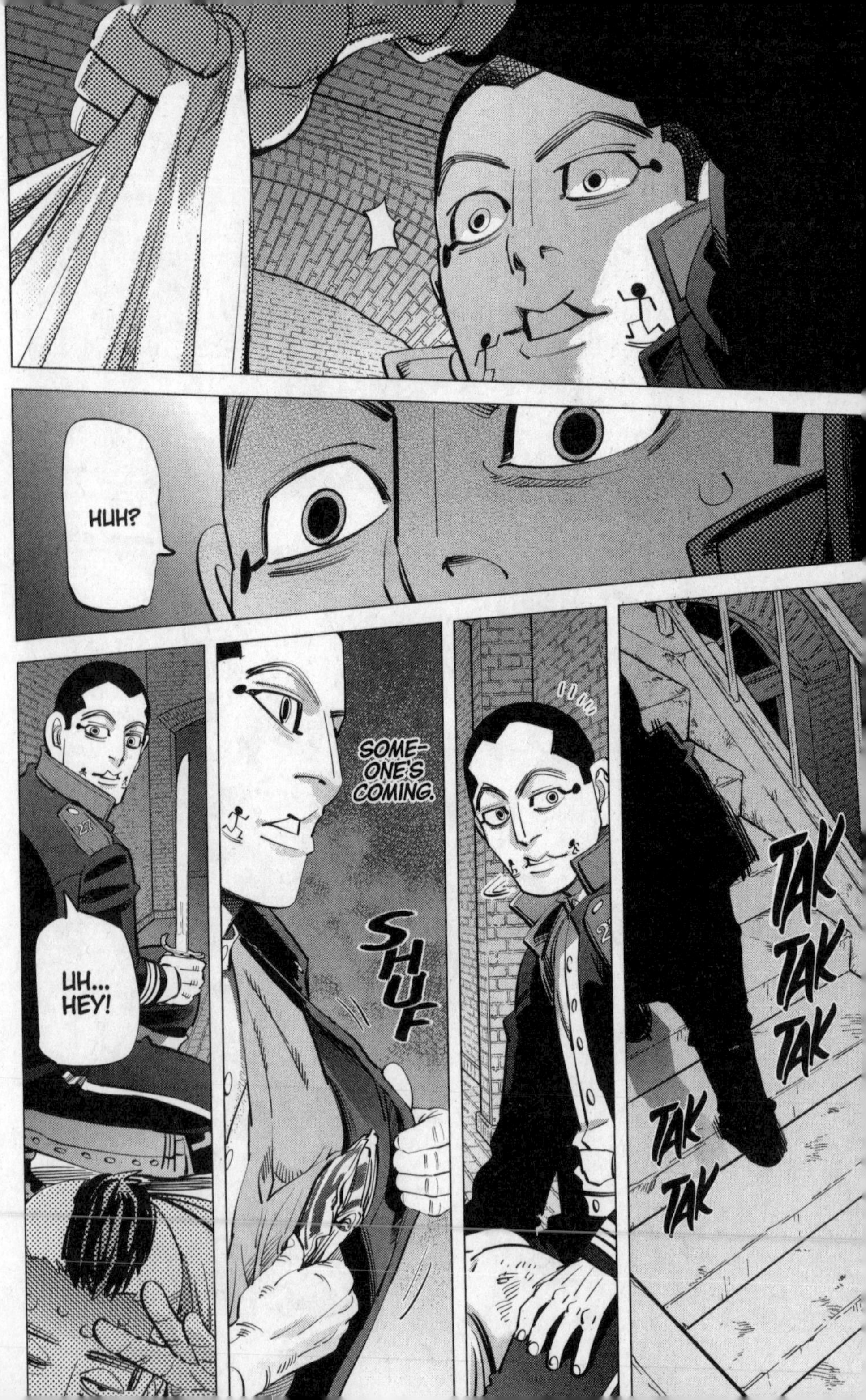
HUH?
TAK TAK TAK
TAK TAK
SOME-ONE'S COMING.
SHUF
UH... HEY!

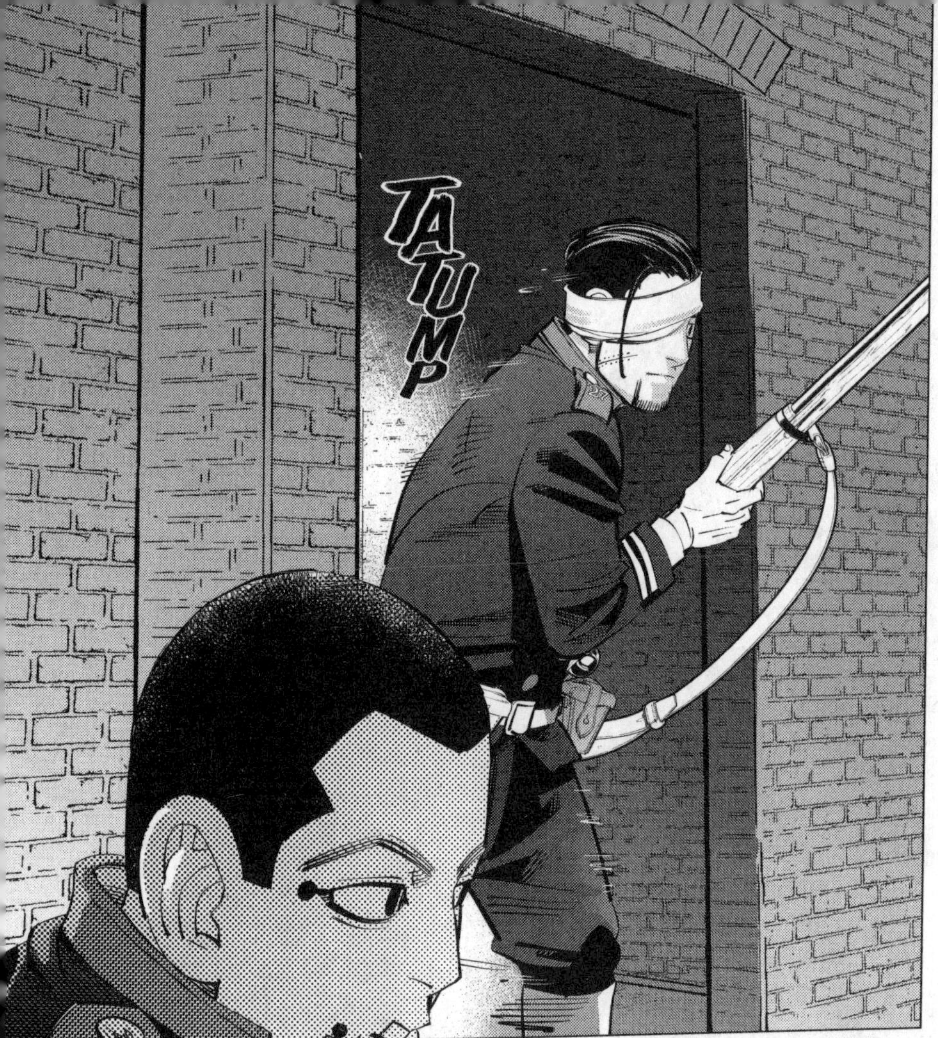
TATUMP
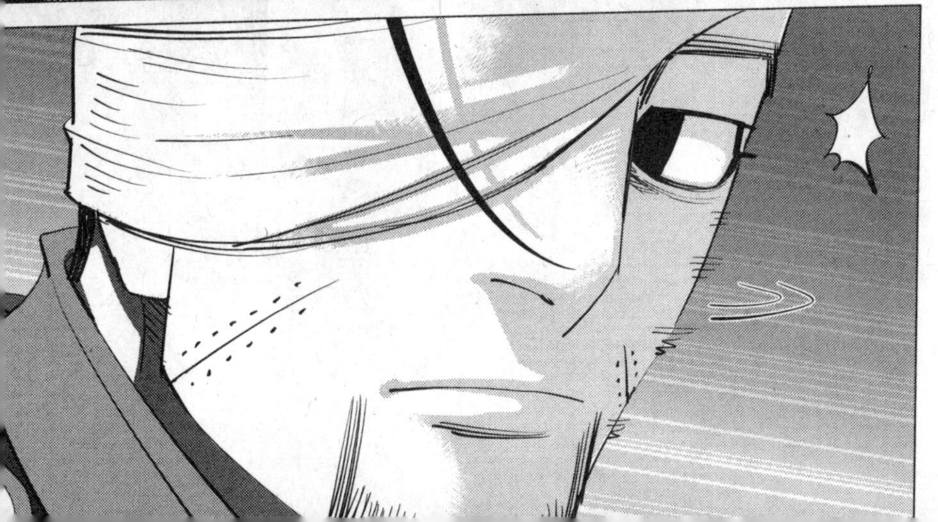

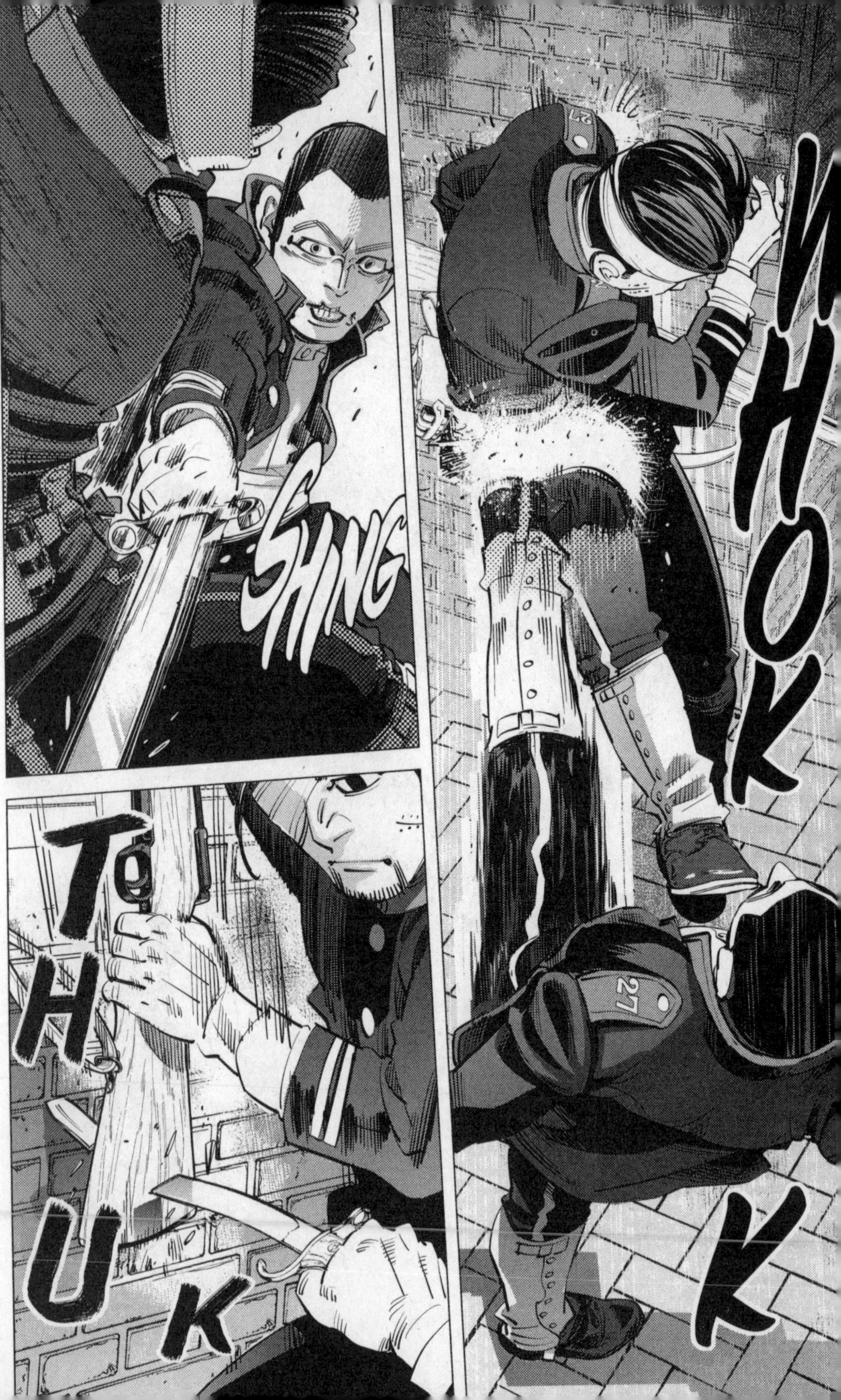
WHOK
K
SHING
THUK

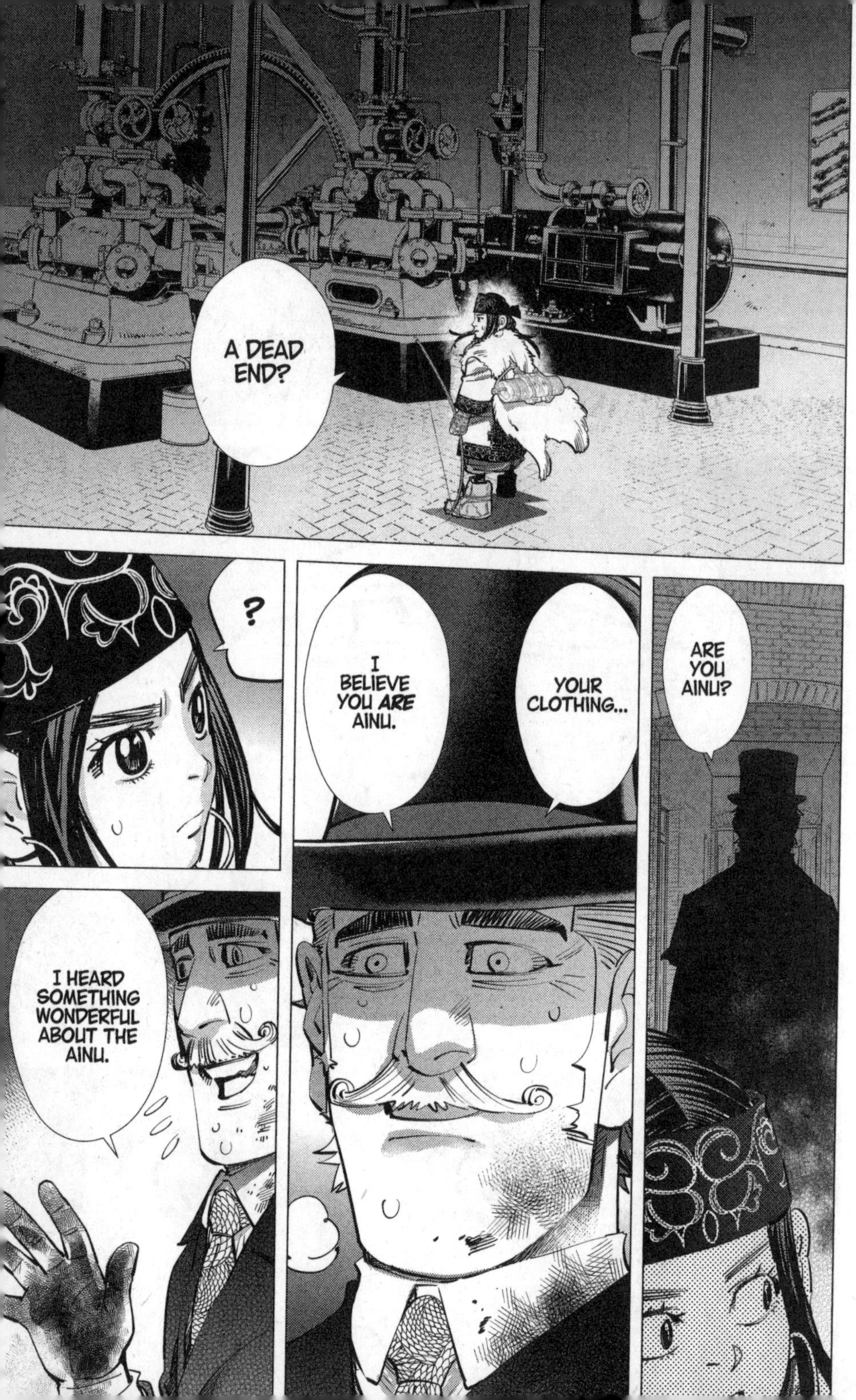
A DEAD END?
ARE YOU AINU?
YOUR CLOTHING...
I BELIEVE YOU *ARE* AINU.
?
I HEARD SOMETHING WONDERFUL ABOUT THE AINU.

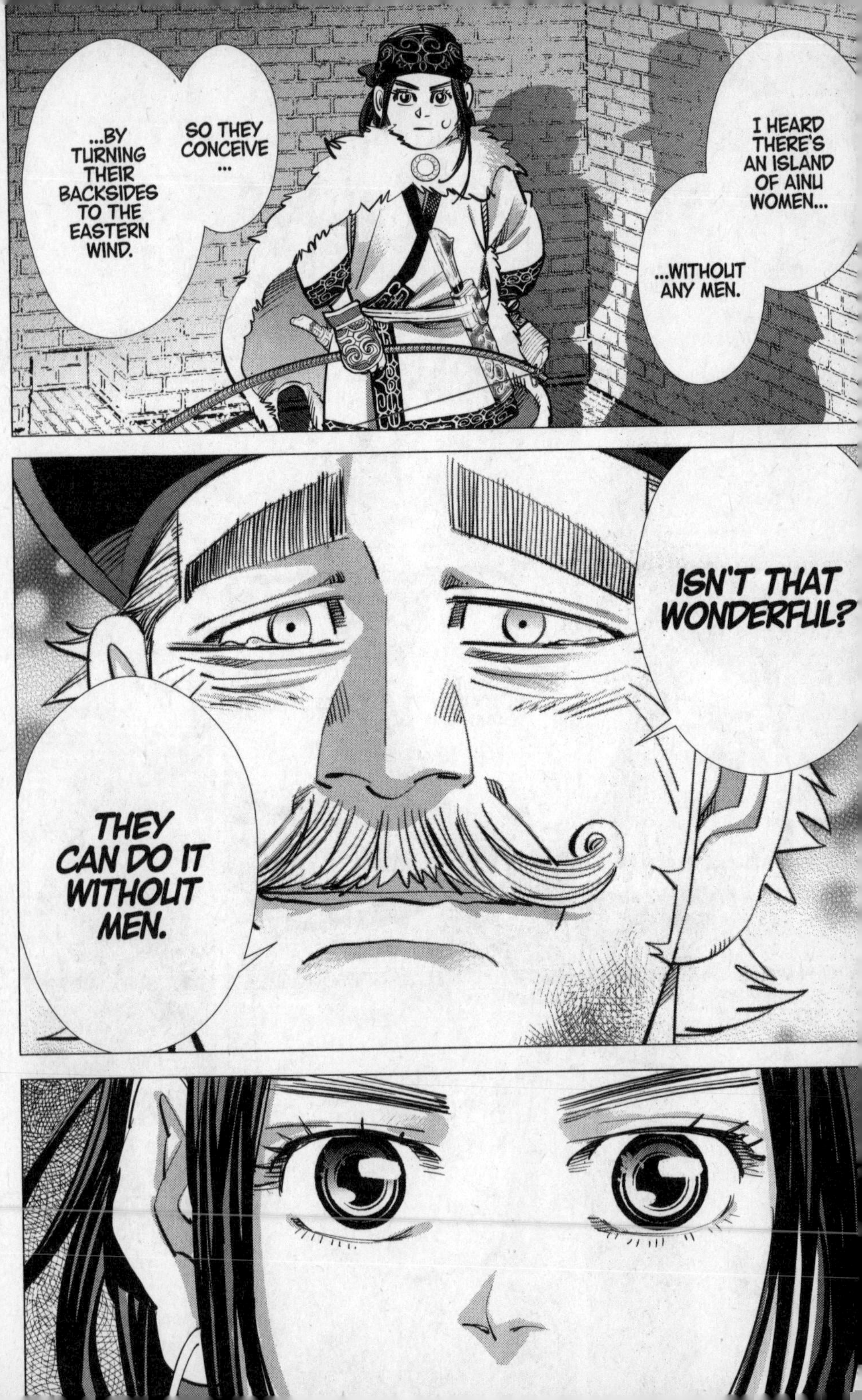
I HEARD THERE'S AN ISLAND OF AINU WOMEN...
...WITHOUT ANY MEN.
SO THEY CONCEIVE...
...BY TURNING THEIR BACKSIDES TO THE EASTERN WIND.
ISN'T THAT WONDERFUL?
THEY CAN DO IT WITHOUT MEN.

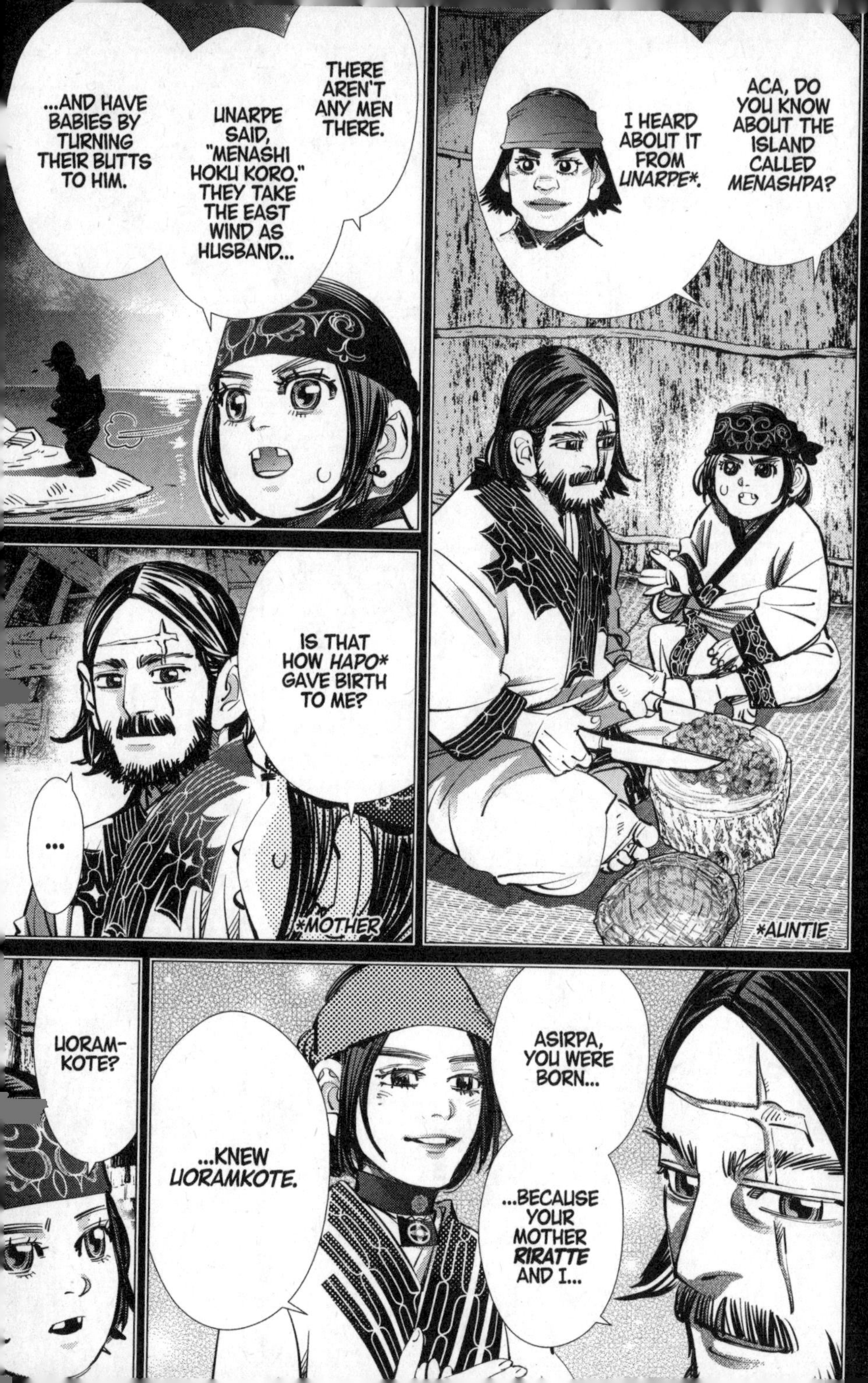
ACA, DO YOU KNOW ABOUT THE ISLAND CALLED MENASHPA?
I HEARD ABOUT IT FROM UNARPE*.
*AUNTIE
THERE AREN'T ANY MEN THERE.
UNARPE SAID, "MENASHI HOKU KORO." THEY TAKE THE EAST WIND AS HUSBAND...
...AND HAVE BABIES BY TURNING THEIR BUTTS TO HIM.
IS THAT HOW HAPO* GAVE BIRTH TO ME?
...
*MOTHER
ASIRPA, YOU WERE BORN...
...BECAUSE YOUR MOTHER RIRATTE AND I...
...KNEW UORAMKOTE.
UORAM-KOTE?

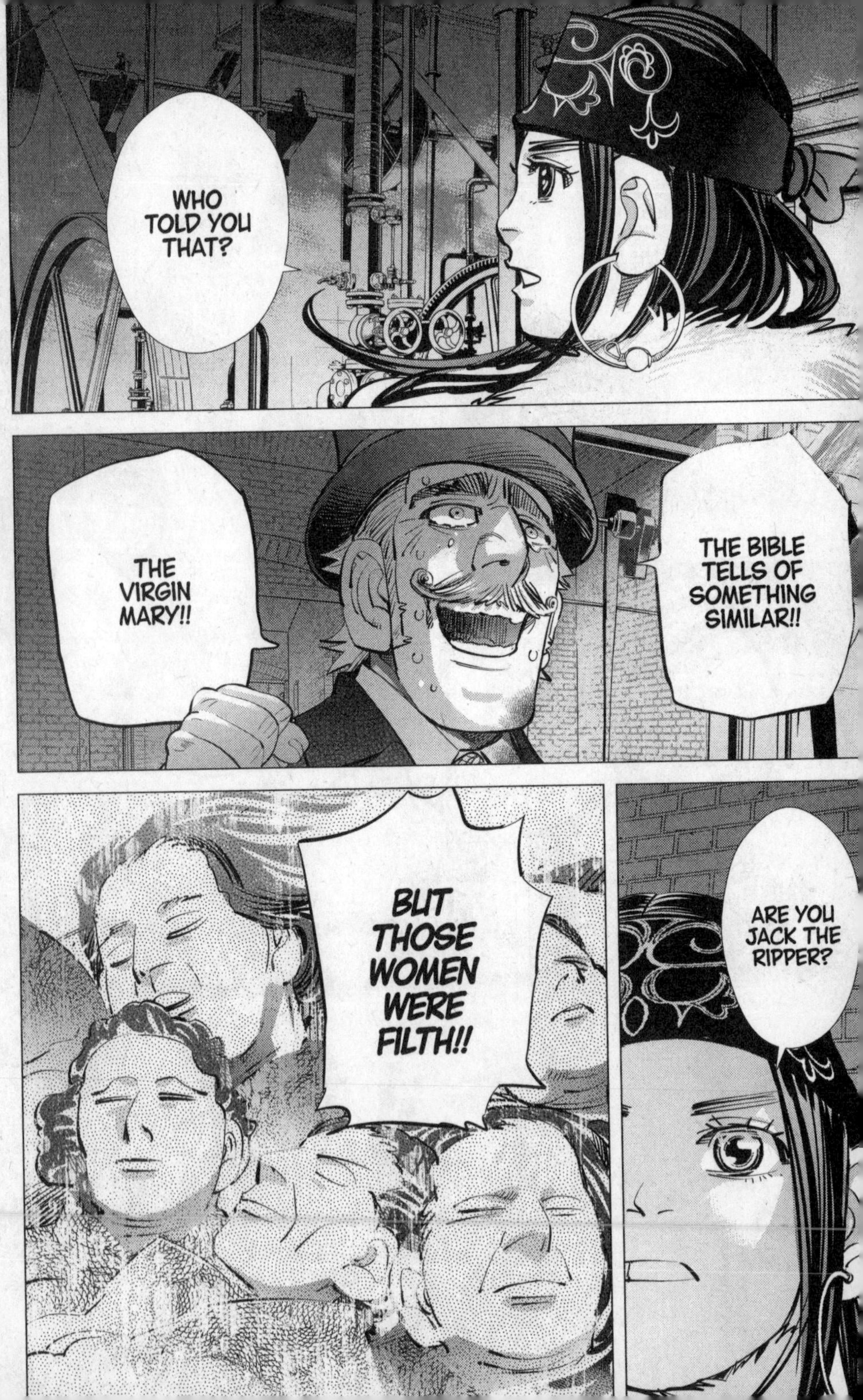
WHO TOLD YOU THAT?
THE BIBLE TELLS OF SOMETHING SIMILAR!!
THE VIRGIN MARY!!
ARE YOU JACK THE RIPPER?
BUT THOSE WOMEN WERE FILTH!!

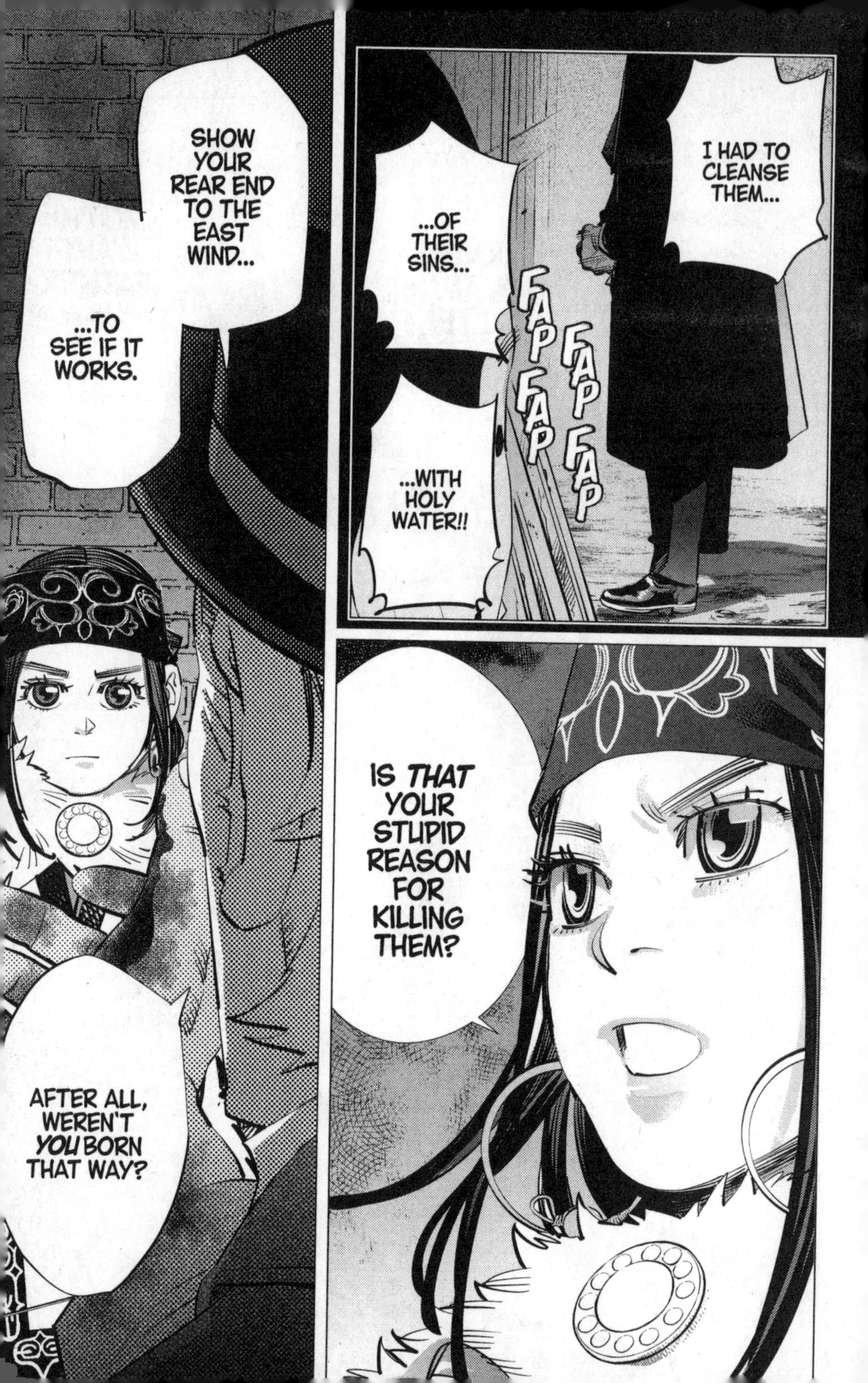
I HAD TO CLEANSE THEM...
...OF THEIR SINS...
FAP FAP
FAP FAP
...WITH HOLY WATER!!
IS *THAT* YOUR STUPID REASON FOR KILLING THEM?
SHOW YOUR REAR END TO THE EAST WIND...
...TO SEE IF IT WORKS.
AFTER ALL, WEREN'T *YOU* BORN THAT WAY?

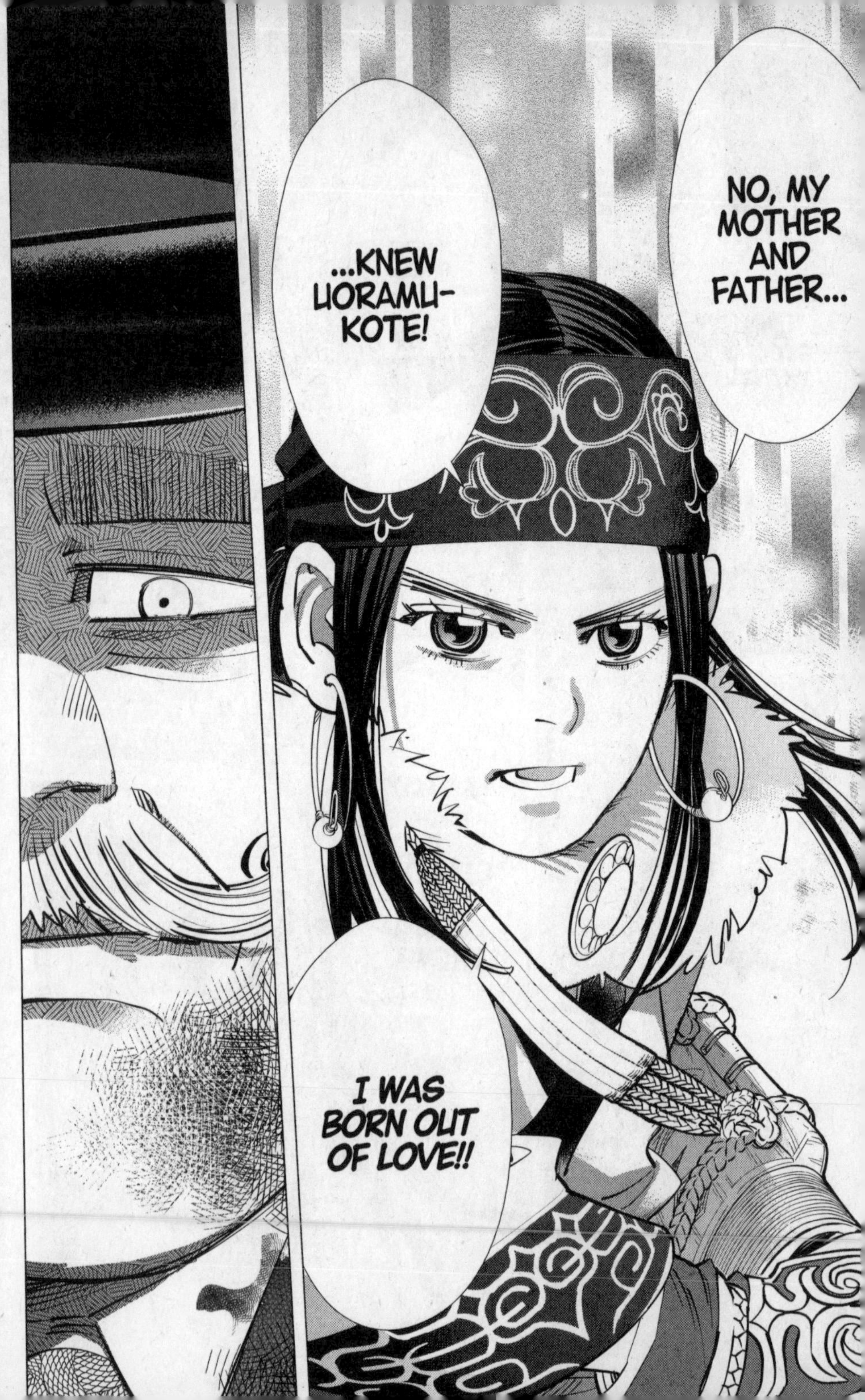
NO, MY MOTHER AND FATHER...
...KNEW WORAMU-KOTE!
I WAS BORN OUT OF LOVE!!

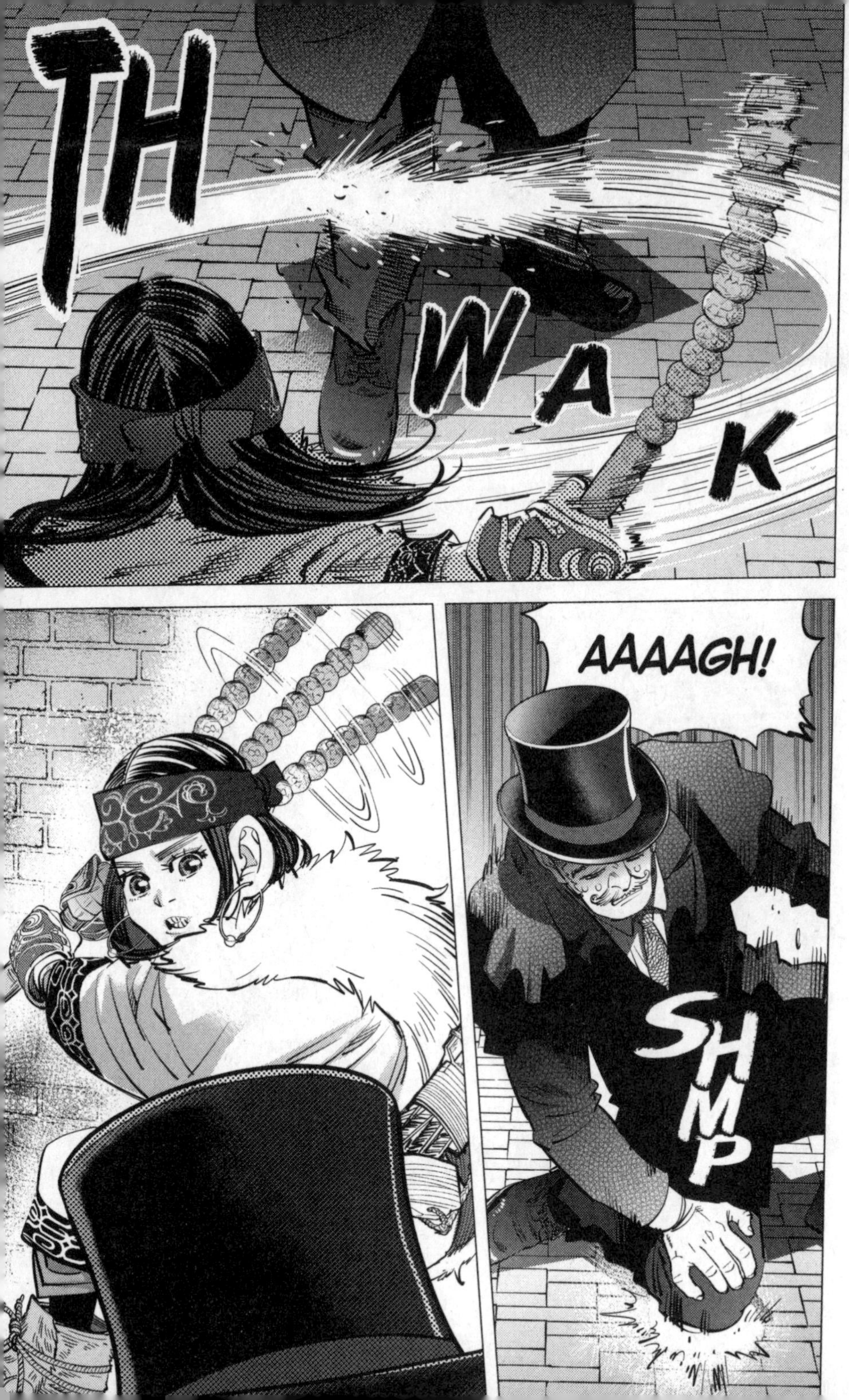
THWAK
AAAAGH!
SHMP

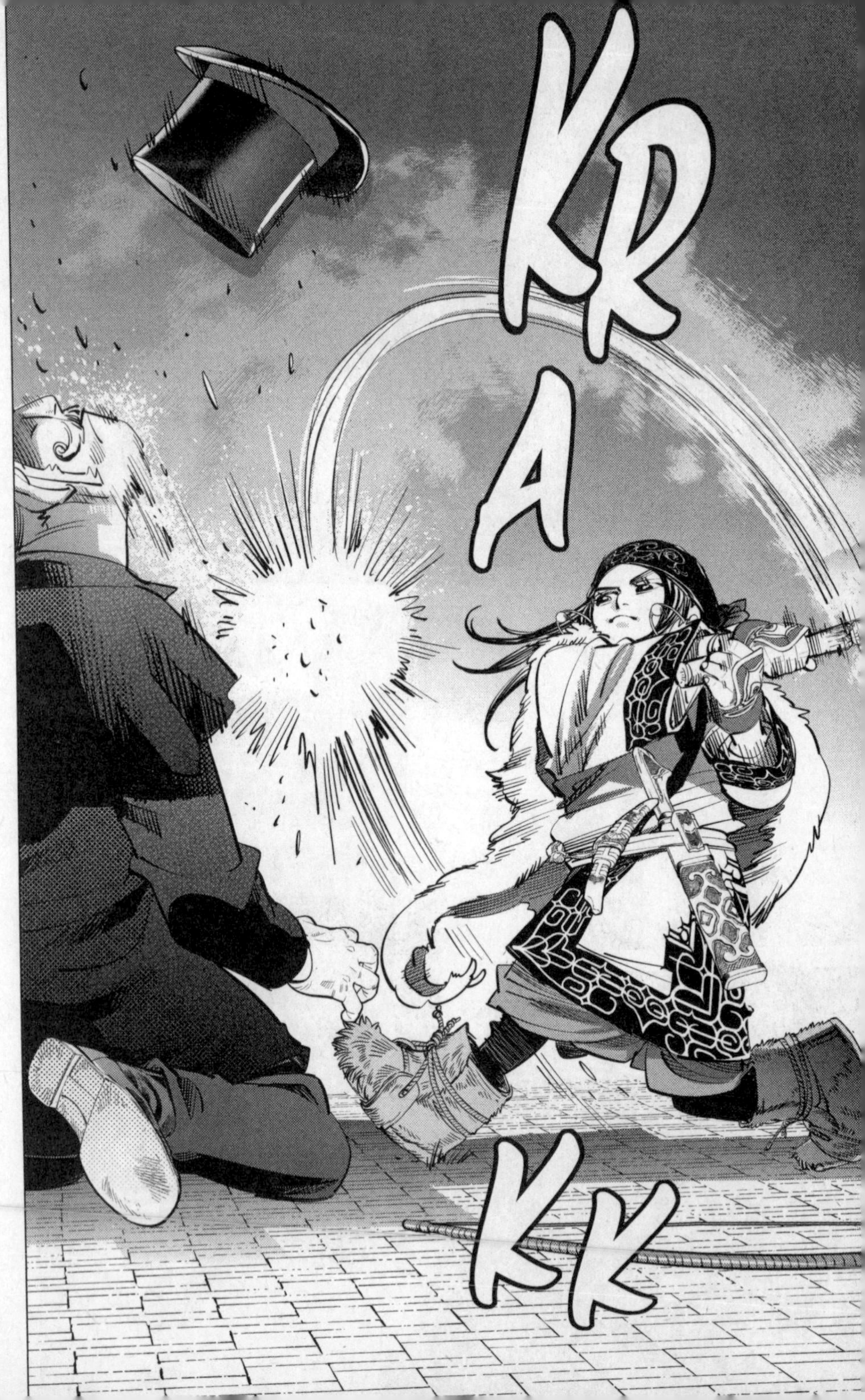
KRAKK

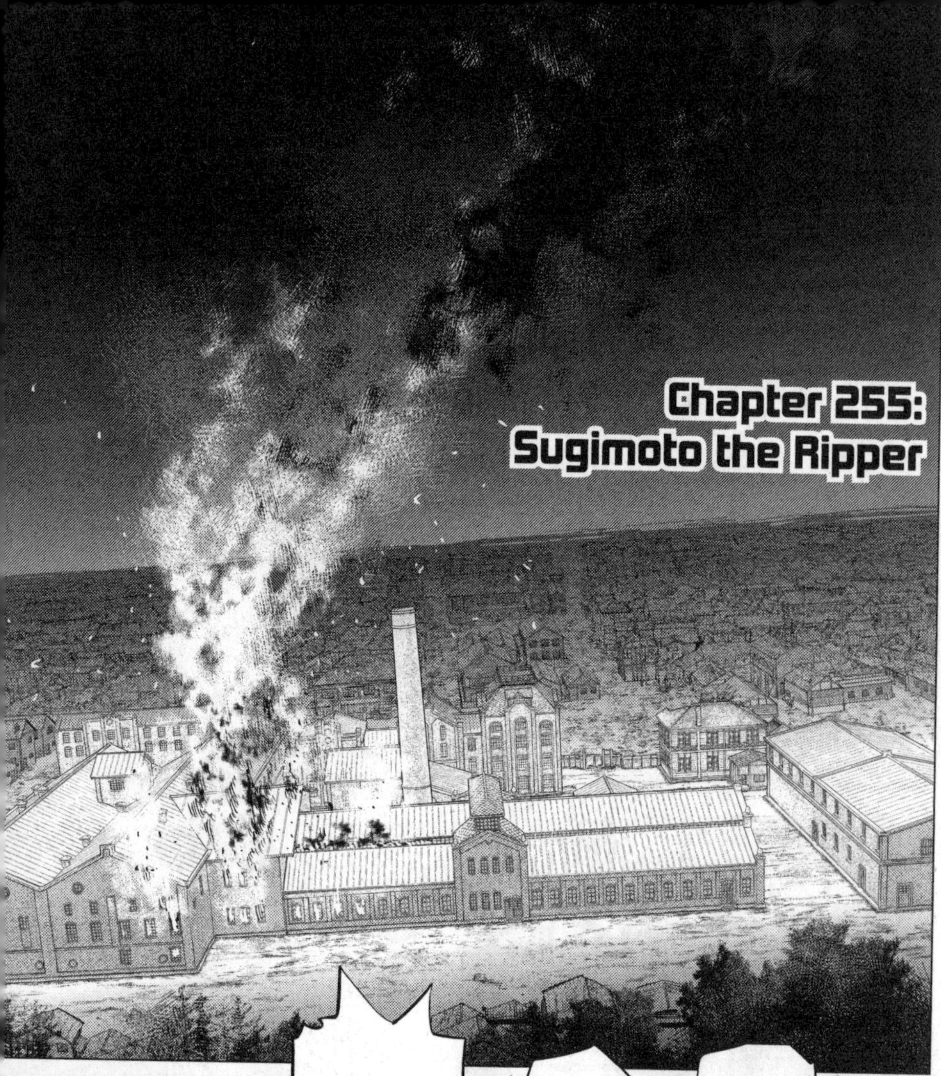
Chapter 255:
Sugimoto the Ripper

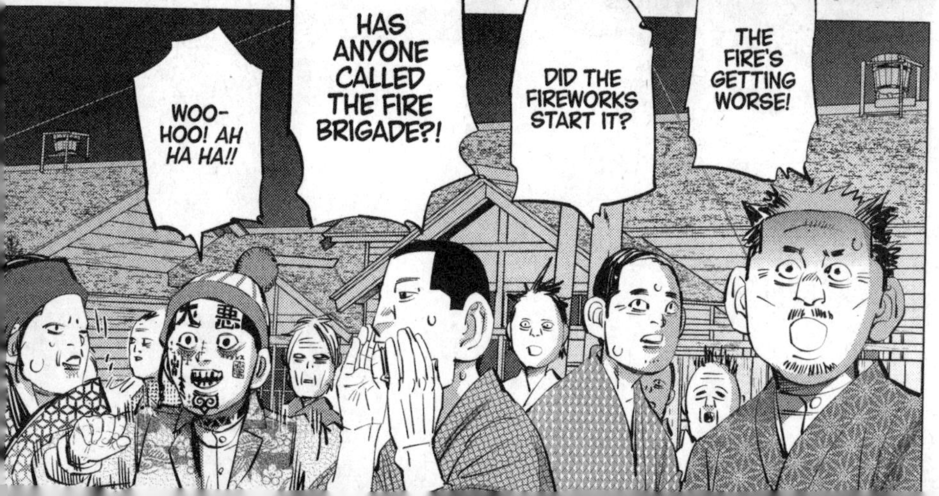
THE FIRE'S GETTING WORSE!
DID THE FIREWORKS START IT?
HAS ANYONE CALLED THE FIRE BRIGADE?!
WOO-HOO! AH HA HA!!

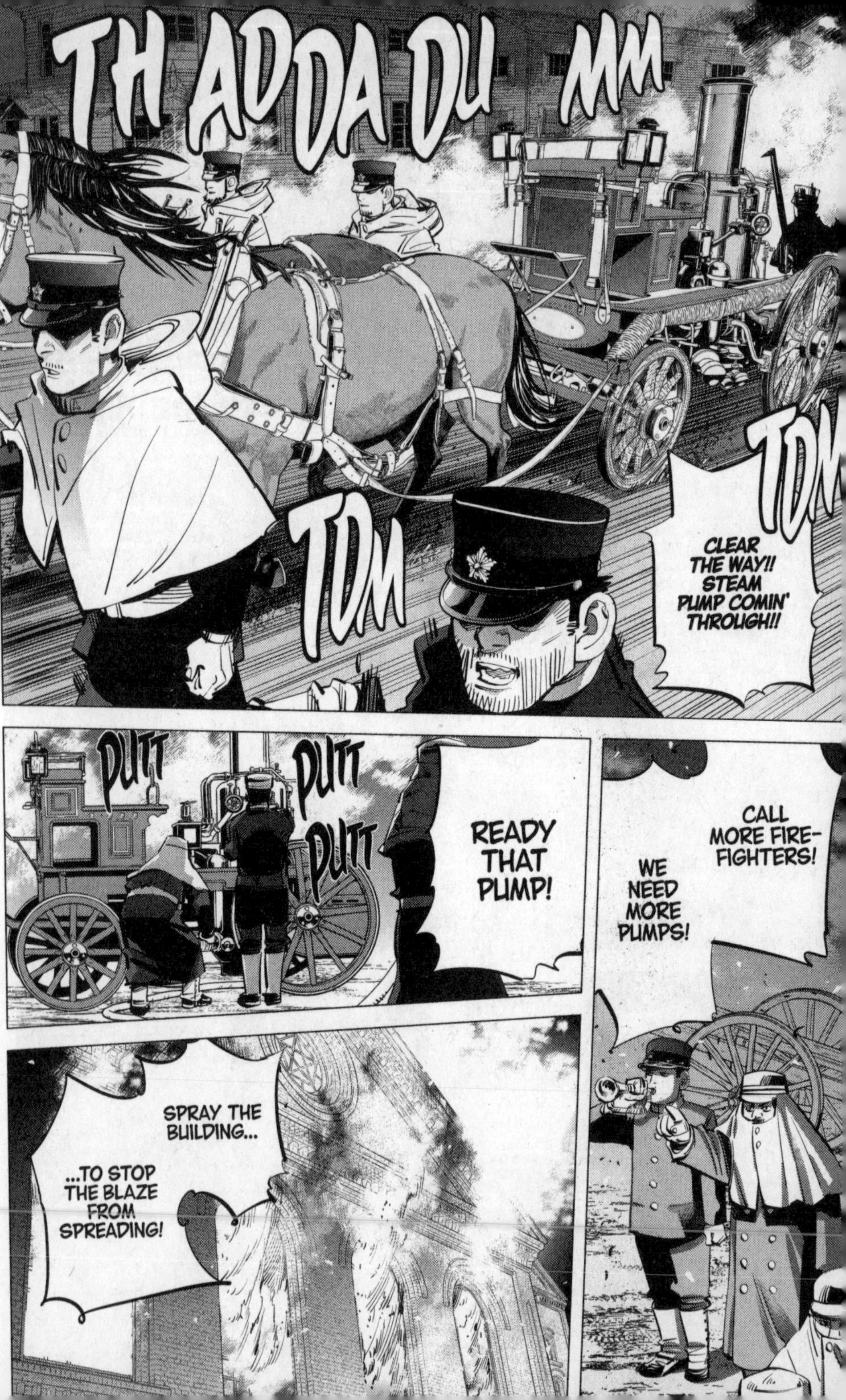
TH ADDA DU MM
TOM
TOM
CLEAR THE WAY!! STEAM PUMP COMIN' THROUGH!!
CALL MORE FIRE-FIGHTERS!
WE NEED MORE PUMPS!
READY THAT PUMP!
PUTT
PUTT
PUTT
SPRAY THE BUILDING...
...TO STOP THE BLAZE FROM SPREADING!

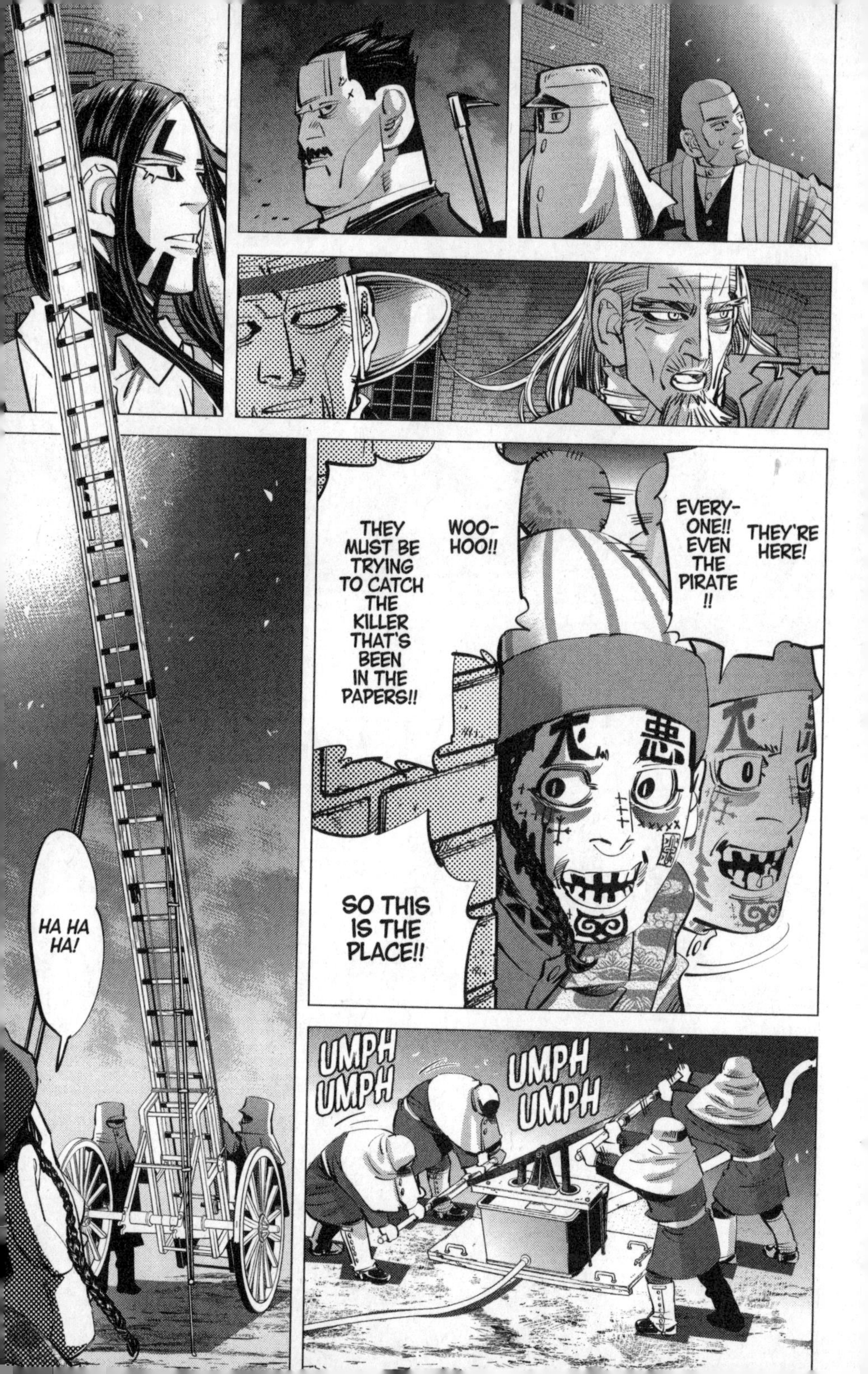
THEY'RE HERE!
EVERY-ONE!! EVEN THE PIRATE!!
WOO-HOO!!
THEY MUST BE TRYING TO CATCH THE KILLER THAT'S BEEN IN THE PAPERS!!
SO THIS IS THE PLACE!!
UMPH UMPH
UMPH UMPH
HA HA HA!

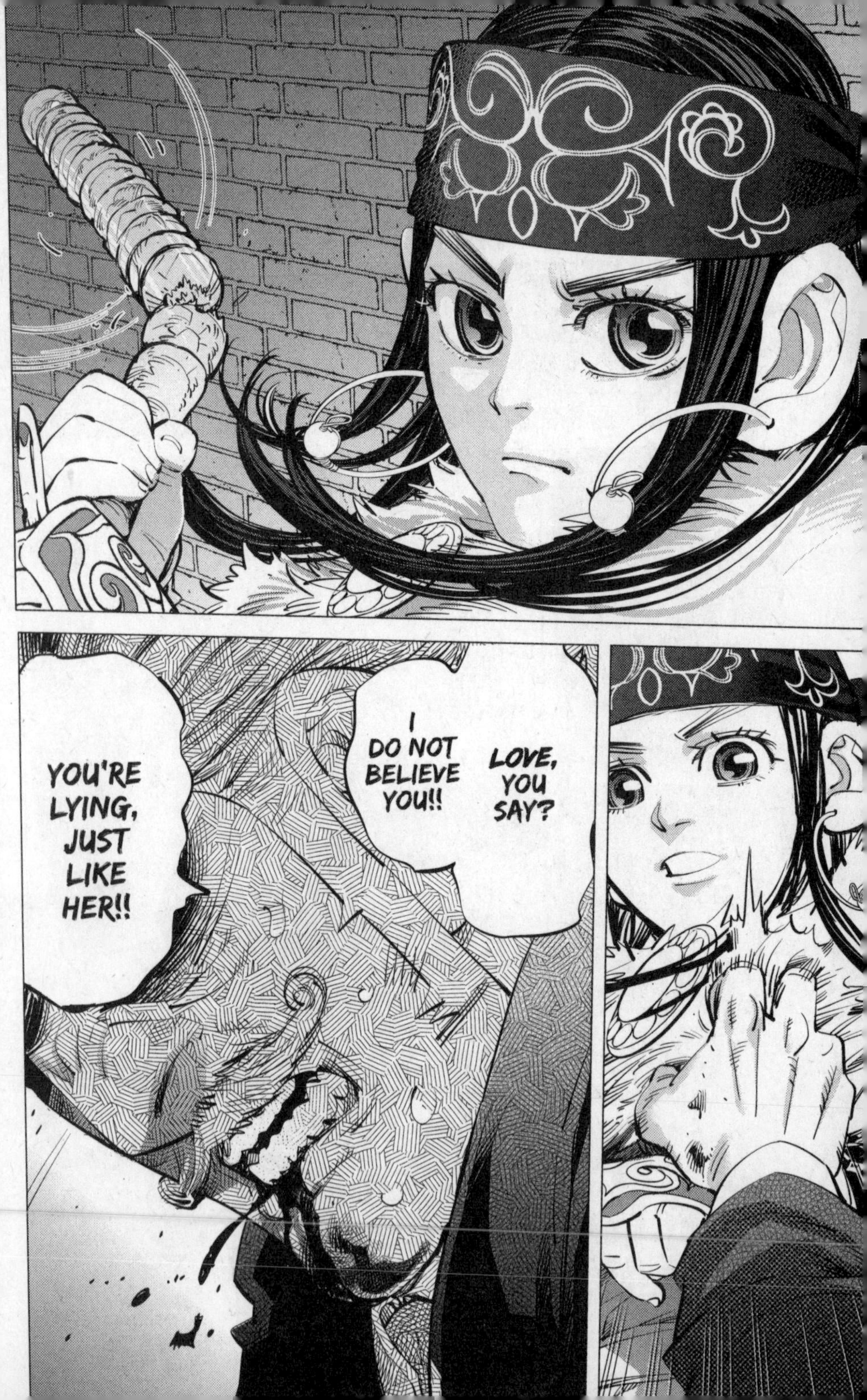
LOVE, YOU SAY?
I DO NOT BELIEVE YOU!!
YOU'RE LYING, JUST LIKE HER!!

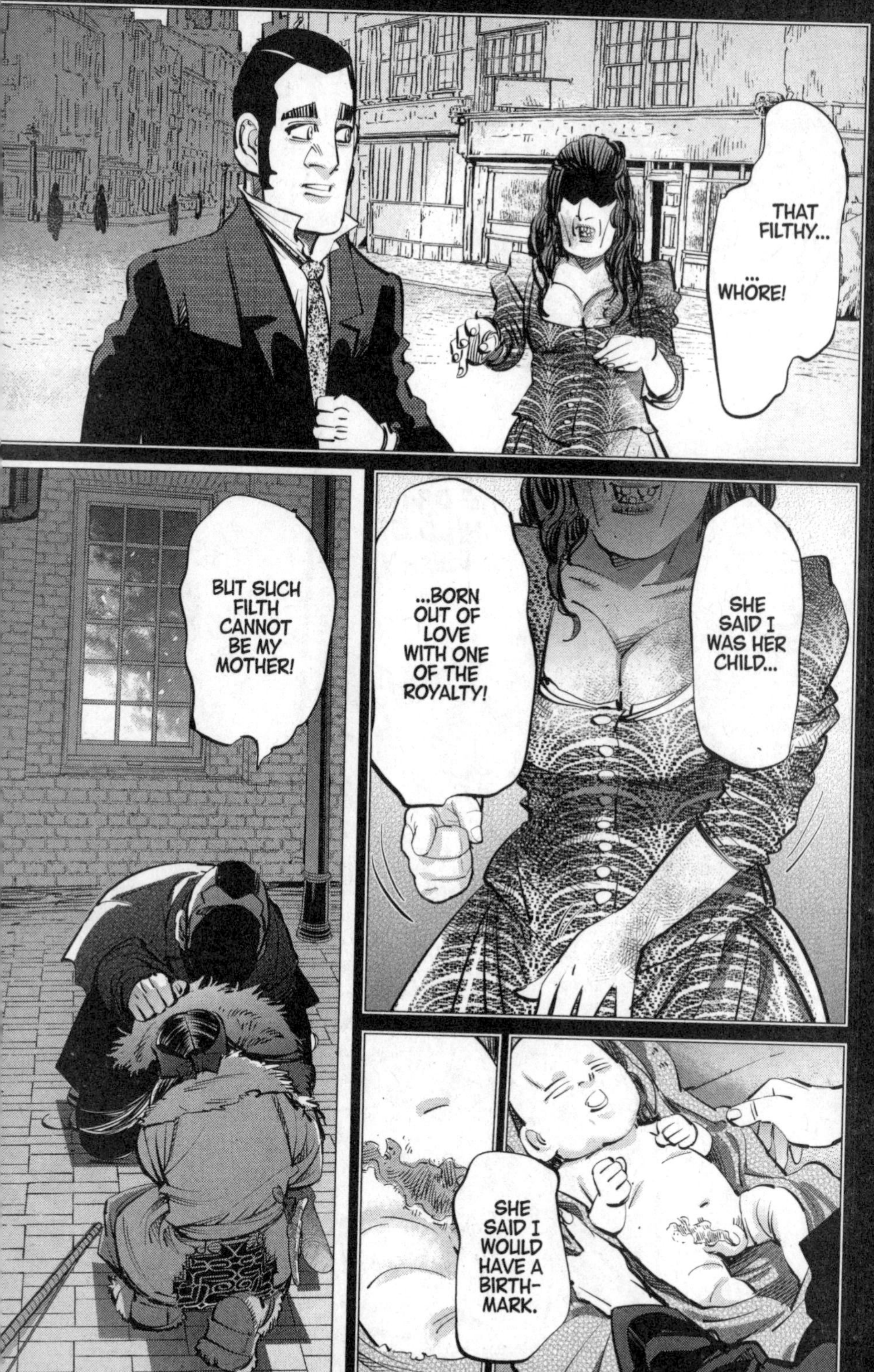
THAT FILTHY... ...WHÖRE!
SHE SAID I WAS HER CHILD...
...BORN OUT OF LOVE WITH ONE OF THE ROYALTY!
SHE SAID I WOULD HAVE A BIRTH-MARK.
BUT SUCH FILTH CANNOT BE MY MOTHER!

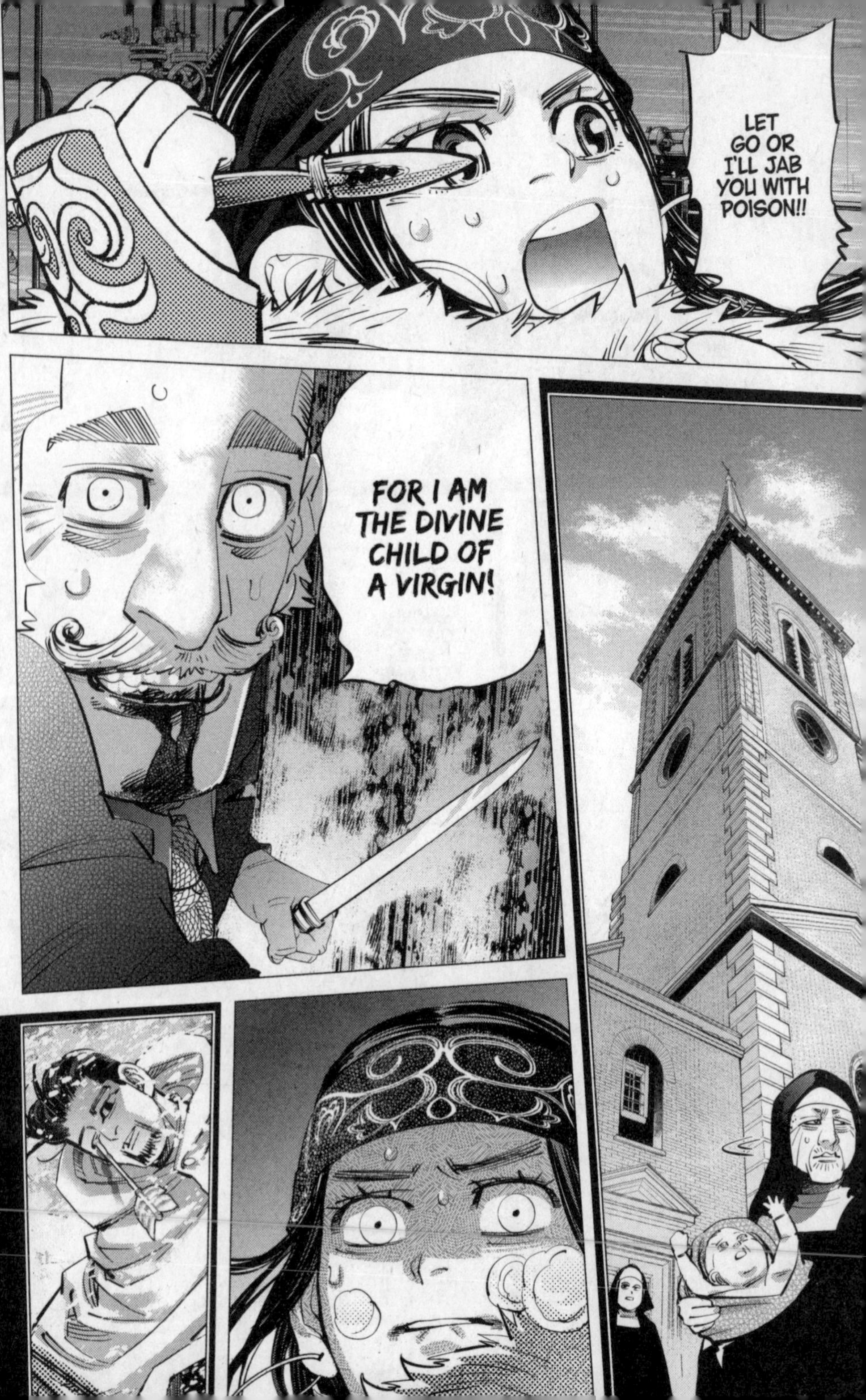
LET GO OR I'LL JAB YOU WITH POISON!!
FOR I AM THE DIVINE CHILD OF A VIRGIN!

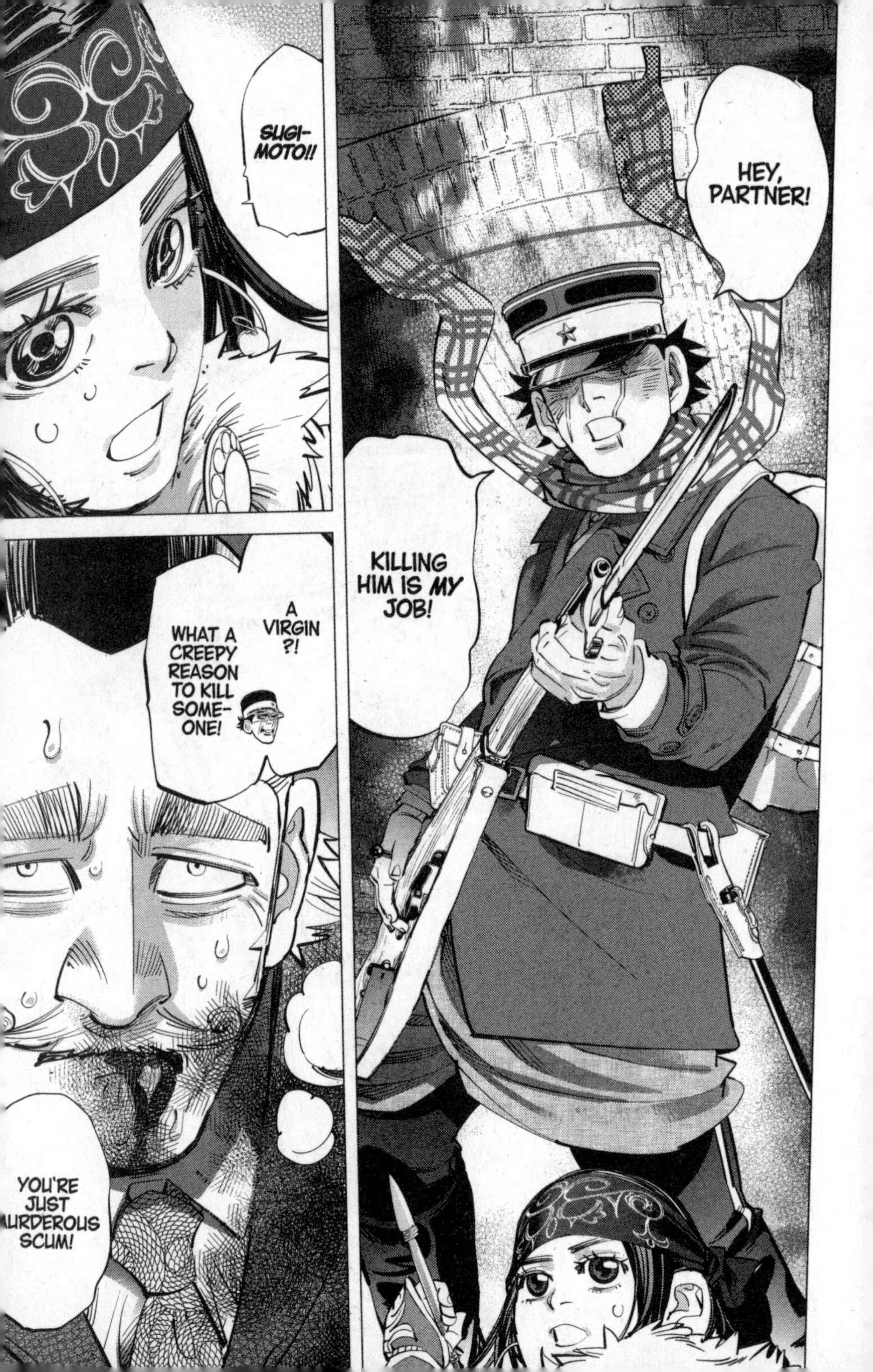
HEY, PARTNER!
KILLING HIM IS MY JOB!
SUGI-MOTO!!
A VIRGIN?!
WHAT A CREEPY REASON TO KILL SOME-ONE!
YOU'RE JUST URDEROUS SCUM!

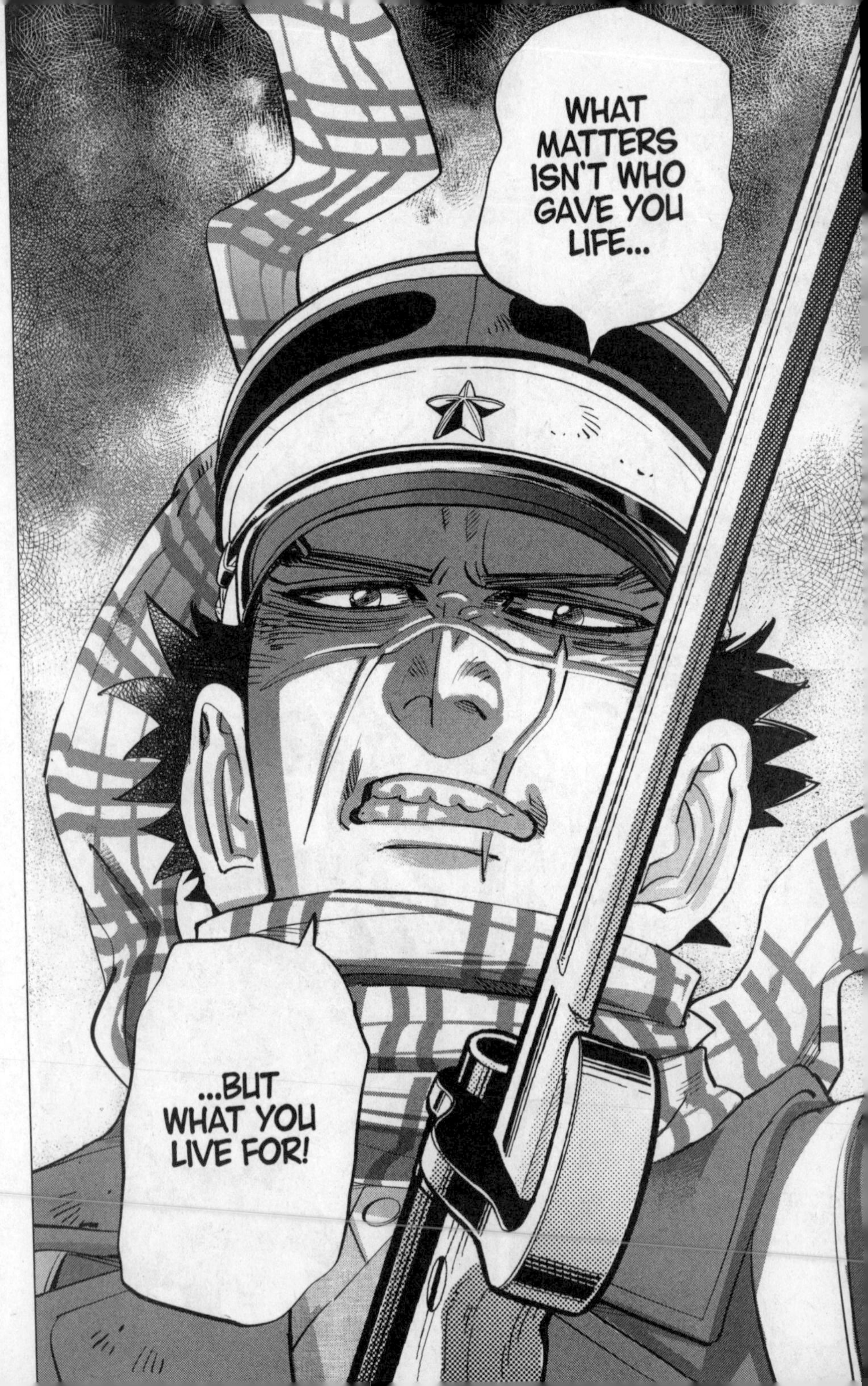
WHAT MATTERS ISN'T WHO GAVE YOU LIFE...
...BUT WHAT YOU LIVE FOR!

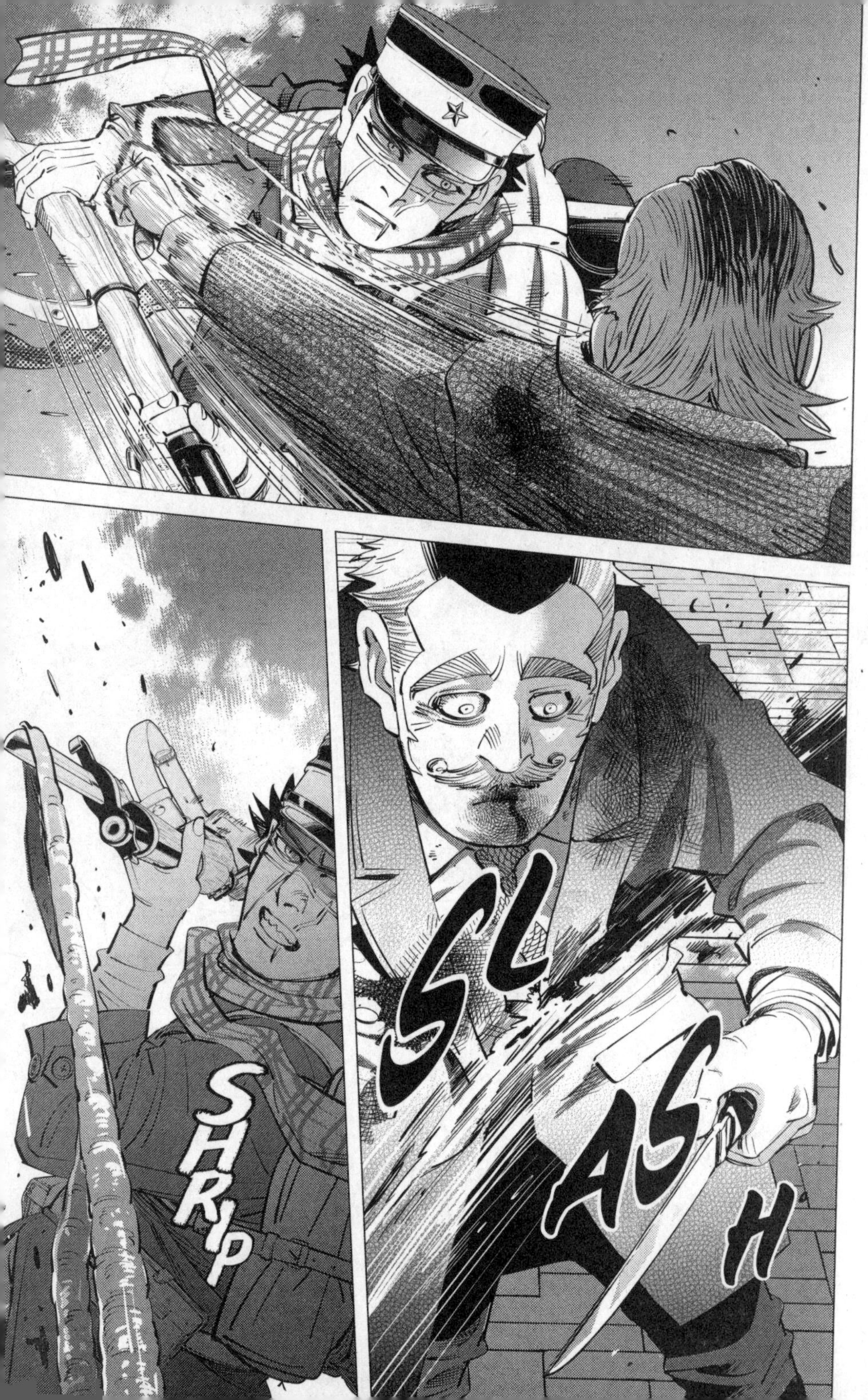
SLASH
SHRIP

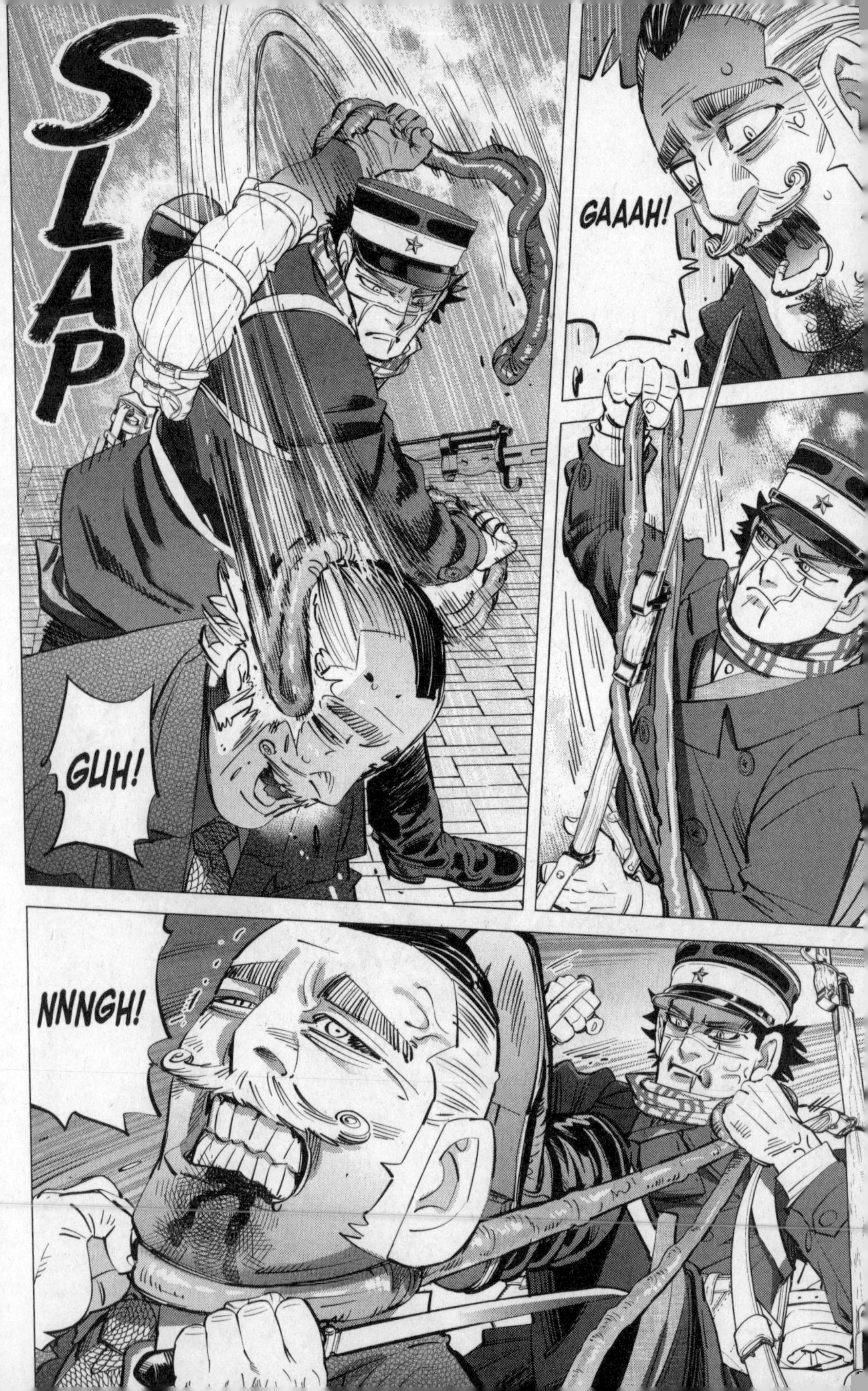
GAAAH!
SLAP
GUH!
NNNGH!

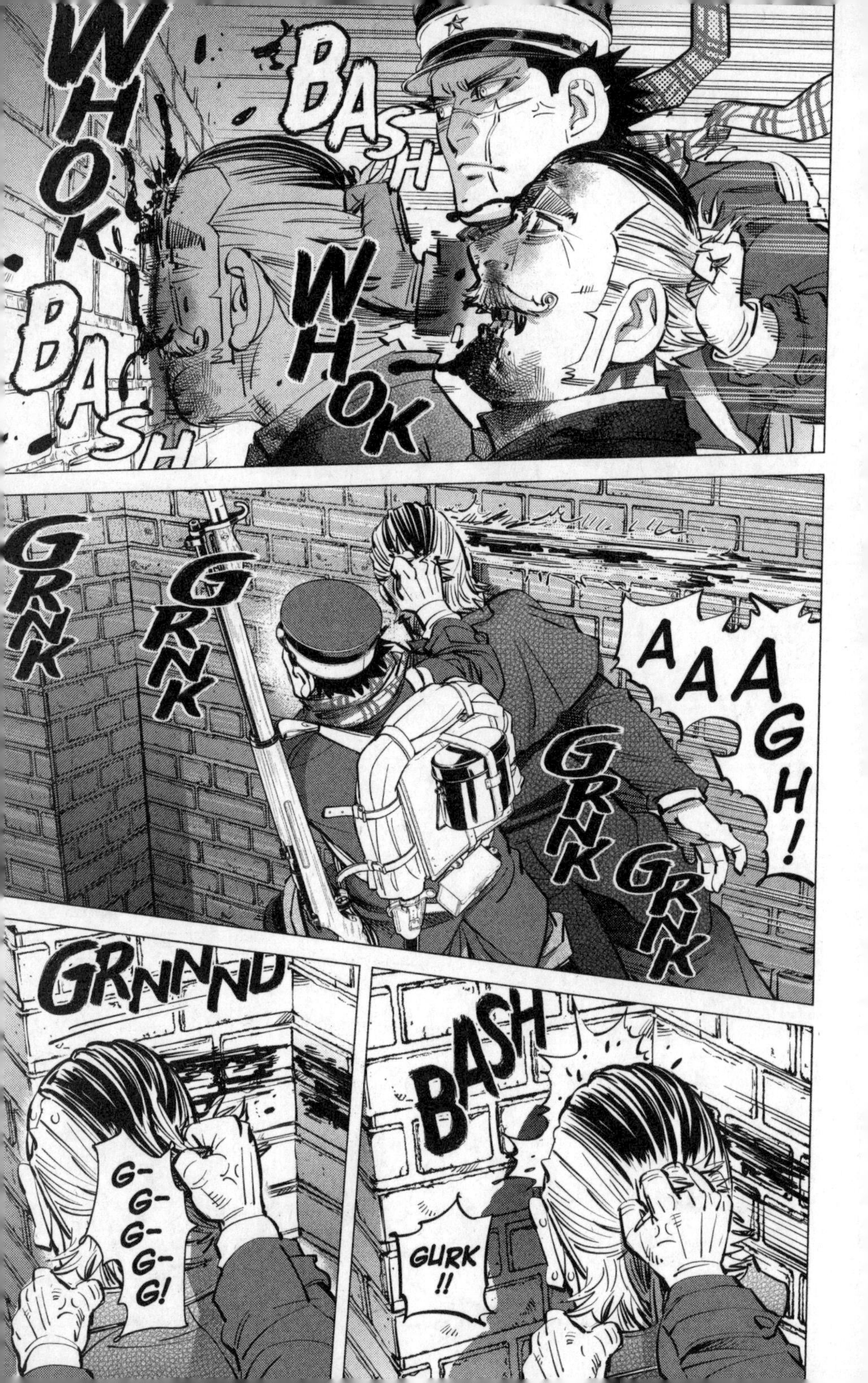
BASH
WHOK
WHOK
BASH
AAAGH!
GRNK
GRNK
GRNK
GRNK
BASH
GURK!!
GRNNND
G-G-G-G-G!

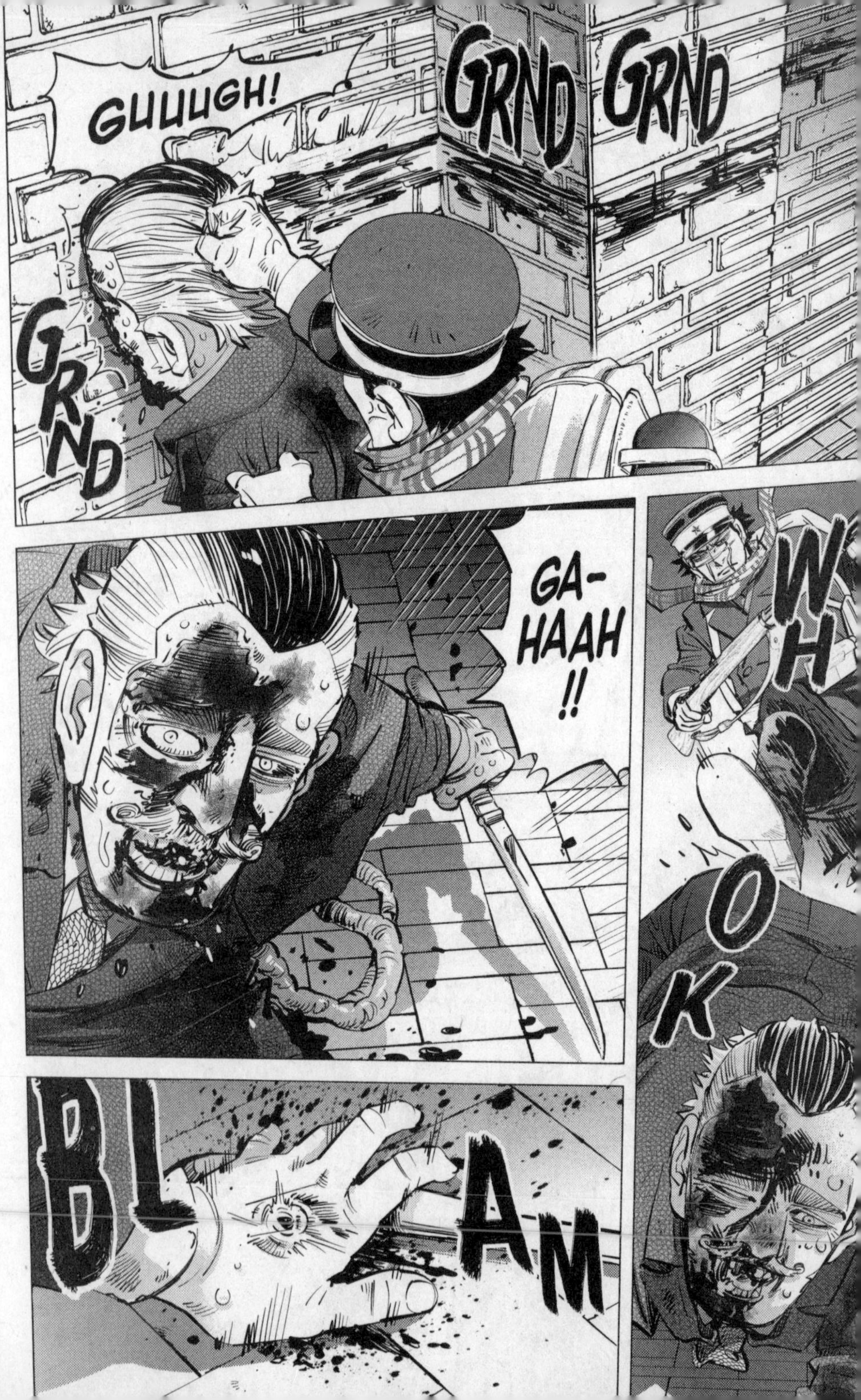
GRND GRND
GUUUGH!
GRND
WHOOK
GA-HAAH!!
BLAM

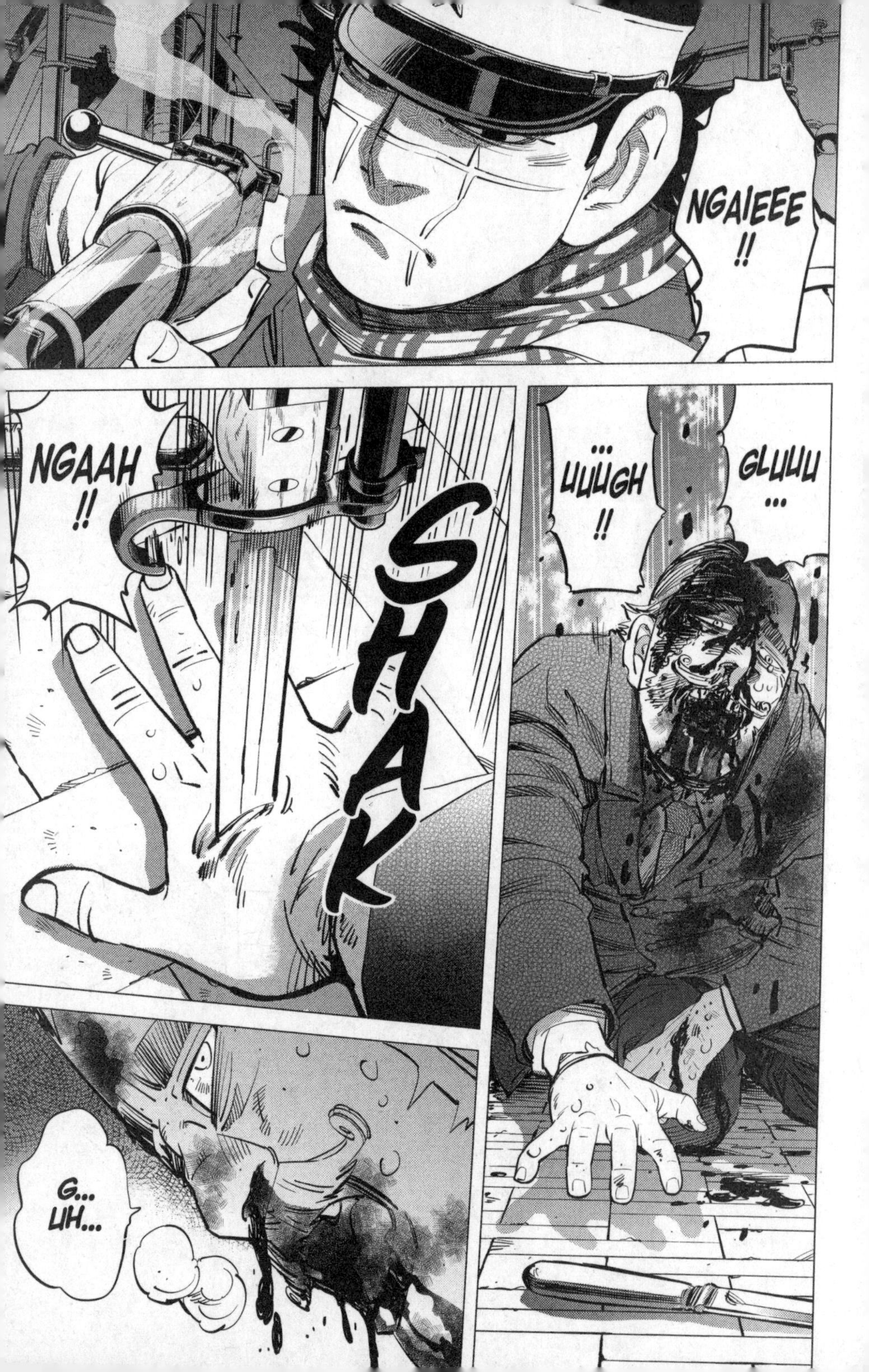
NGAIEEE !!
GLUUU ...
... UUUGH !!
NGAAH !!
SHAK
G... UH...

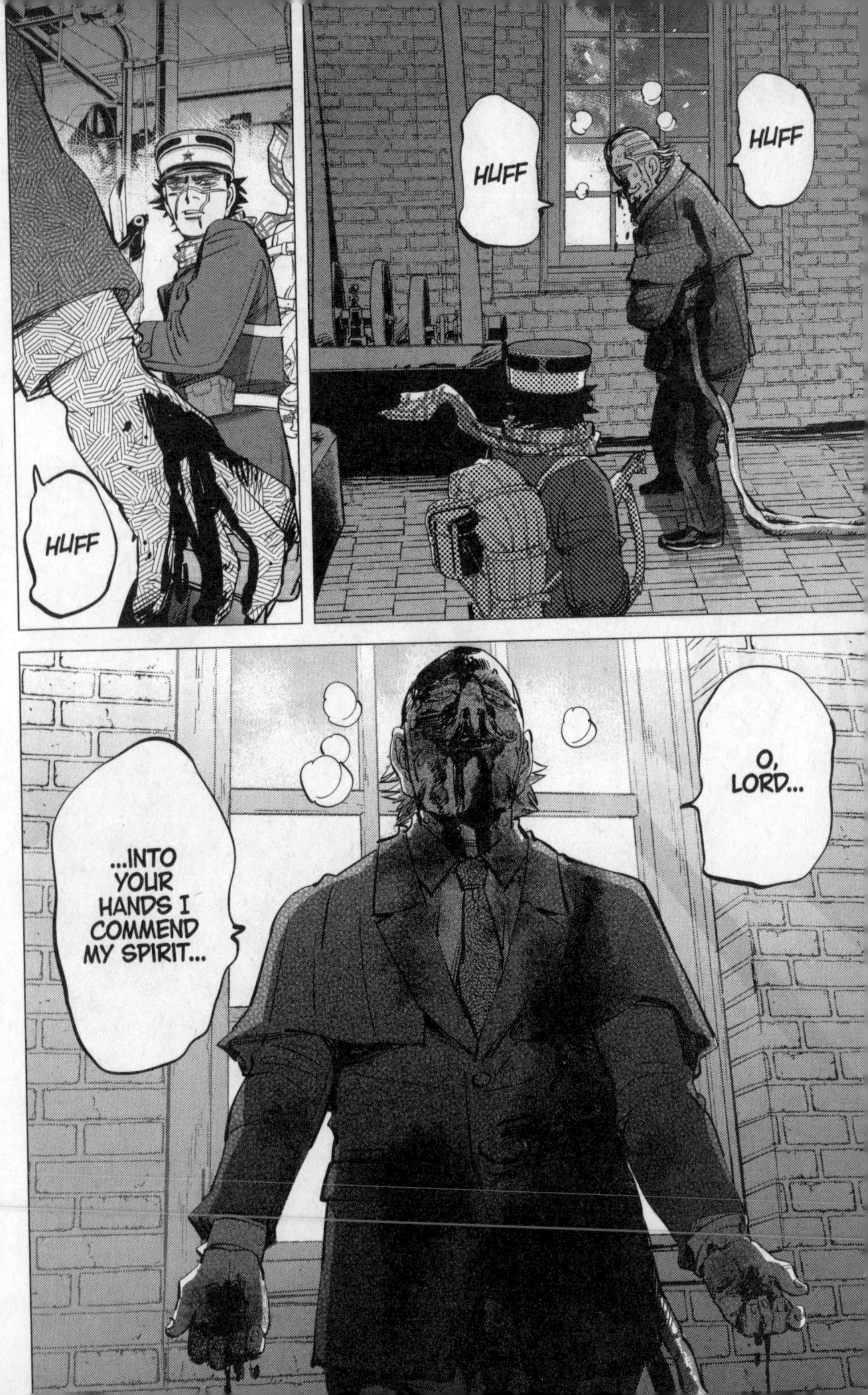
HUFF
HUFF
HUFF
O, LORD...
...INTO YOUR HANDS I COMMEND MY SPIRIT...

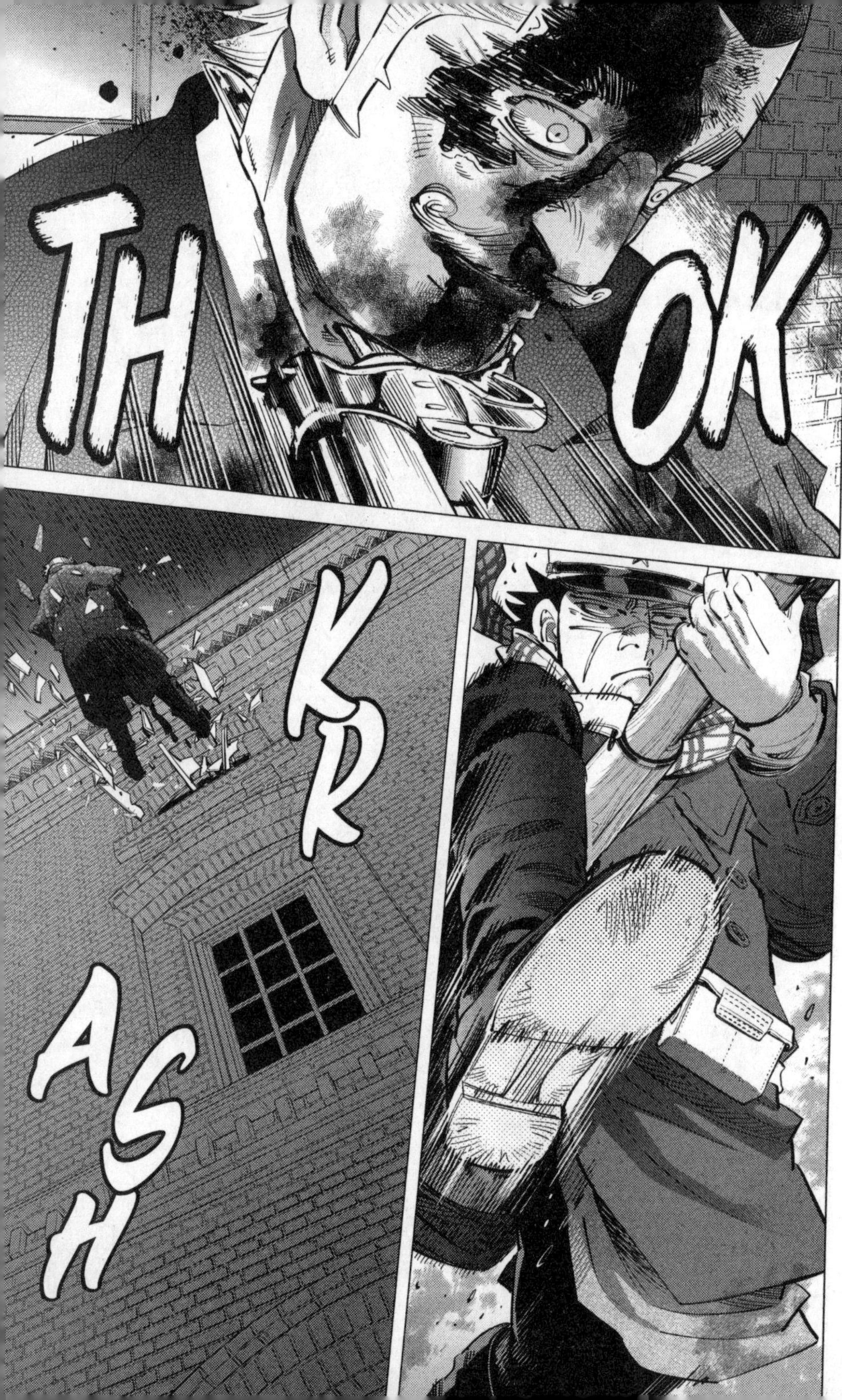
THOK
KRASH

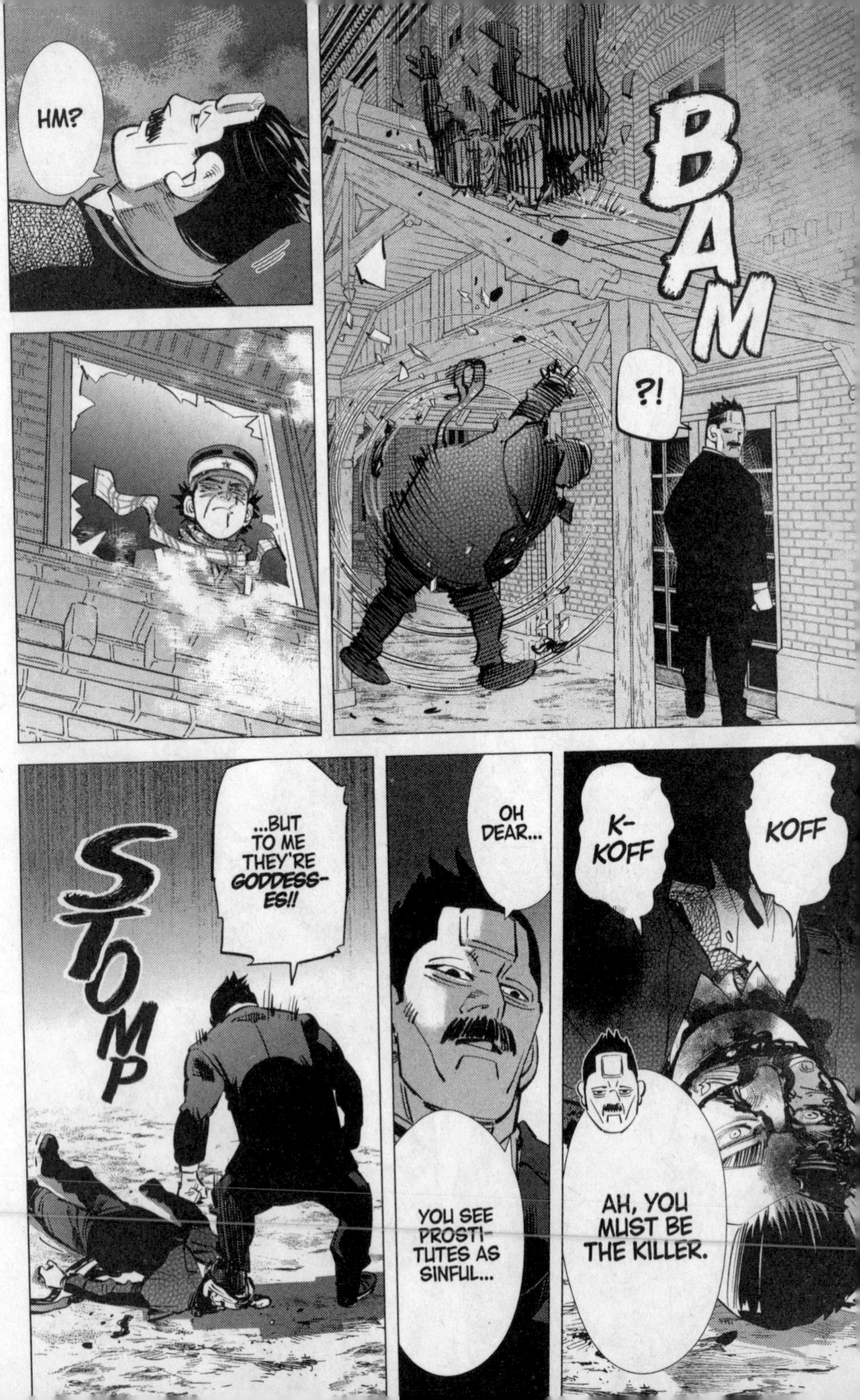
BAM
?!
HM?
KOFF
K-KOFF
AH, YOU MUST BE THE KILLER.
OH DEAR...
YOU SEE PROSTITUTES AS SINFUL...
...BUT TO ME THEY'RE GODDESSES!!
STOMP

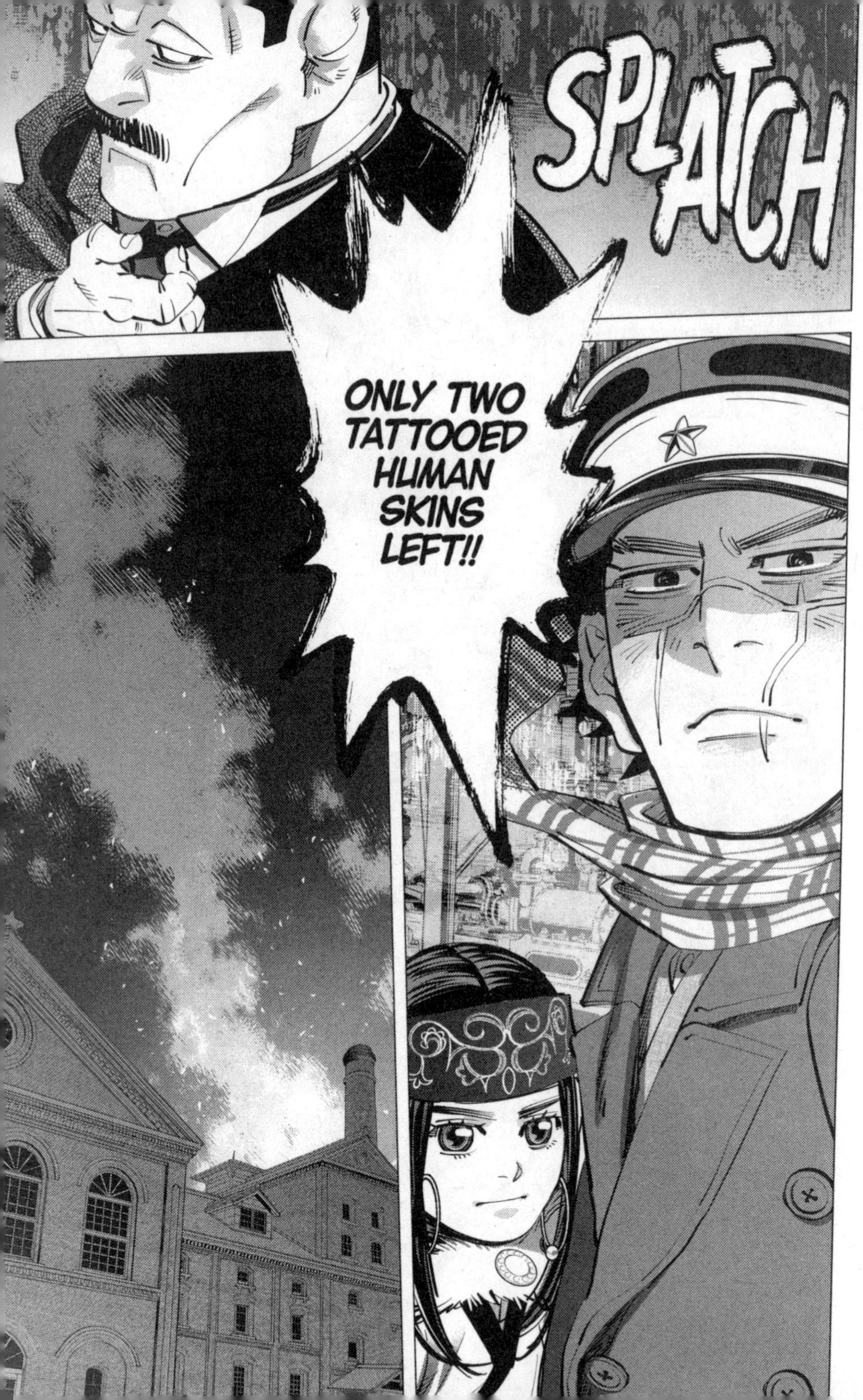
SPLATCH
ONLY TWO TATTOOED HUMAN SKINS LEFT!!

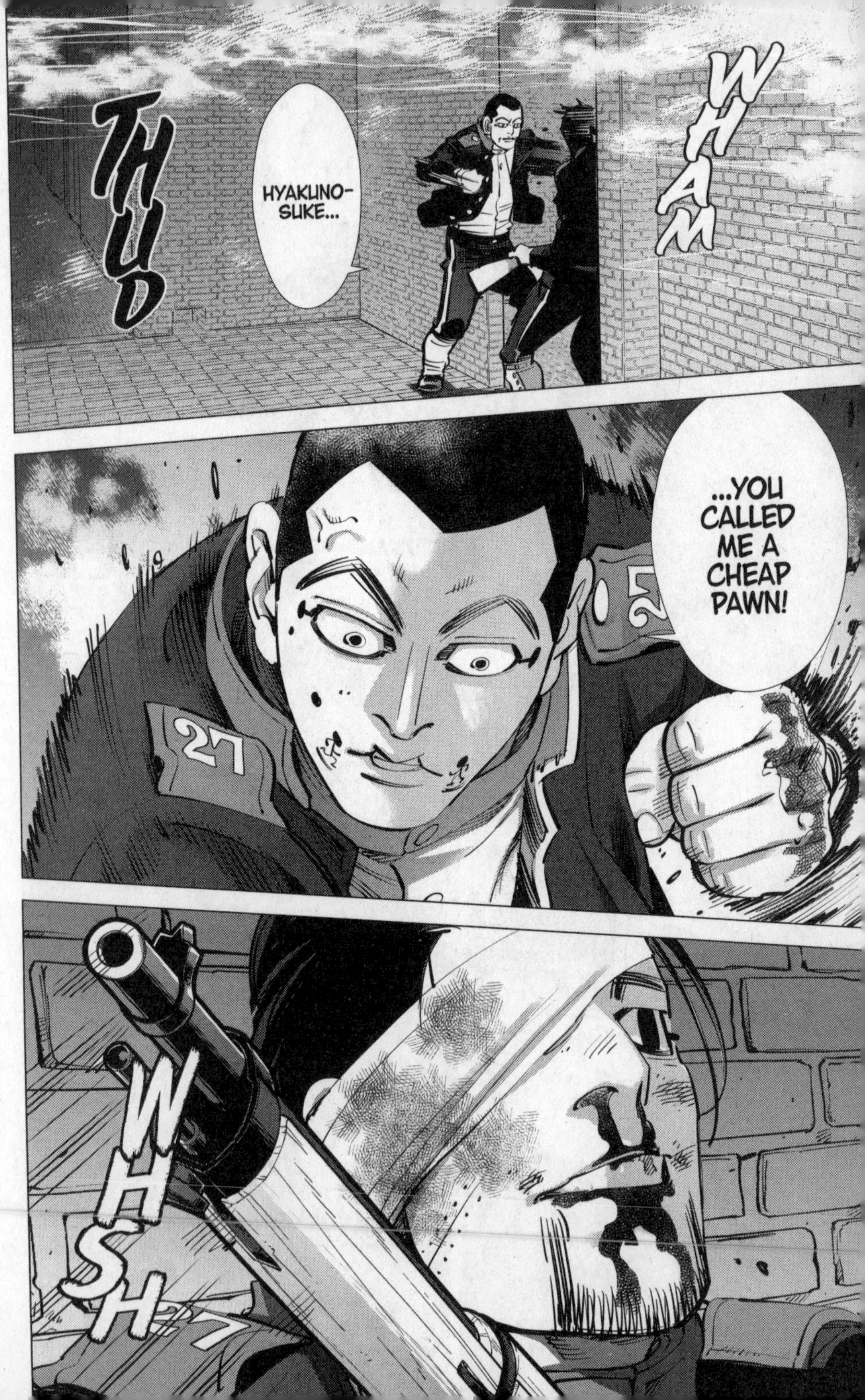
WHAM
HYAKUNOSUKE...
THUD
...YOU CALLED ME A CHEAP PAWN!
WHSH

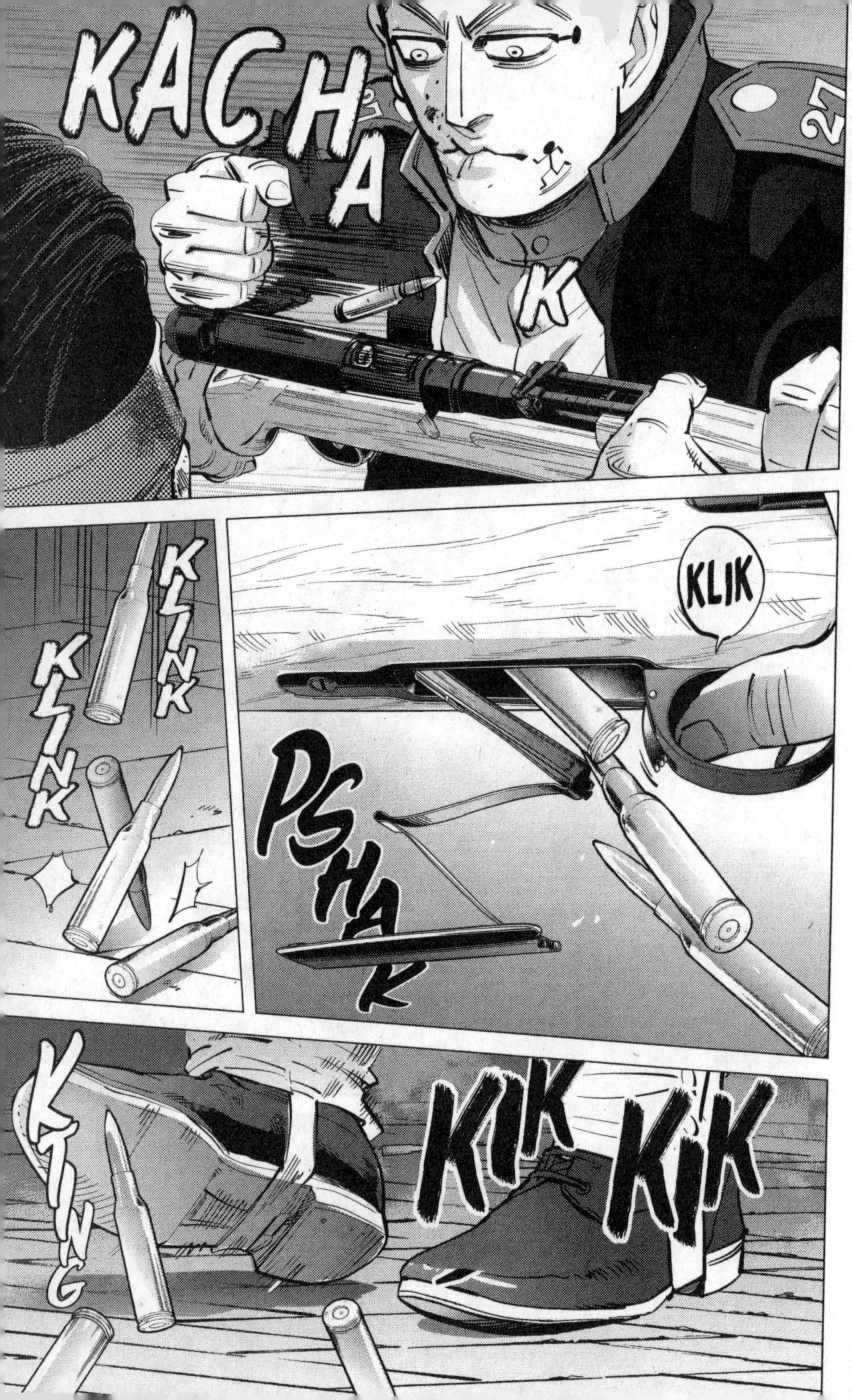
KACHAK
KLIK
PSHAK
KLINK
KLINK
KIK KIK
KTING

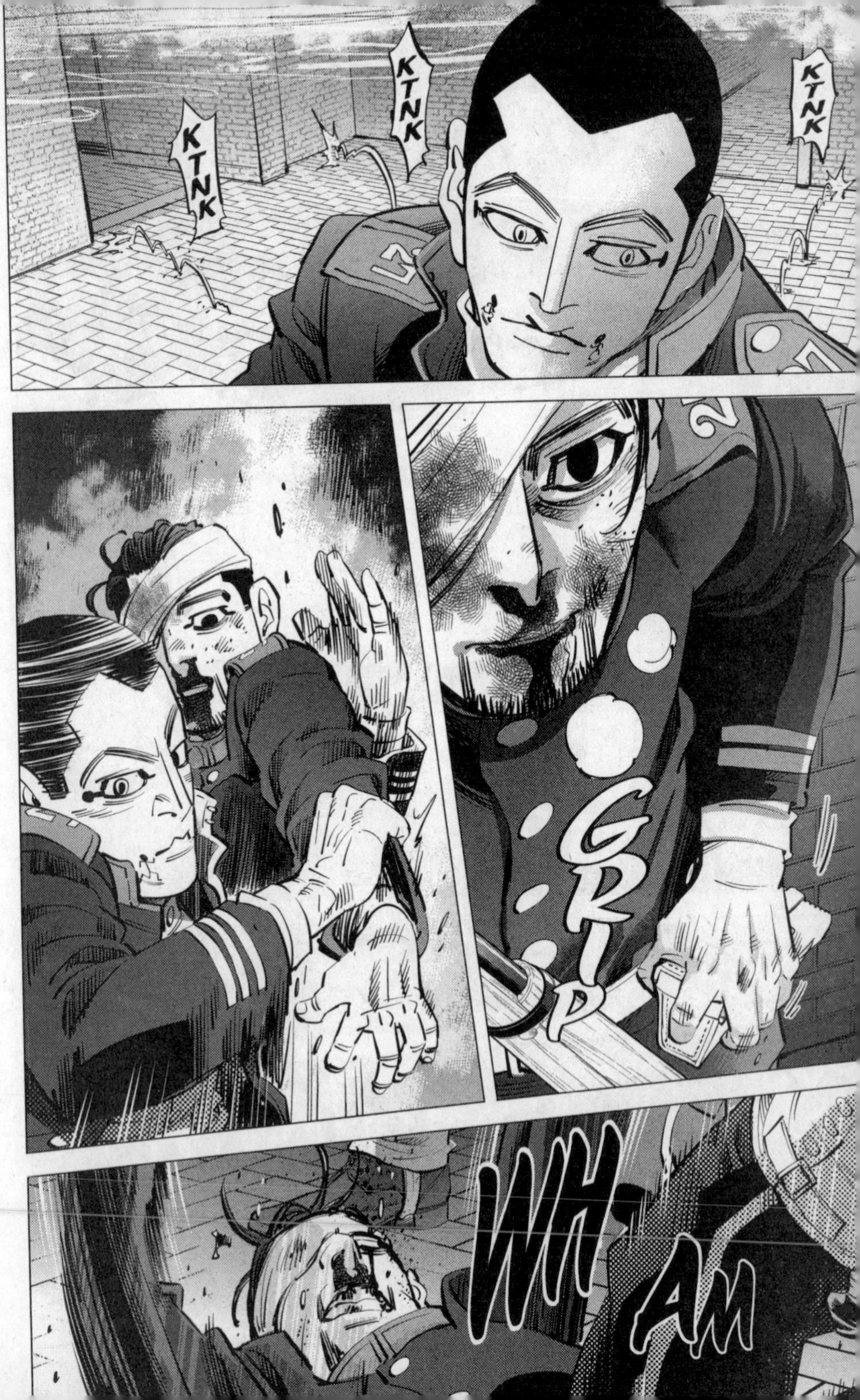
KTNK
KTNK
KTNK
GRIP
WHAM

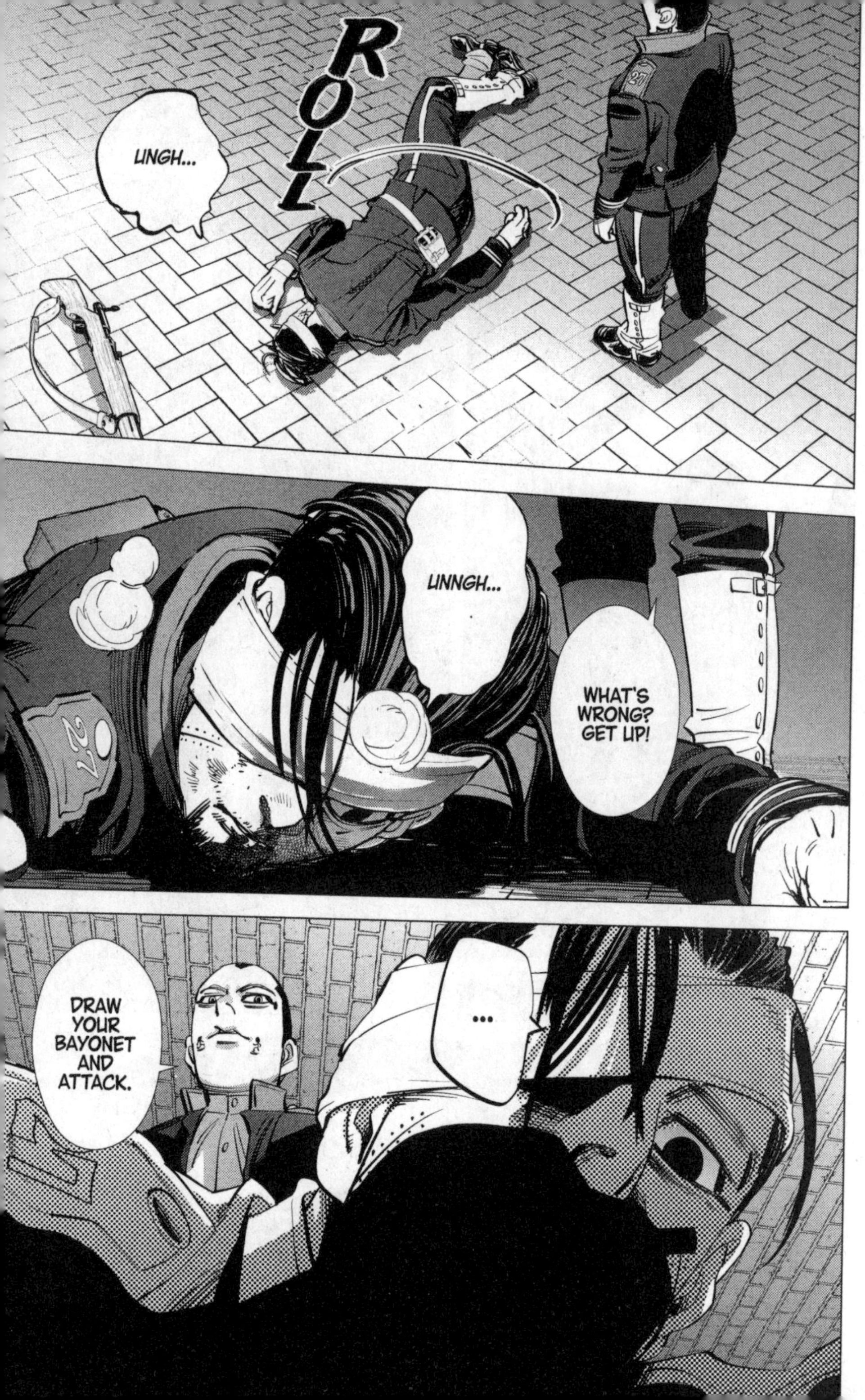
ROLL
UNGH...
UNNGH...
WHAT'S WRONG? GET UP!
...
DRAW YOUR BAYONET AND ATTACK.

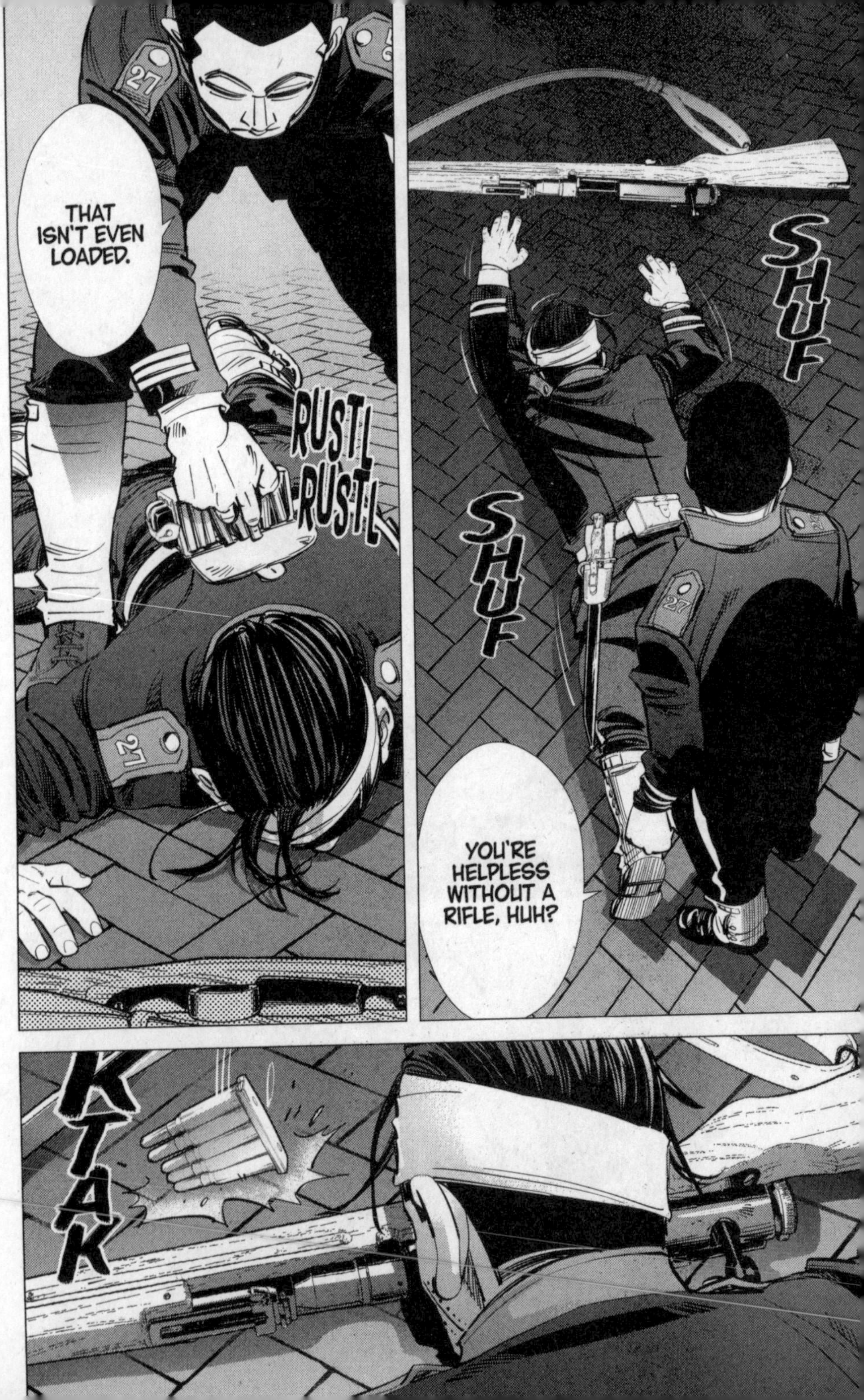
SHUF
SHUF
YOU'RE HELPLESS WITHOUT A RIFLE, HUH?
THAT ISN'T EVEN LOADED.
RUSTL
RUSTL
KTAK

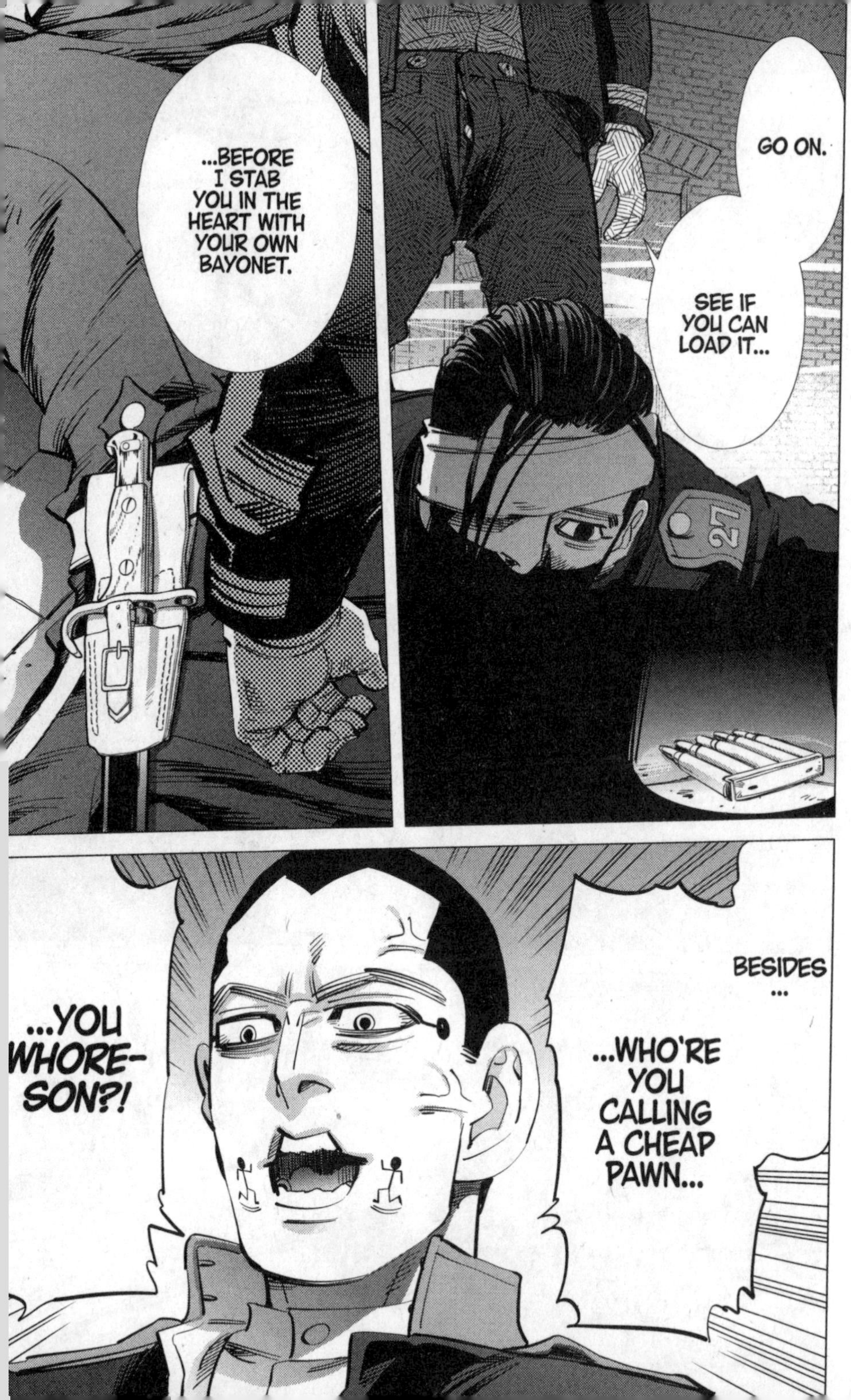
GO ON.
SEE IF YOU CAN LOAD IT...
...BEFORE I STAB YOU IN THE HEART WITH YOUR OWN BAYONET.
BESIDES...
...WHO'RE YOU CALLING A CHEAP PAWN...
...YOU WHORE-SON?!

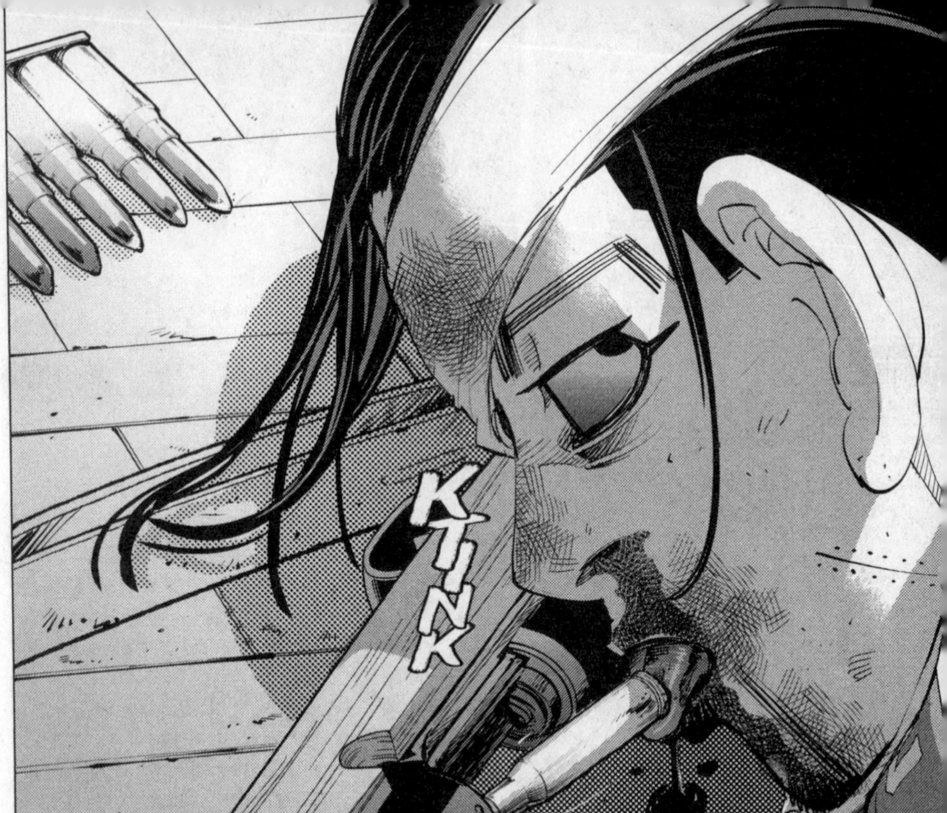
KTINK
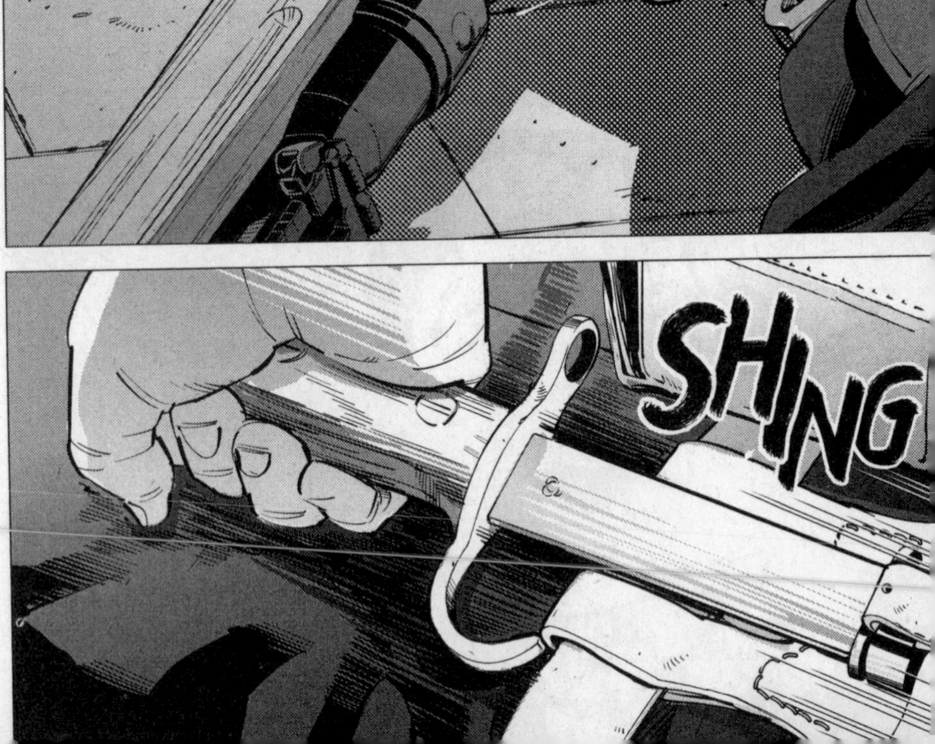
SHING

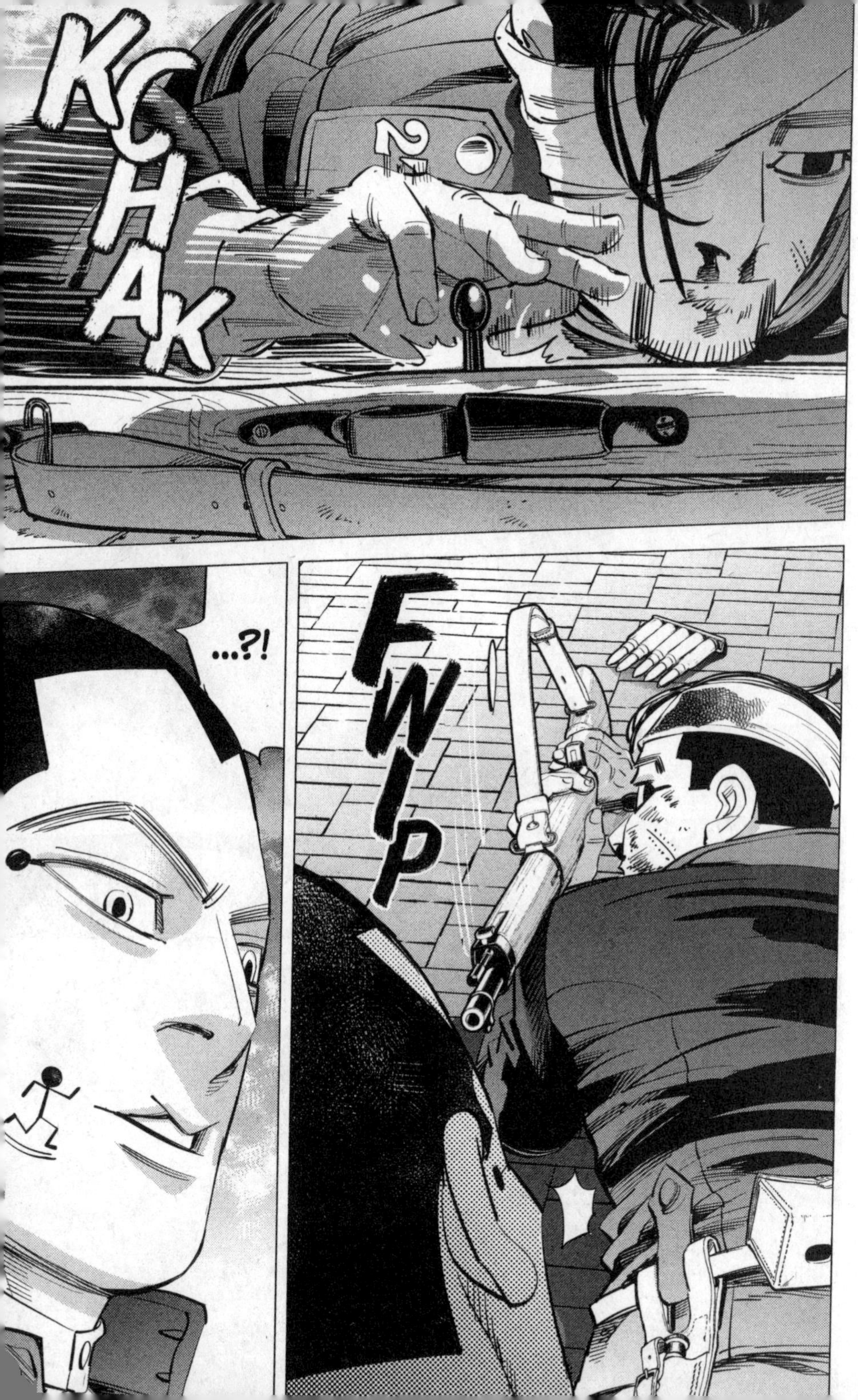
KCHAK
FWIP
...?!

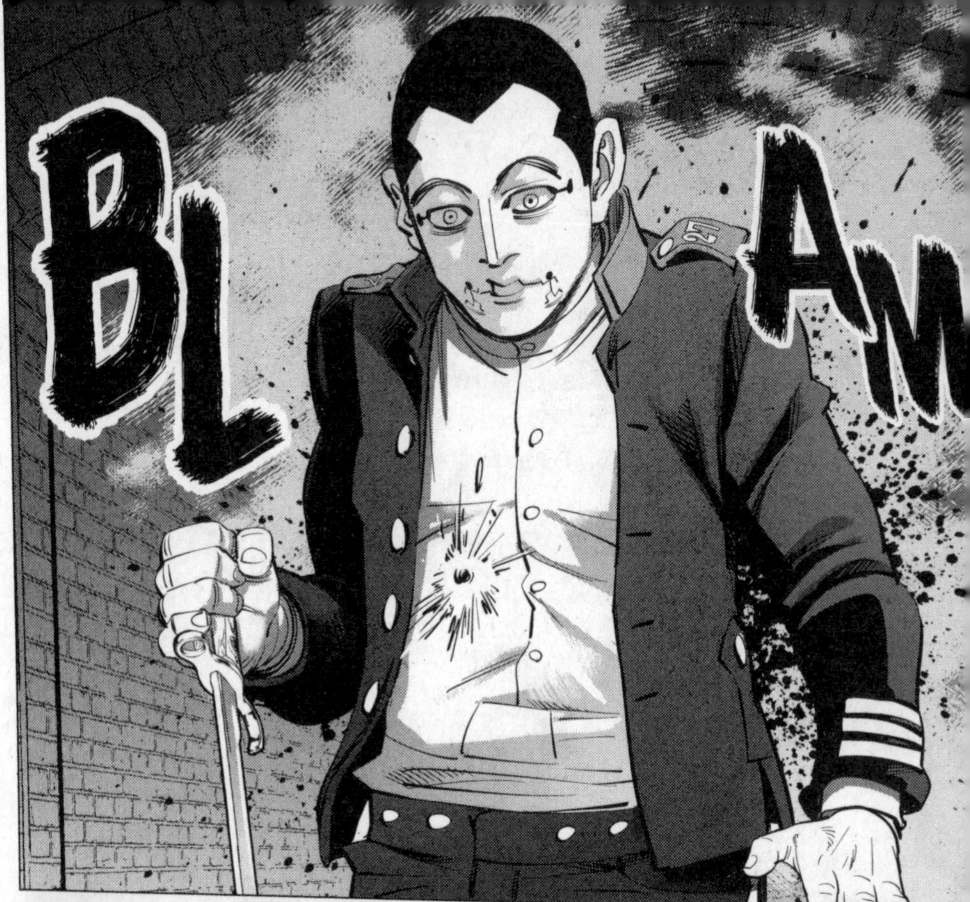
BLAM
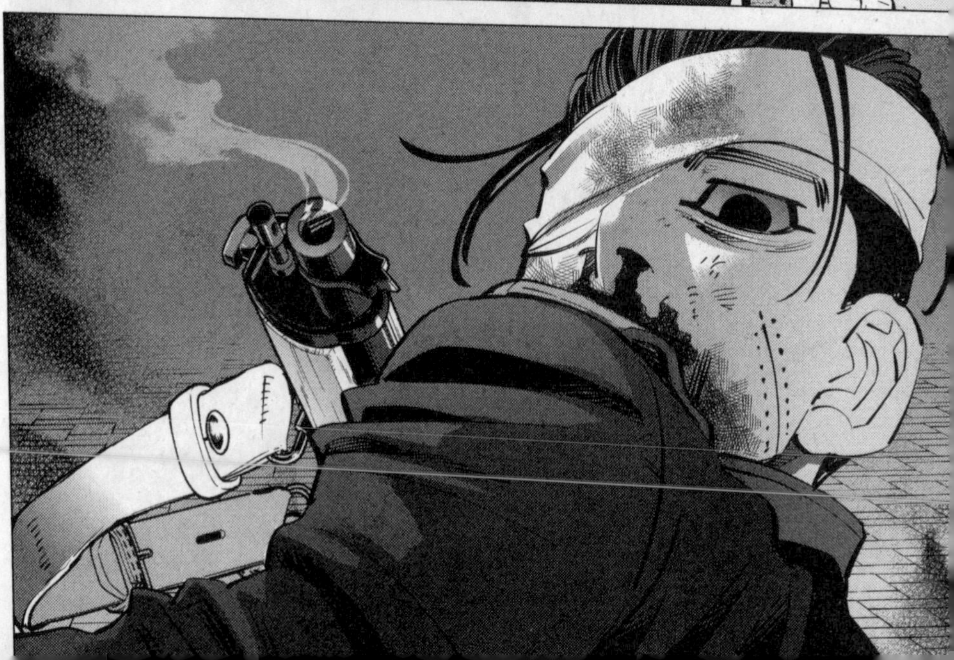

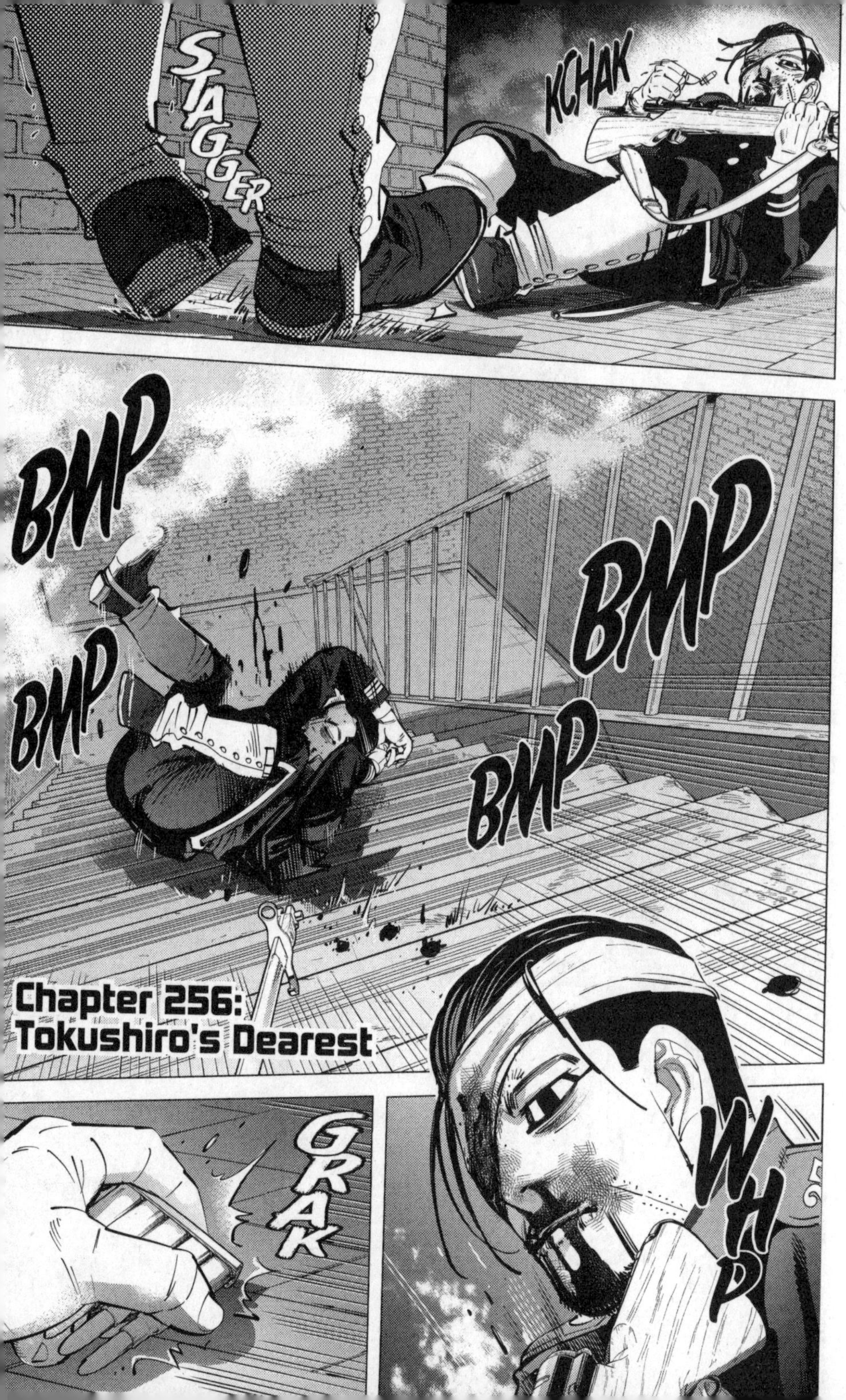
KCHAK
STAGGER
BMP
BMP
BMP
BMP
Chapter 256:
Tokushiro's Dearest
WHP
GRAK

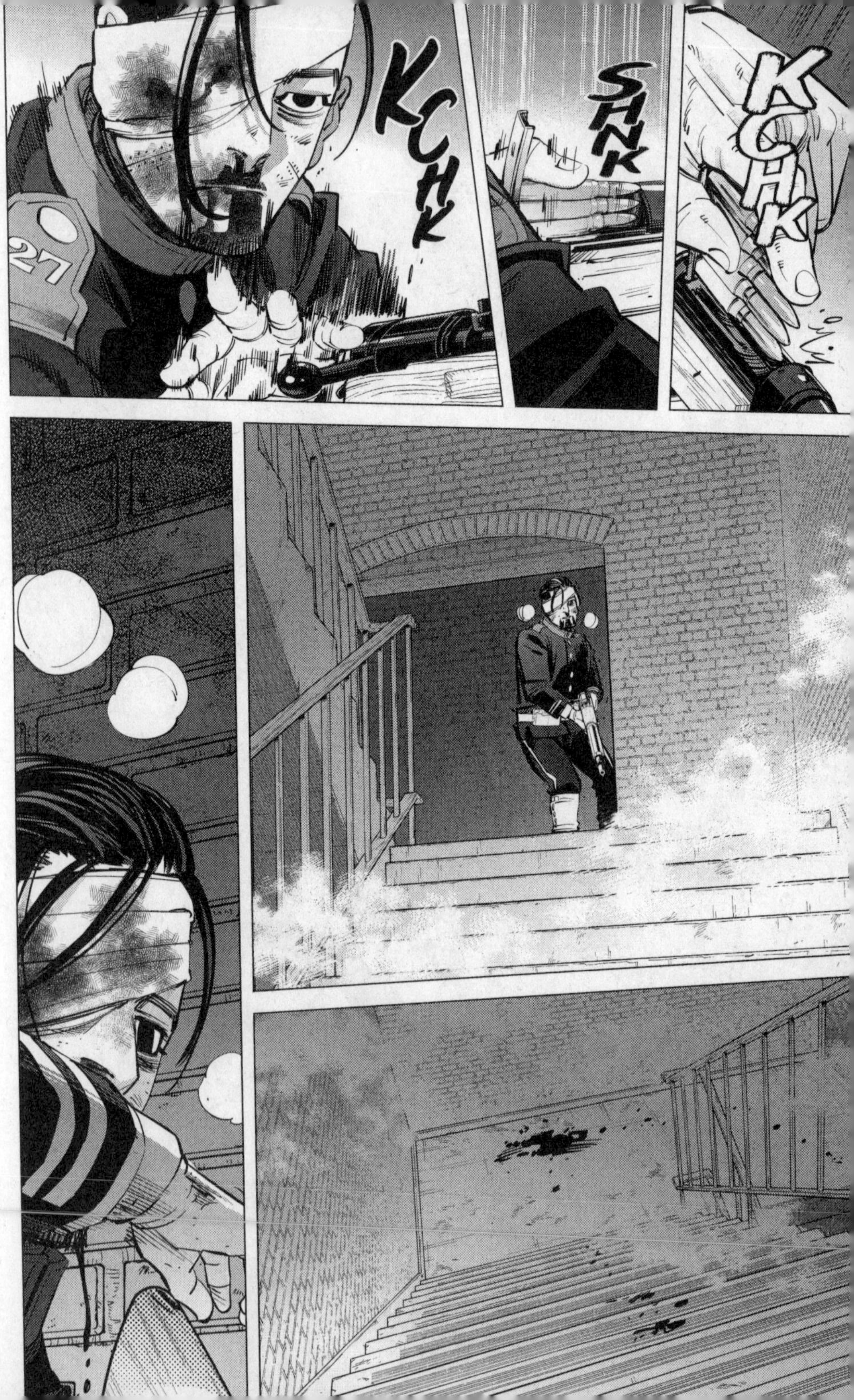
KCHK
SHNK
KCHK

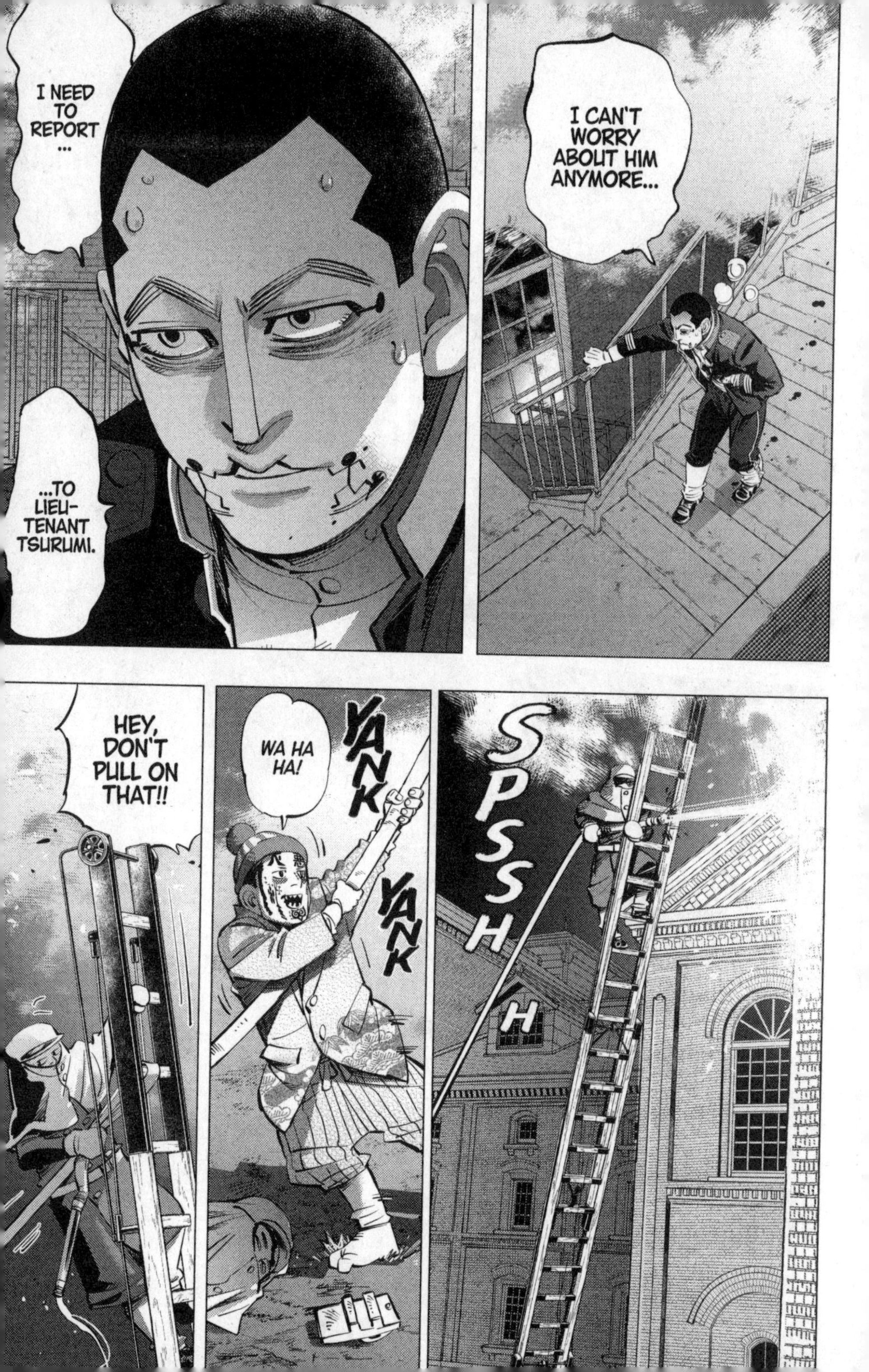
I CAN'T WORRY ABOUT HIM ANYMORE...
I NEED TO REPORT ...
...TO LIEU-TENANT TSURUMI.
SPSSH
H
WA HA HA!
YANK
YANK
YANK
HEY, DON'T PULL ON THAT!!

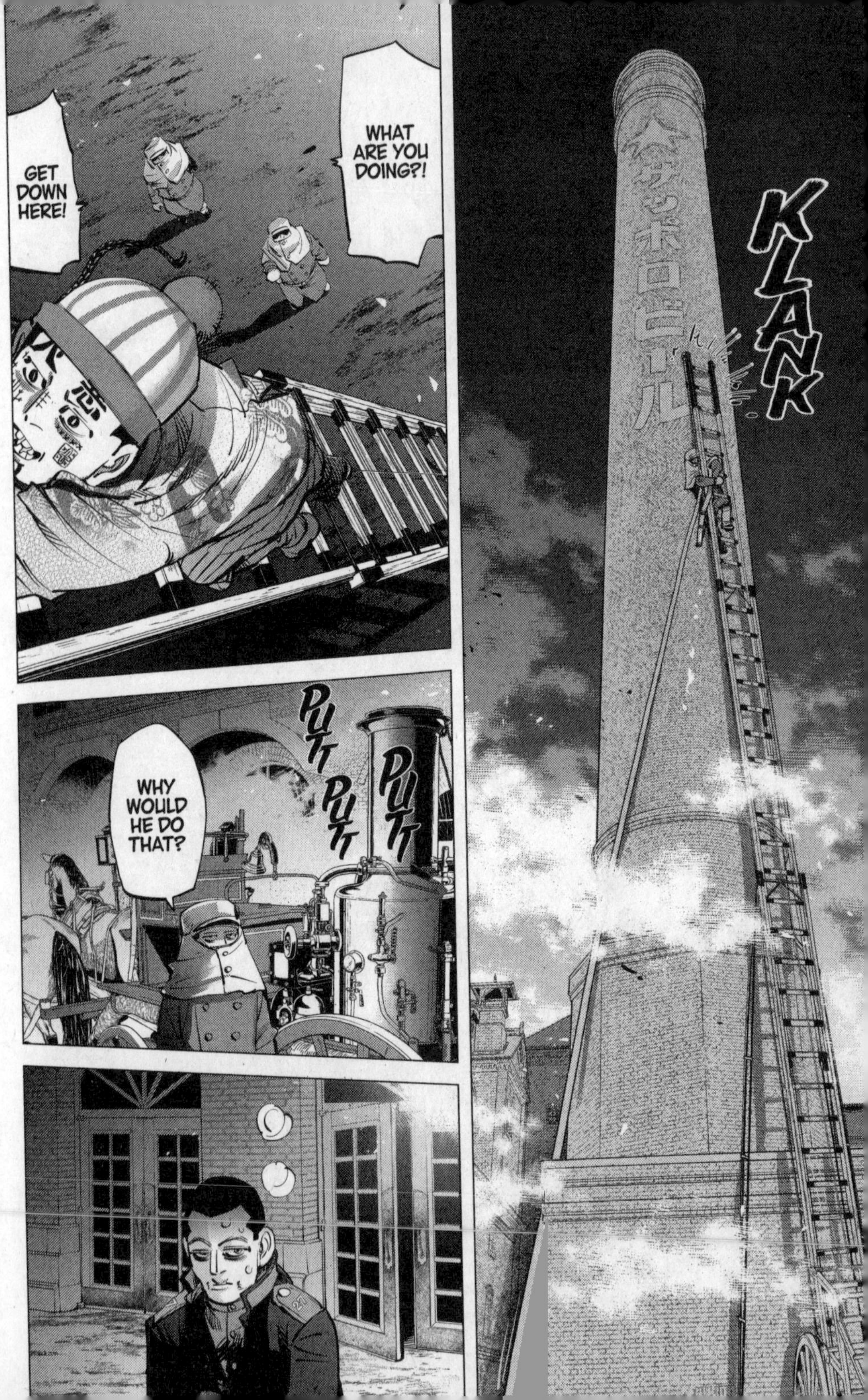
KLANK
WHAT ARE YOU DOING?!
GET DOWN HERE!
PUTT PUTT PUTT
WHY WOULD HE DO THAT?

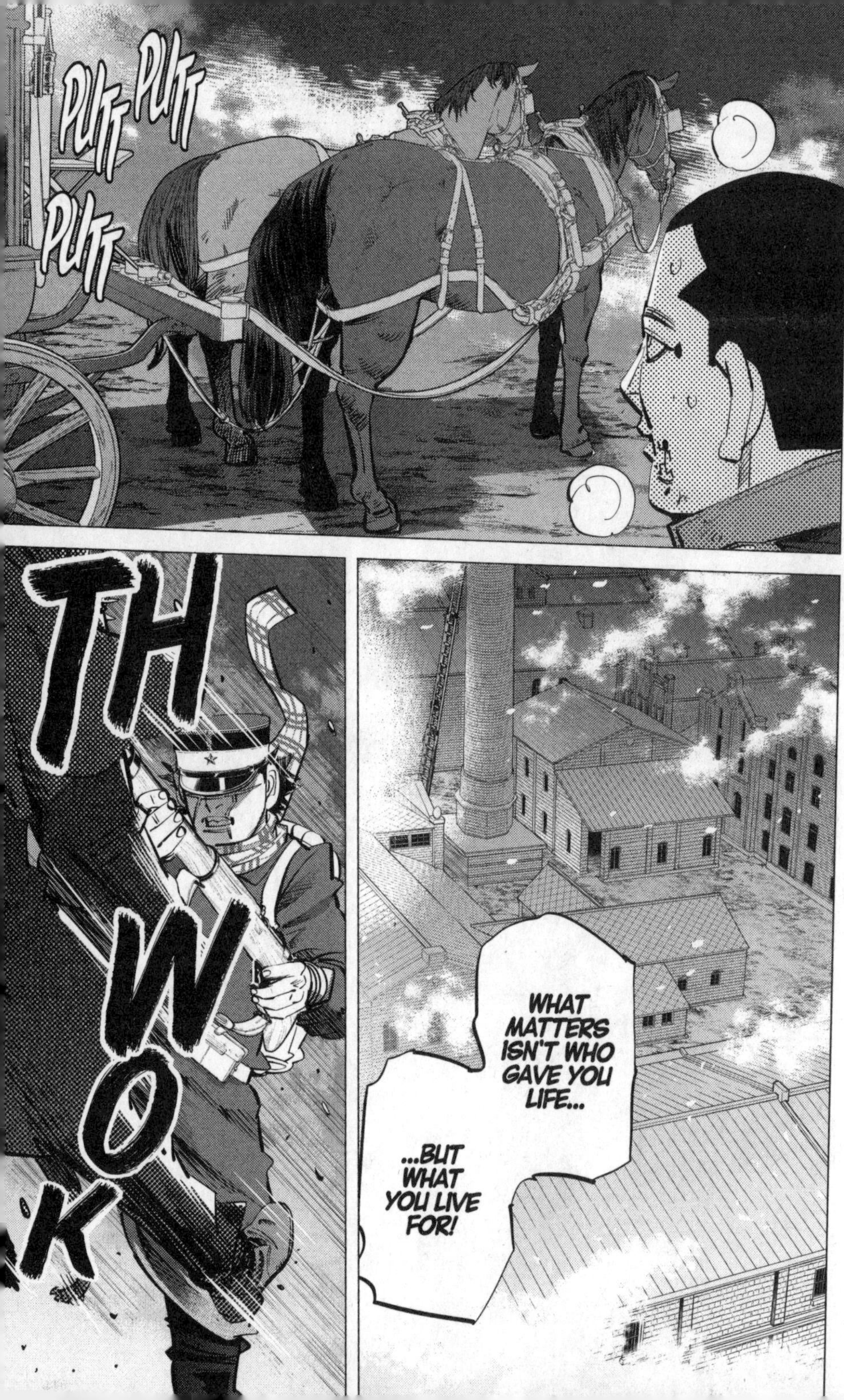
PUTT PUTT
PUTT
WHAT MATTERS ISN'T WHO GAVE YOU LIFE...
...BUT WHAT YOU LIVE FOR!
THWOK

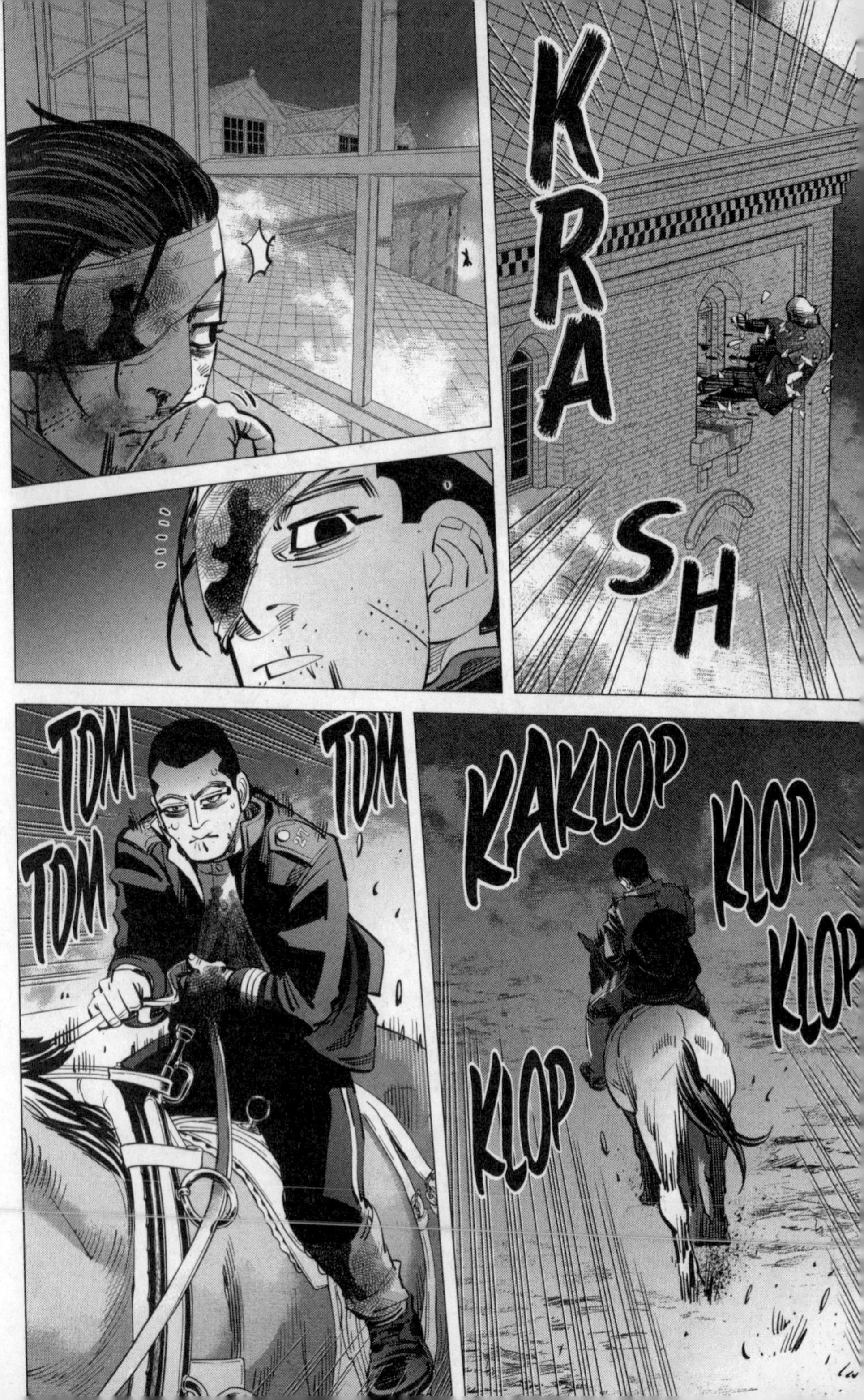
KRASH
KAKLOP
KLOP
KLOP
KLOP
TOM
TOM TOM

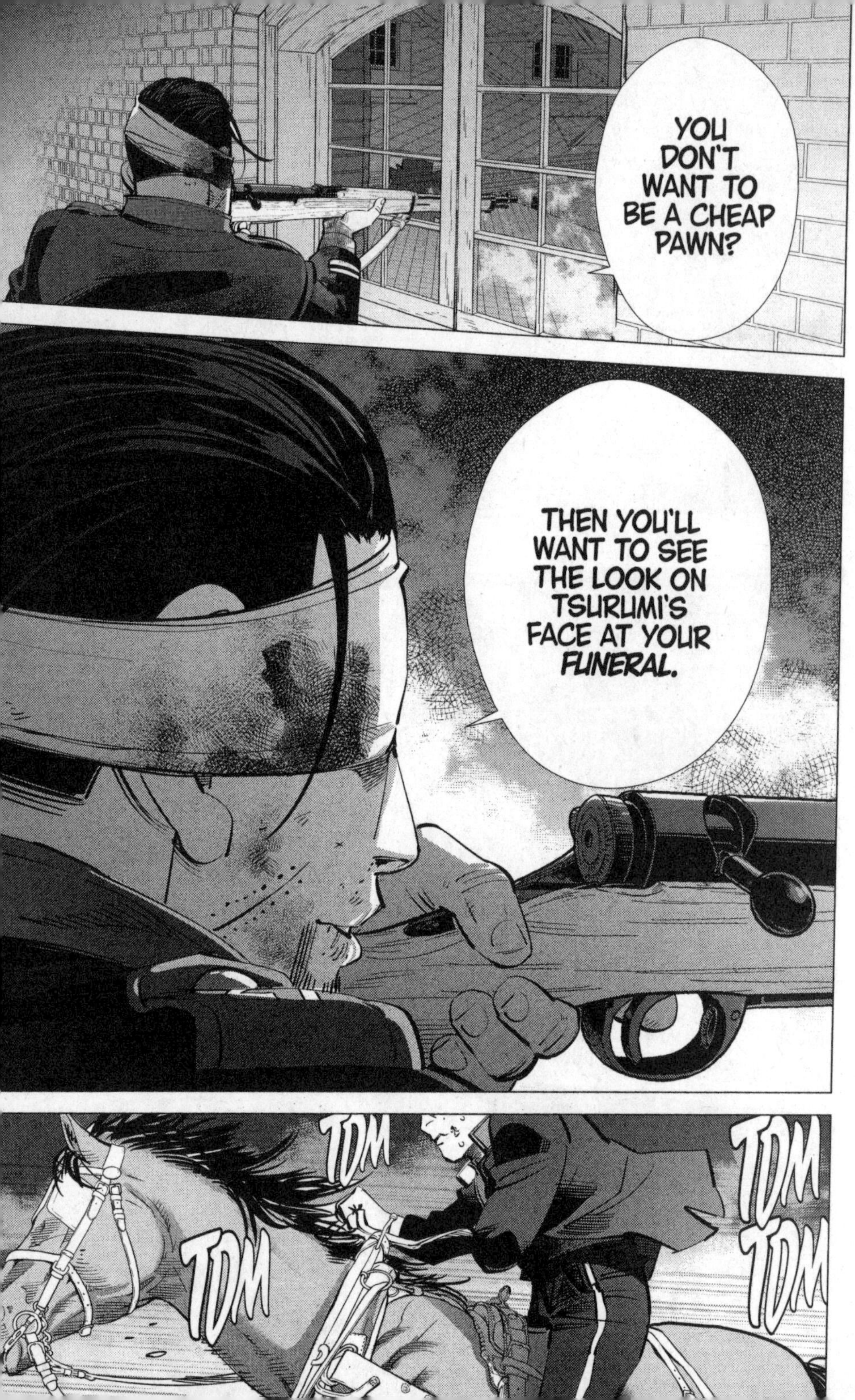
YOU DON'T WANT TO BE A CHEAP PAWN?
THEN YOU'LL WANT TO SEE THE LOOK ON TSURUMI'S FACE AT YOUR FUNERAL.
TOM TOM
TOM
TOM

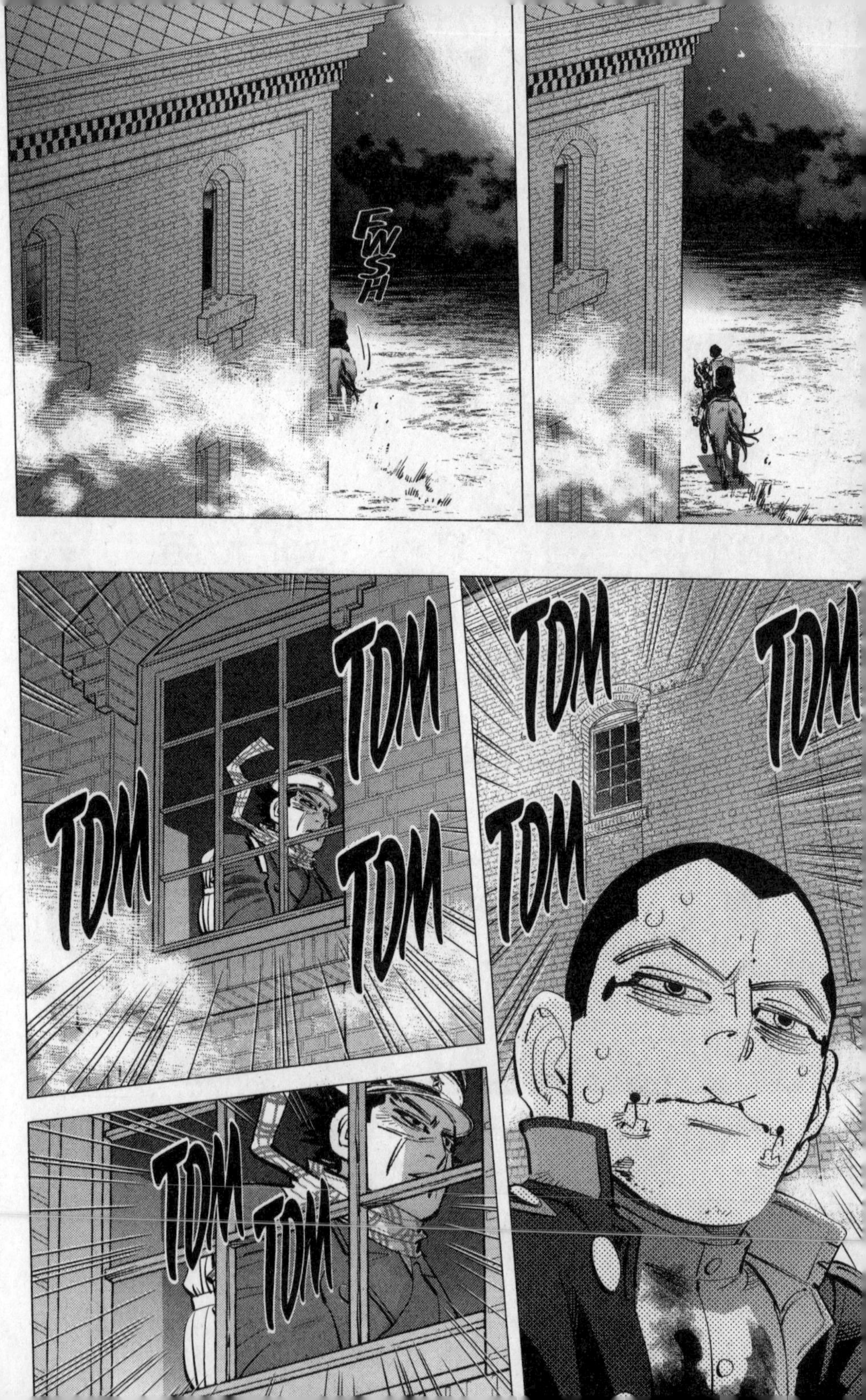
FWSH
TOM
TOM
TOM
TOM
TOM
TOM
TOM
TOM

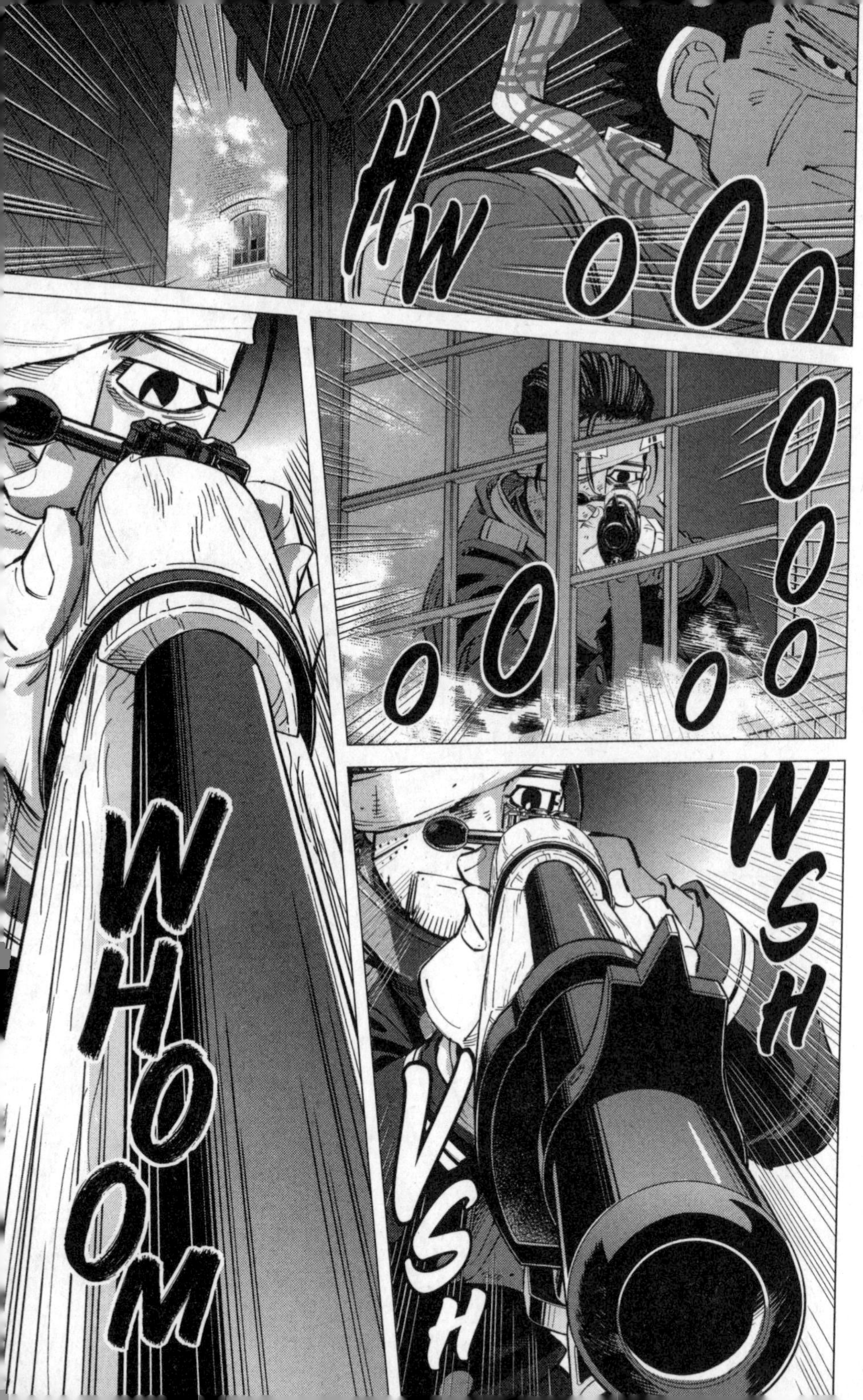
HWOOOOOOOOOOOO
WSH
VSH
WHOOOM

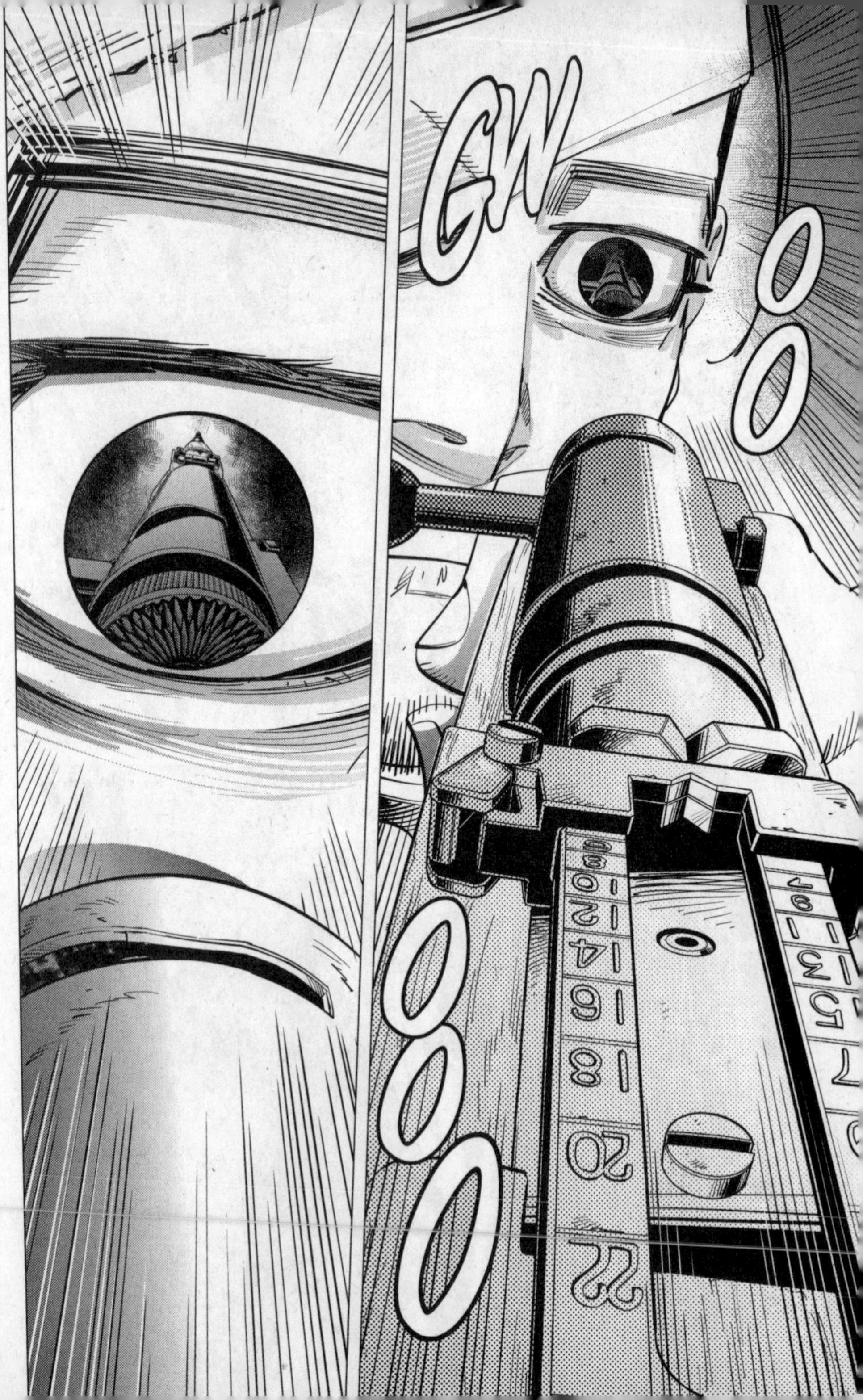
GWOOOOOO

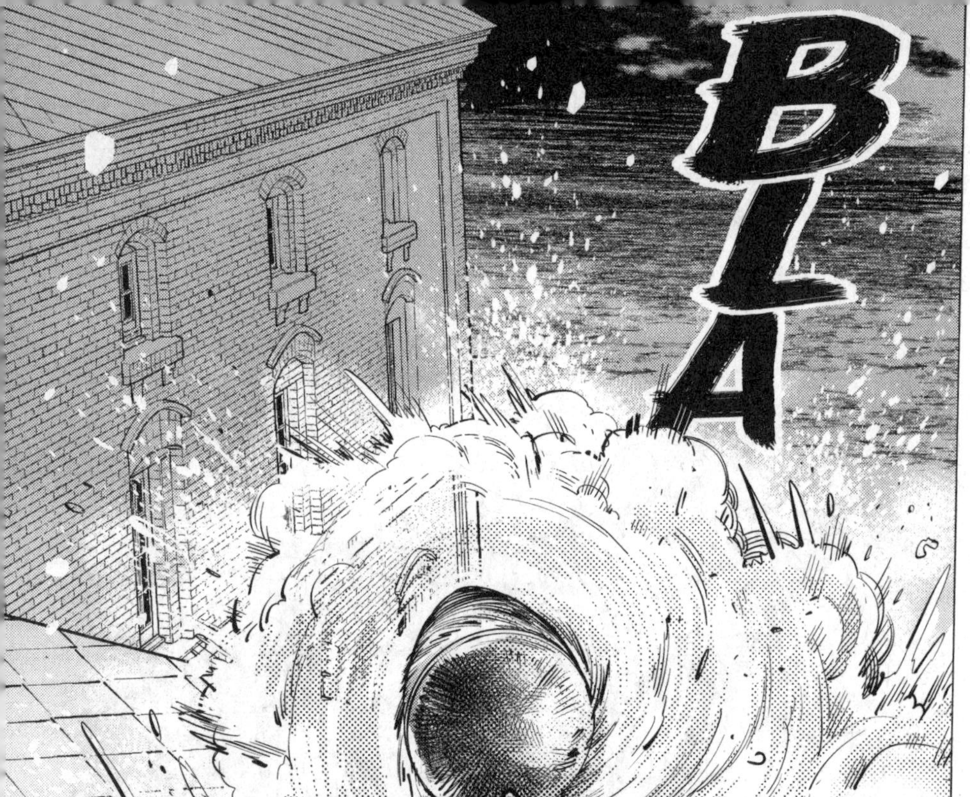
BLAMM
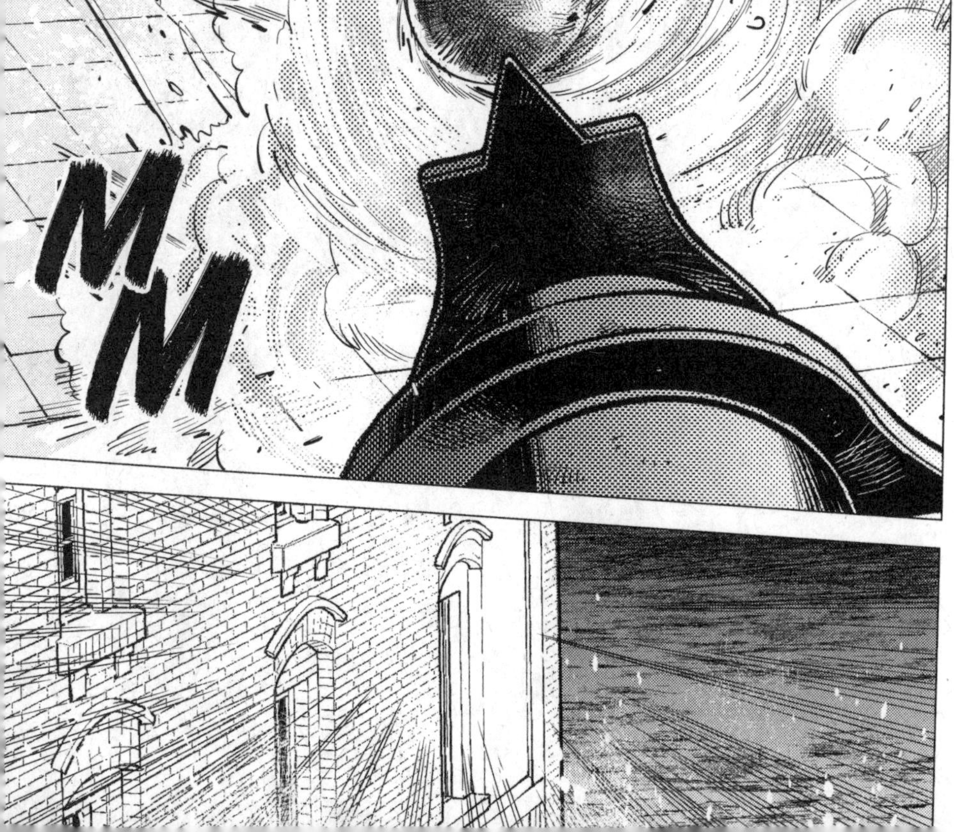

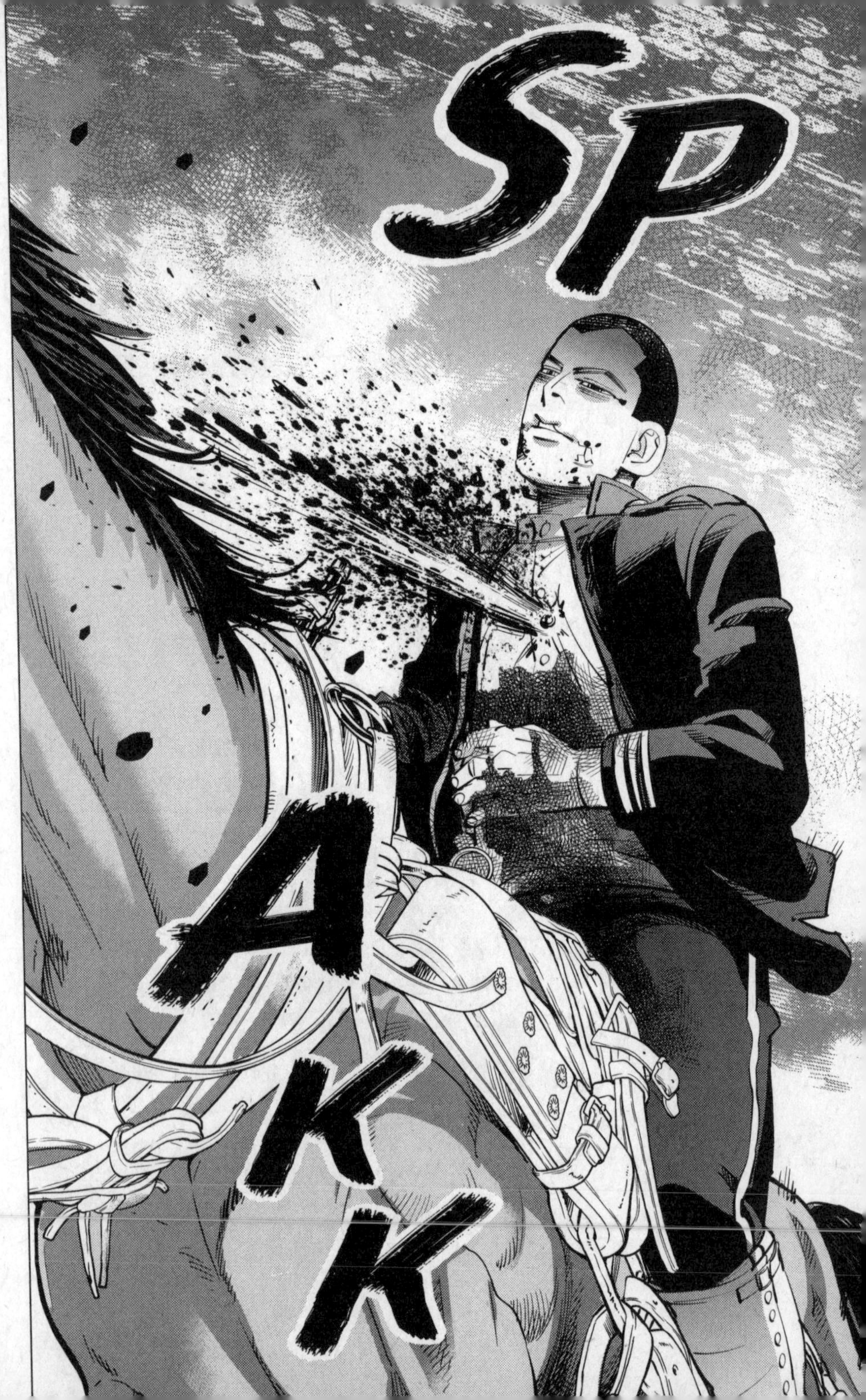
SPAKK

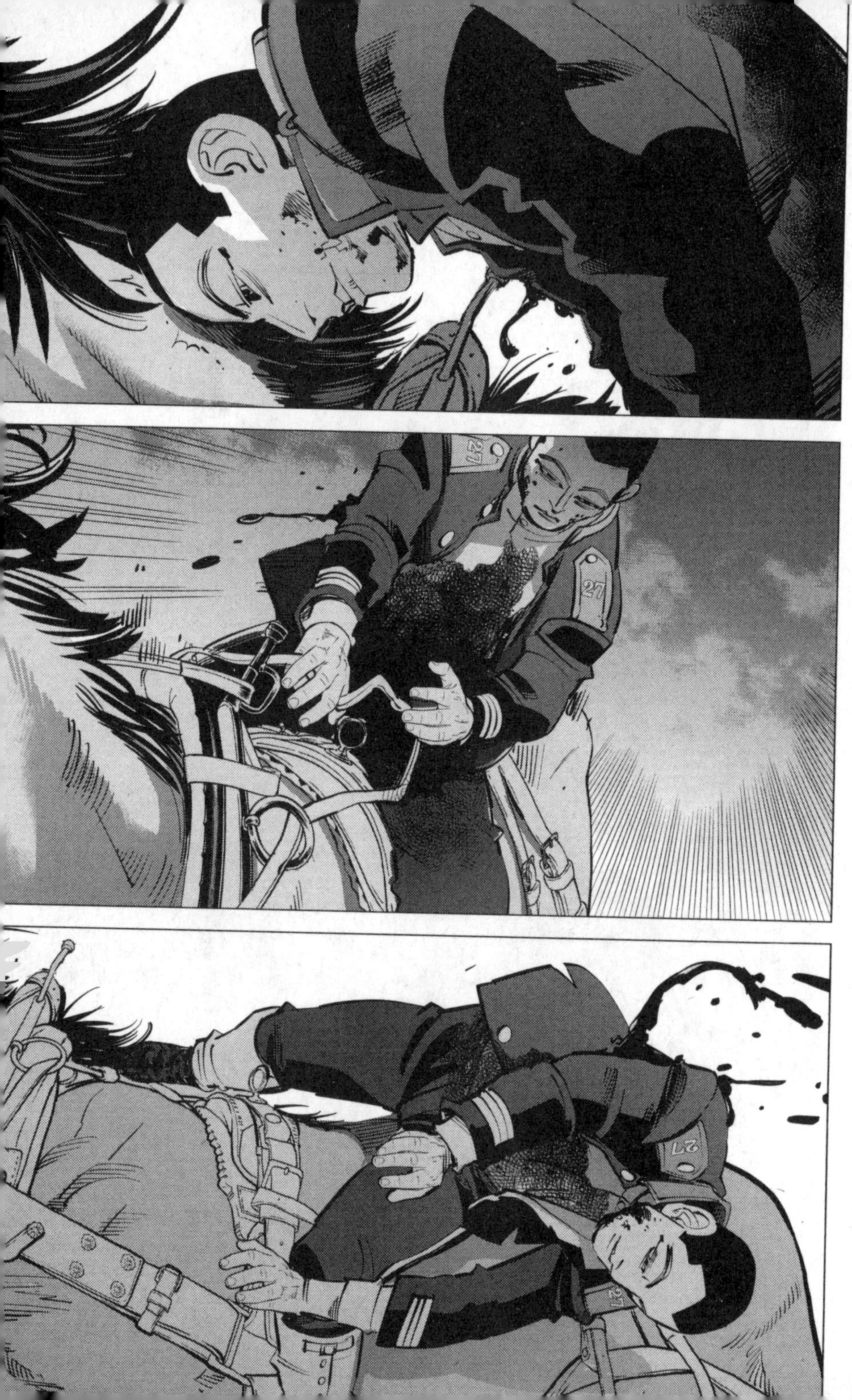

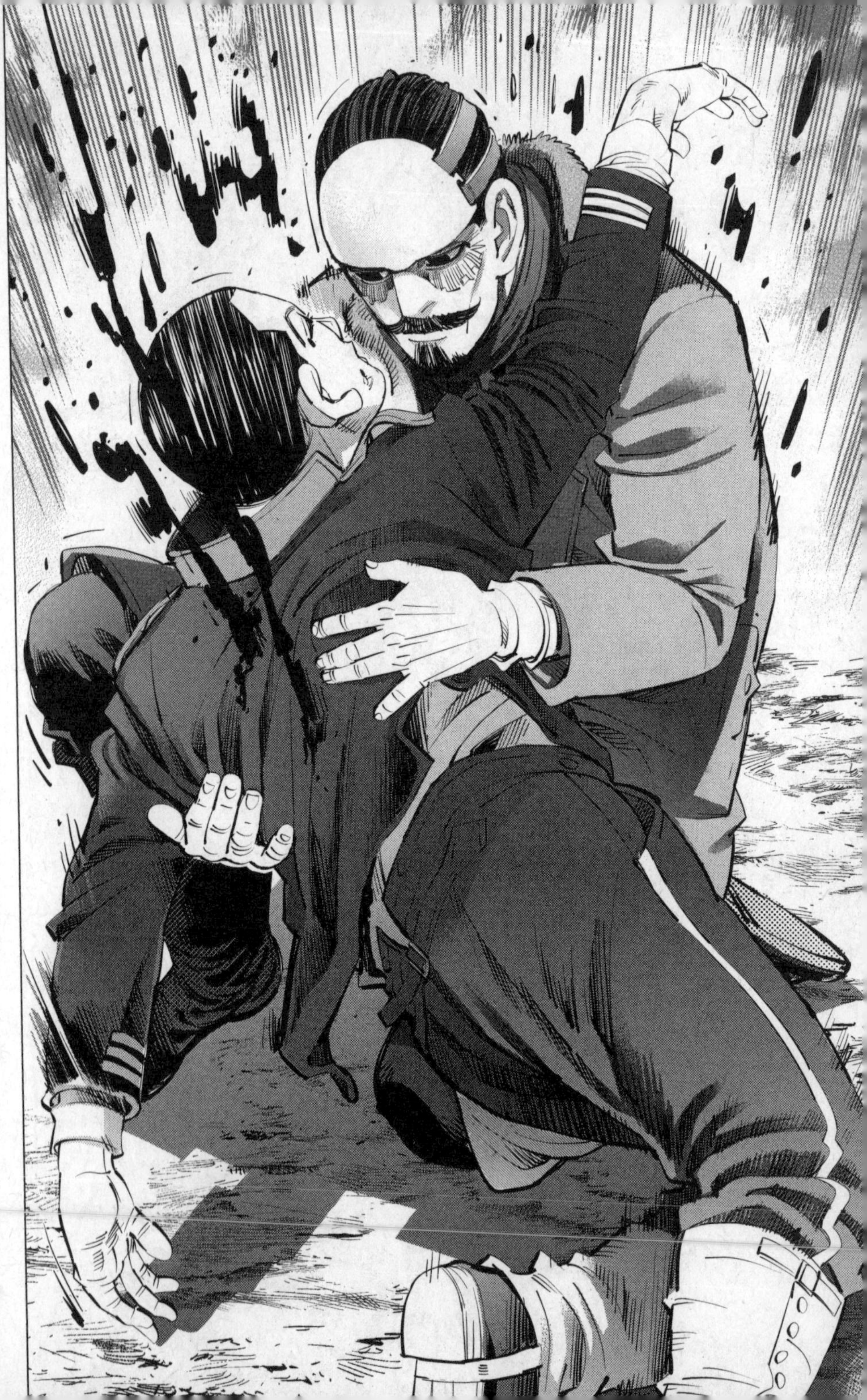

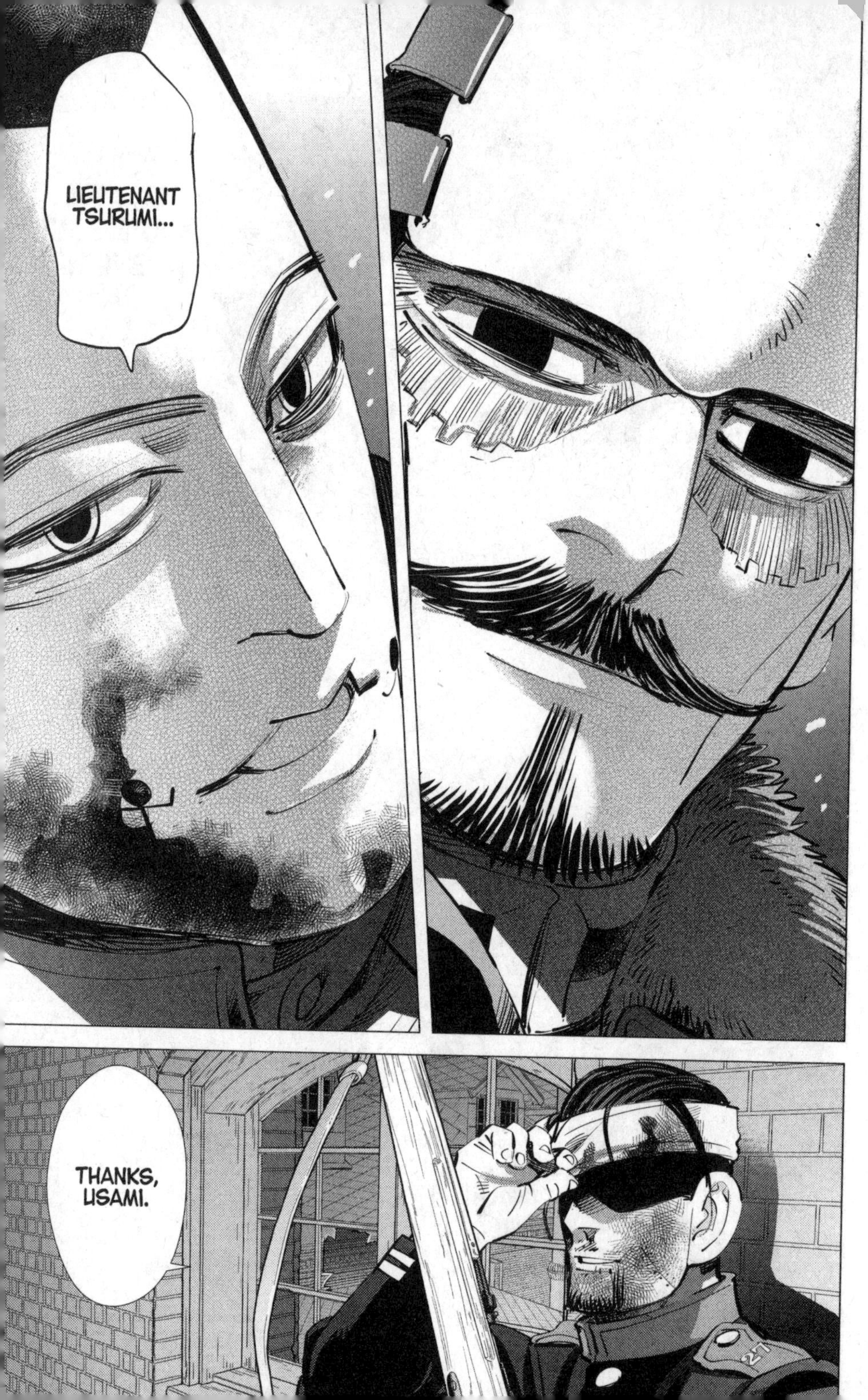
LIEUTENANT TSURUMI...
THANKS, USAMI.

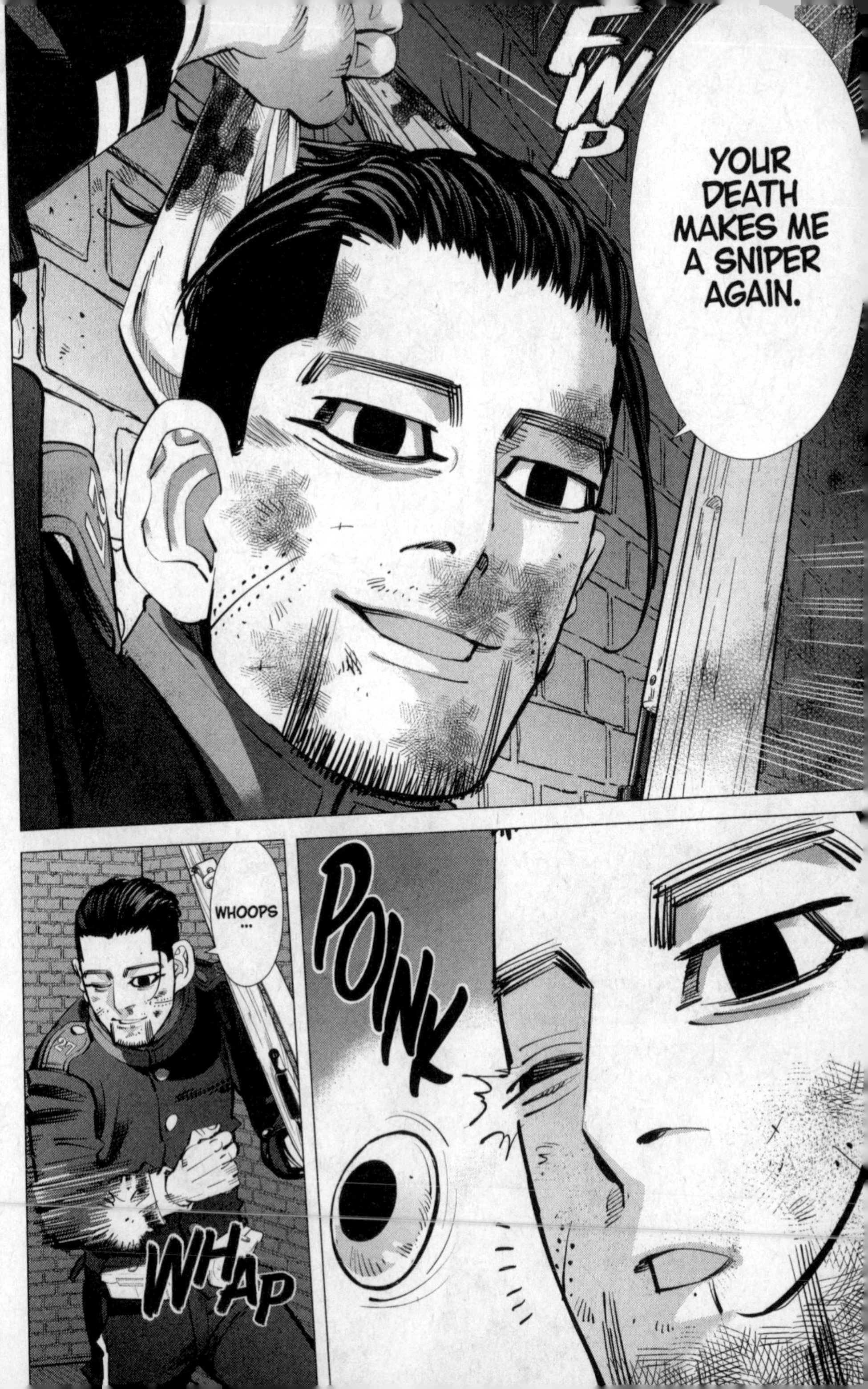
FWP
YOUR DEATH MAKES ME A SNIPER AGAIN.
POINK
WHOOPS ...
WHAP

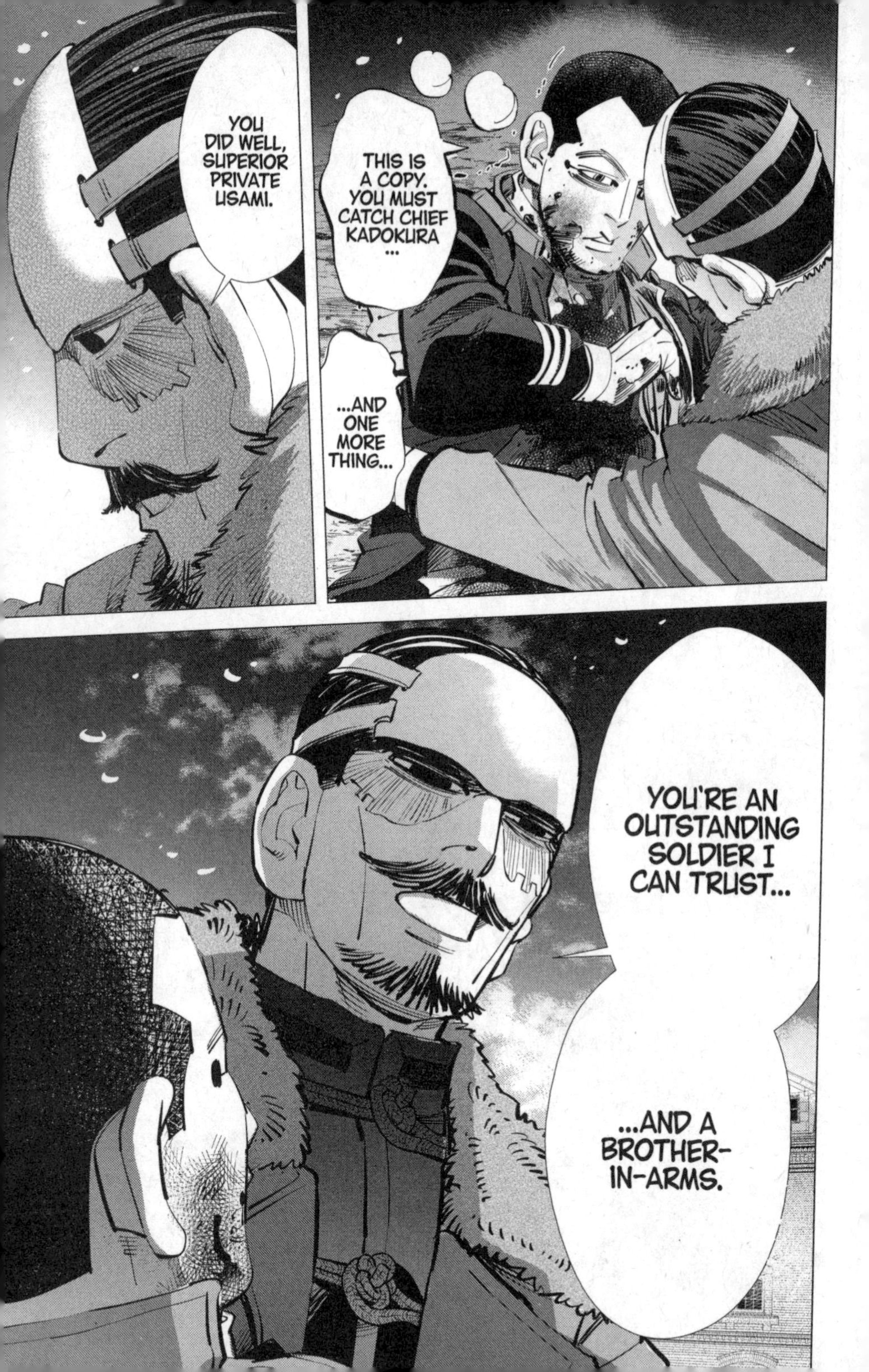
THIS IS A COPY. YOU MUST CATCH CHIEF KADOKURA ...
...AND ONE MORE THING...
YOU DID WELL, SUPERIOR PRIVATE USAMI.
YOU'RE AN OUTSTANDING SOLDIER I CAN TRUST...
...AND A BROTHER-IN-ARMS.

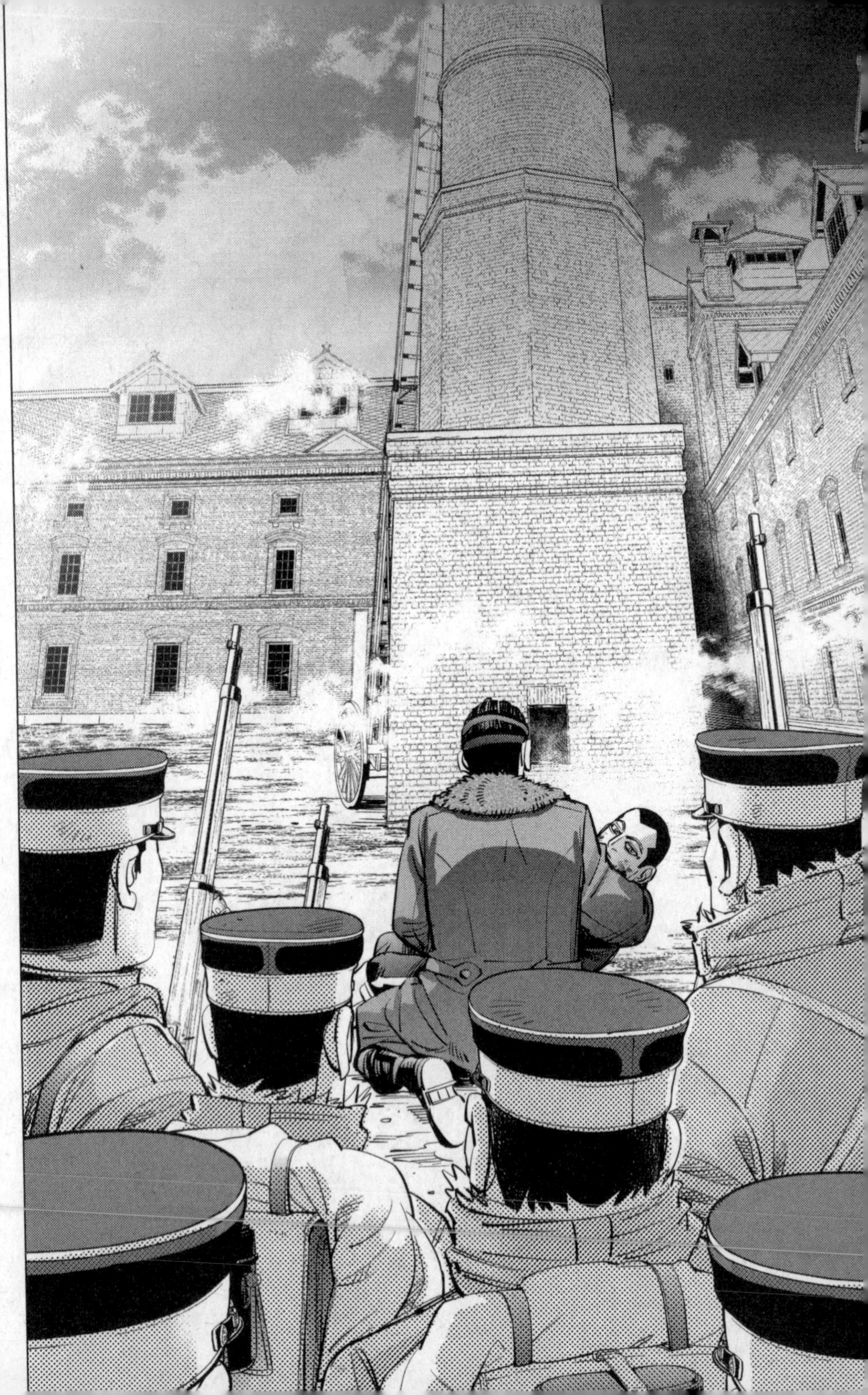

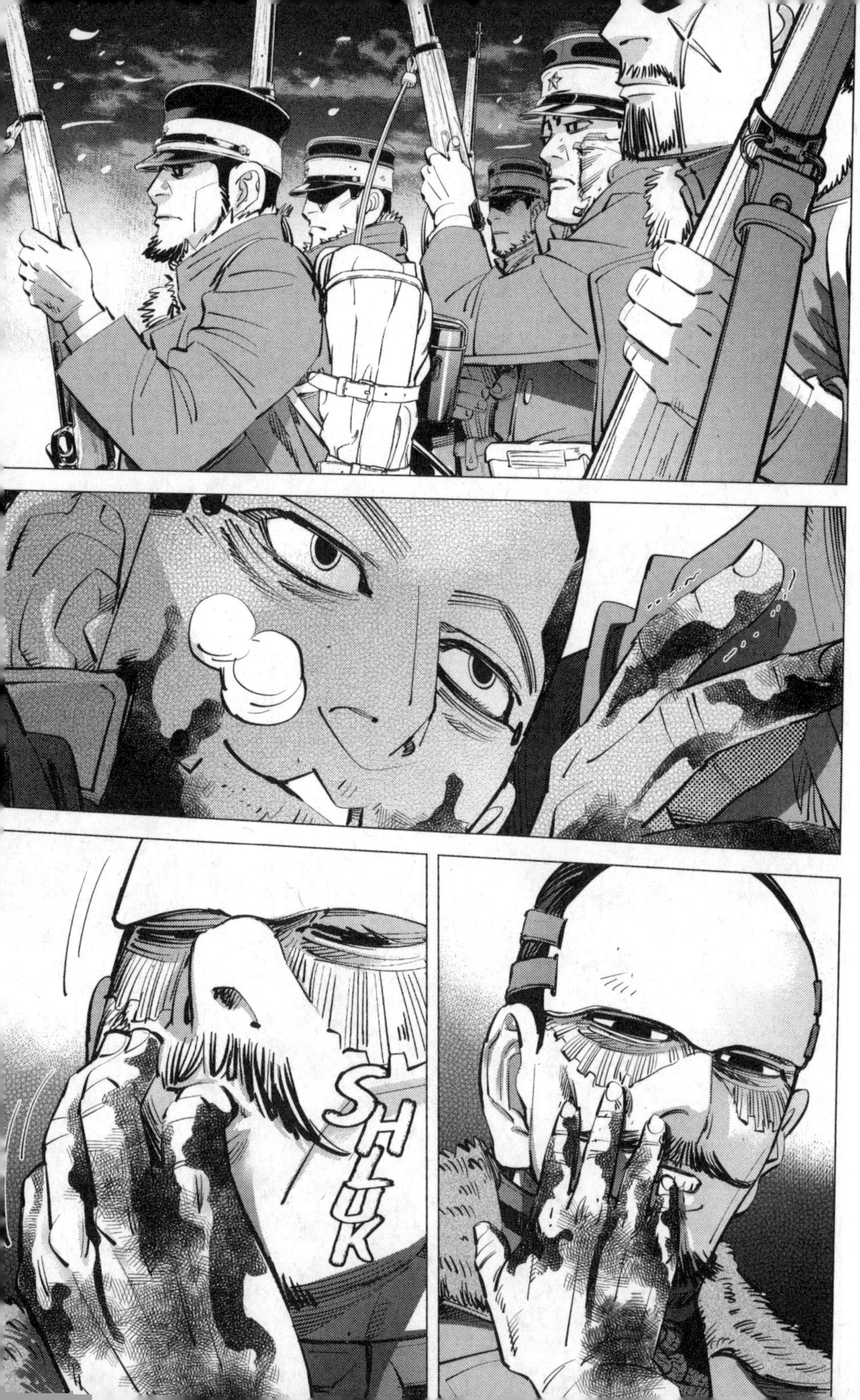
SHLUK

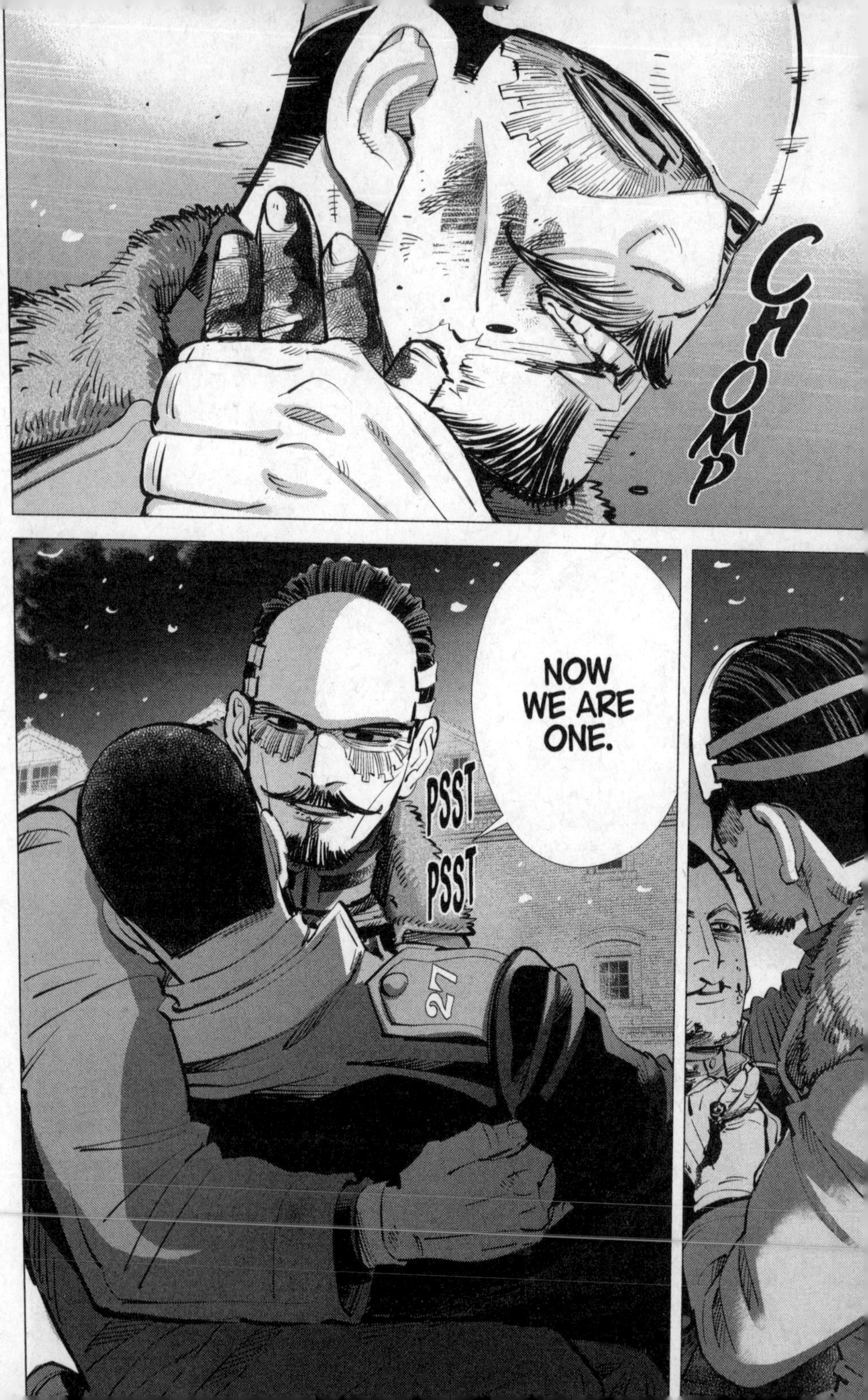
CHOMP
NOW WE ARE ONE.
PSST
PSST

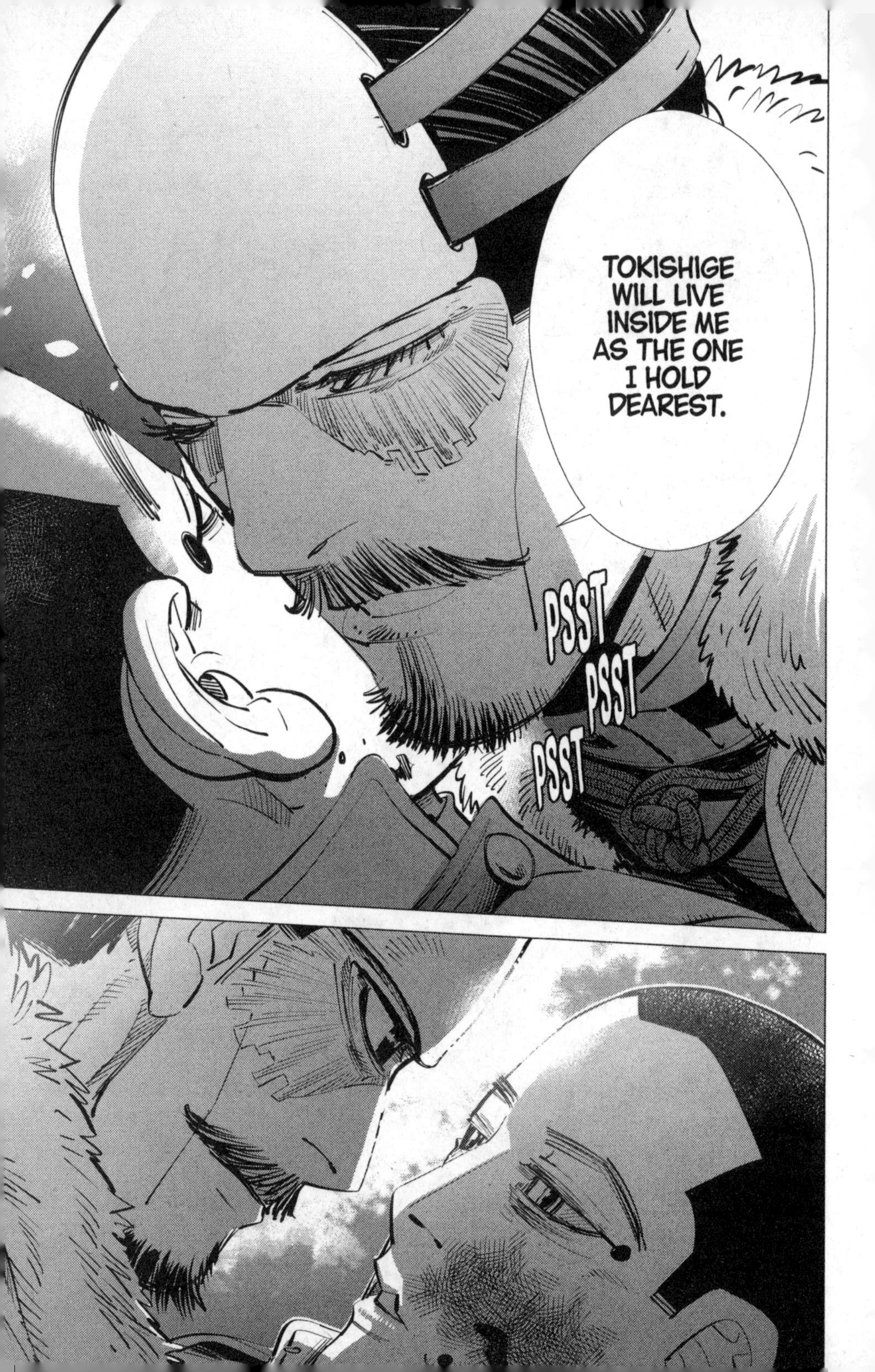

TOKISHIGE WILL LIVE INSIDE ME AS THE ONE I HOLD DEAREST.
PSST PSST PSST

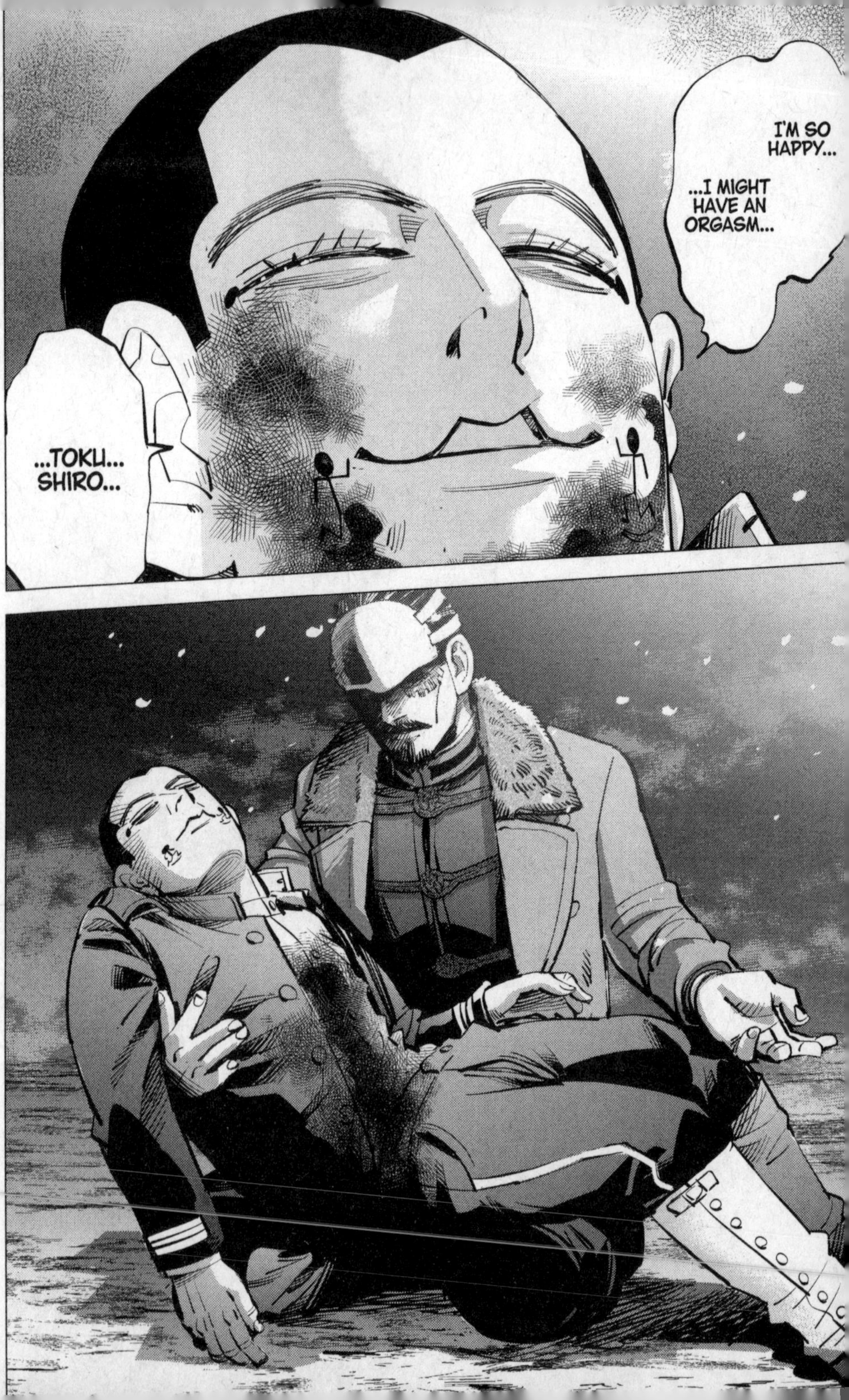
I'M SO HAPPY...
...I MIGHT HAVE AN ORGASM...
...TOKU... SHIRO...

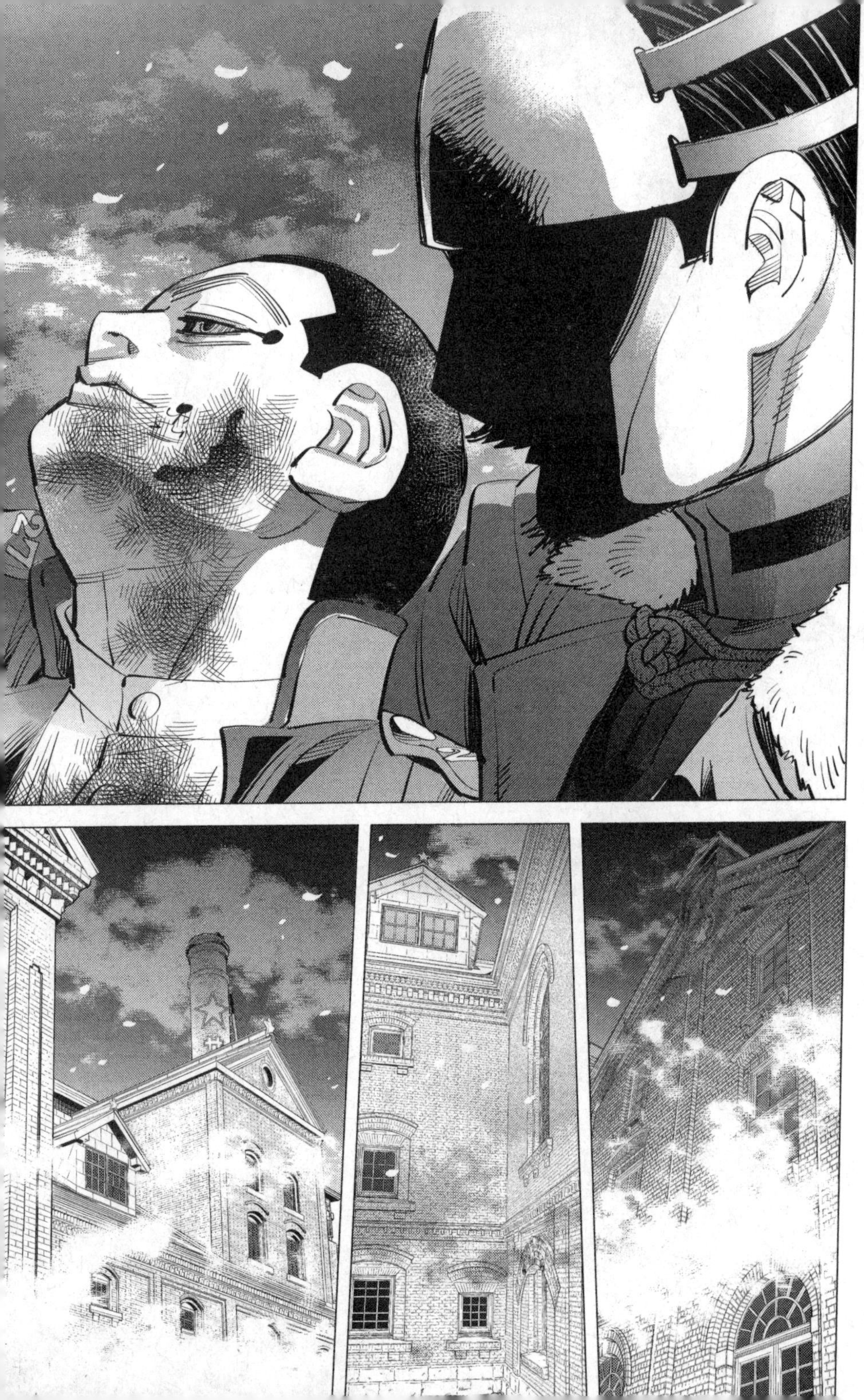

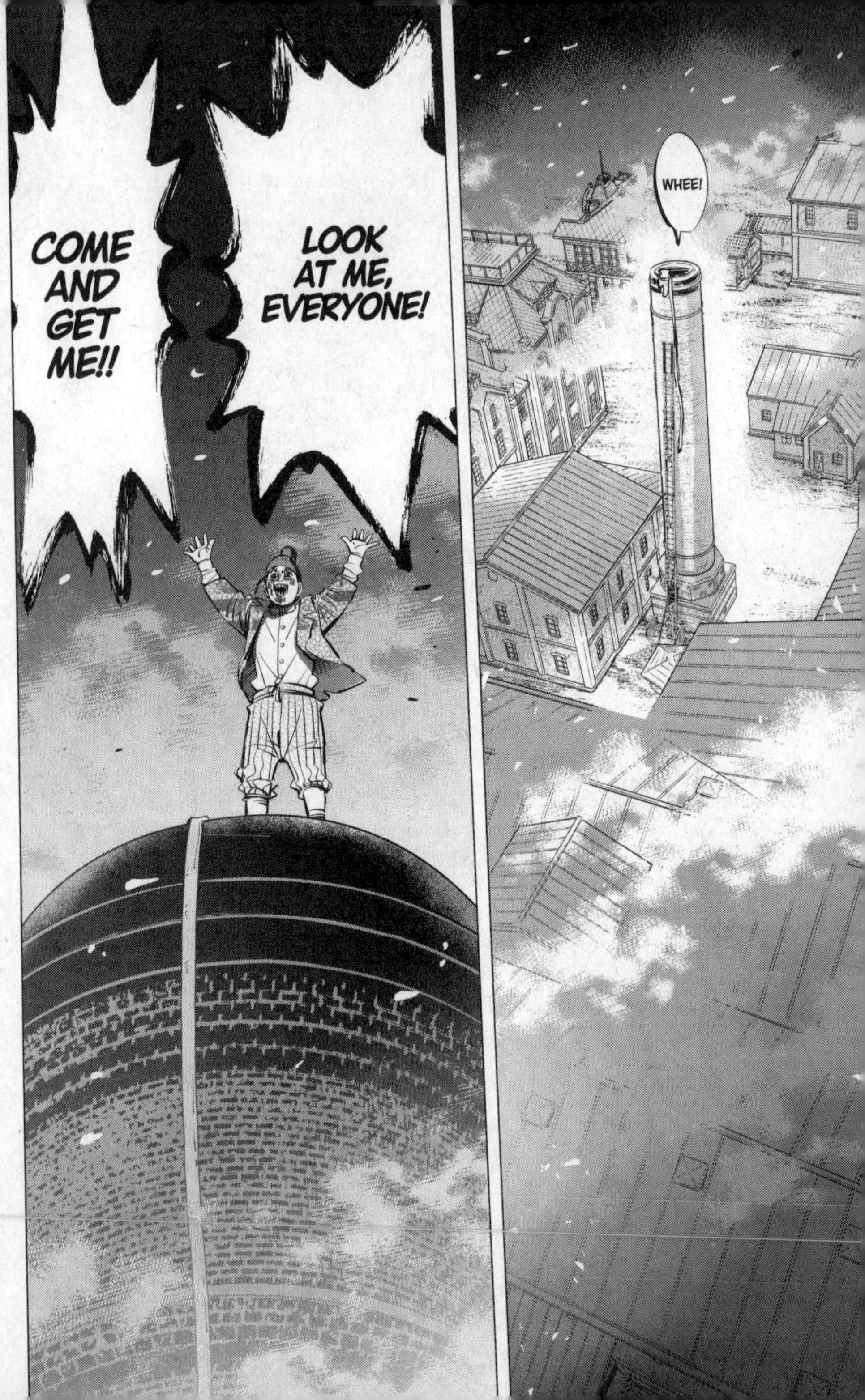
WHEE!
LOOK AT ME, EVERYONE!
COME AND GET ME!!

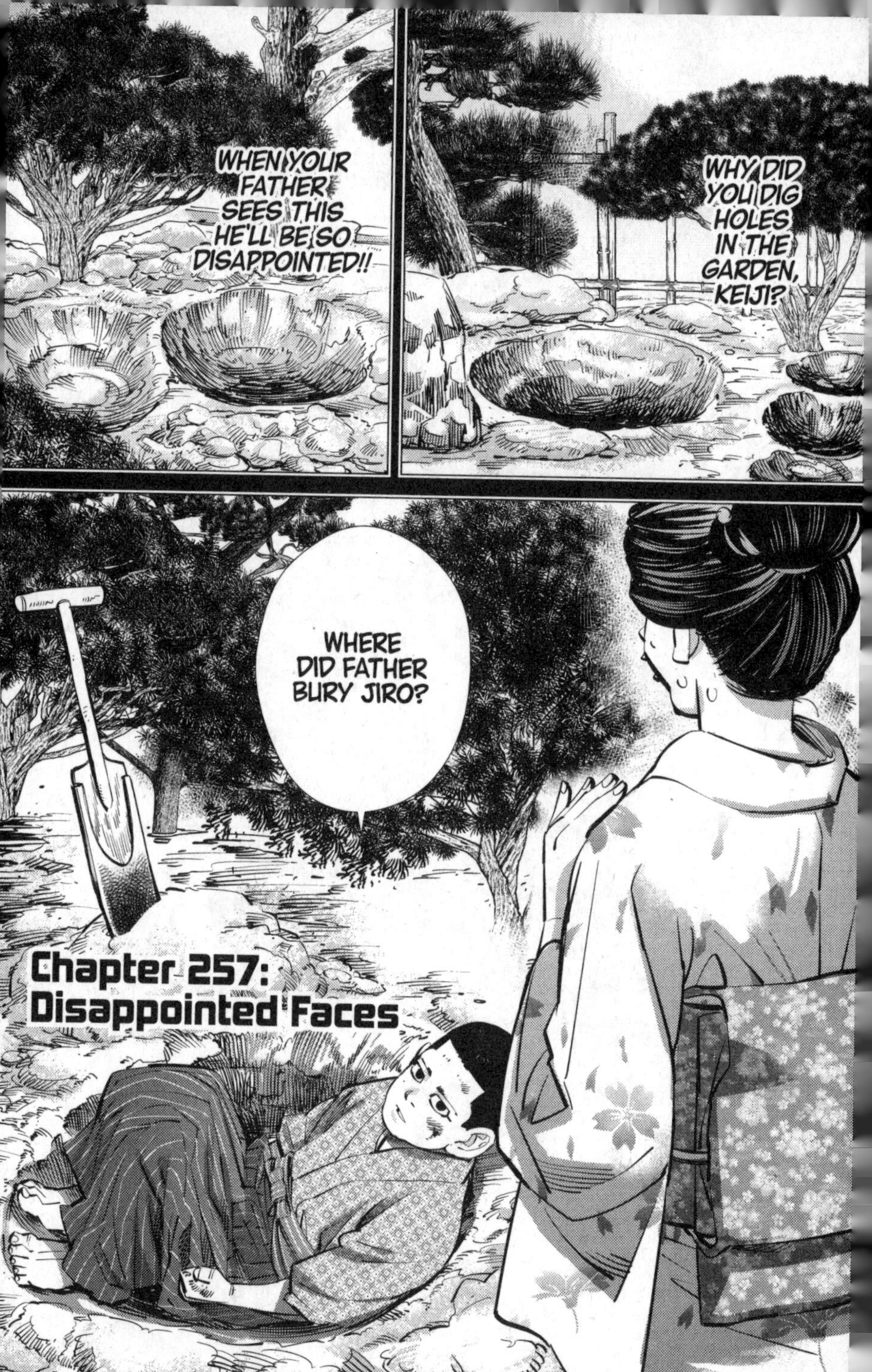
WHY DID YOU DIG HOLES IN THE GARDEN, KEIJI?
WHEN YOUR FATHER SEES THIS HE'LL BE SO DISAPPOINTED!!
WHERE DID FATHER BURY JIRO?
Chapter 257: Disappointed Faces

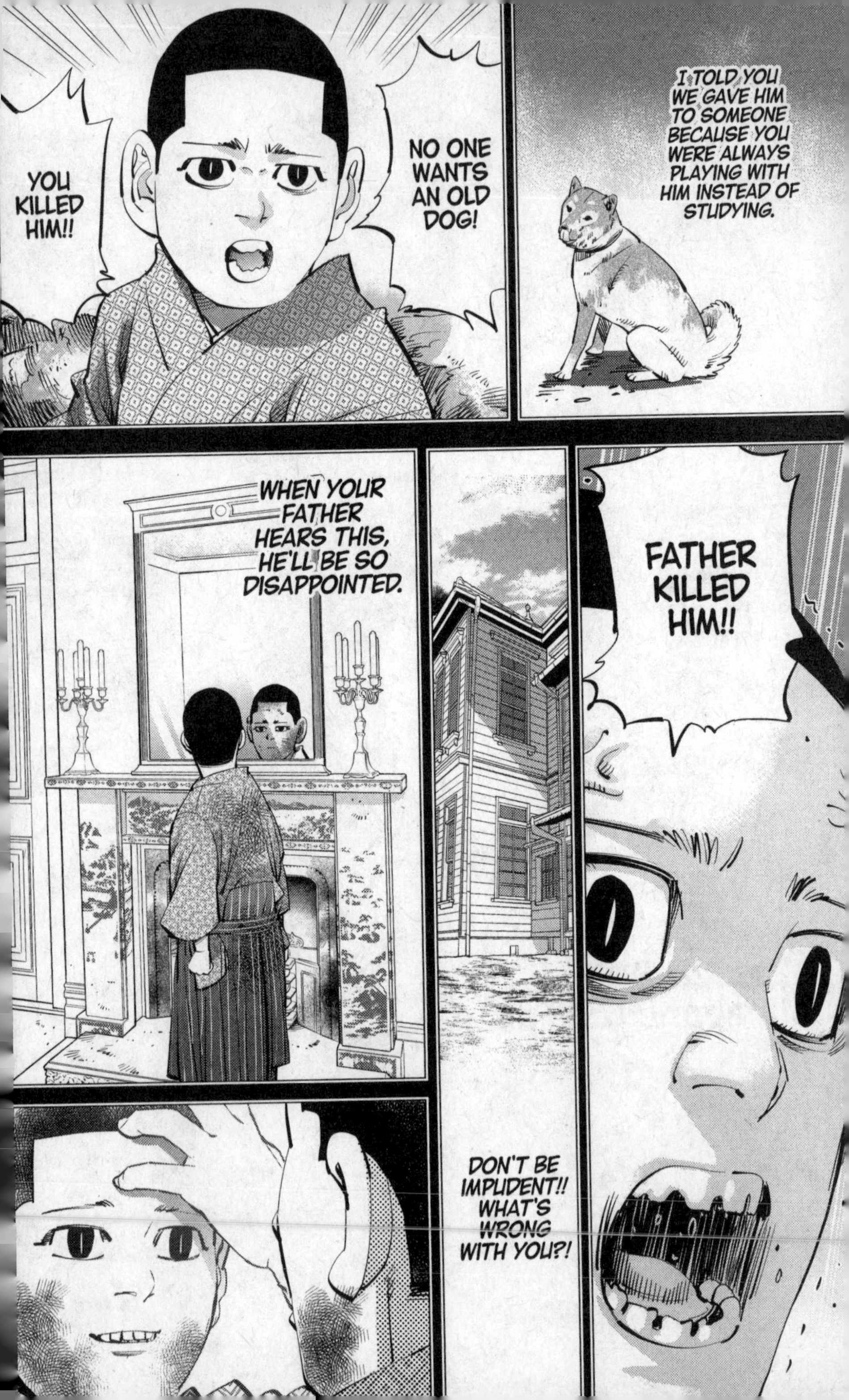
I TOLD YOU WE GAVE HIM TO SOMEONE BECAUSE YOU WERE ALWAYS PLAYING WITH HIM INSTEAD OF STUDYING.
NO ONE WANTS AN OLD DOG!
YOU KILLED HIM!!
FATHER KILLED HIM!!
DON'T BE IMPUDENT!! WHAT'S WRONG WITH YOU?!
WHEN YOUR FATHER HEARS THIS, HE'LL BE SO DISAPPOINTED.

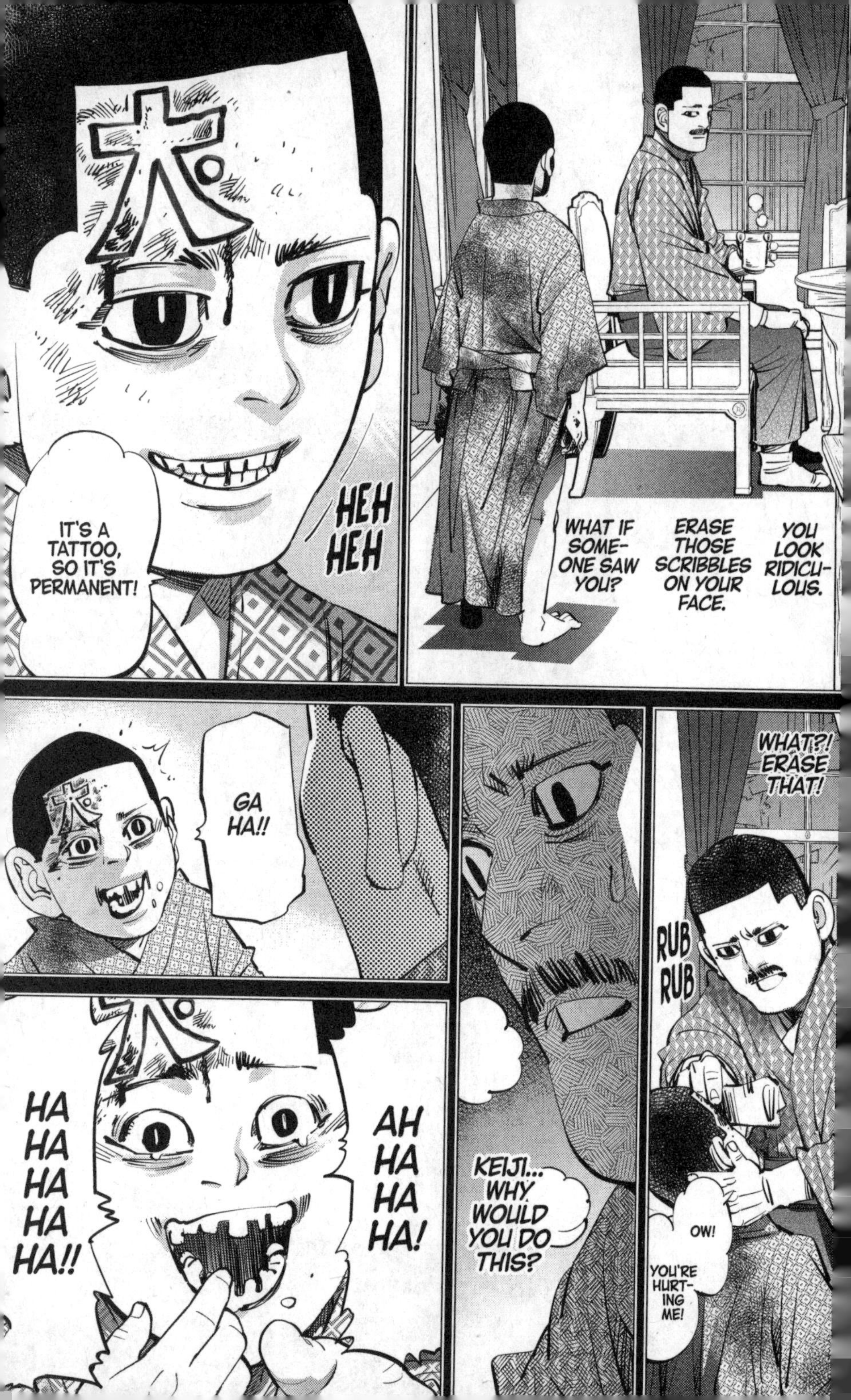
YOU LOOK RIDICULOUS.
ERASE THOSE SCRIBBLES ON YOUR FACE.
WHAT IF SOMEONE SAW YOU?
HEH HEH
IT'S A TATTOO, SO IT'S PERMANENT!
WHAT?! ERASE THAT!
RUB RUB
OW!
YOU'RE HURTING ME!
KEIJI... WHY WOULD YOU DO THIS?
GA HA!!
AH HA HA HA HA!
HA HA HA HA HA HA!!

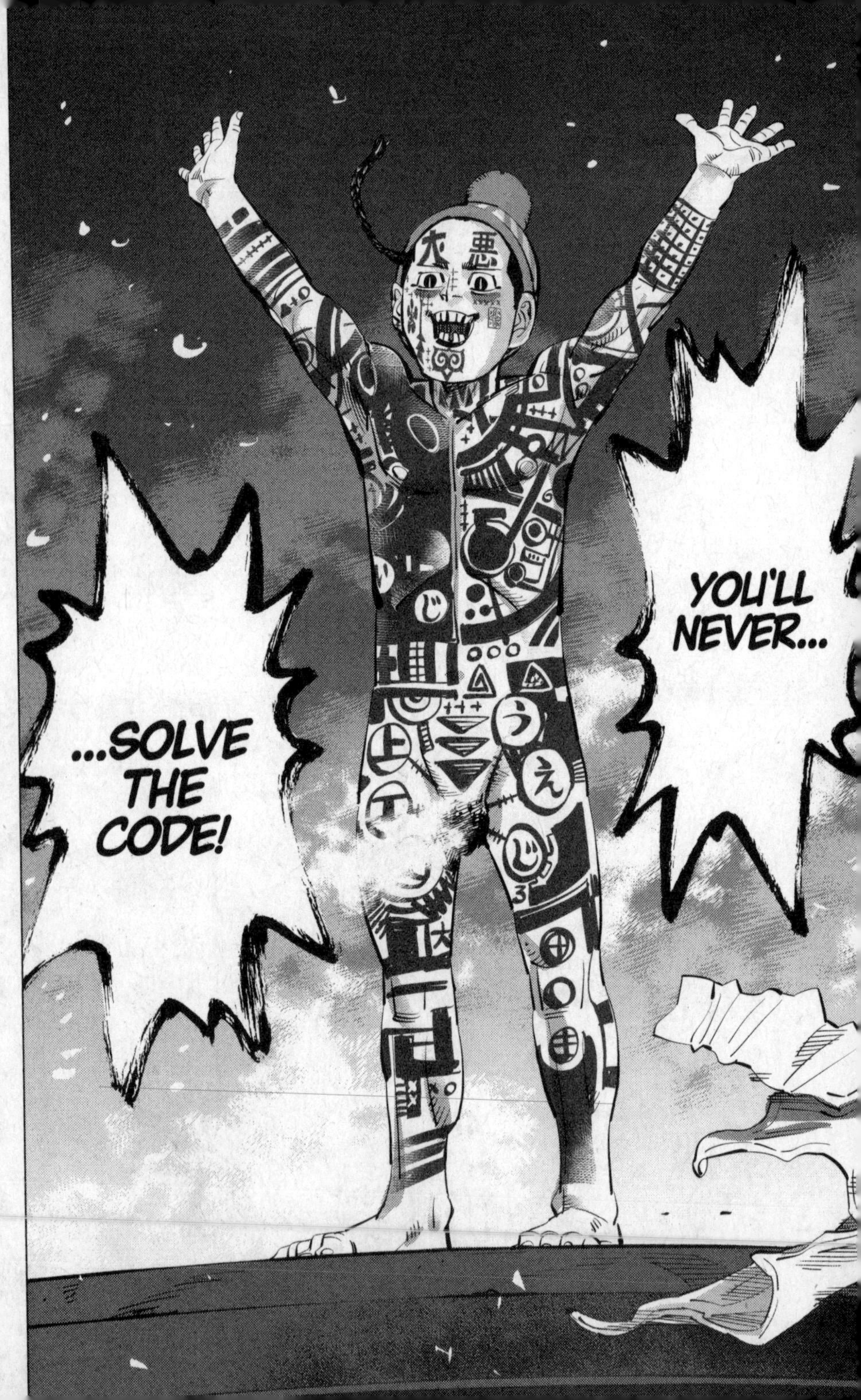
YOU'LL NEVER...
...SOLVE THE CODE!

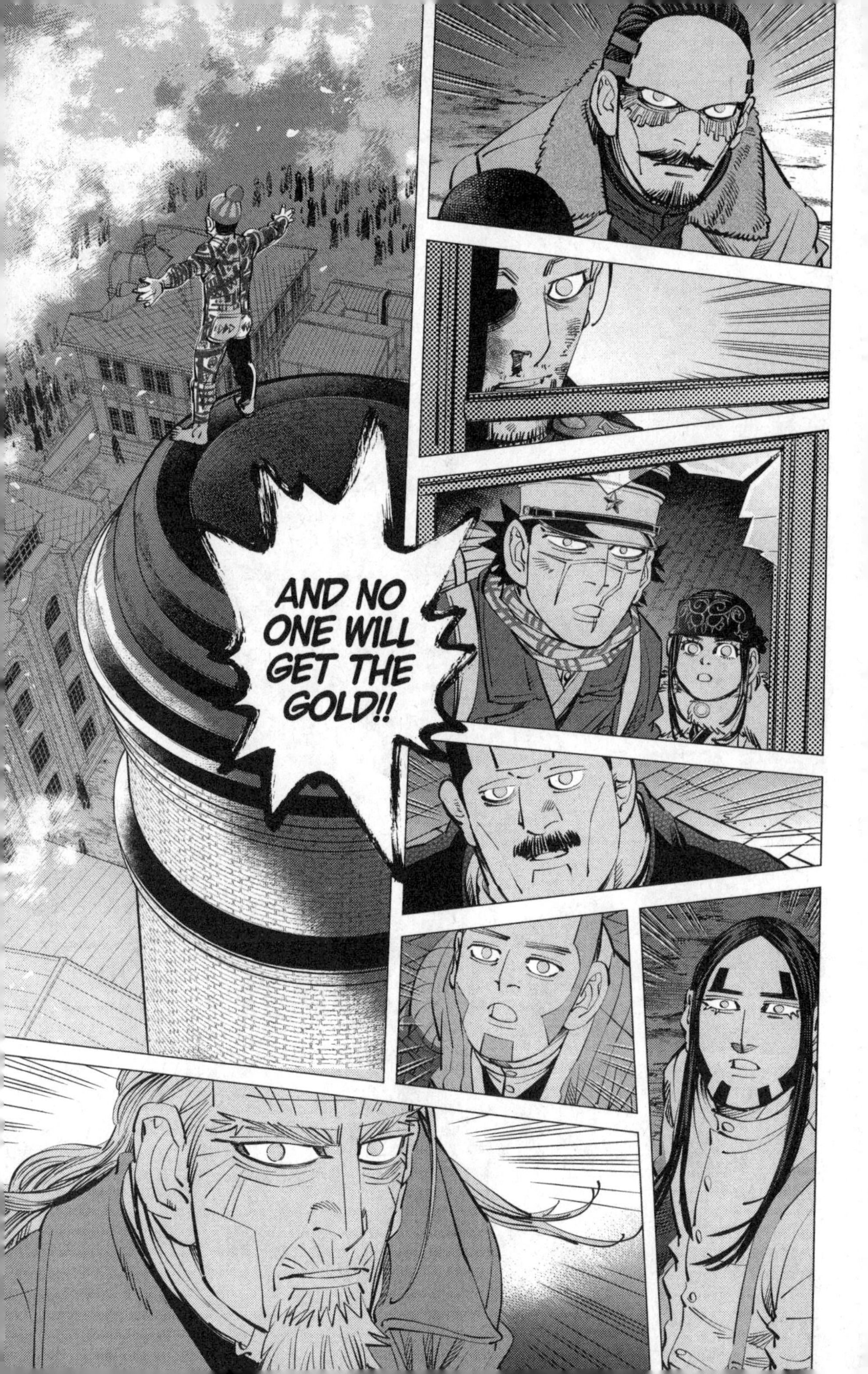
AND NO ONE WILL GET THE GOLD!!

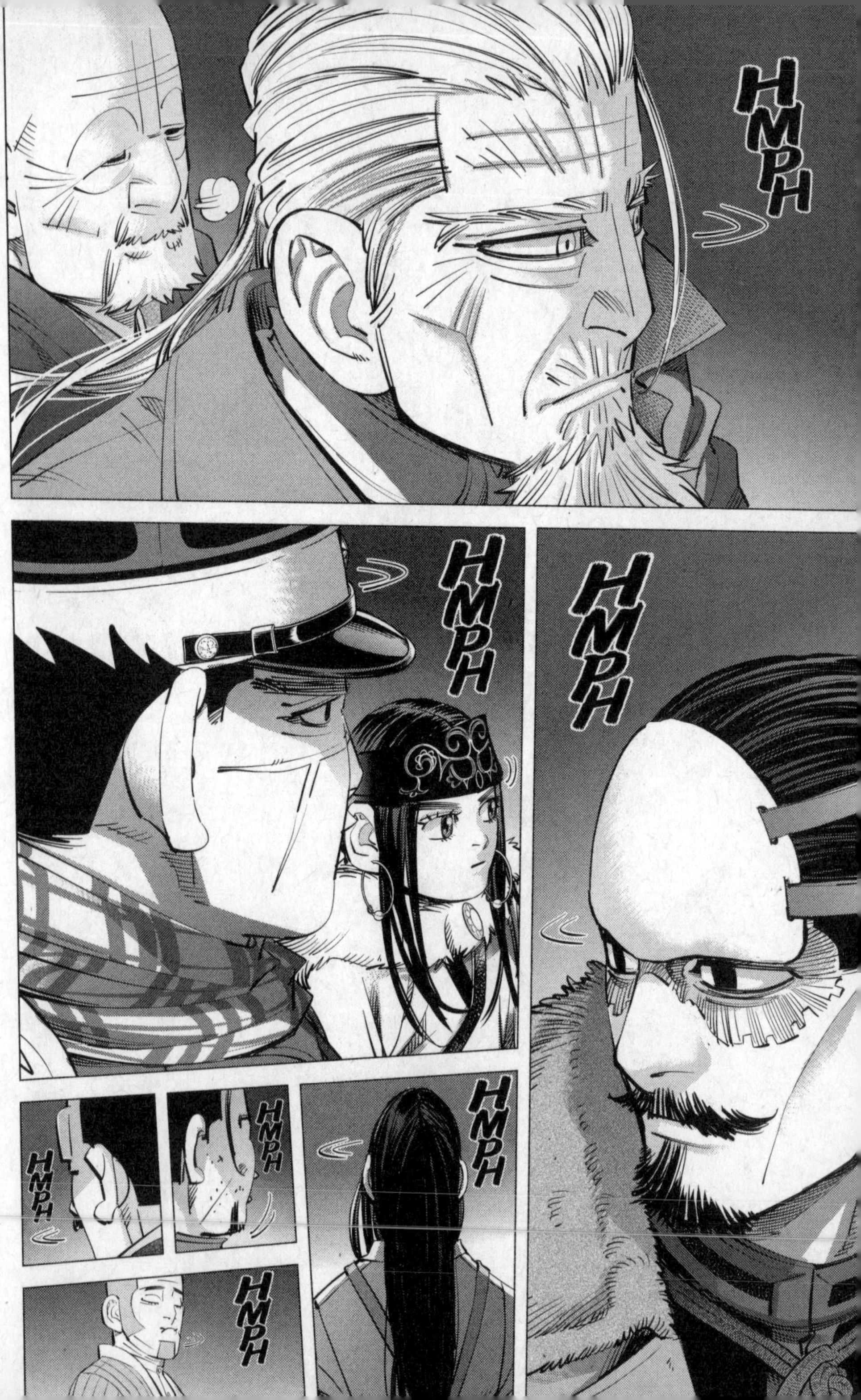
HMPH
HMPH
HMPH
HMPH
HMPH
HMPH
HMPH

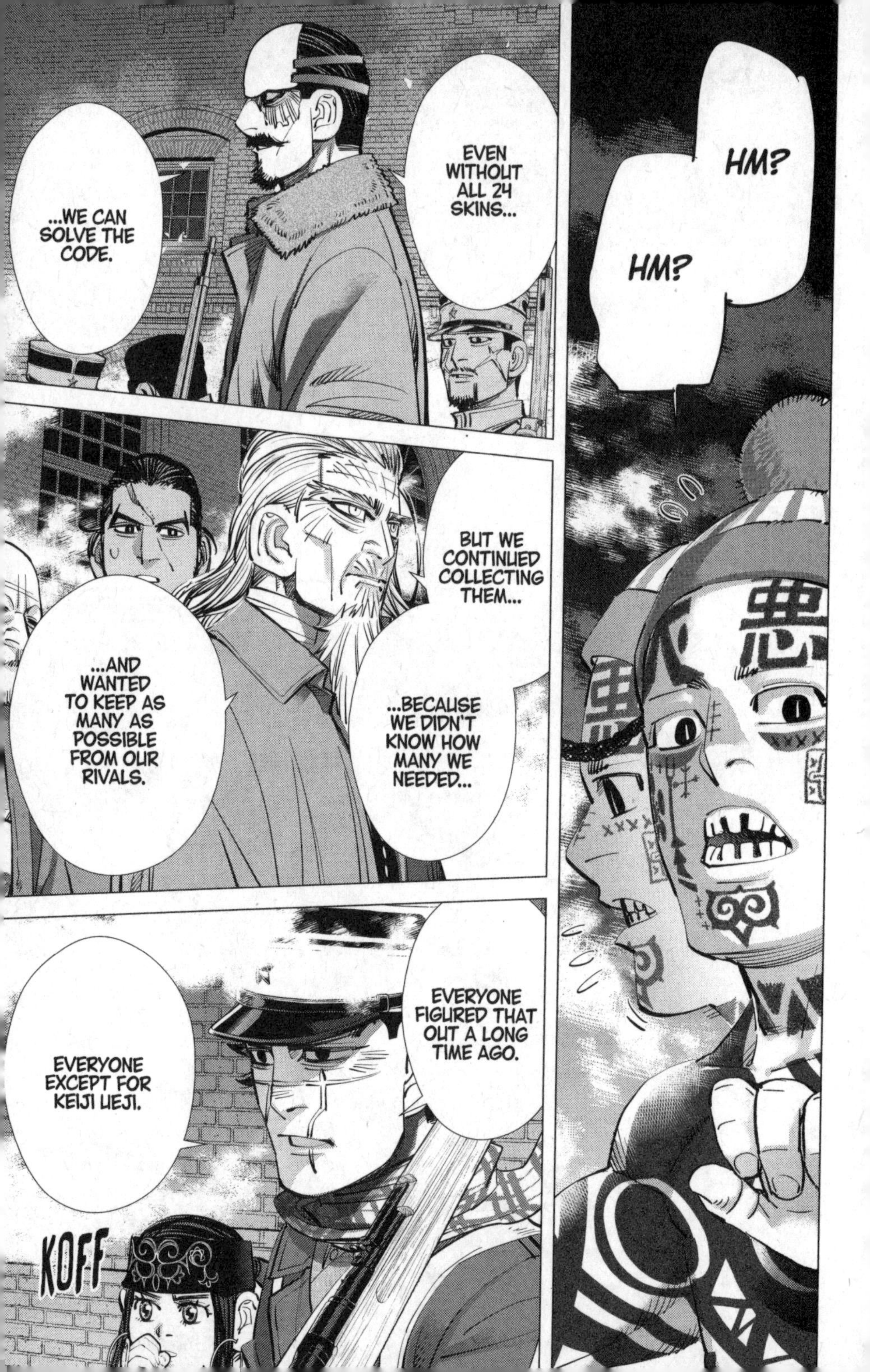
HM?
HM?
EVEN WITHOUT ALL 24 SKINS...
...WE CAN SOLVE THE CODE.
BUT WE CONTINUED COLLECTING THEM...
...BECAUSE WE DIDN'T KNOW HOW MANY WE NEEDED...
...AND WANTED TO KEEP AS MANY AS POSSIBLE FROM OUR RIVALS.
EVERYONE FIGURED THAT OUT A LONG TIME AGO.
EVERYONE EXCEPT FOR KEIJI UEJI.
KOFF

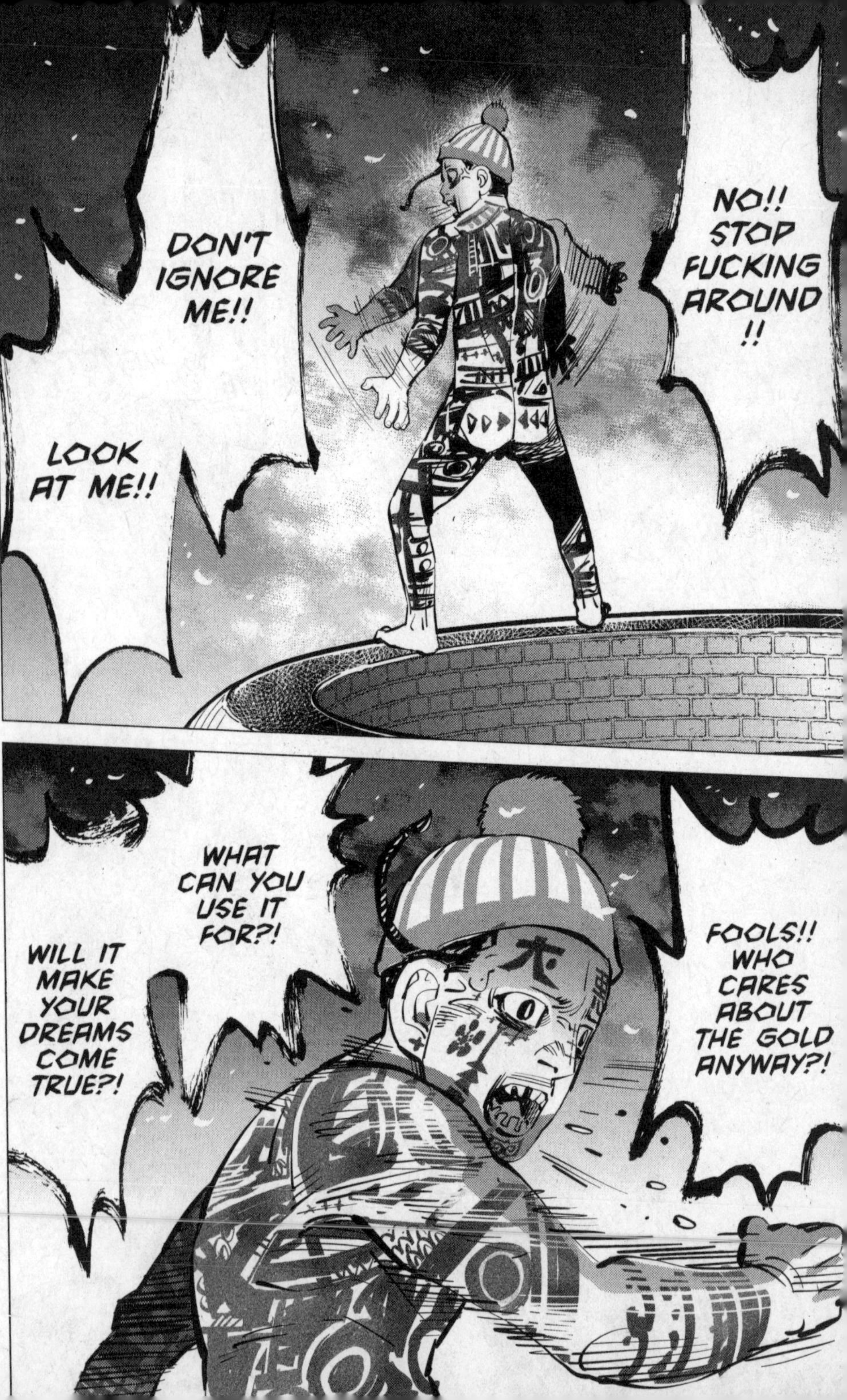
NO!! STOP FUCKING AROUND!!
DON'T IGNORE ME!!
LOOK AT ME!!
FOOLS!! WHO CARES ABOUT THE GOLD ANYWAY?!
WHAT CAN YOU USE IT FOR?!
WILL IT MAKE YOUR DREAMS COME TRUE?!

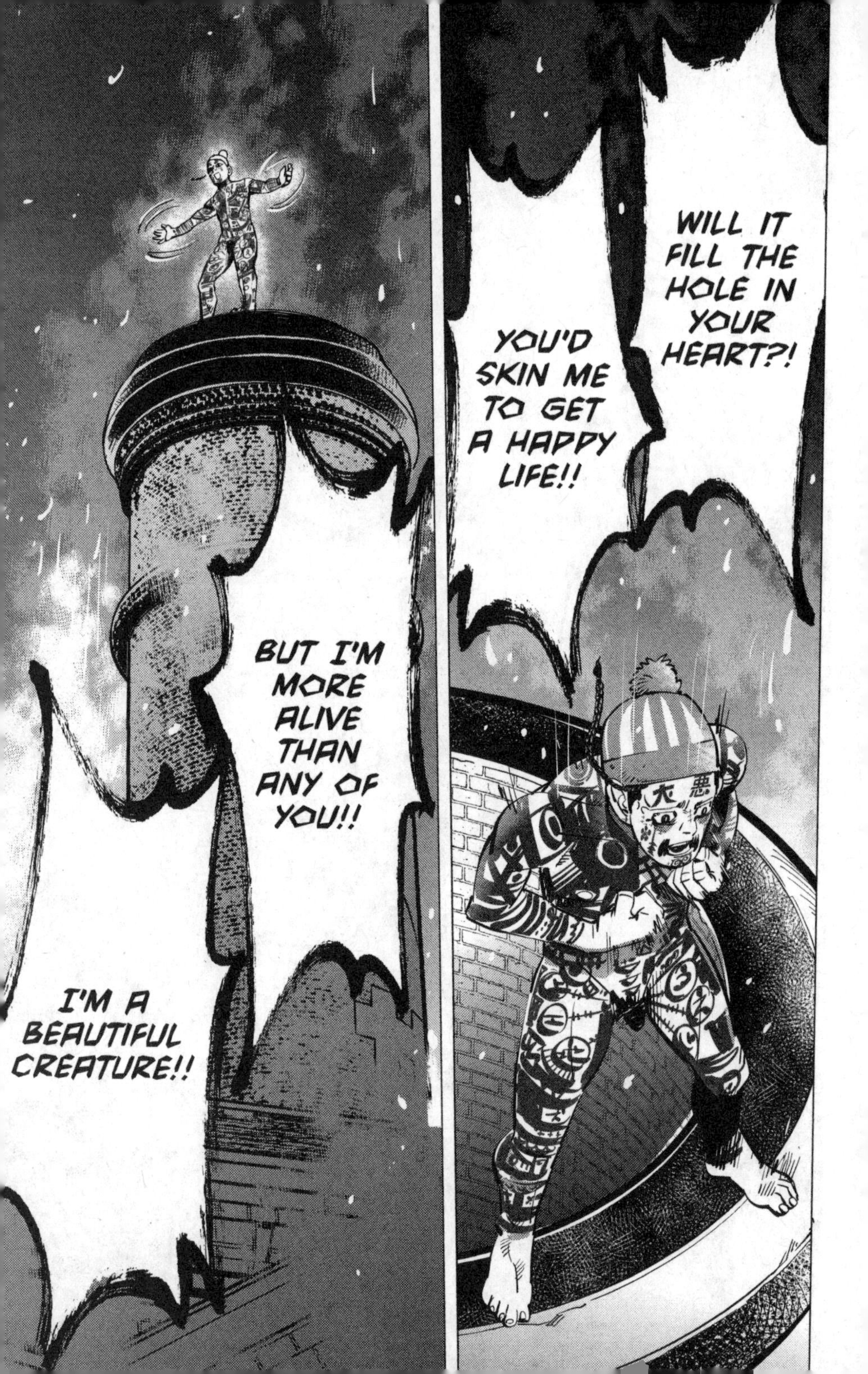
WILL IT FILL THE HOLE IN YOUR HEART?!
YOU'D SKIN ME TO GET A HAPPY LIFE!!
BUT I'M MORE ALIVE THAN ANY OF YOU!!
I'M A BEAUTIFUL CREATURE!!

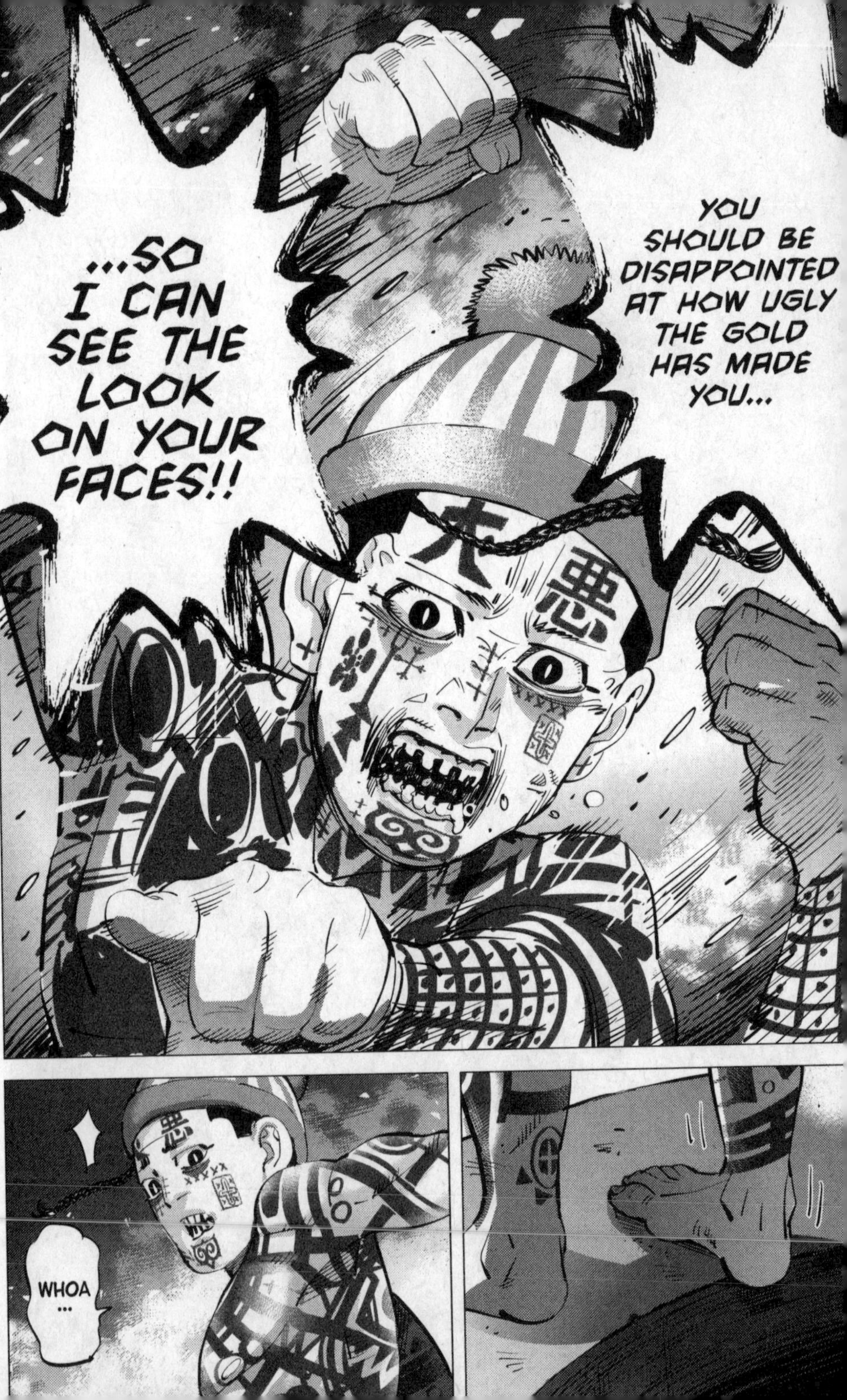
YOU SHOULD BE DISAPPOINTED AT HOW UGLY THE GOLD HAS MADE YOU...
...SO I CAN SEE THE LOOK ON YOUR FACES!!
WHOA ...

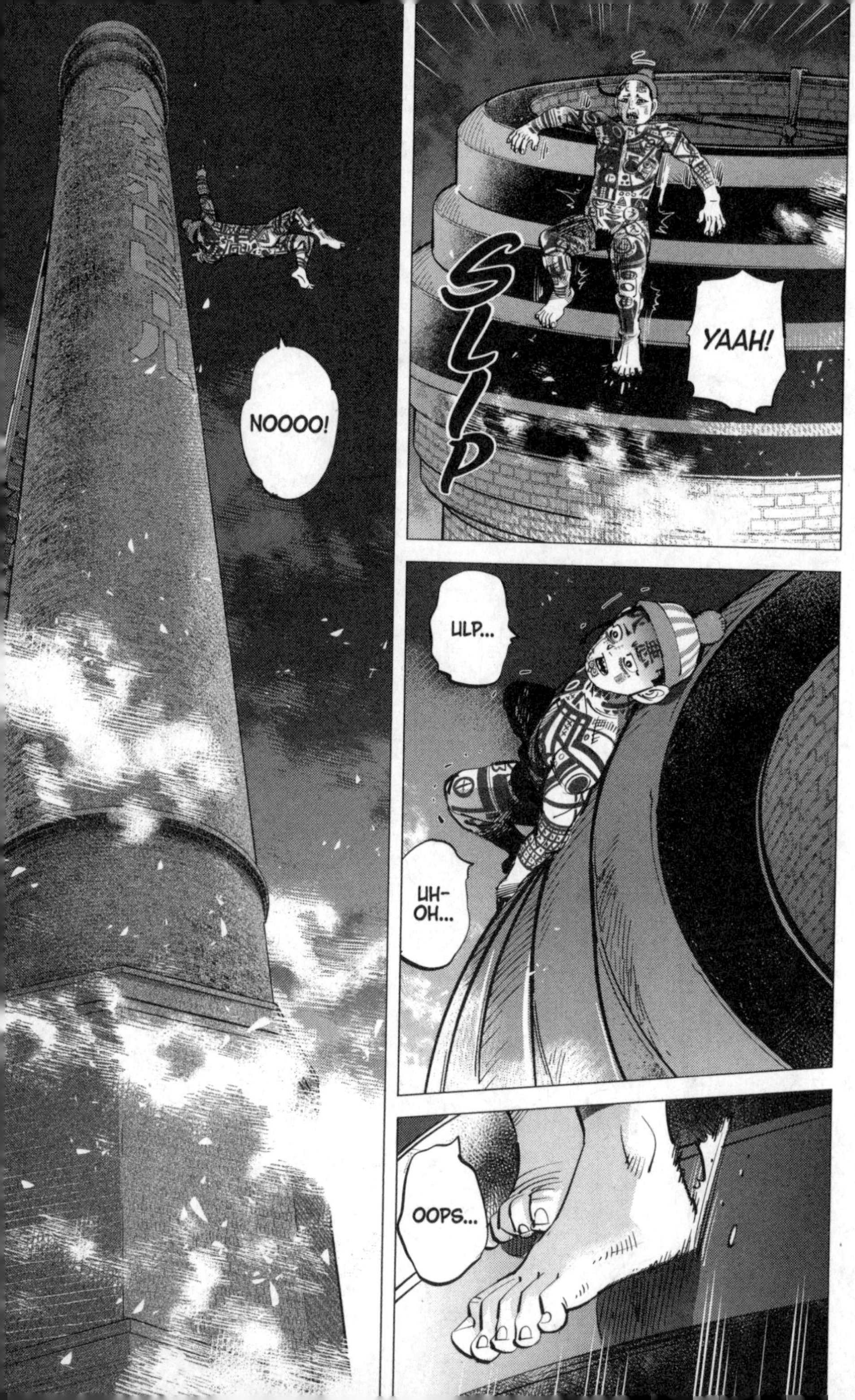
SLIP
YAAH!
ULP...
UH-OH...
OOPS...
NOOOO!

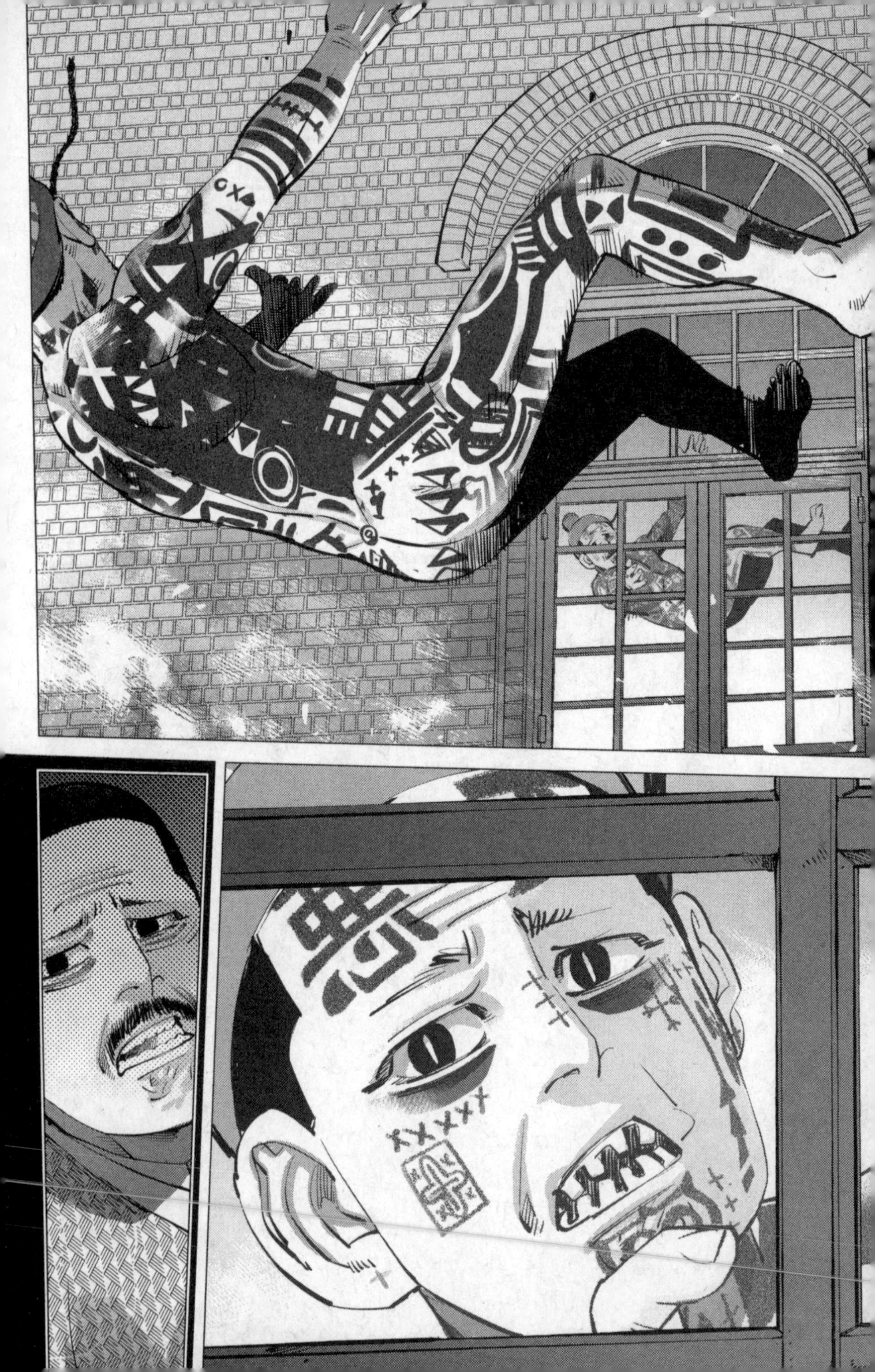

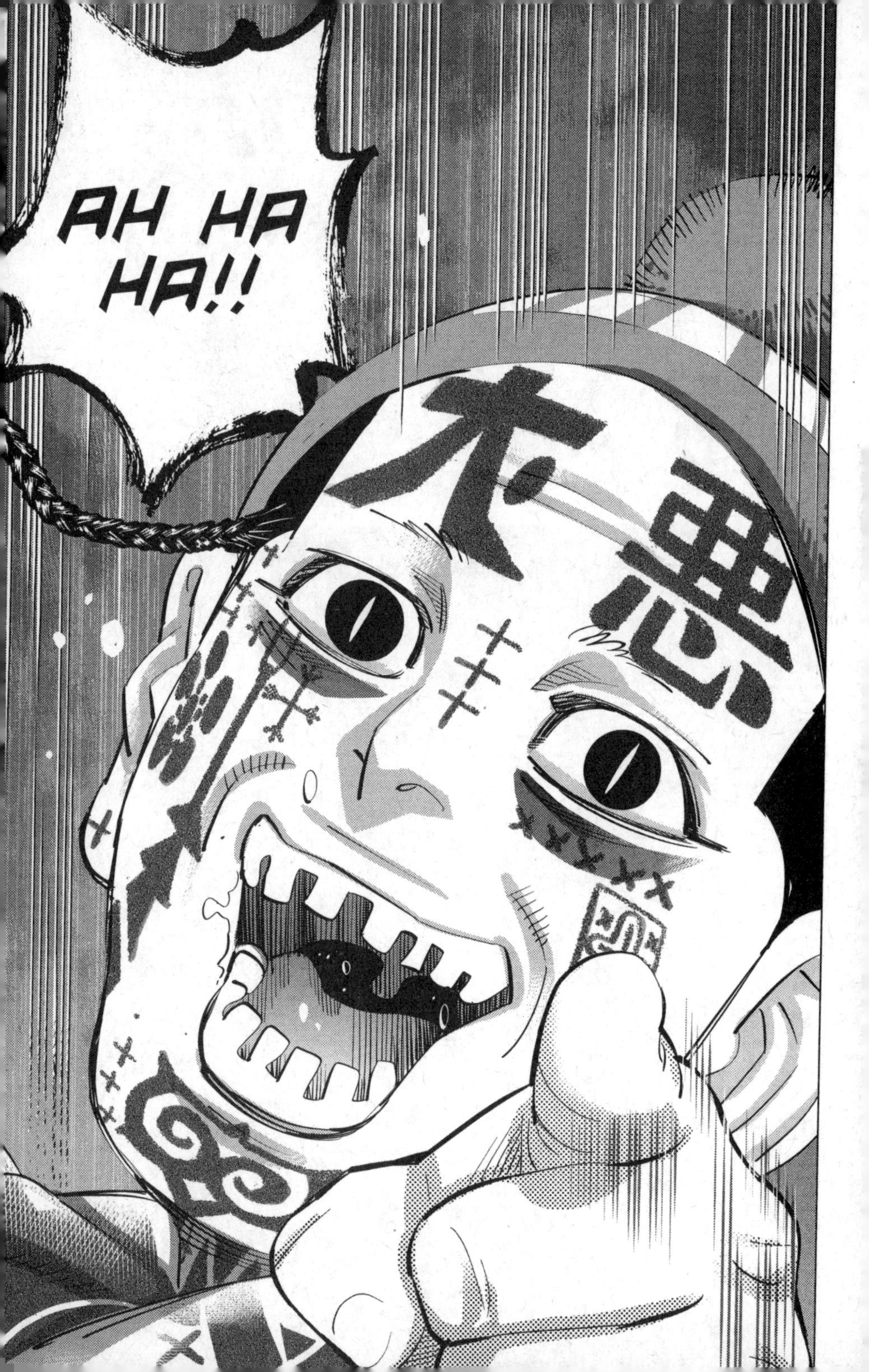
AH HA HA!!
大悪

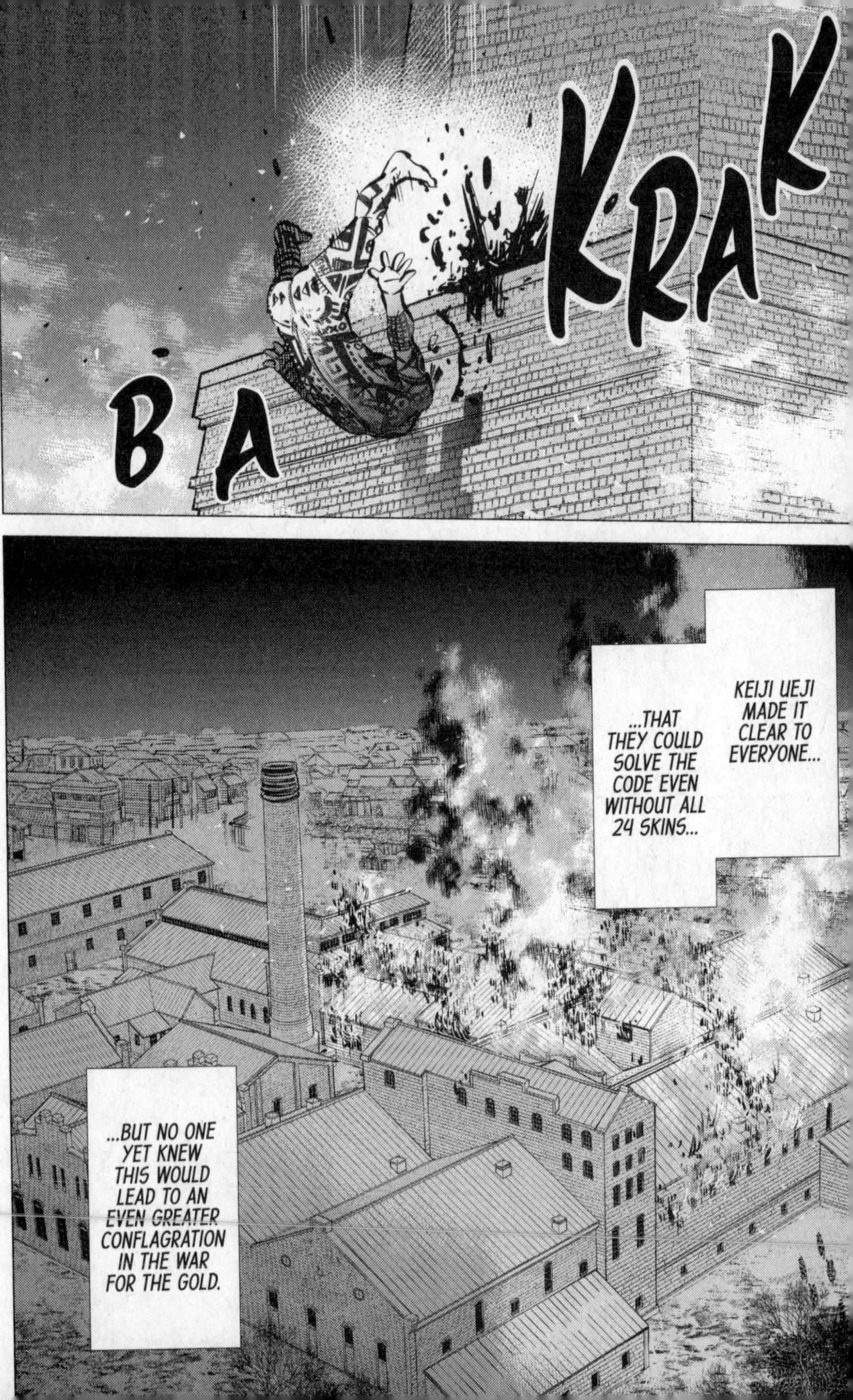
BA
KRAK
KEIJI UEJI MADE IT CLEAR TO EVERYONE...
...THAT THEY COULD SOLVE THE CODE EVEN WITHOUT ALL 24 SKINS...
...BUT NO ONE YET KNEW THIS WOULD LEAD TO AN EVEN GREATER CONFLAGRATION IN THE WAR FOR THE GOLD.

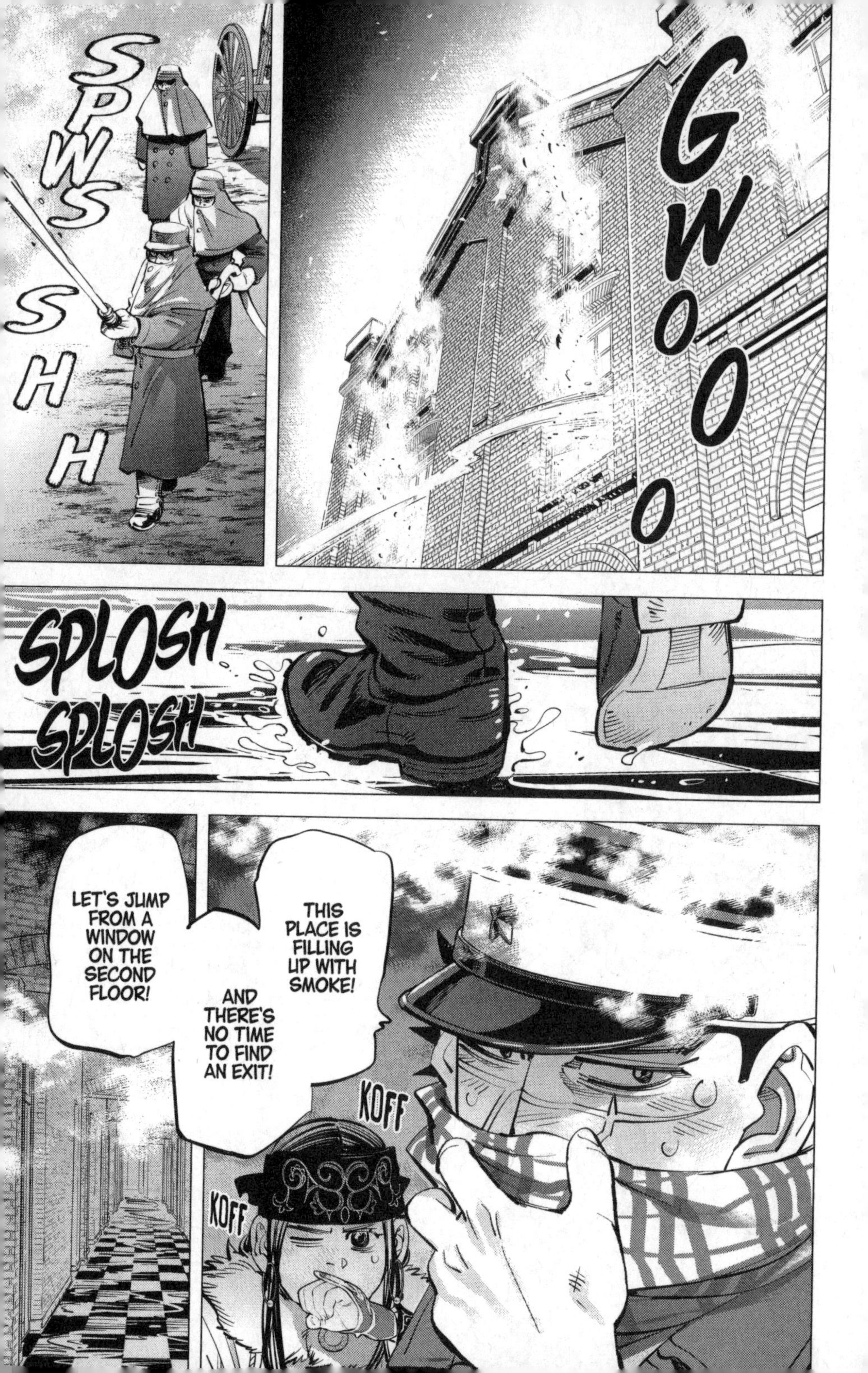
GWOOO
SPWSSHH
SPLOSH
SPLOSH
THIS PLACE IS FILLING UP WITH SMOKE!
AND THERE'S NO TIME TO FIND AN EXIT!
LET'S JUMP FROM A WINDOW ON THE SECOND FLOOR!
KOFF
KOFF

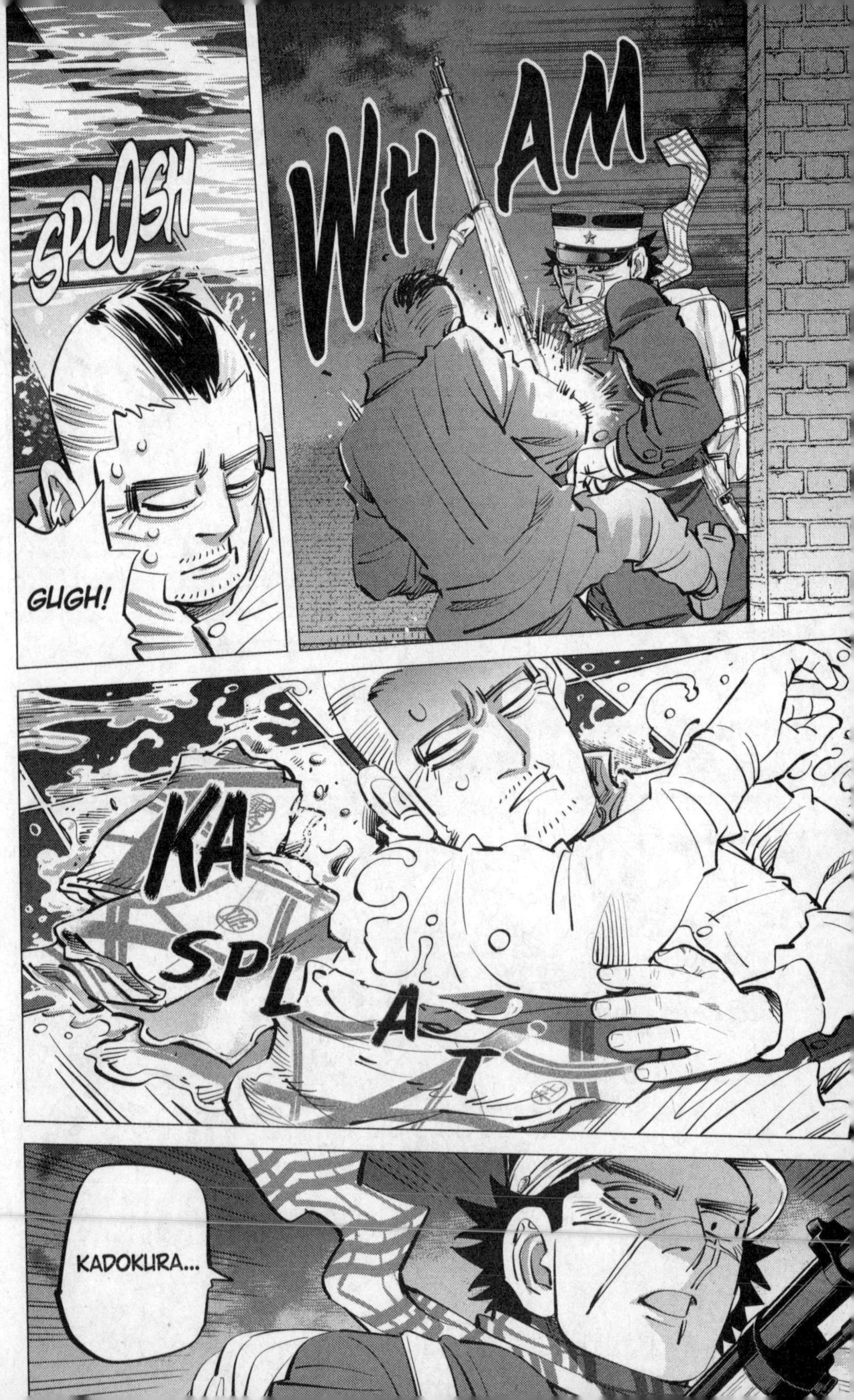
WHAM
SPLOSH
GUGH!
KA
SPLAT
KADOKURA...

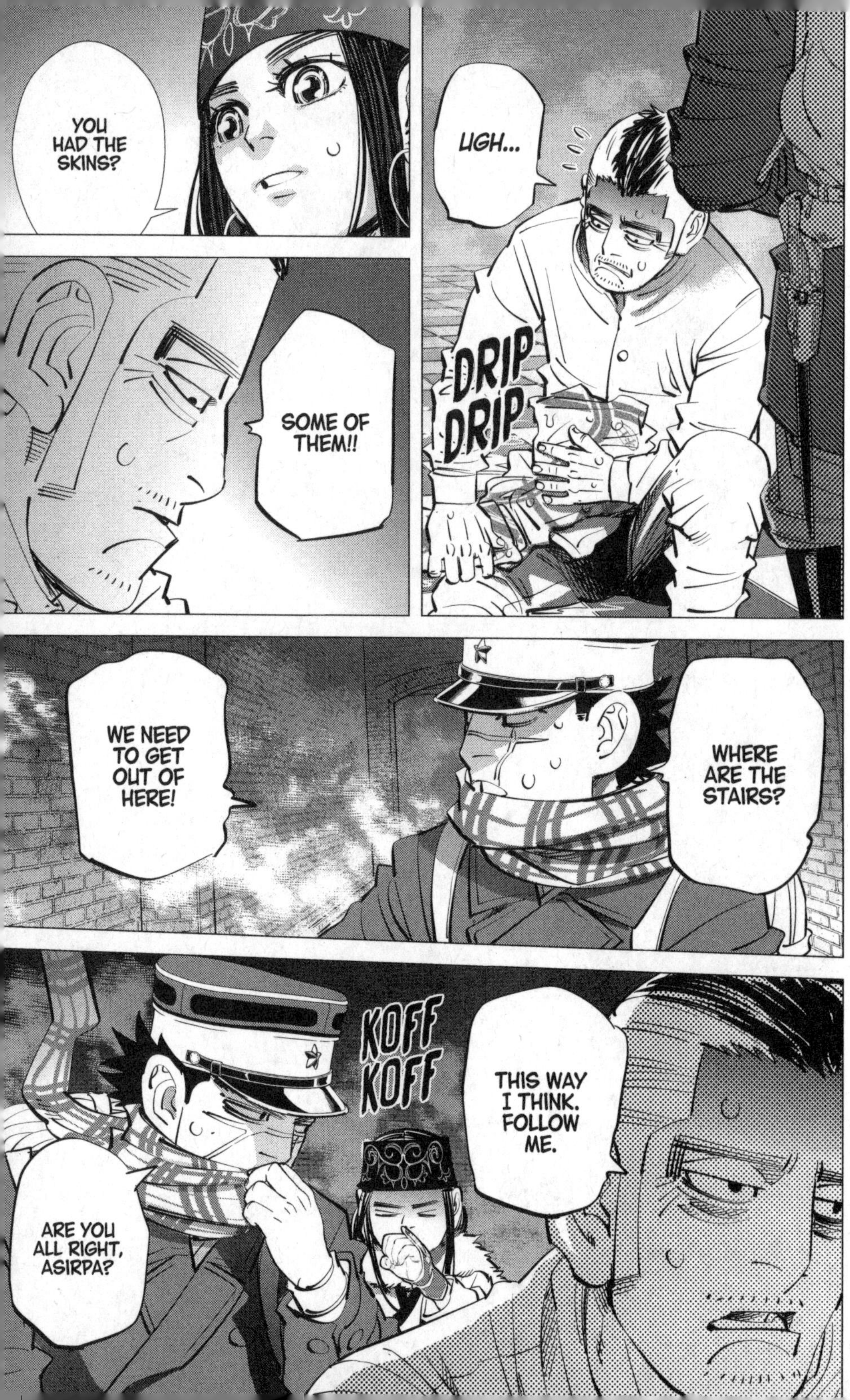
UGH...
DRIP DRIP
YOU HAD THE SKINS?
SOME OF THEM!!
WHERE ARE THE STAIRS?
WE NEED TO GET OUT OF HERE!
THIS WAY I THINK. FOLLOW ME.
KOFF KOFF
ARE YOU ALL RIGHT, ASIRPA?

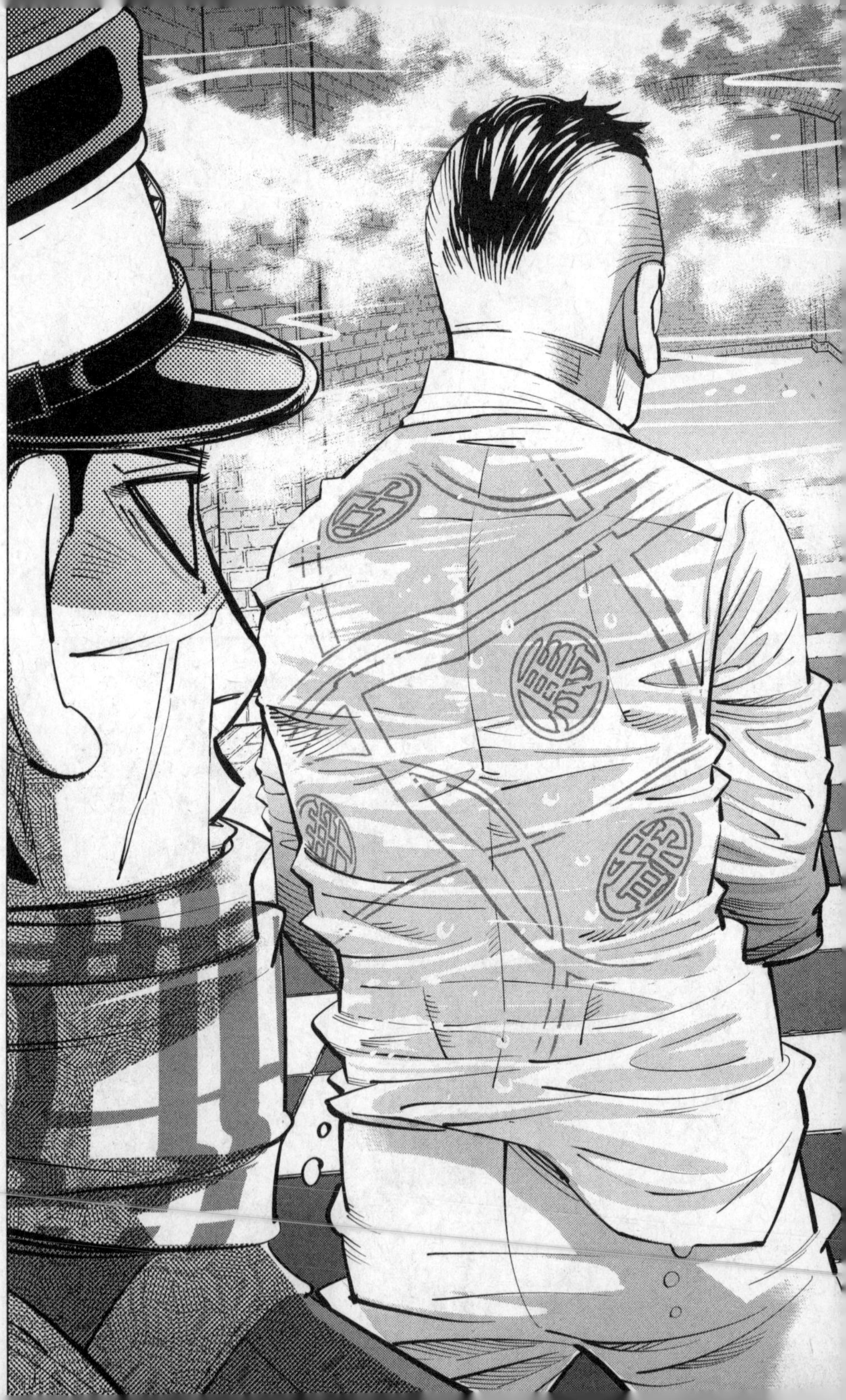

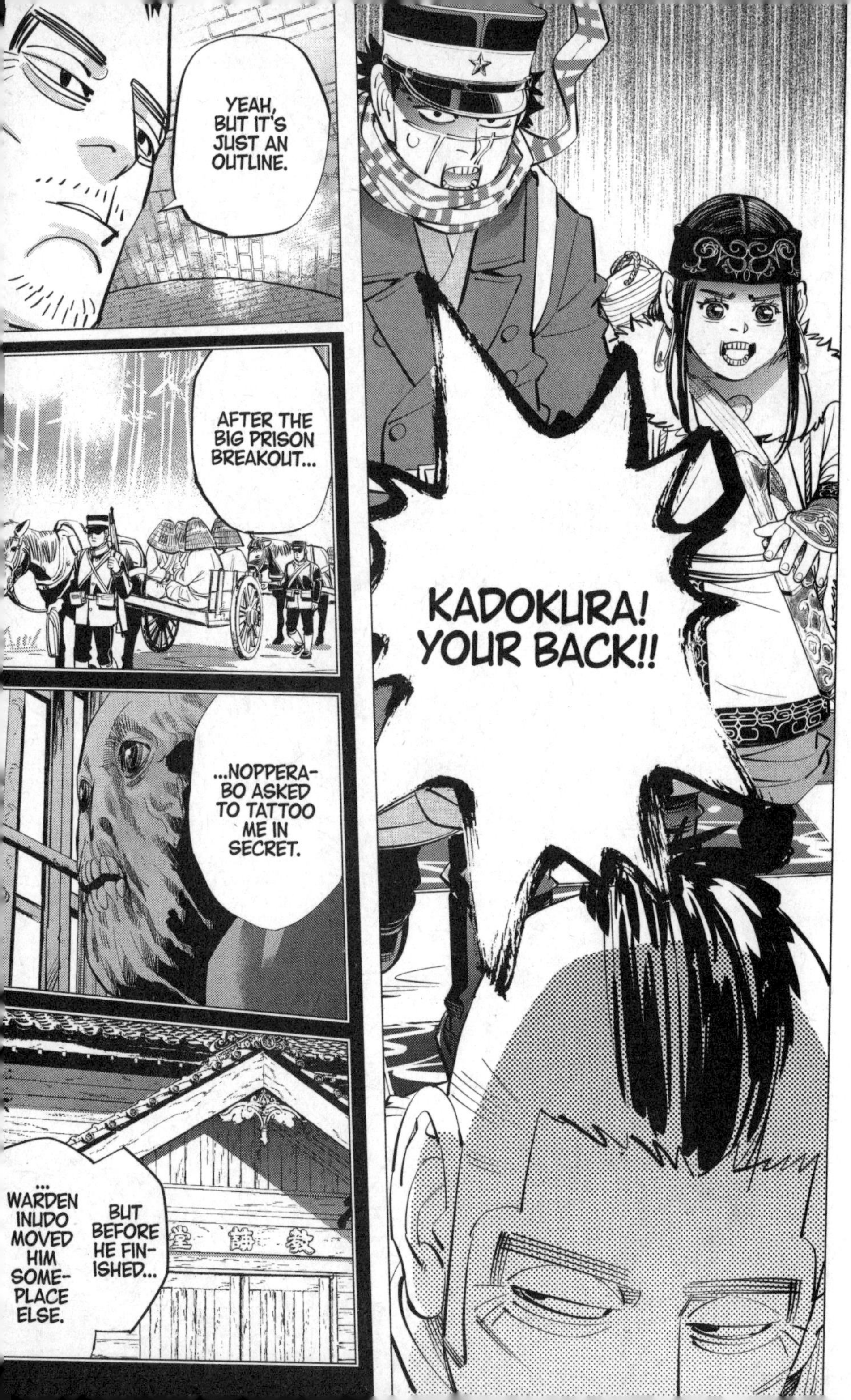
KADOKURA! YOUR BACK!!
YEAH, BUT IT'S JUST AN OUTLINE.
AFTER THE BIG PRISON BREAKOUT...
...NOPPERA-BO ASKED TO TATTOO ME IN SECRET.
BUT BEFORE HE FIN-ISHED...
...WARDEN INUDO MOVED HIM SOME-PLACE ELSE.

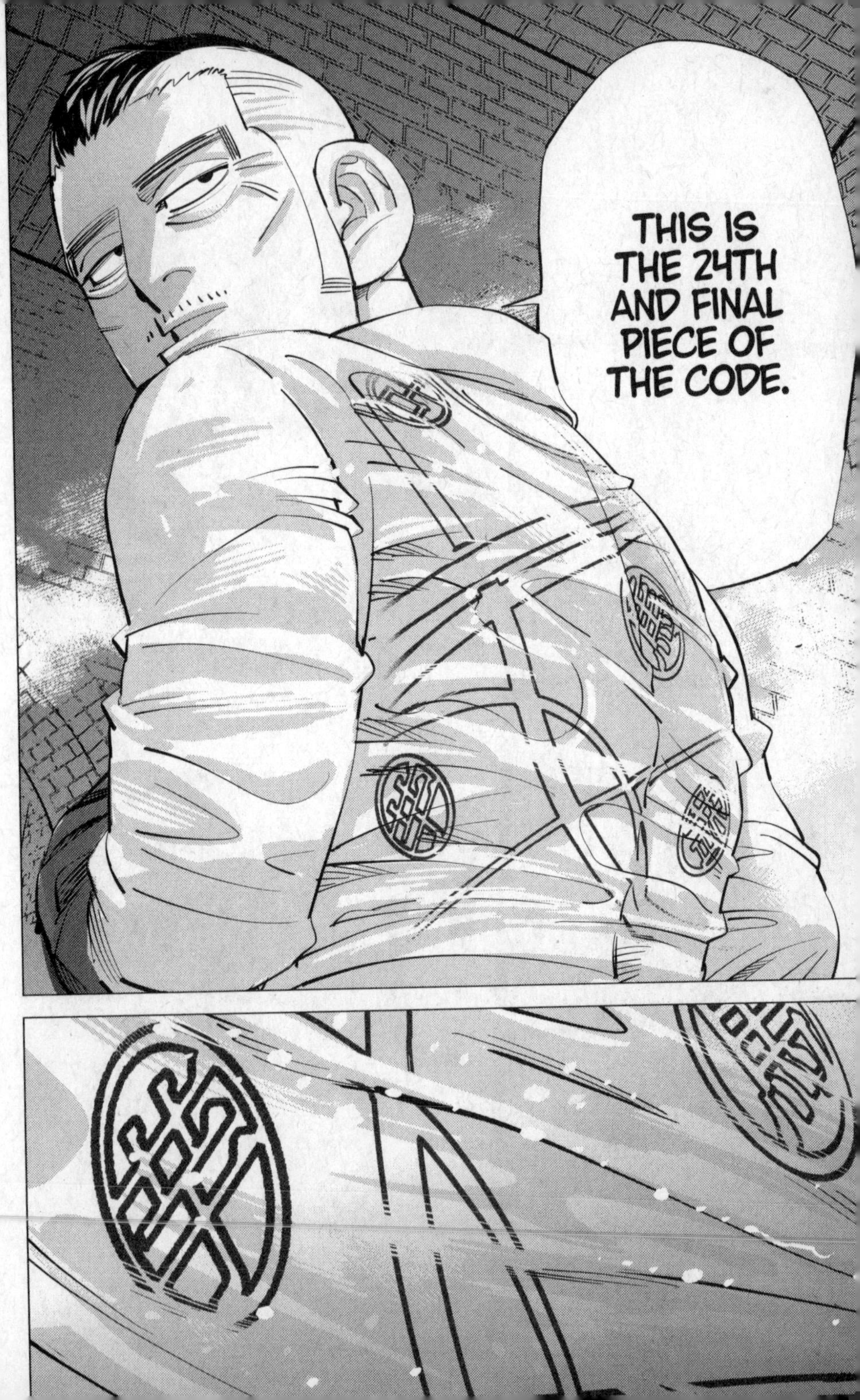
THIS IS THE 24TH AND FINAL PIECE OF THE CODE.

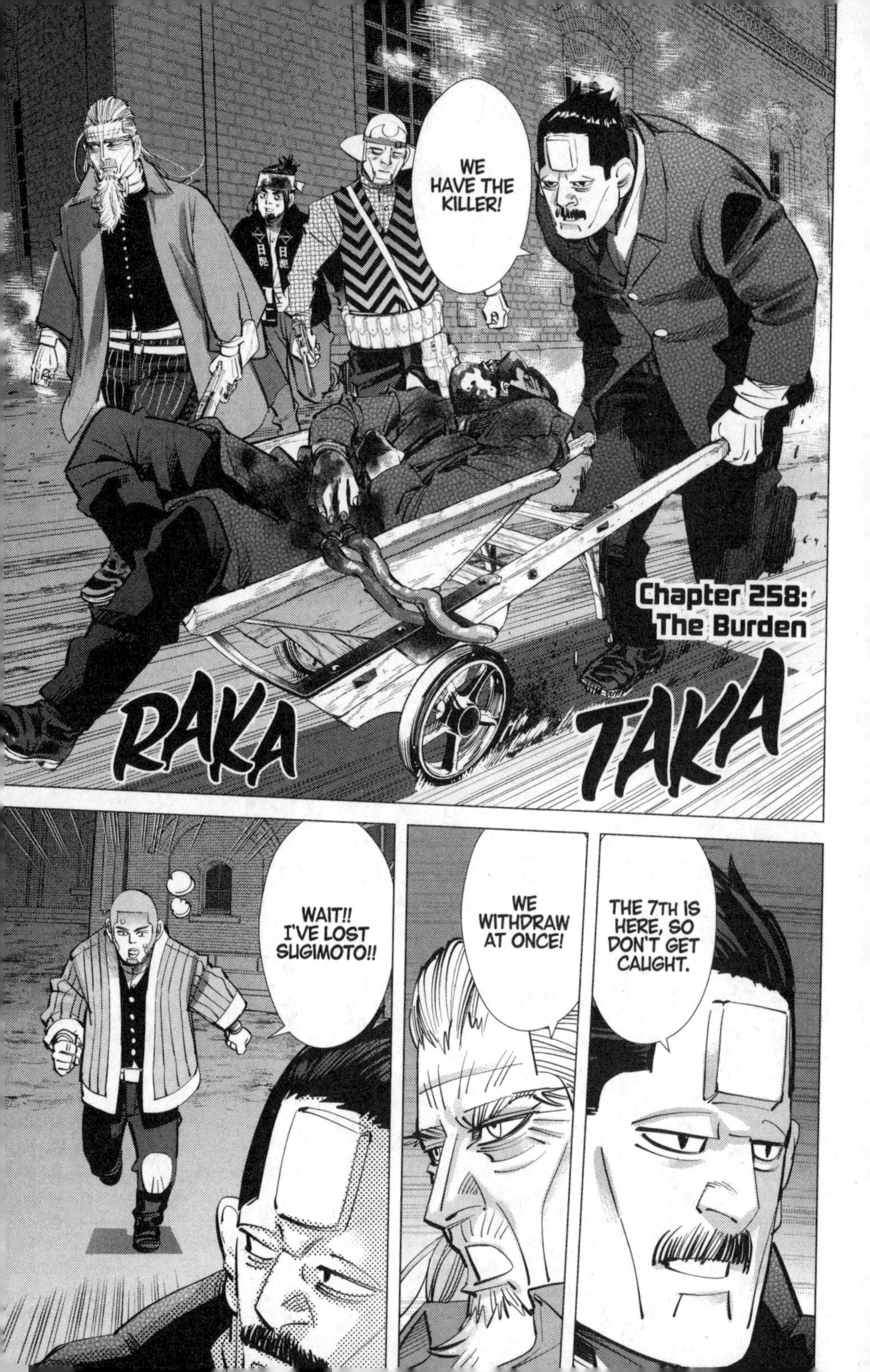
WE HAVE THE KILLER!
Chapter 258: The Burden
RAKA TAKA
THE 7TH IS HERE, SO DON'T GET CAUGHT.
WE WITHDRAW AT ONCE!
WAIT!! I'VE LOST SUGIMOTO!!

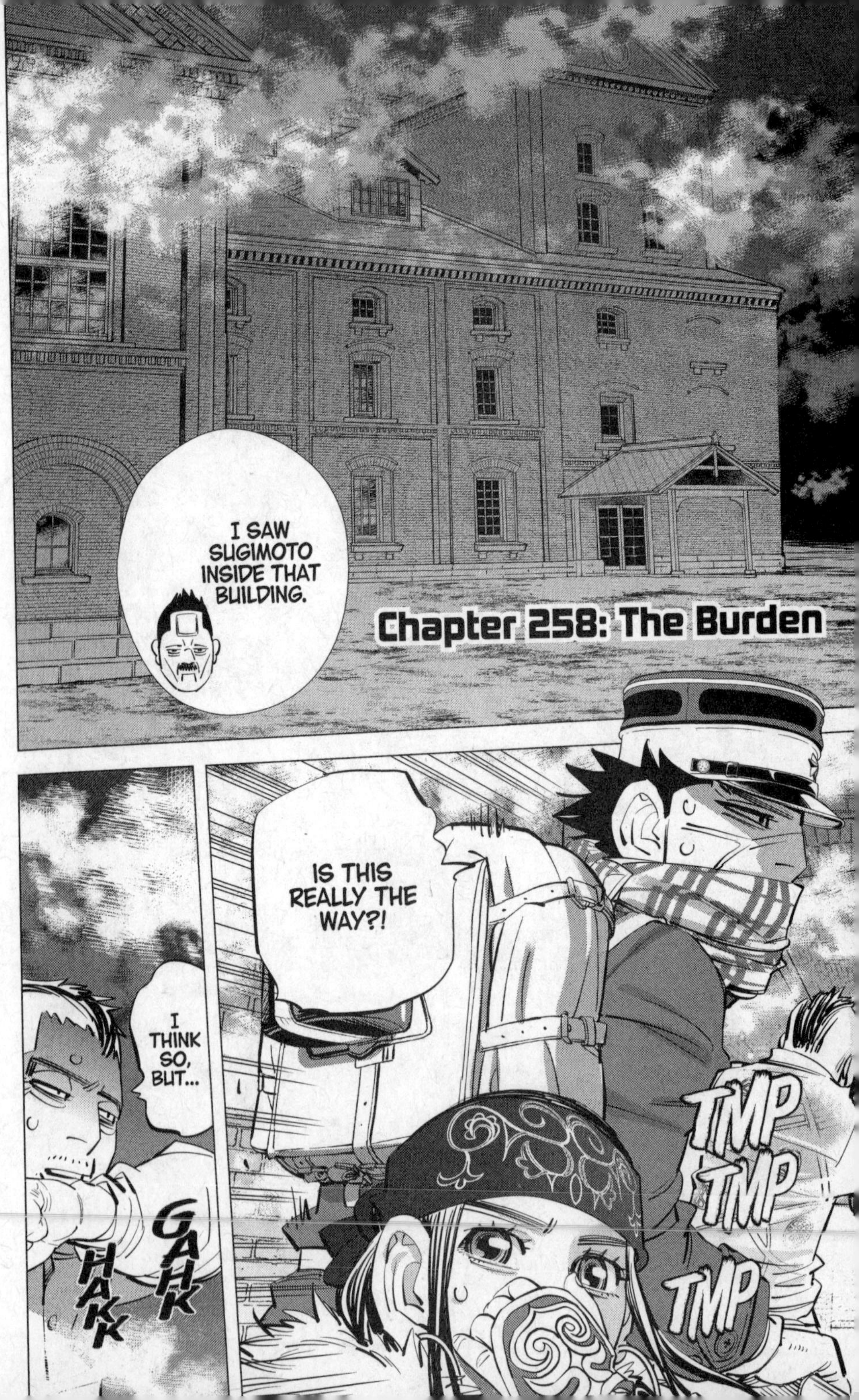
I SAW SUGIMOTO INSIDE THAT BUILDING.
Chapter 258: The Burden
IS THIS REALLY THE WAY?!
TMP
TMP
TMP
I THINK SO, BUT...
GAHK
HAKK

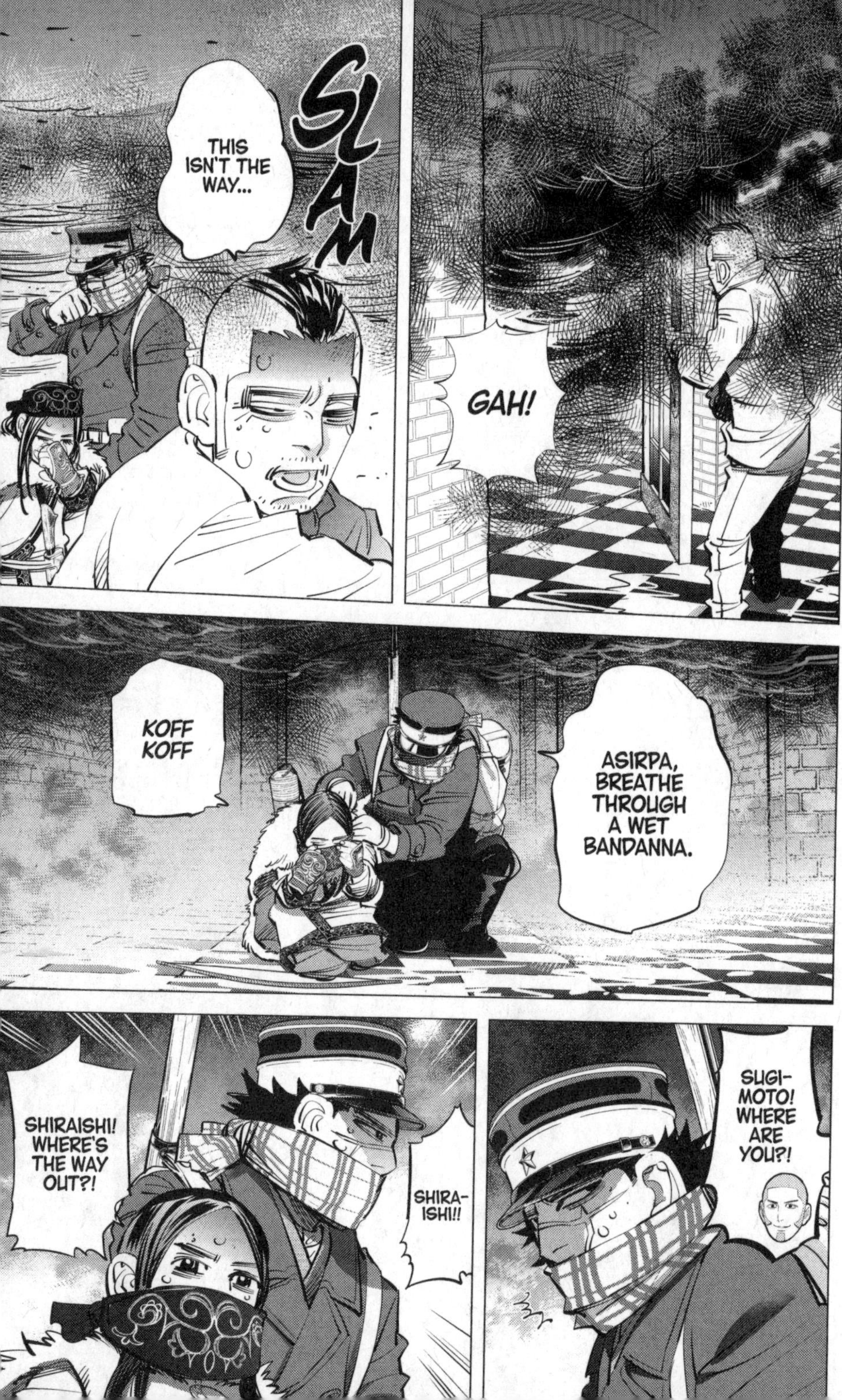
GAH!
SLAM
THIS ISN'T THE WAY...
ASIRPA, BREATHE THROUGH A WET BANDANNA.
KOFF KOFF
SUGI-MOTO! WHERE ARE YOU?!
SHIRA-ISHI!!
SHIRAISHI! WHERE'S THE WAY OUT?!

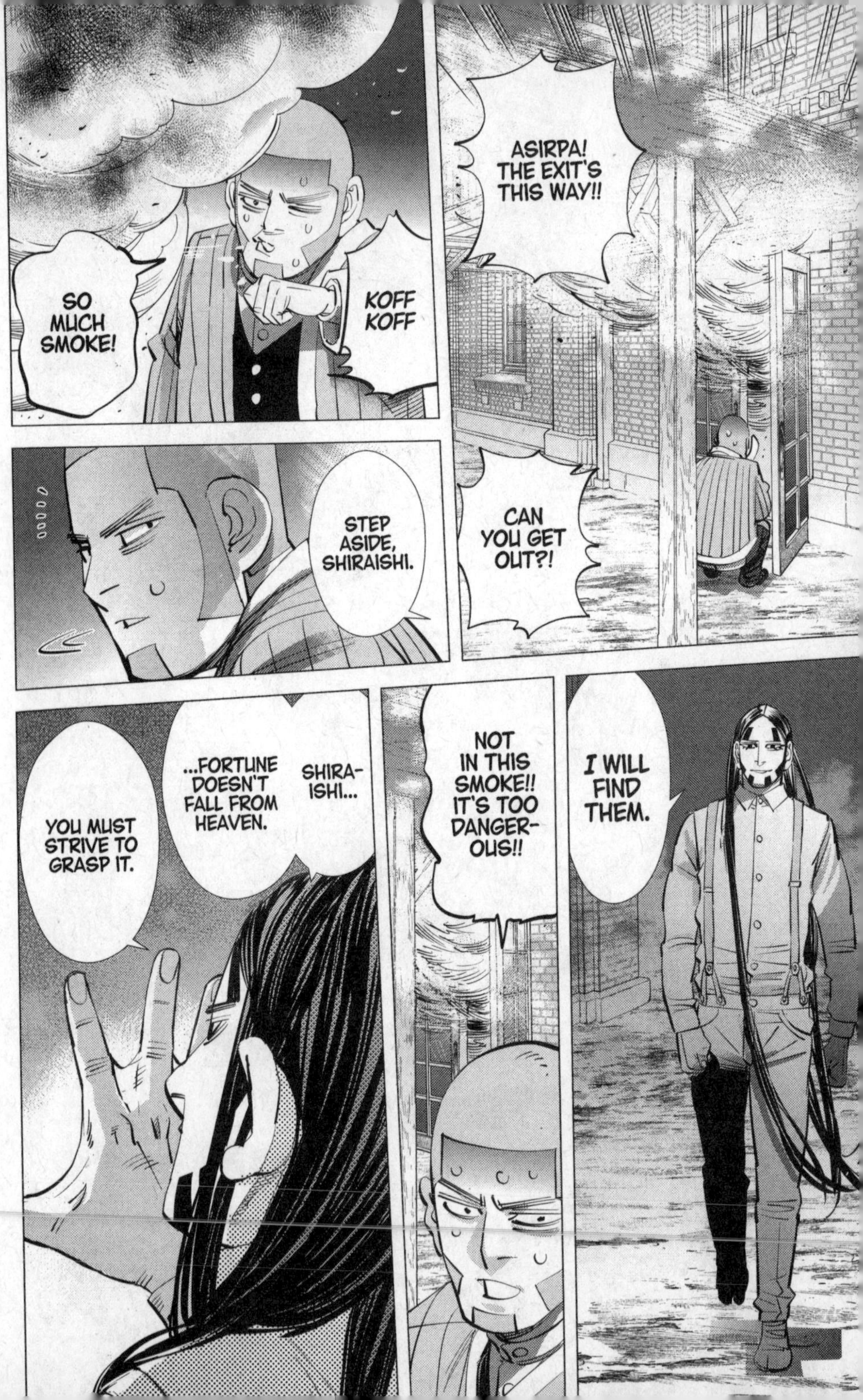
ASIRPA! THE EXIT'S THIS WAY!!
CAN YOU GET OUT?!
KOFF KOFF
SO MUCH SMOKE!
STEP ASIDE, SHIRAISHI.
I WILL FIND THEM.
NOT IN THIS SMOKE!! IT'S TOO DANGER-OUS!!
SHIRA-ISHI...
...FORTUNE DOESN'T FALL FROM HEAVEN.
YOU MUST STRIVE TO GRASP IT.

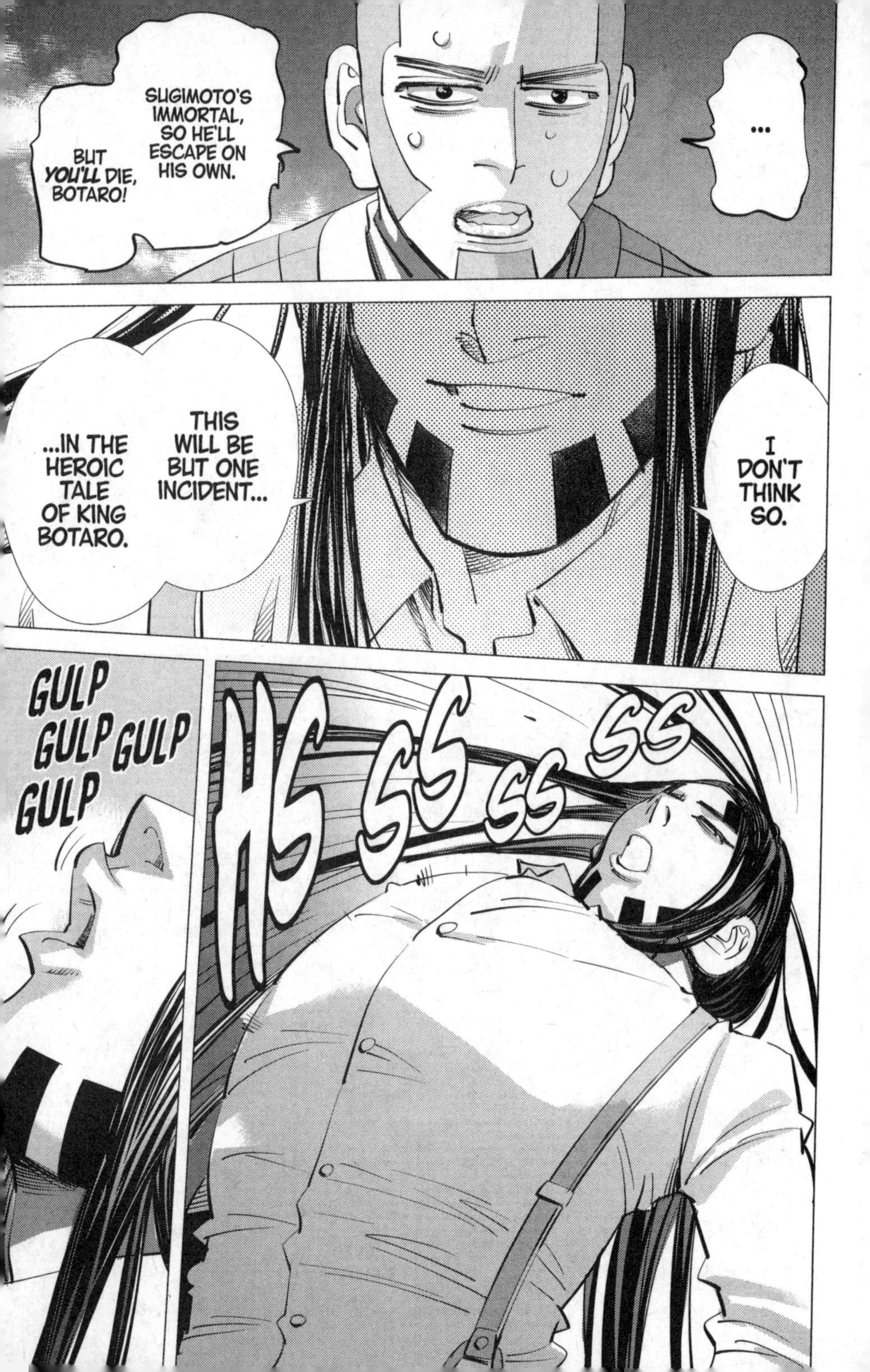
...
SUGIMOTO'S IMMORTAL, SO HE'LL ESCAPE ON HIS OWN.
BUT *YOU'LL* DIE, BOTARO!
I DON'T THINK SO.
THIS WILL BE BUT ONE INCIDENT...
...IN THE HEROIC TALE OF KING BOTARO.
HSSSSSSSS
GULP GULP GULP GULP

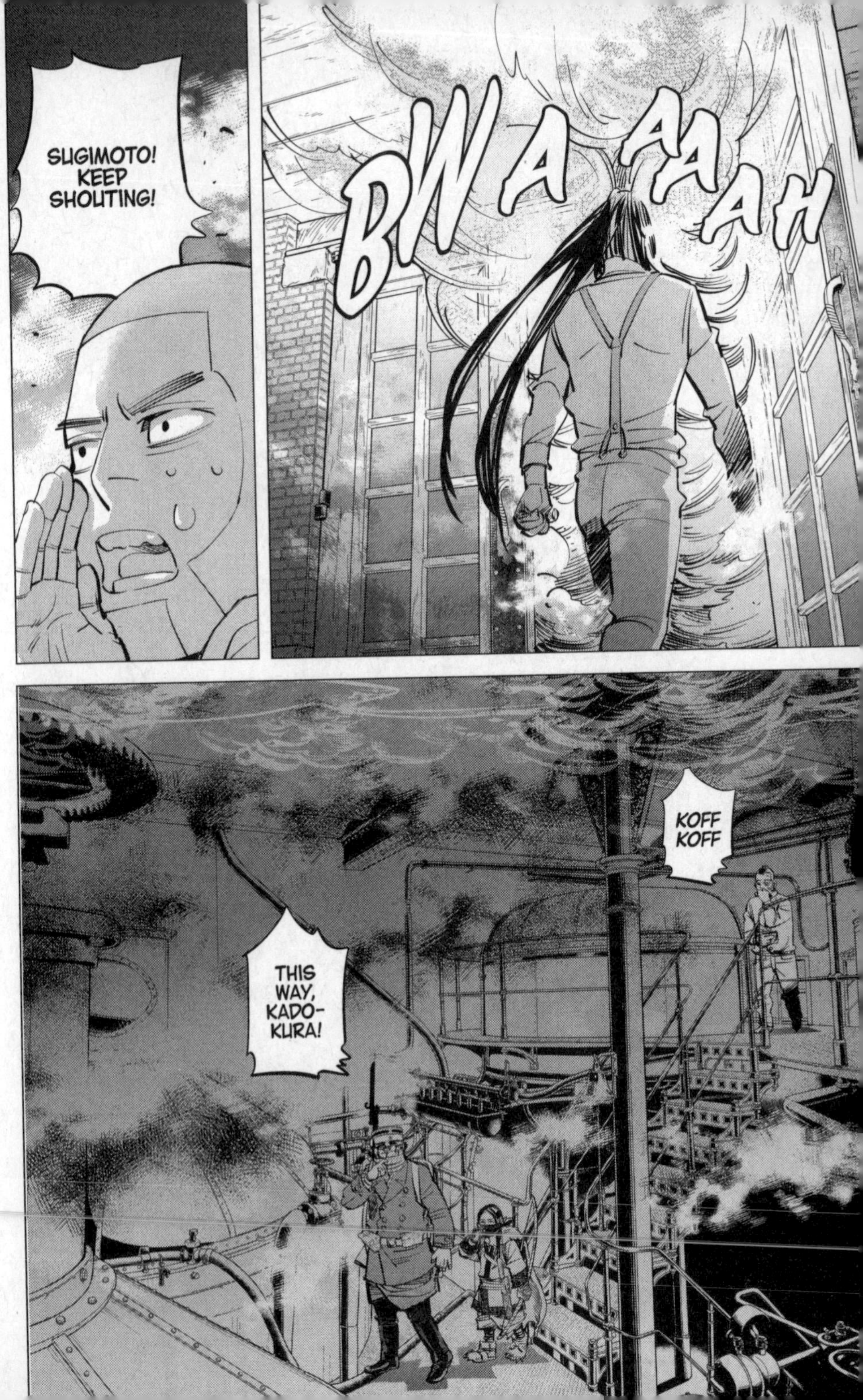
BWAAAAAH
SUGIMOTO! KEEP SHOUTING!
KOFF KOFF
THIS WAY, KADO-KURA!

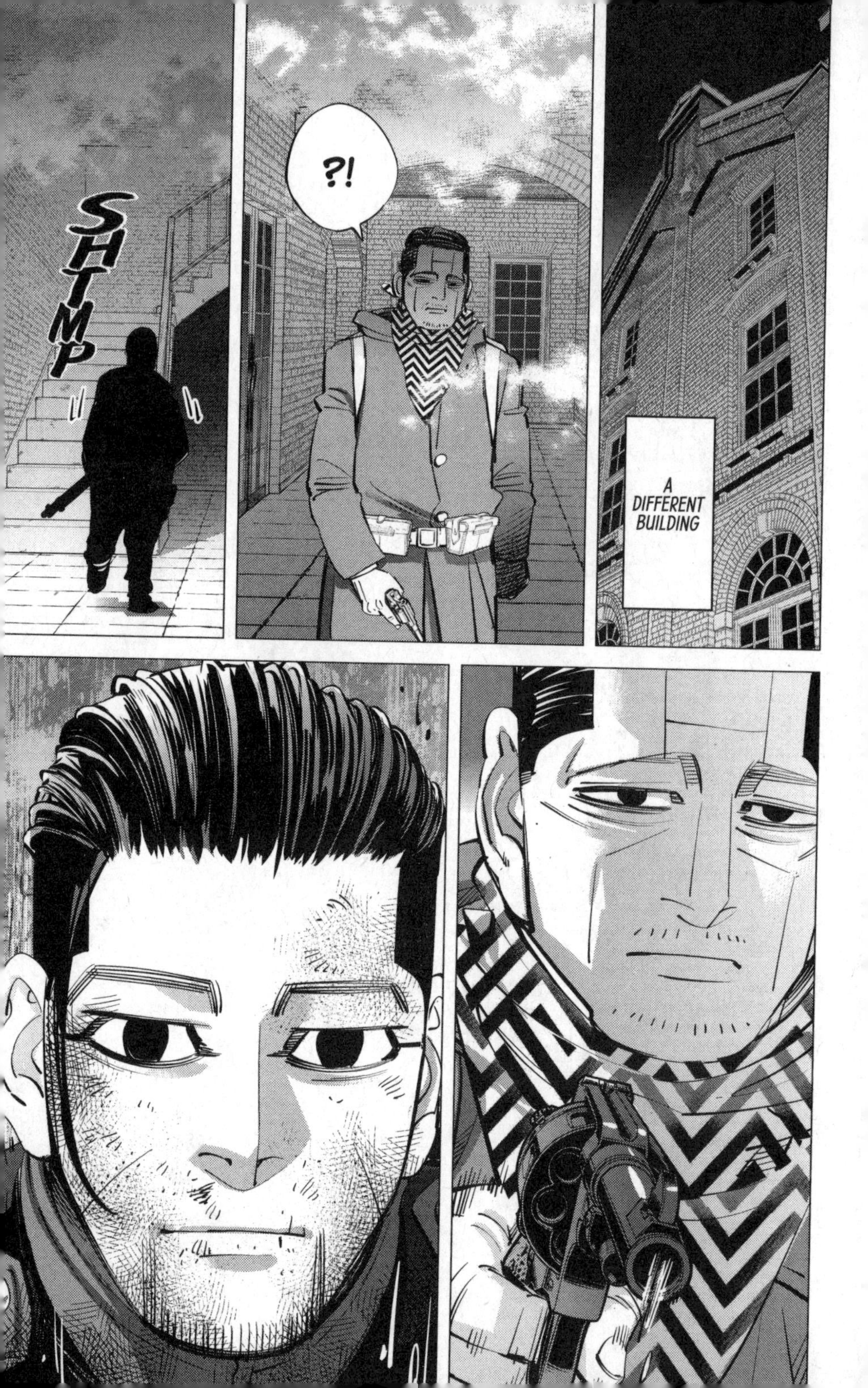
A DIFFERENT BUILDING
?!
SHTIMP

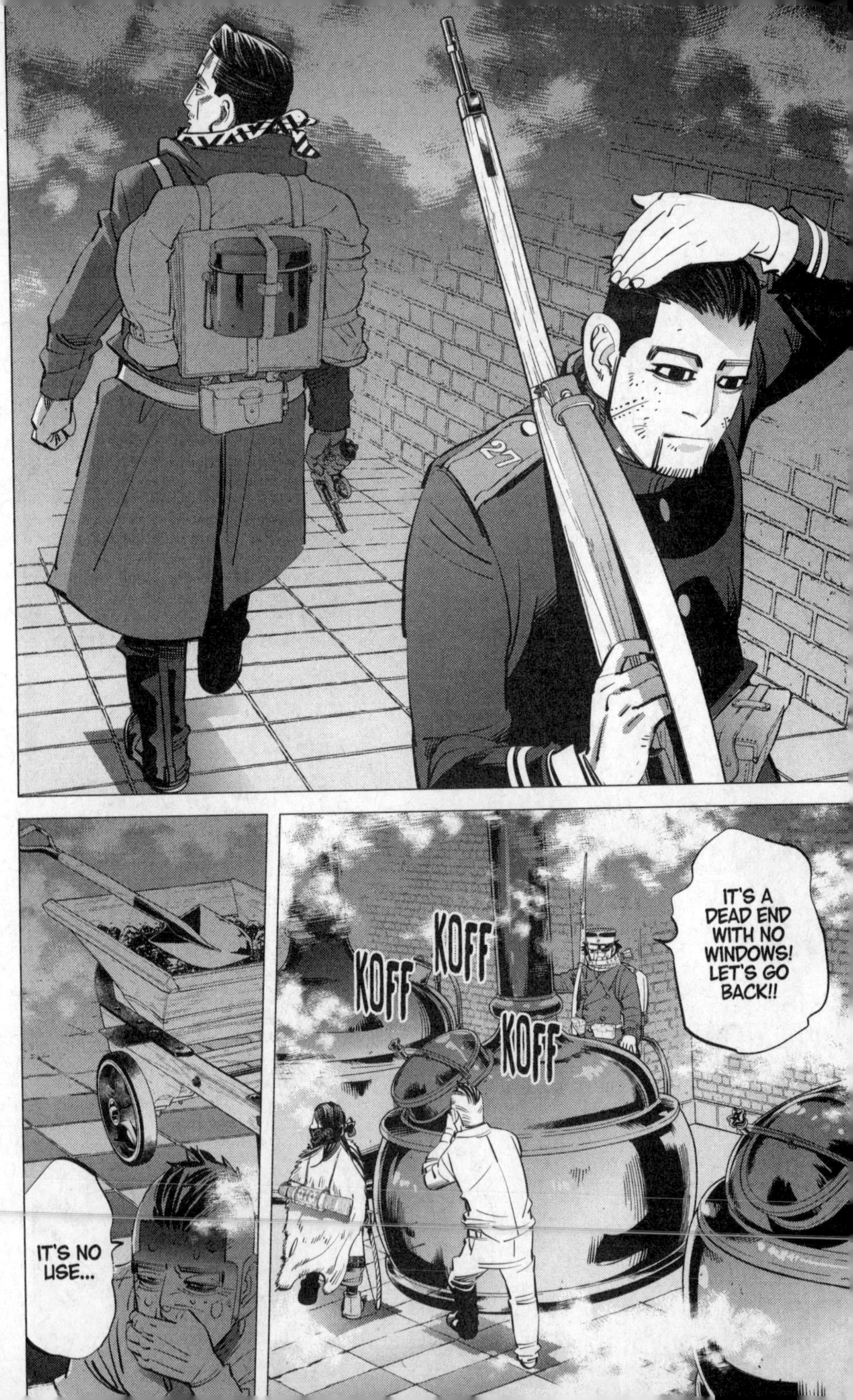
IT'S A DEAD END WITH NO WINDOWS! LET'S GO BACK!!
KOFF
KOFF
KOFF
IT'S NO USE...

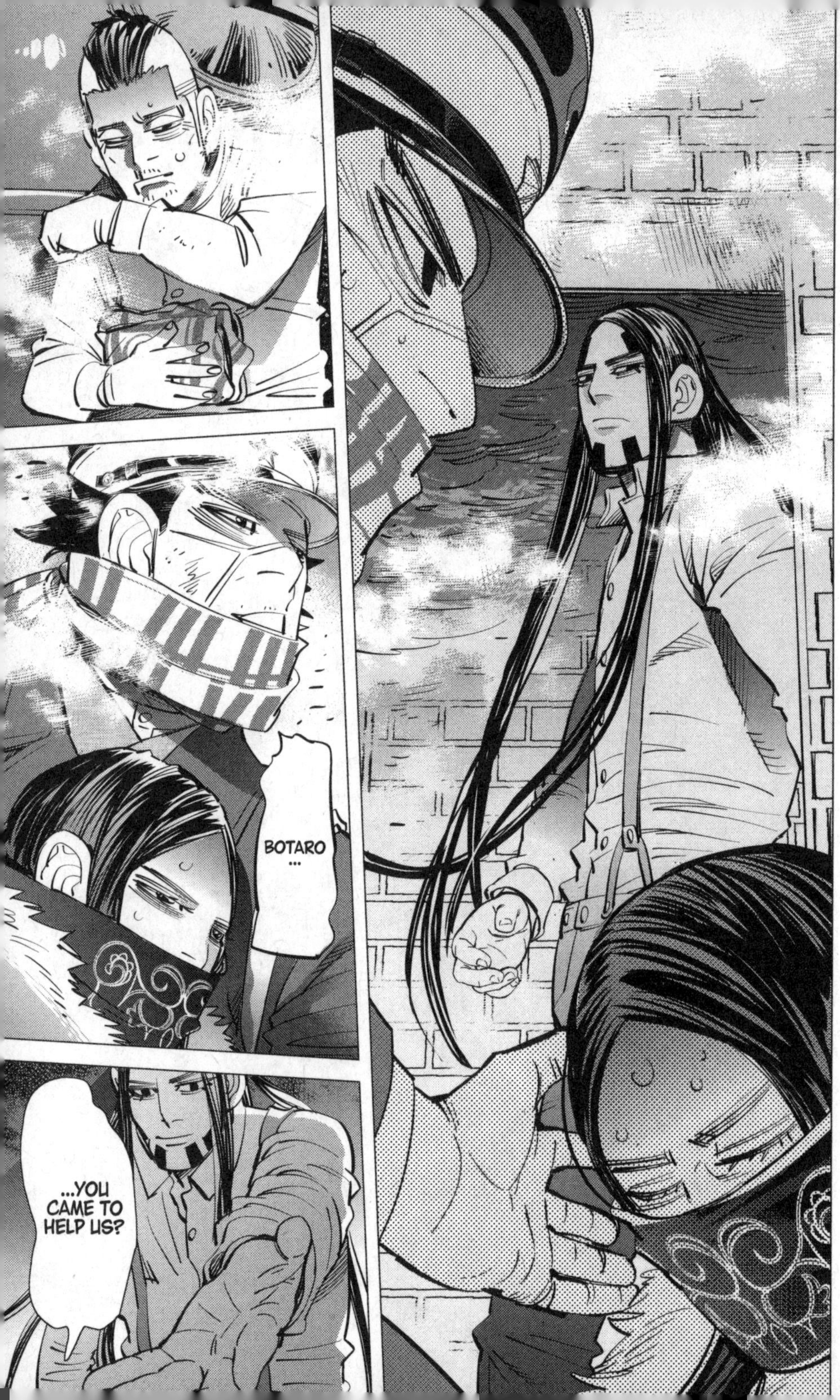
BOTARO
...
...YOU CAME TO HELP US?

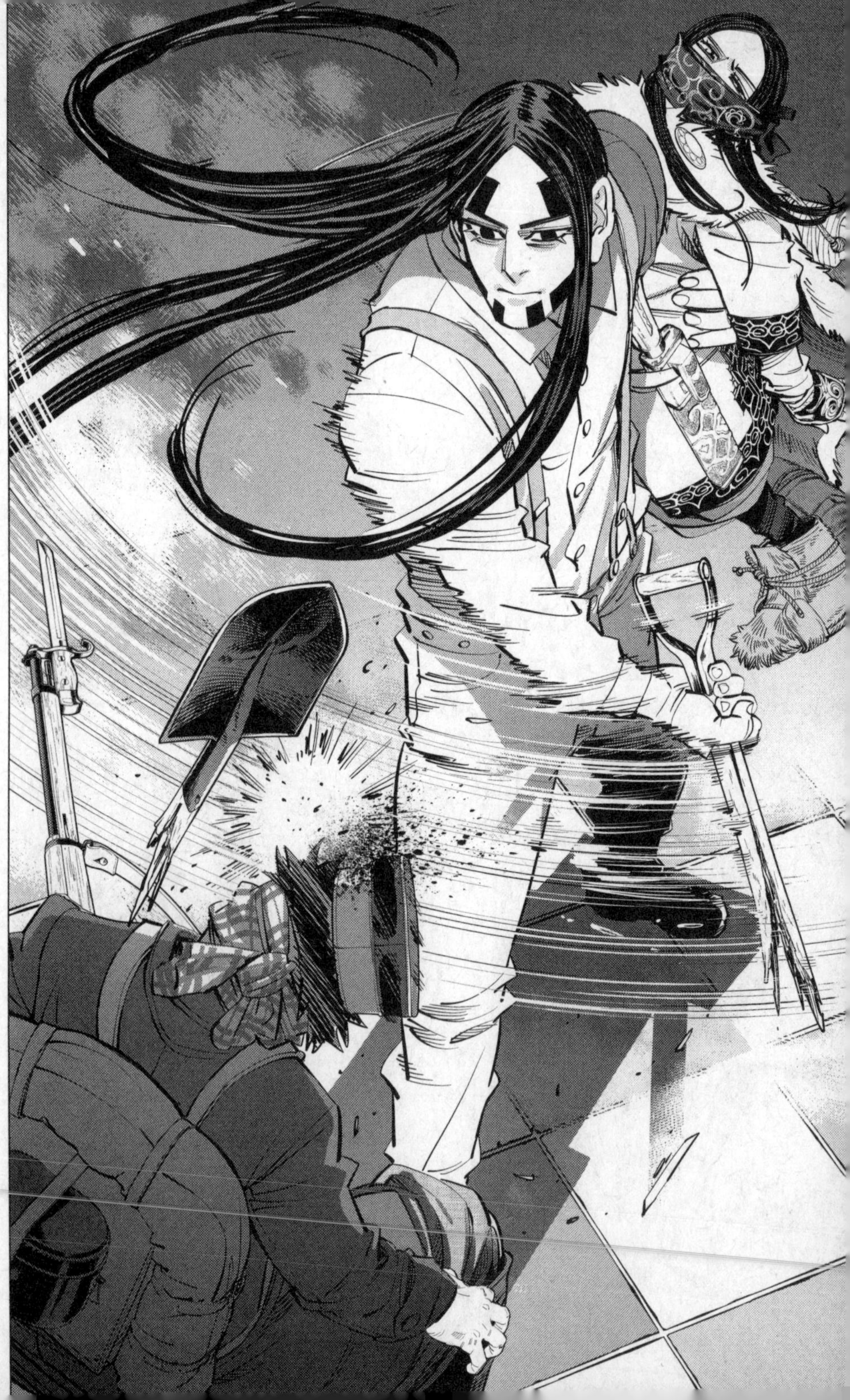

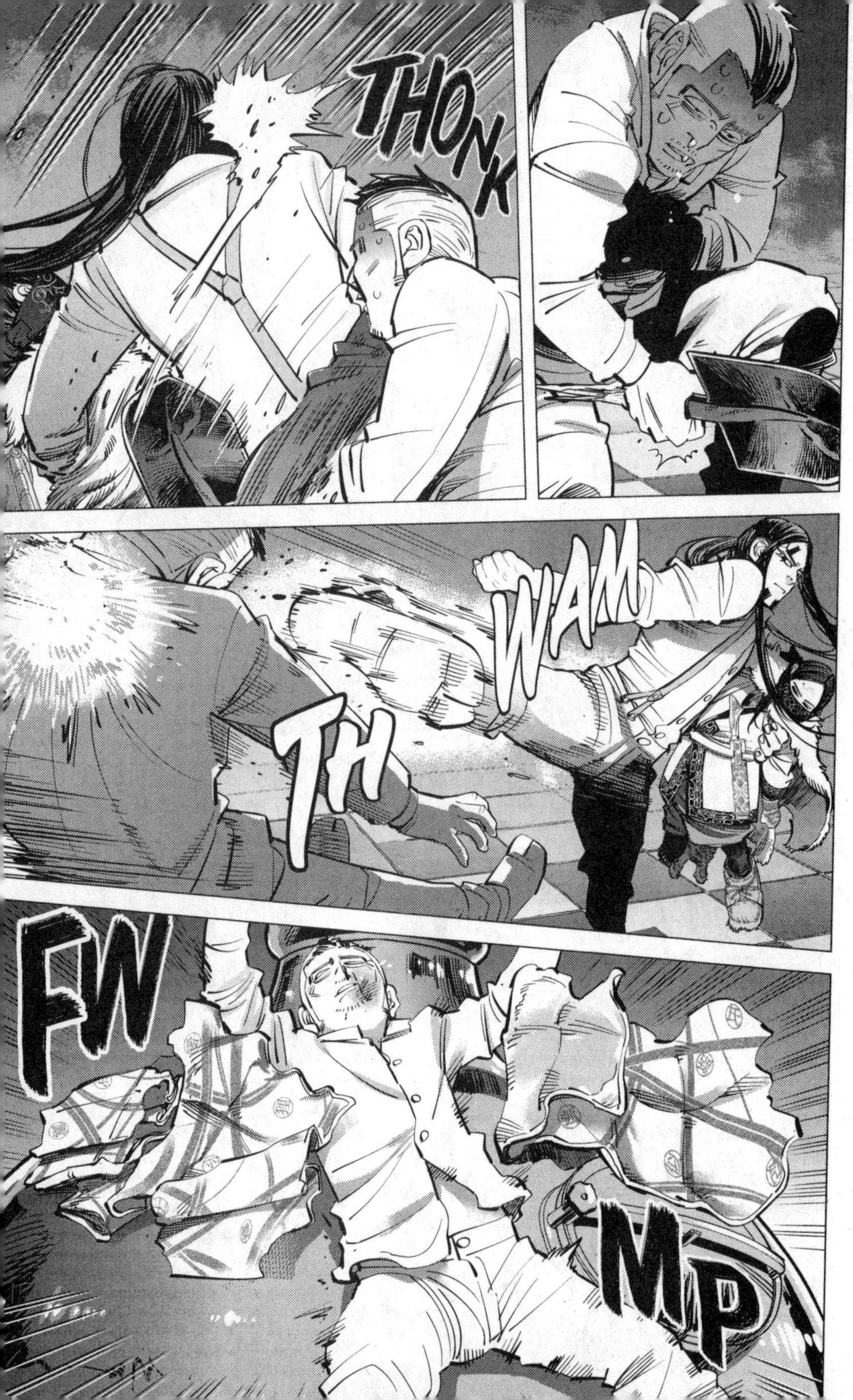
THONK
WAM
TH
FW
MP

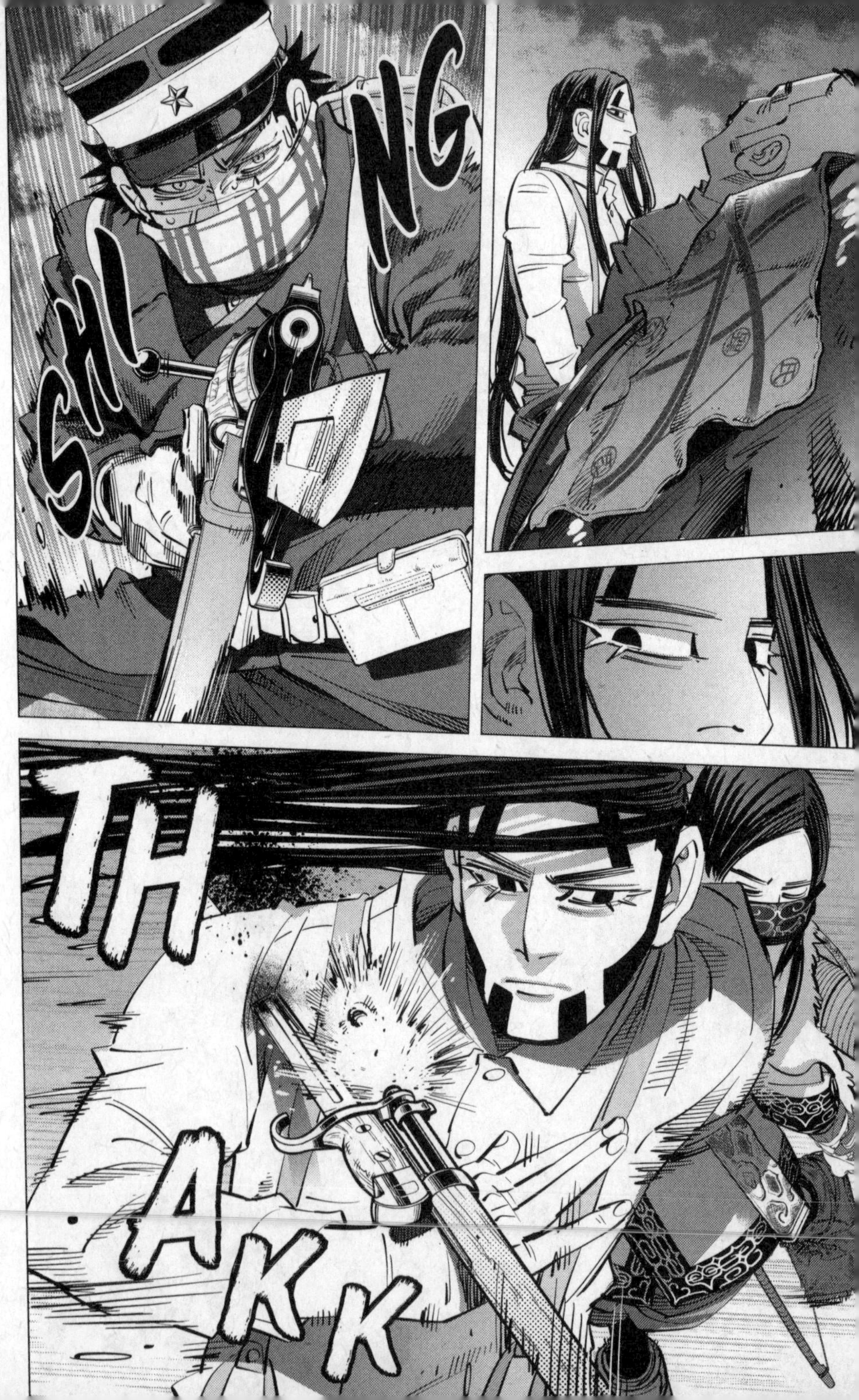
SHING
THAKK

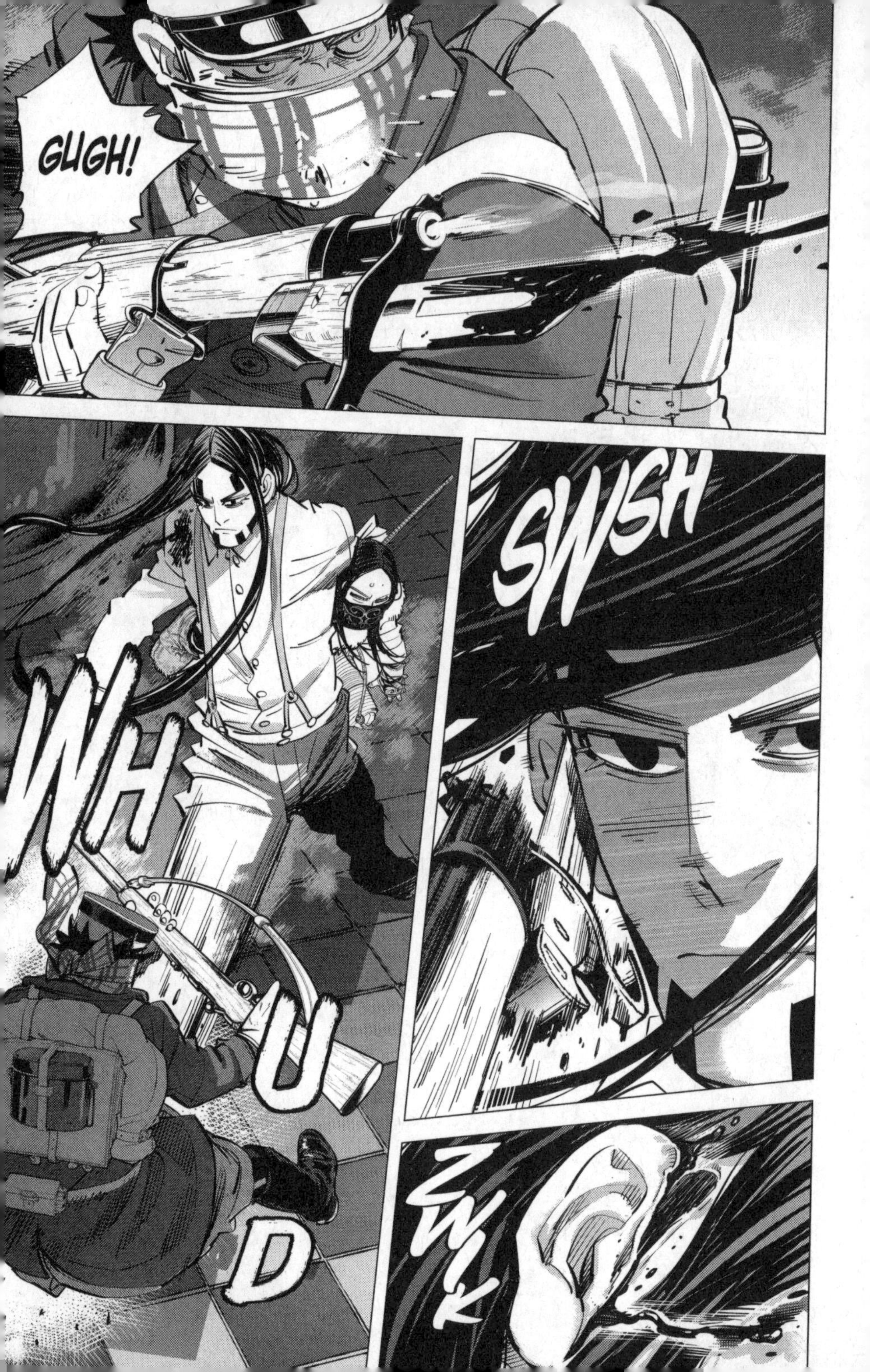
GUGH!
SWISH
ZWK
WHUD

FWUP

KOFF KOFF!

I CAN'T MOVE!

GAHK!

BOTARO...

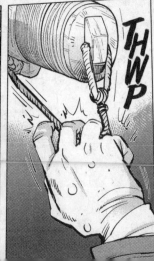

THWP

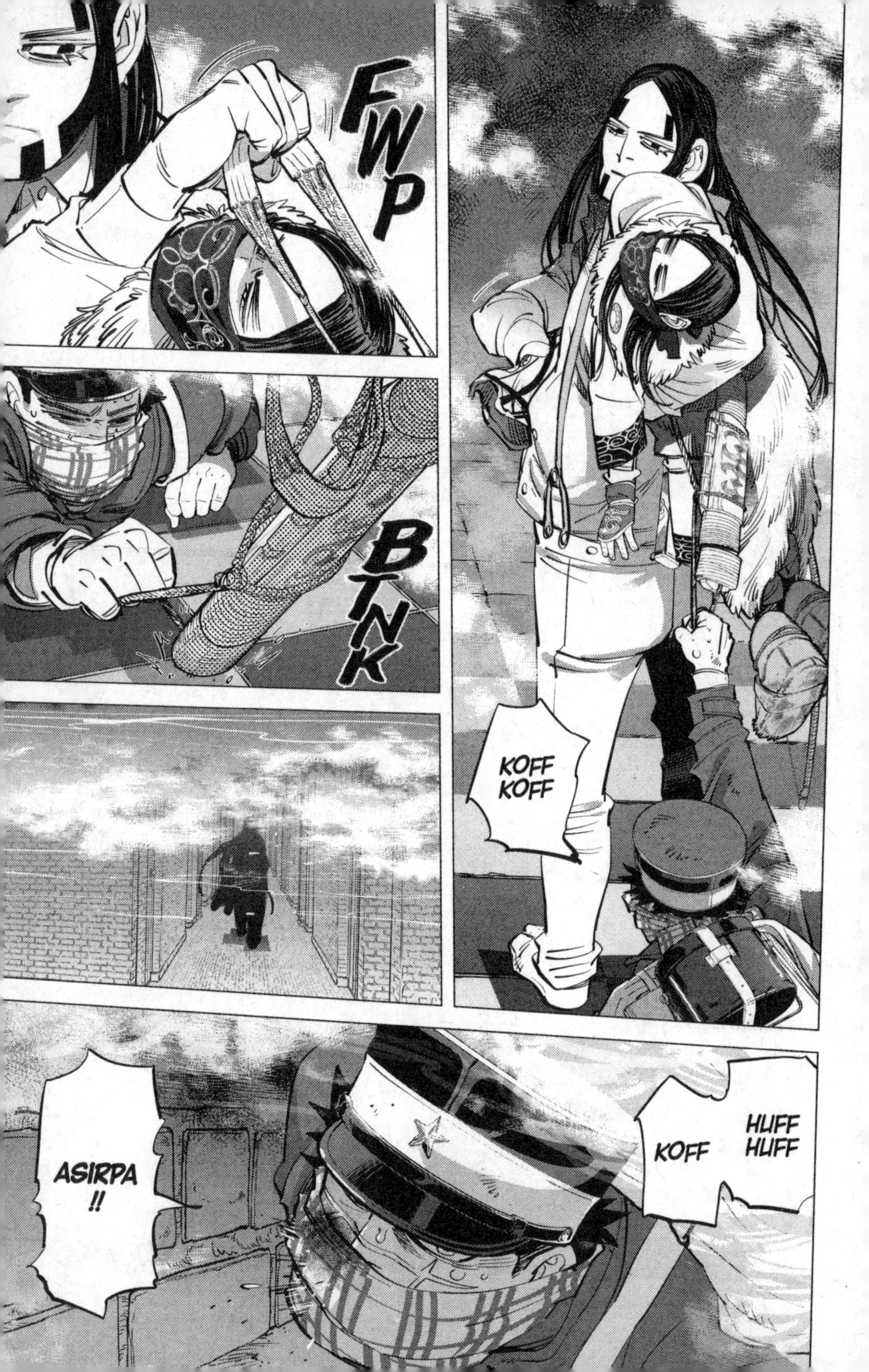
KOFF KOFF
FWP
BTNK
HUFF HUFF
KOFF
ASIRPA!!

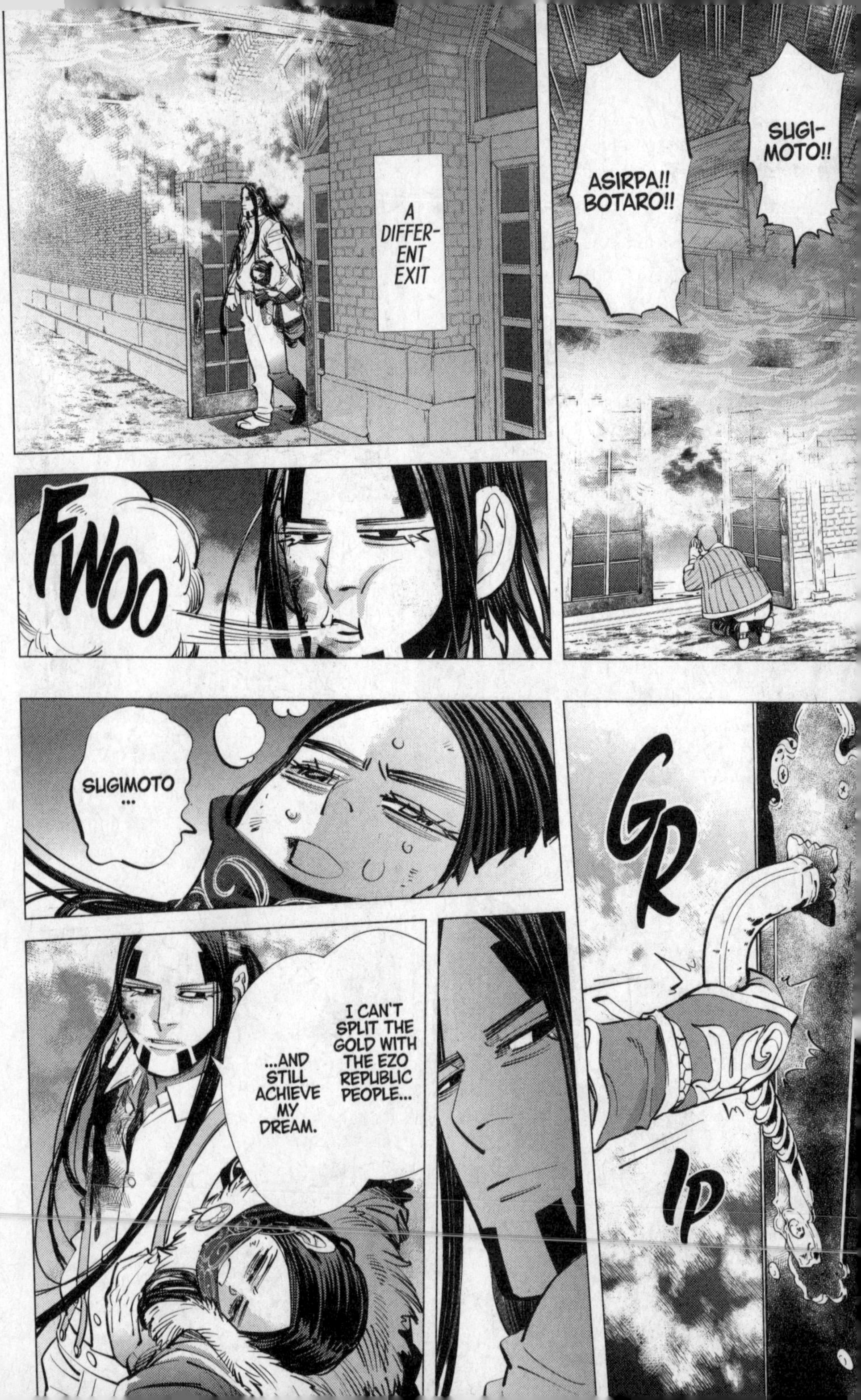
SUGI-MOTO!!
ASIRPA!! BOTARO!!
A DIFFER-ENT EXIT
FWOO
GR
IP
SUGIMOTO ...
I CAN'T SPLIT THE GOLD WITH THE EZO REPUBLIC PEOPLE...
...AND STILL ACHIEVE MY DREAM.

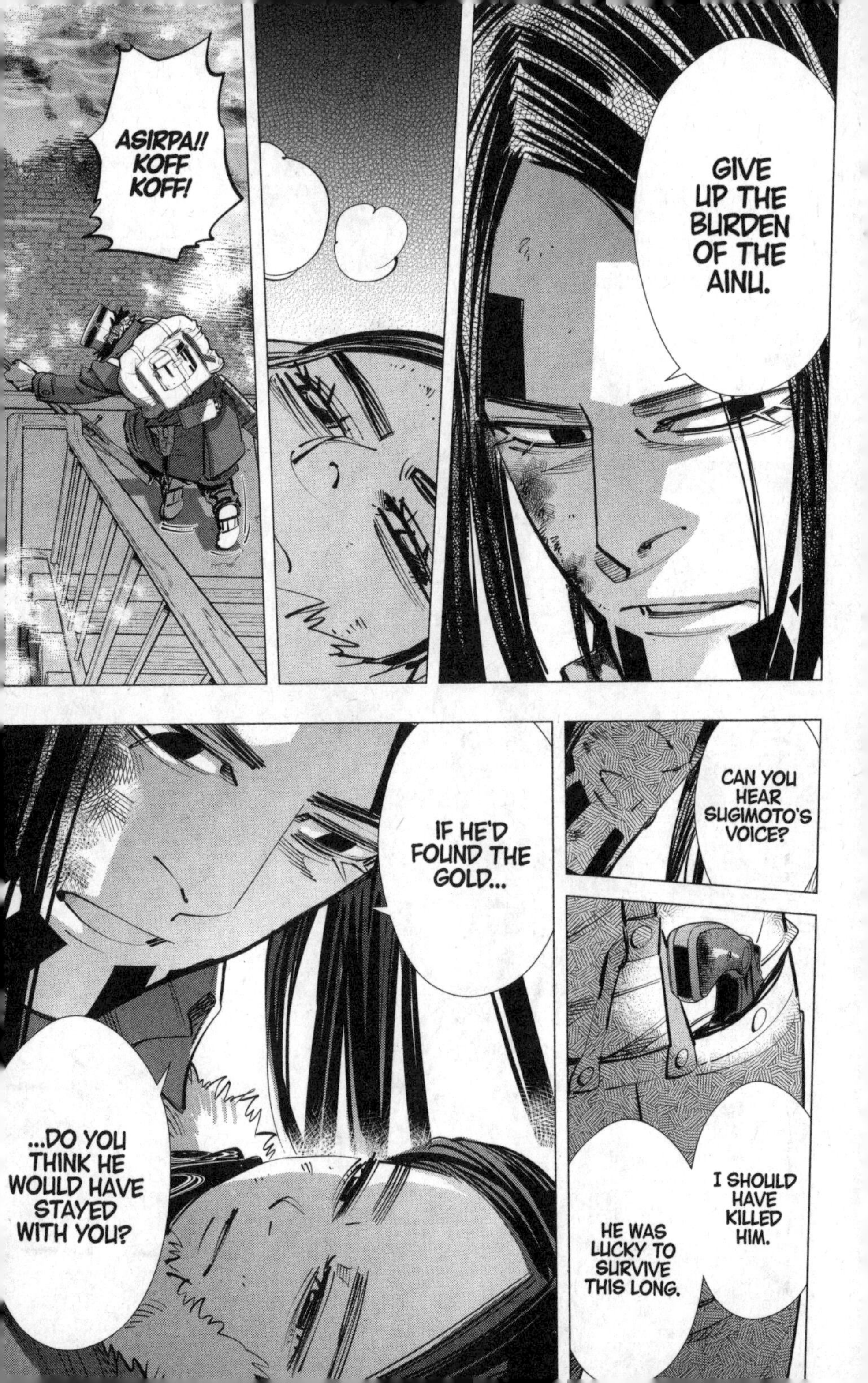
GIVE UP THE BURDEN OF THE AINU.
ASIRPA!! KOFF KOFF!
CAN YOU HEAR SUGIMOTO'S VOICE?
I SHOULD HAVE KILLED HIM.
HE WAS LUCKY TO SURVIVE THIS LONG.
IF HE'D FOUND THE GOLD...
...DO YOU THINK HE WOULD HAVE STAYED WITH YOU?

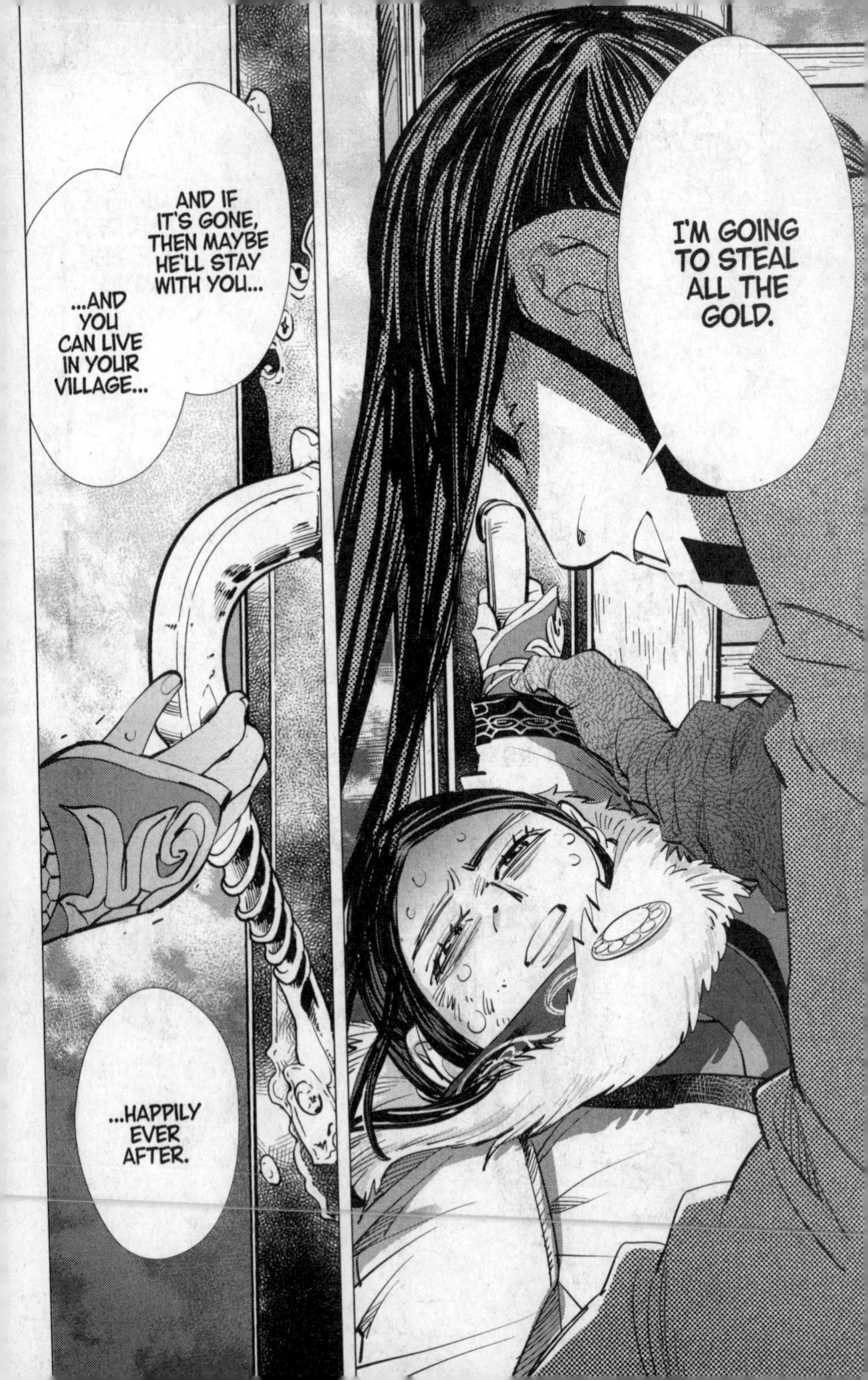
I'M GOING TO STEAL ALL THE GOLD.
AND IF IT'S GONE, THEN MAYBE HE'LL STAY WITH YOU...
...AND YOU CAN LIVE IN YOUR VILLAGE...
...HAPPILY EVER AFTER.

Chapter 259: Making a Home

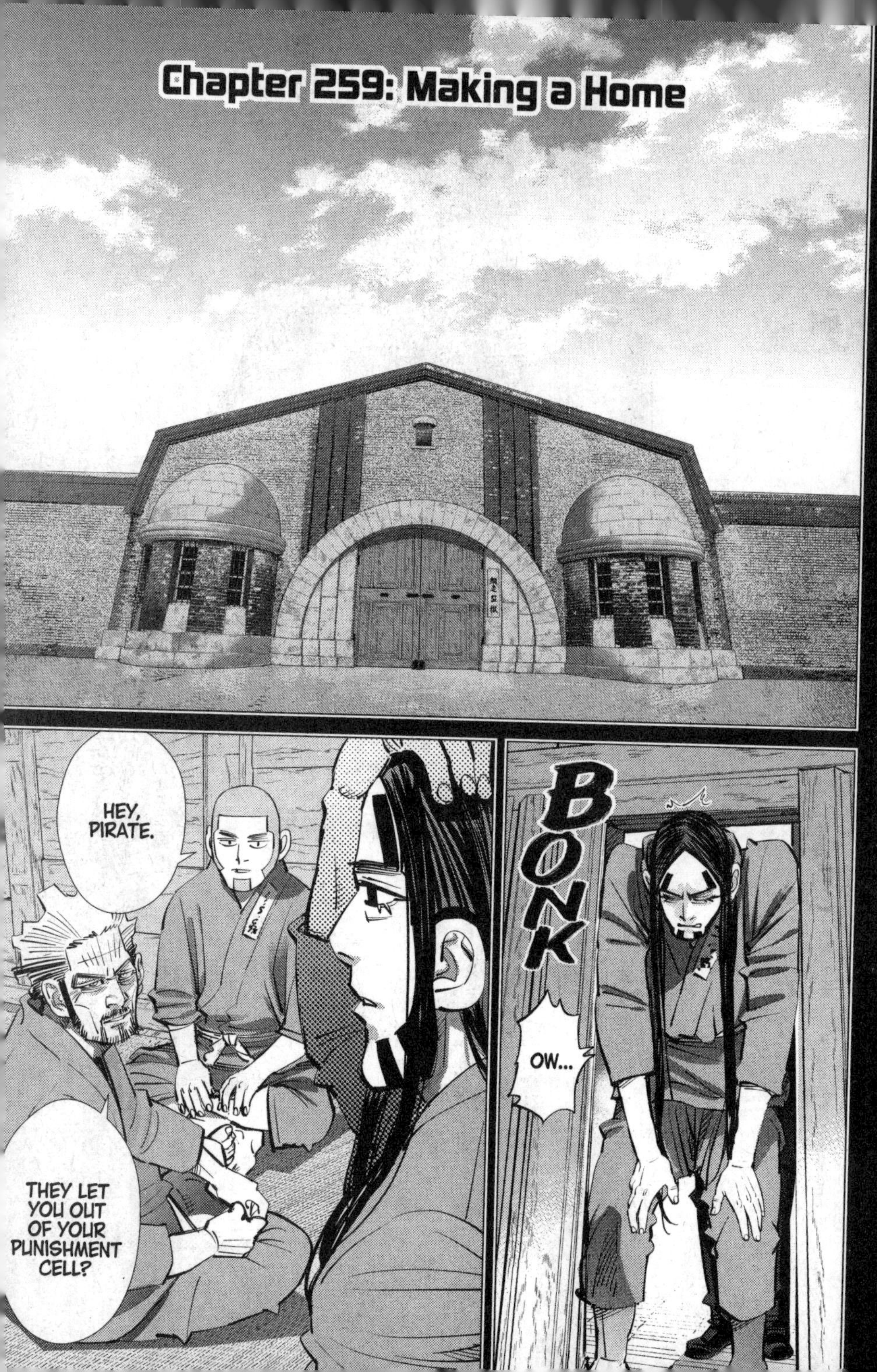
BONK
OW...
HEY, PIRATE.
THEY LET YOU OUT OF YOUR PUNISHMENT CELL?

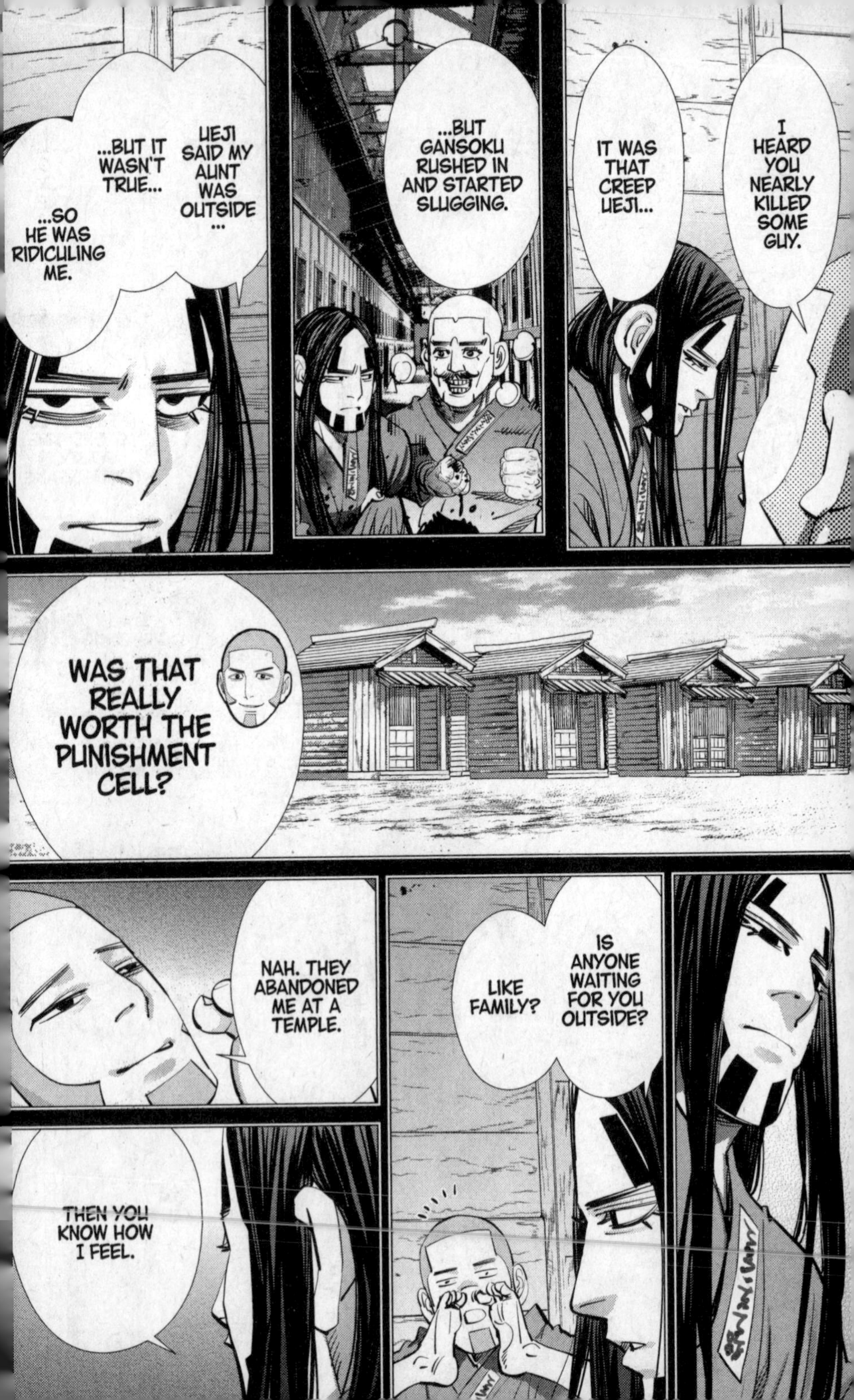
I HEARD YOU NEARLY KILLED SOME GUY.
IT WAS THAT CREEP UEJI...
...BUT GANSOKU RUSHED IN AND STARTED SLUGGING.
UEJI SAID MY AUNT WAS OUTSIDE...
...BUT IT WASN'T TRUE...
...SO HE WAS RIDICULING ME.
WAS THAT REALLY WORTH THE PUNISHMENT CELL?
IS ANYONE WAITING FOR YOU OUTSIDE?
LIKE FAMILY?
NAH. THEY ABANDONED ME AT A TEMPLE.
THEN YOU KNOW HOW I FEEL.

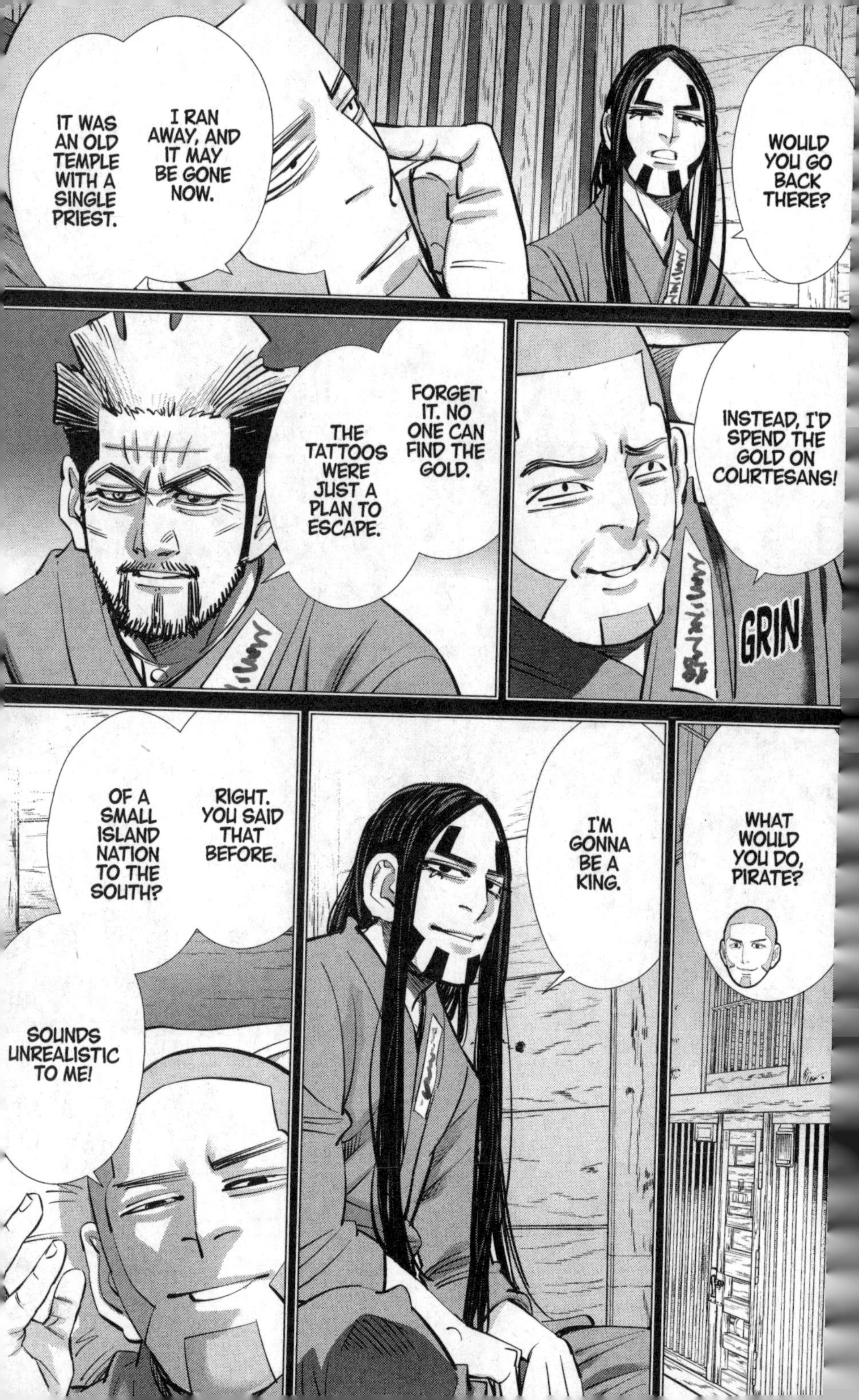
WOULD YOU GO BACK THERE?
I RAN AWAY, AND IT MAY BE GONE NOW.
IT WAS AN OLD TEMPLE WITH A SINGLE PRIEST.
INSTEAD, I'D SPEND THE GOLD ON COURTESANS!
GRIN
FORGET IT. NO ONE CAN FIND THE GOLD.
THE TATTOOS WERE JUST A PLAN TO ESCAPE.
WHAT WOULD YOU DO, PIRATE?
I'M GONNA BE A KING.
RIGHT. YOU SAID THAT BEFORE.
OF A SMALL ISLAND NATION TO THE SOUTH?
SOUNDS UNREALISTIC TO ME!

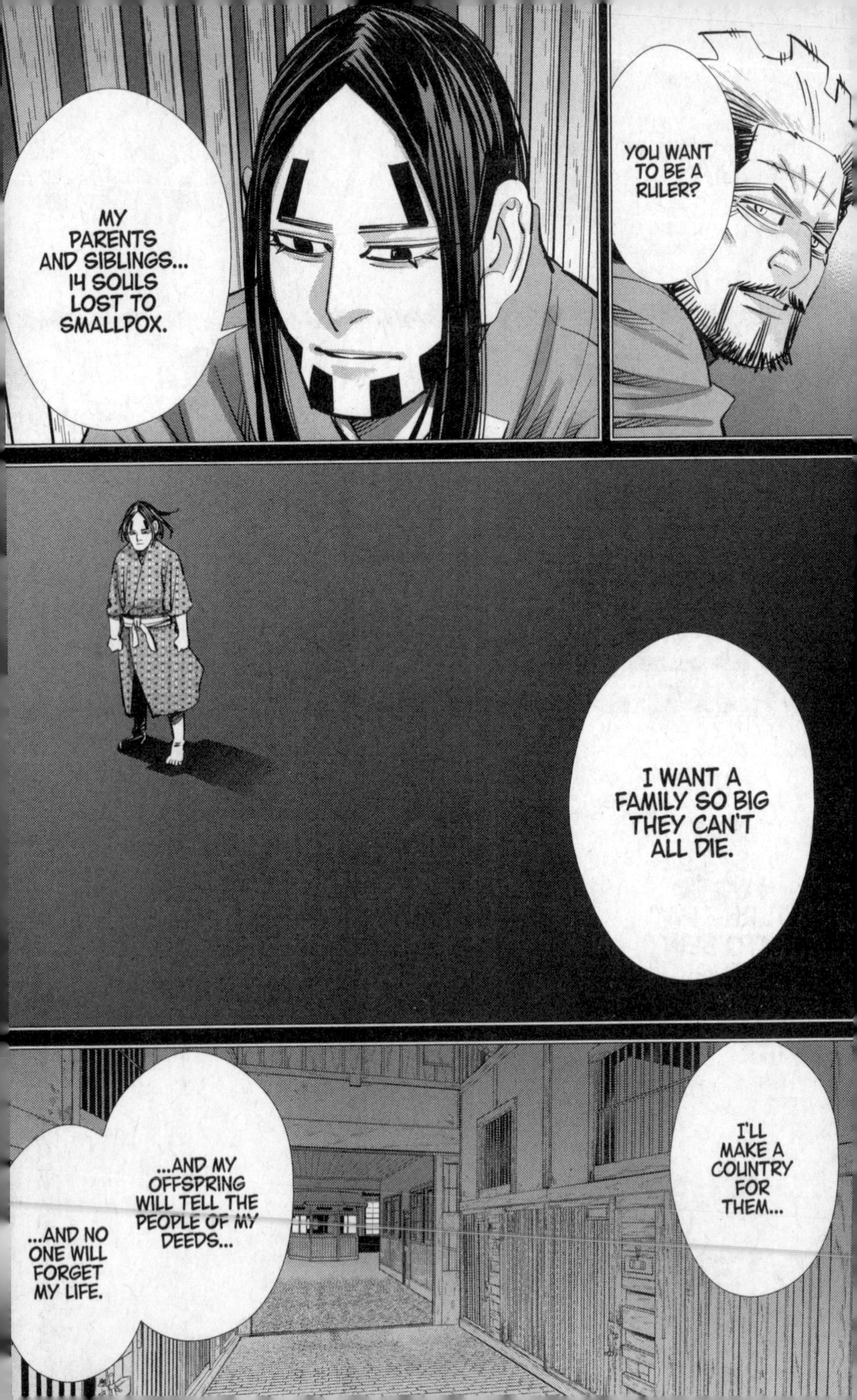
YOU WANT TO BE A RULER?
MY PARENTS AND SIBLINGS... 14 SOULS LOST TO SMALLPOX.
I WANT A FAMILY SO BIG THEY CAN'T ALL DIE.
I'LL MAKE A COUNTRY FOR THEM...
...AND MY OFFSPRING WILL TELL THE PEOPLE OF MY DEEDS...
...AND NO ONE WILL FORGET MY LIFE.

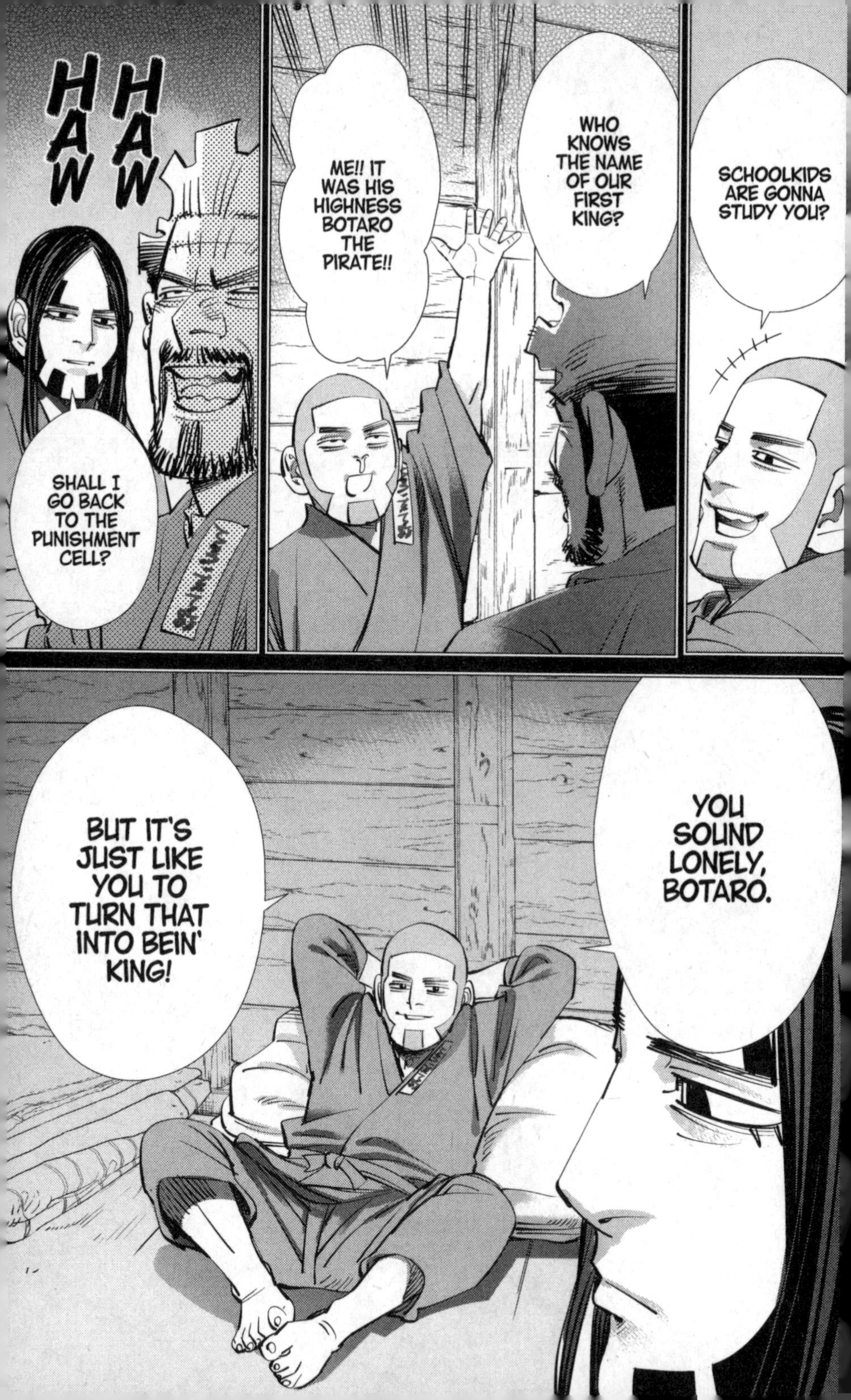
SCHOOLKIDS ARE GONNA STUDY YOU?
WHO KNOWS THE NAME OF OUR FIRST KING?
ME!! IT WAS HIS HIGHNESS BOTARO THE PIRATE!!
HAW HAW
SHALL I GO BACK TO THE PUNISHMENT CELL?
YOU SOUND LONELY, BOTARO.
BUT IT'S JUST LIKE YOU TO TURN THAT INTO BEIN' KING!

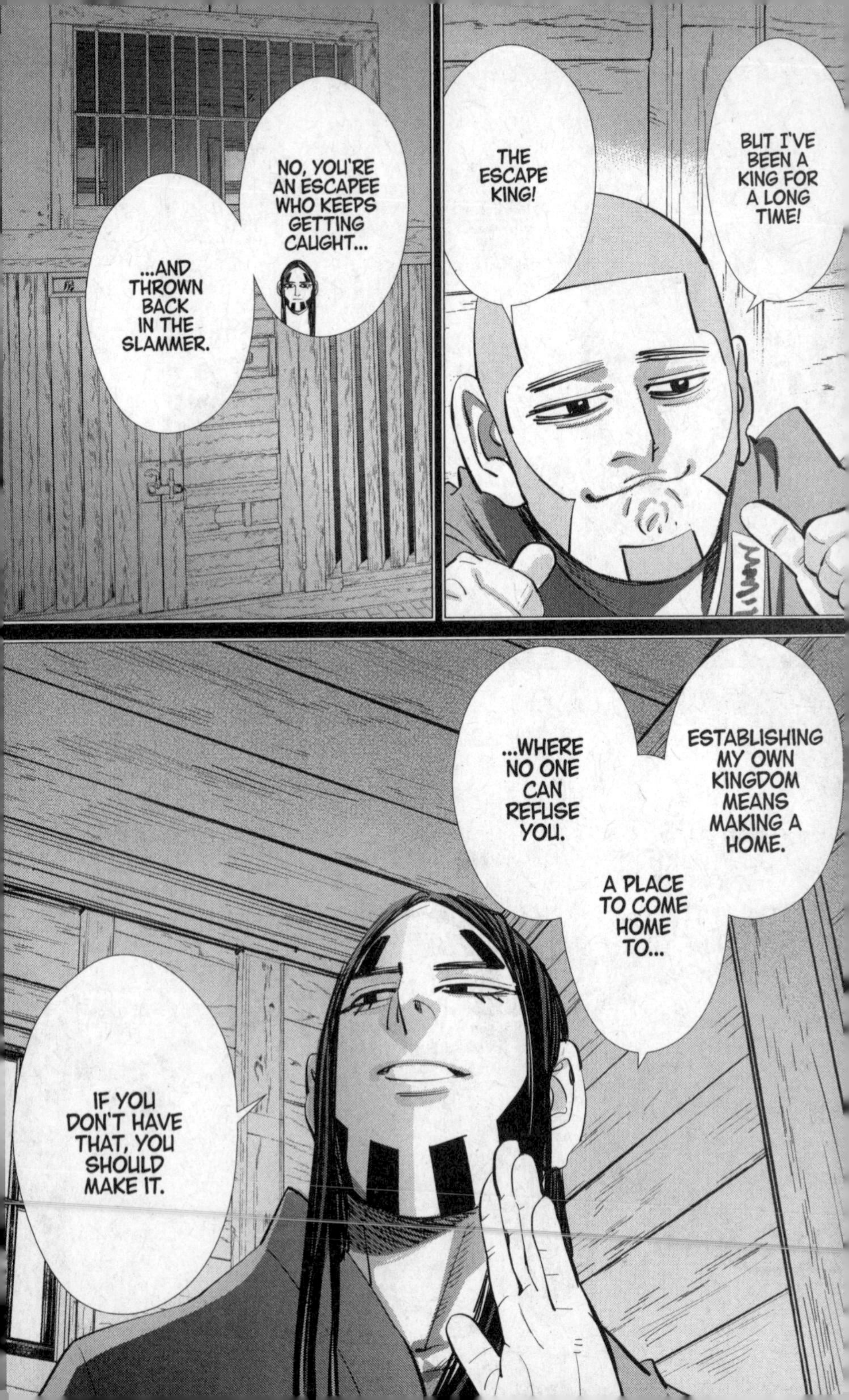
BUT I'VE BEEN A KING FOR A LONG TIME!
THE ESCAPE KING!
NO, YOU'RE AN ESCAPEE WHO KEEPS GETTING CAUGHT...
...AND THROWN BACK IN THE SLAMMER.
ESTABLISHING MY OWN KINGDOM MEANS MAKING A HOME.
A PLACE TO COME HOME TO...
...WHERE NO ONE CAN REFUSE YOU.
IF YOU DON'T HAVE THAT, YOU SHOULD MAKE IT.

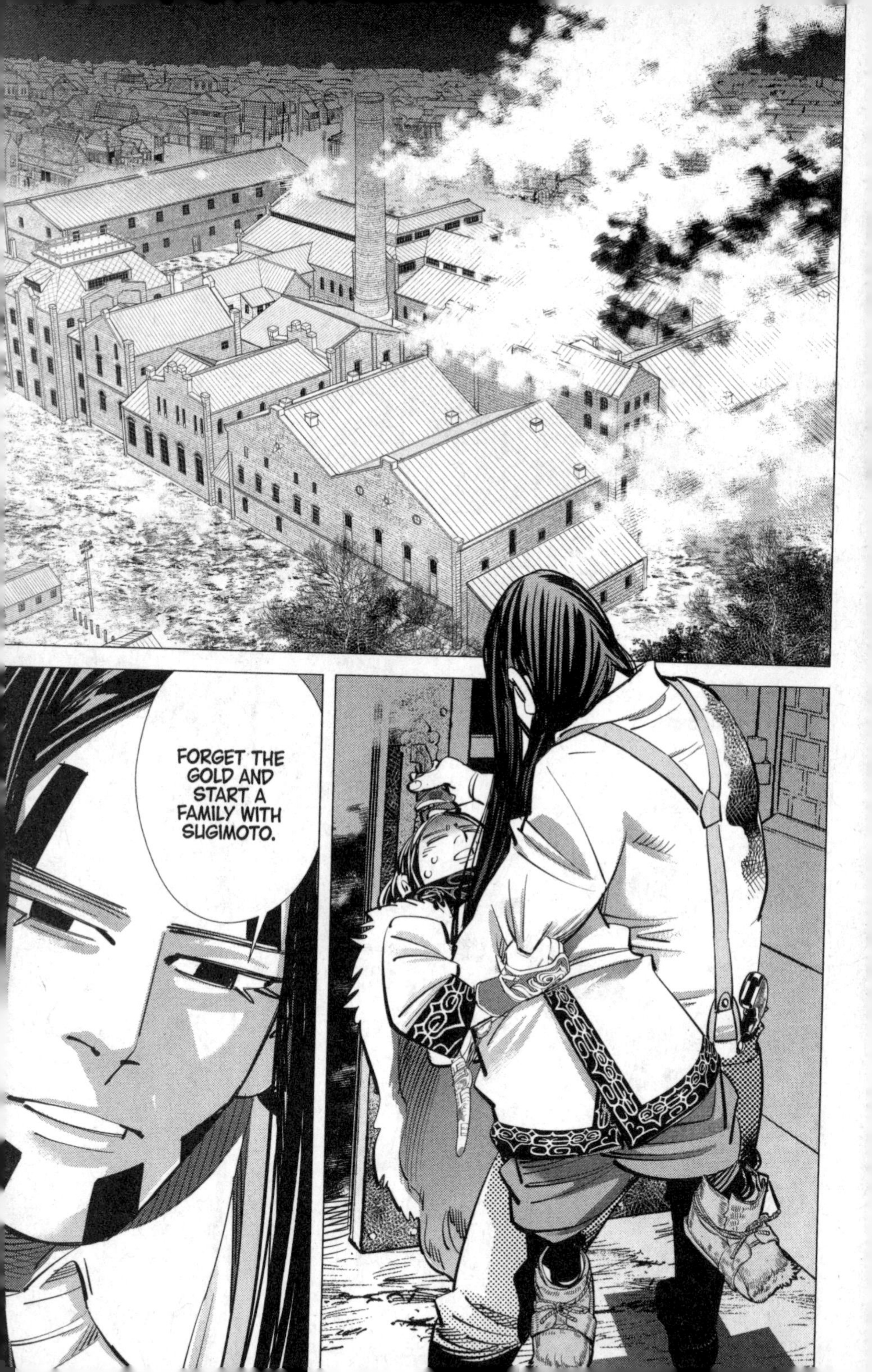
FORGET THE GOLD AND START A FAMILY WITH SUGIMOTO.

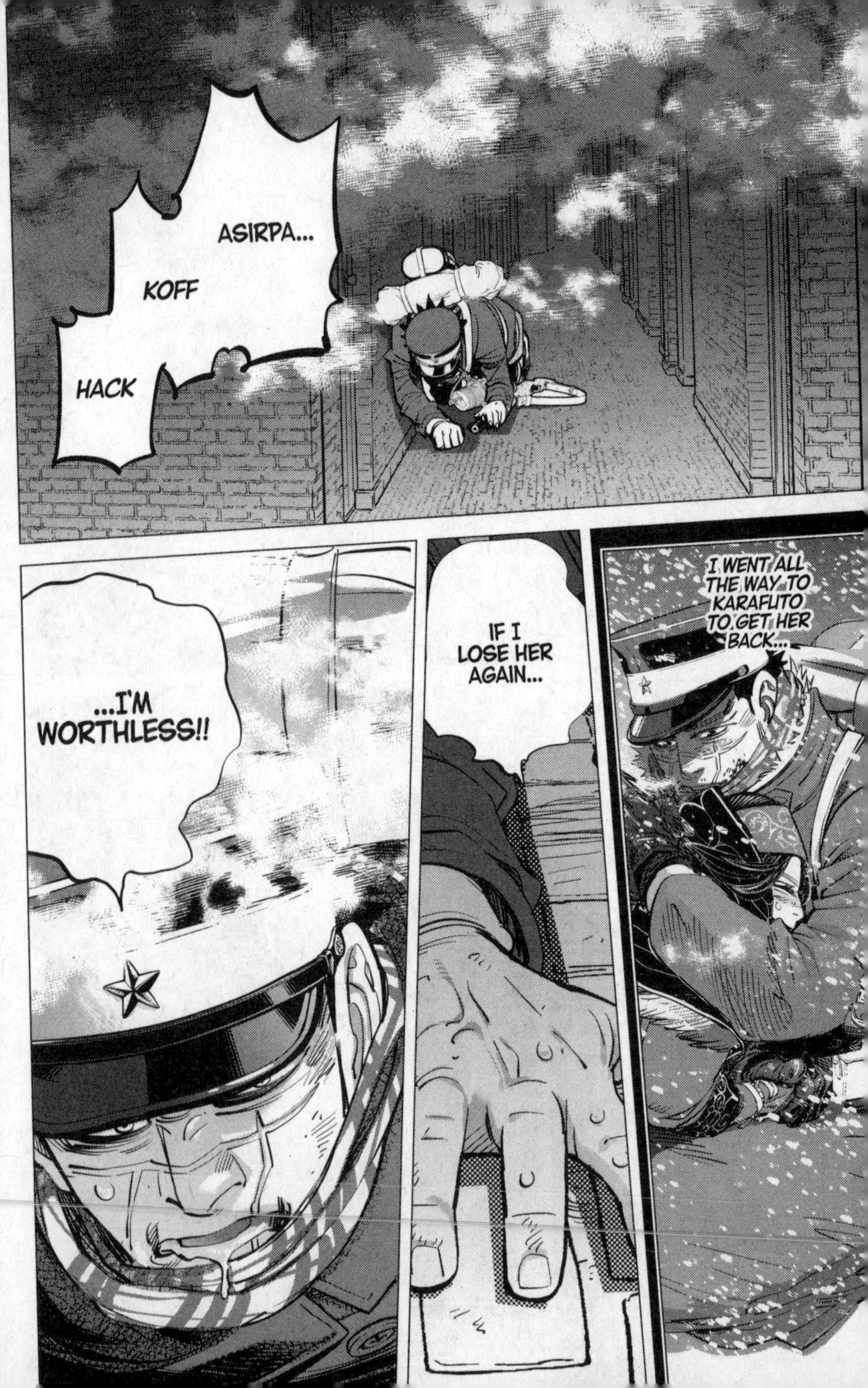
ASIRPA...
KOFF
HACK
I WENT ALL THE WAY TO KARAFUTO TO GET HER BACK...
IF I LOSE HER AGAIN...
...I'M WORTHLESS!!

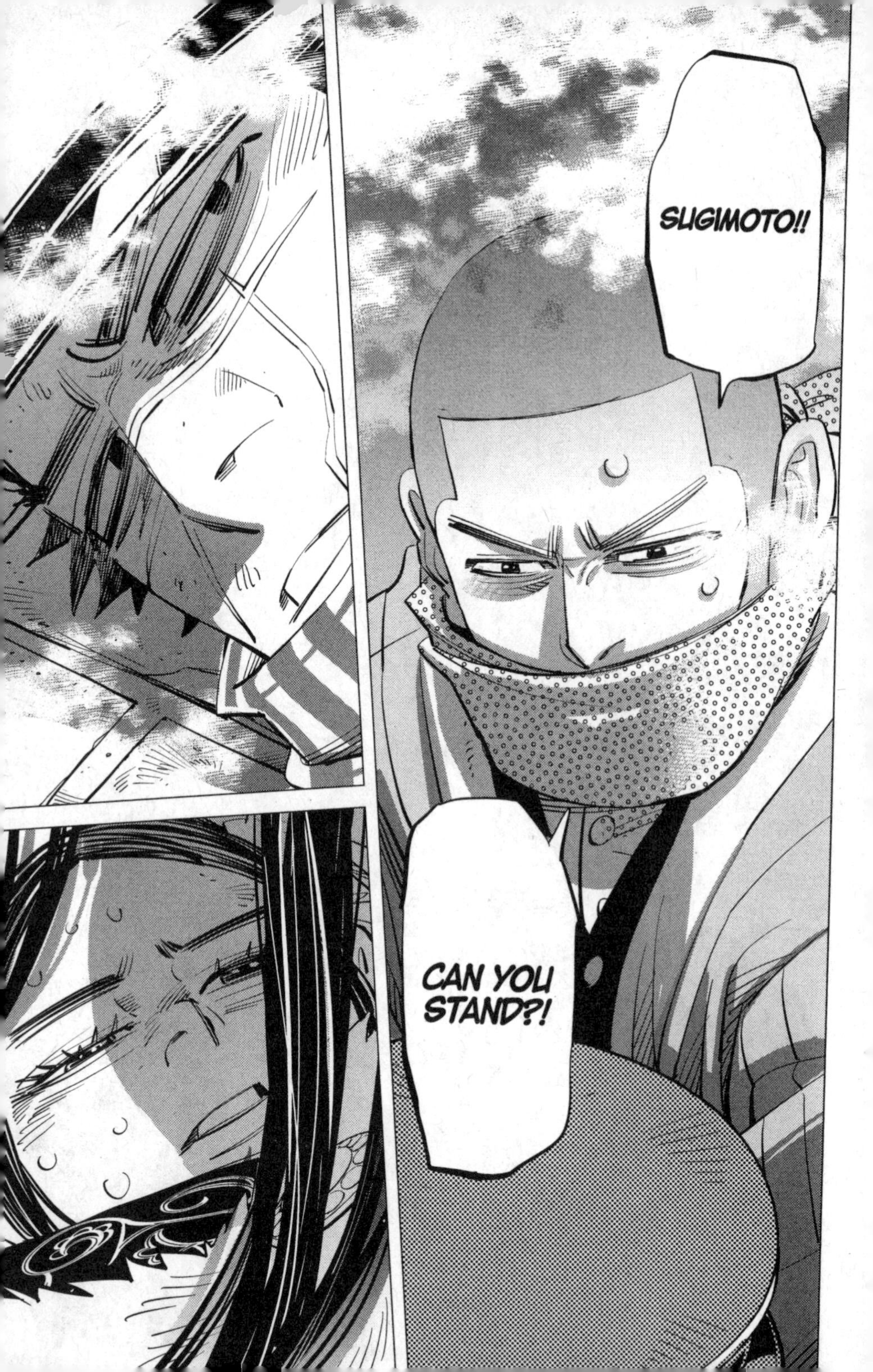
SUGIMOTO!!
CAN YOU STAND?!

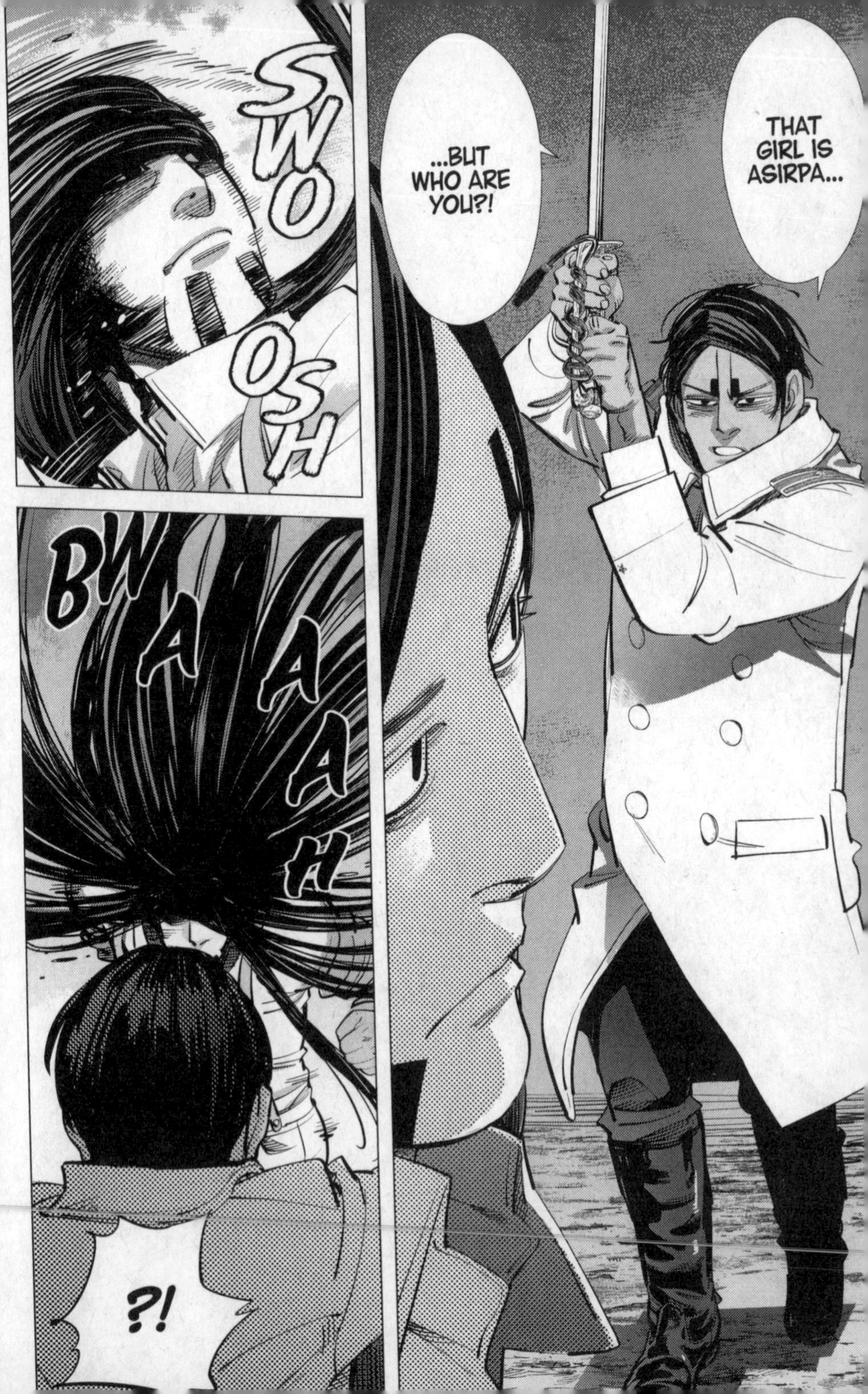
THAT GIRL IS ASIRPA...
...BUT WHO ARE YOU?!
SWOOSH
BWAAAAH
?!

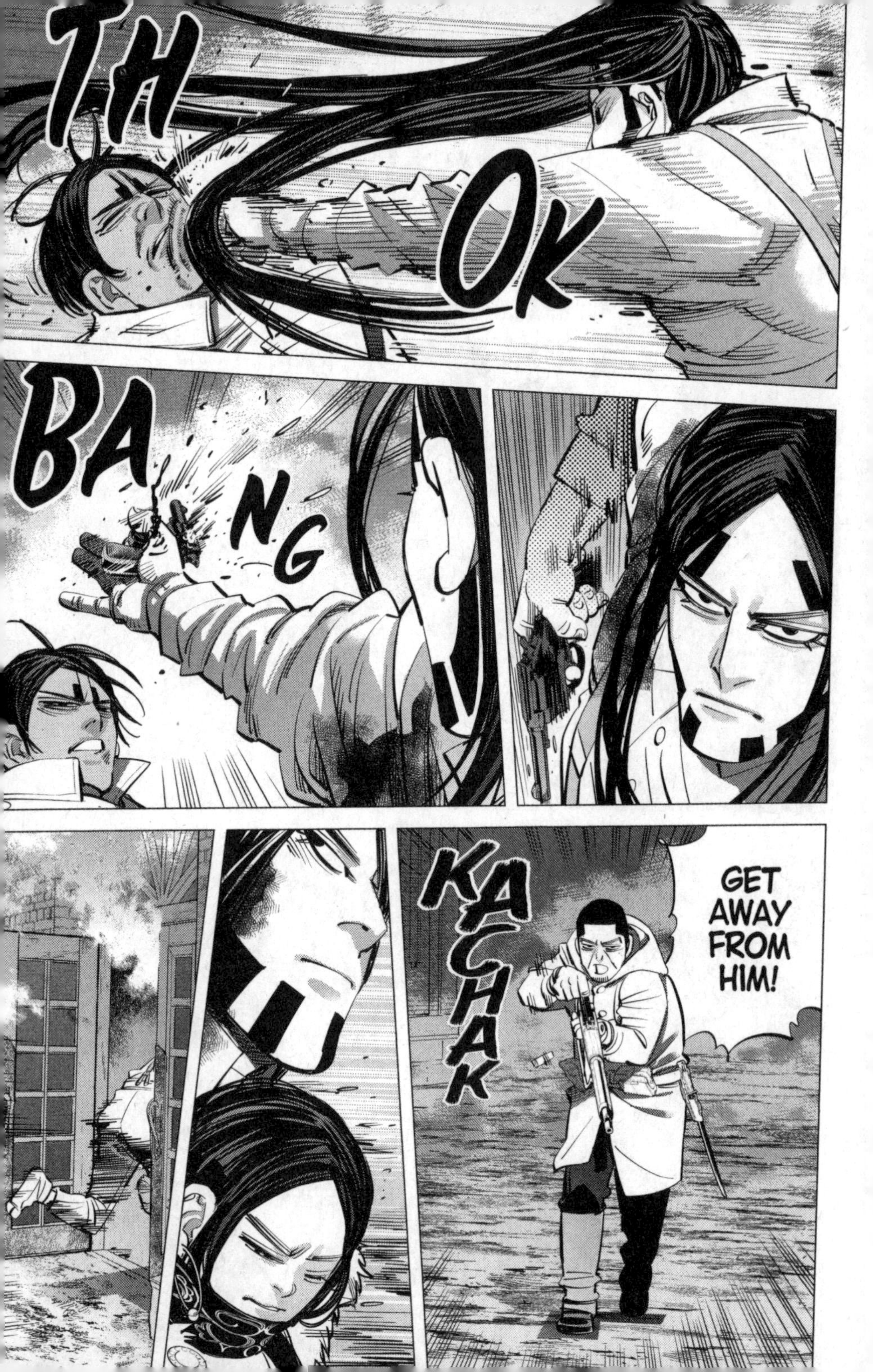
THOK
BANG
GET AWAY FROM HIM!
KACHAK

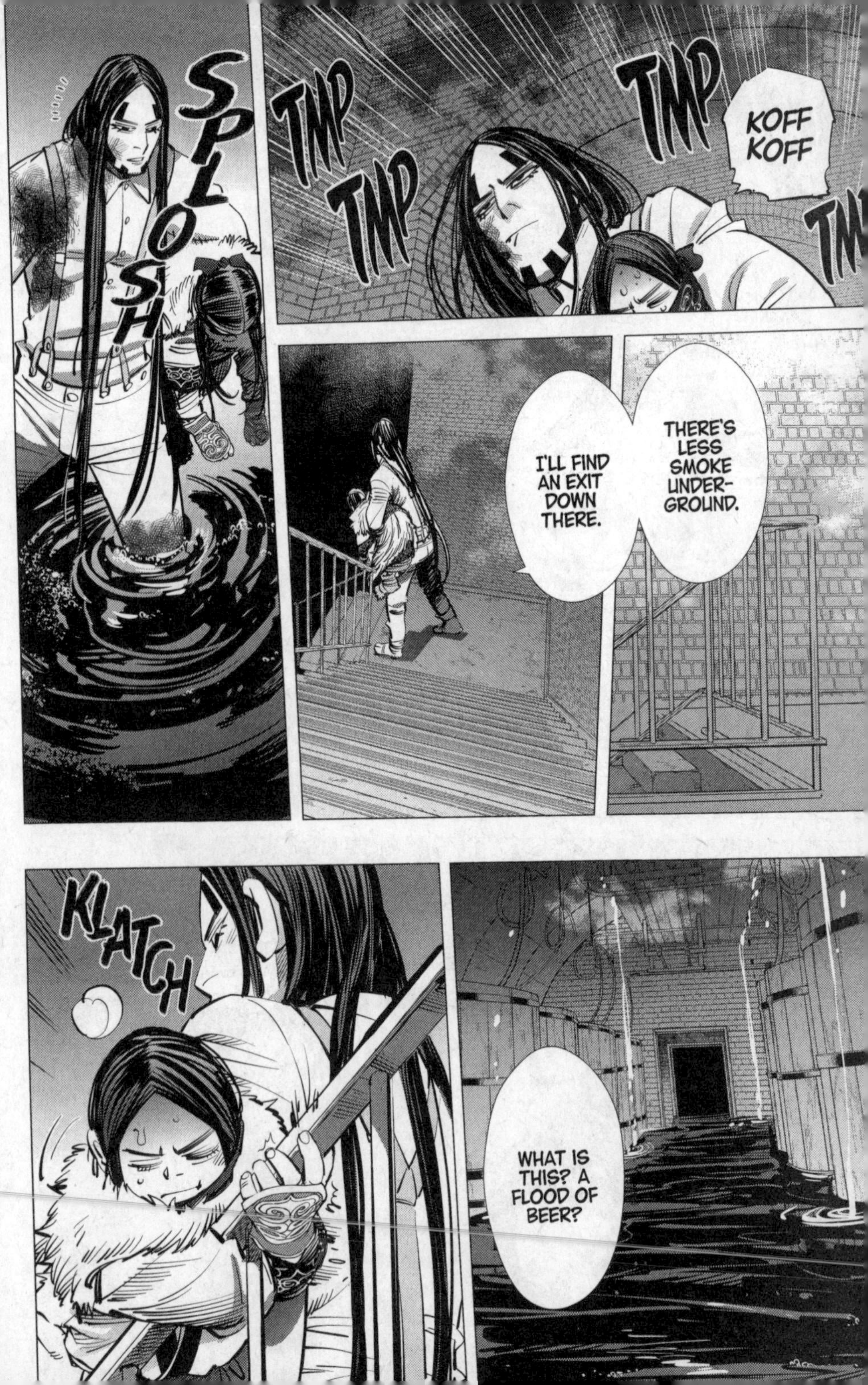
TMP
KOFF KOFF
TMP
TMP
THERE'S LESS SMOKE UNDER-GROUND.
I'LL FIND AN EXIT DOWN THERE.
SPLOSH
WHAT IS THIS? A FLOOD OF BEER?
KLATCH

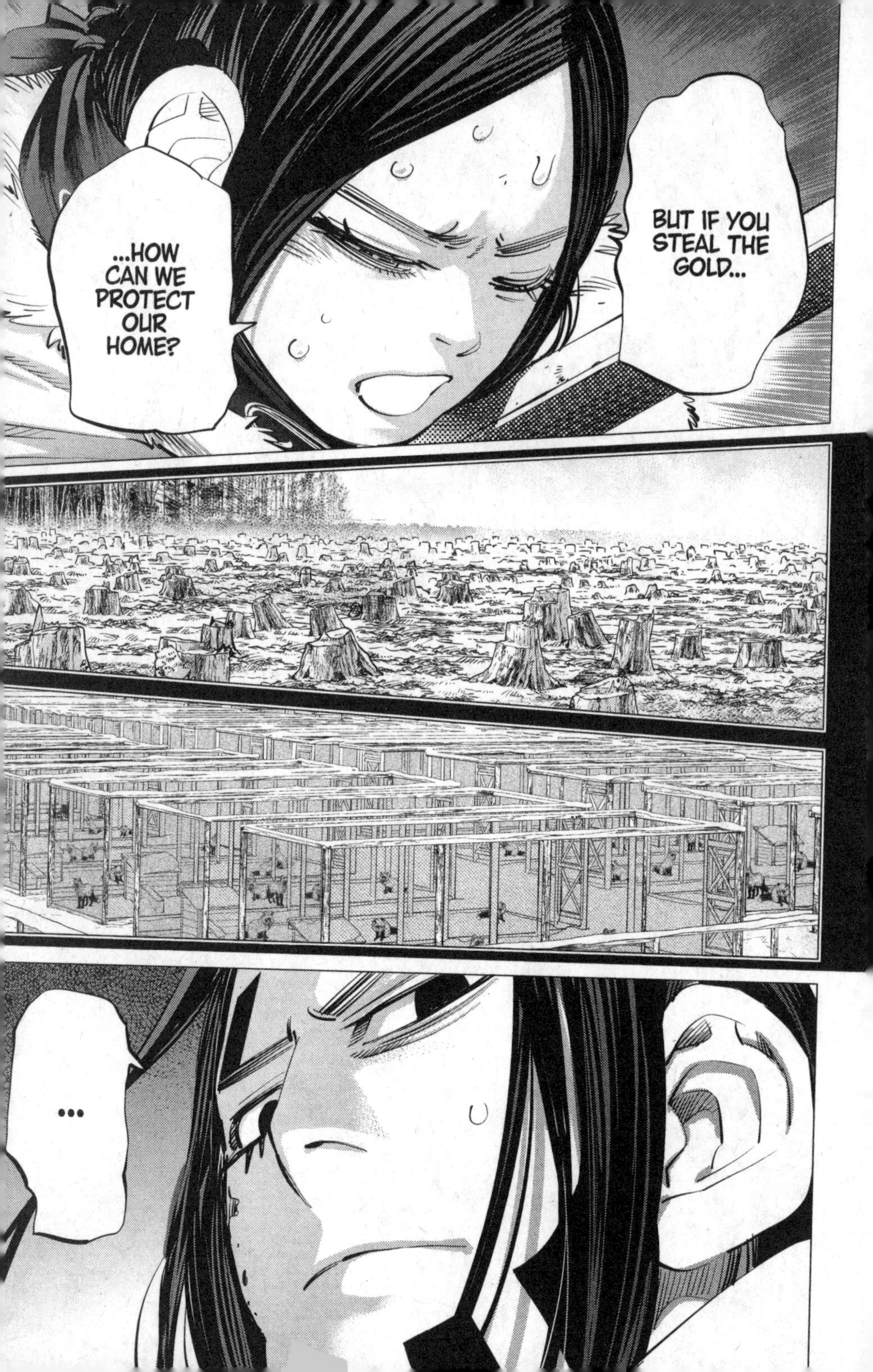
BUT IF YOU STEAL THE GOLD...
...HOW CAN WE PROTECT OUR HOME?
...

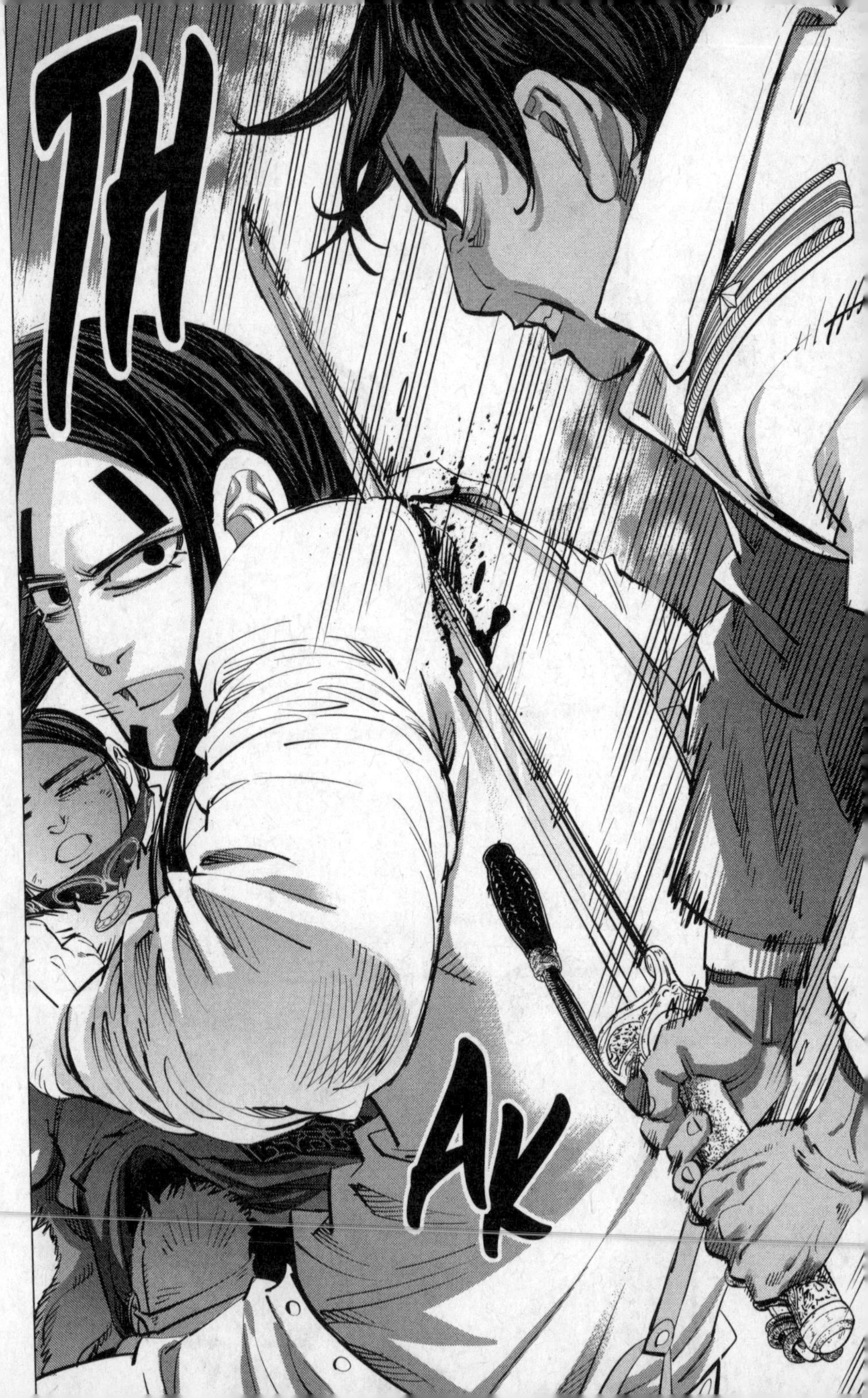
THAK

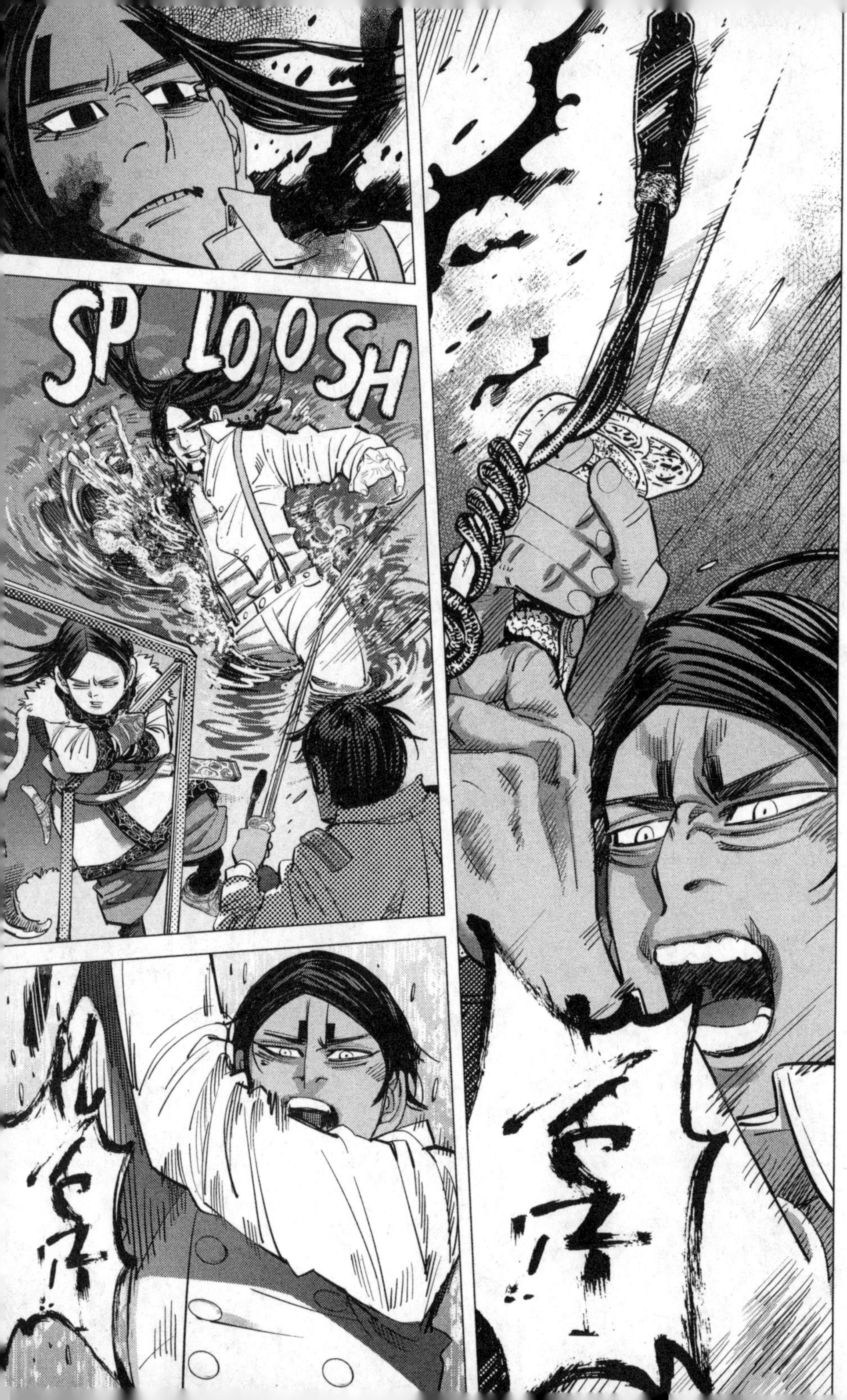
SPLOOSH

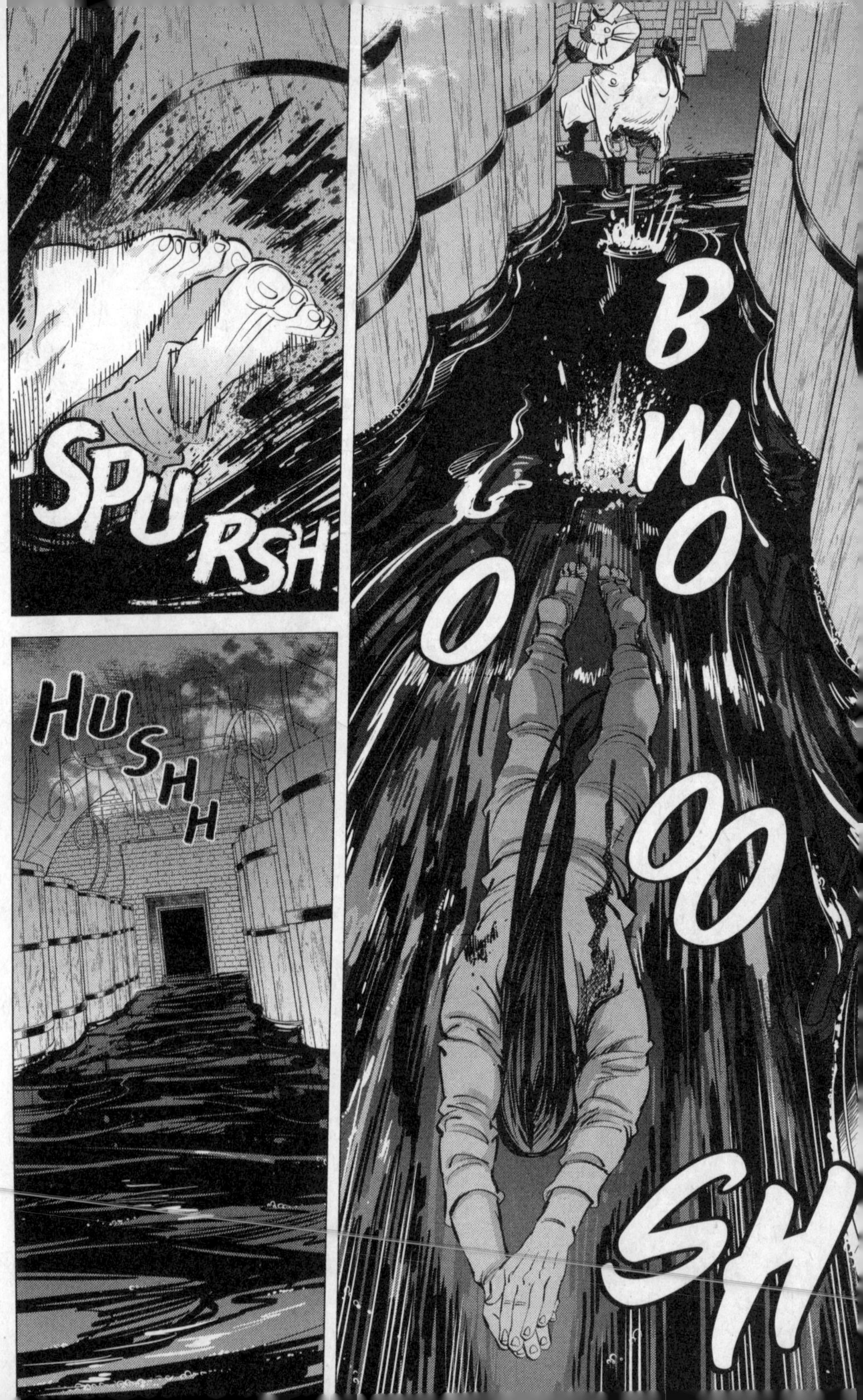
BWOOOOSH
SPURSH
HUSHH

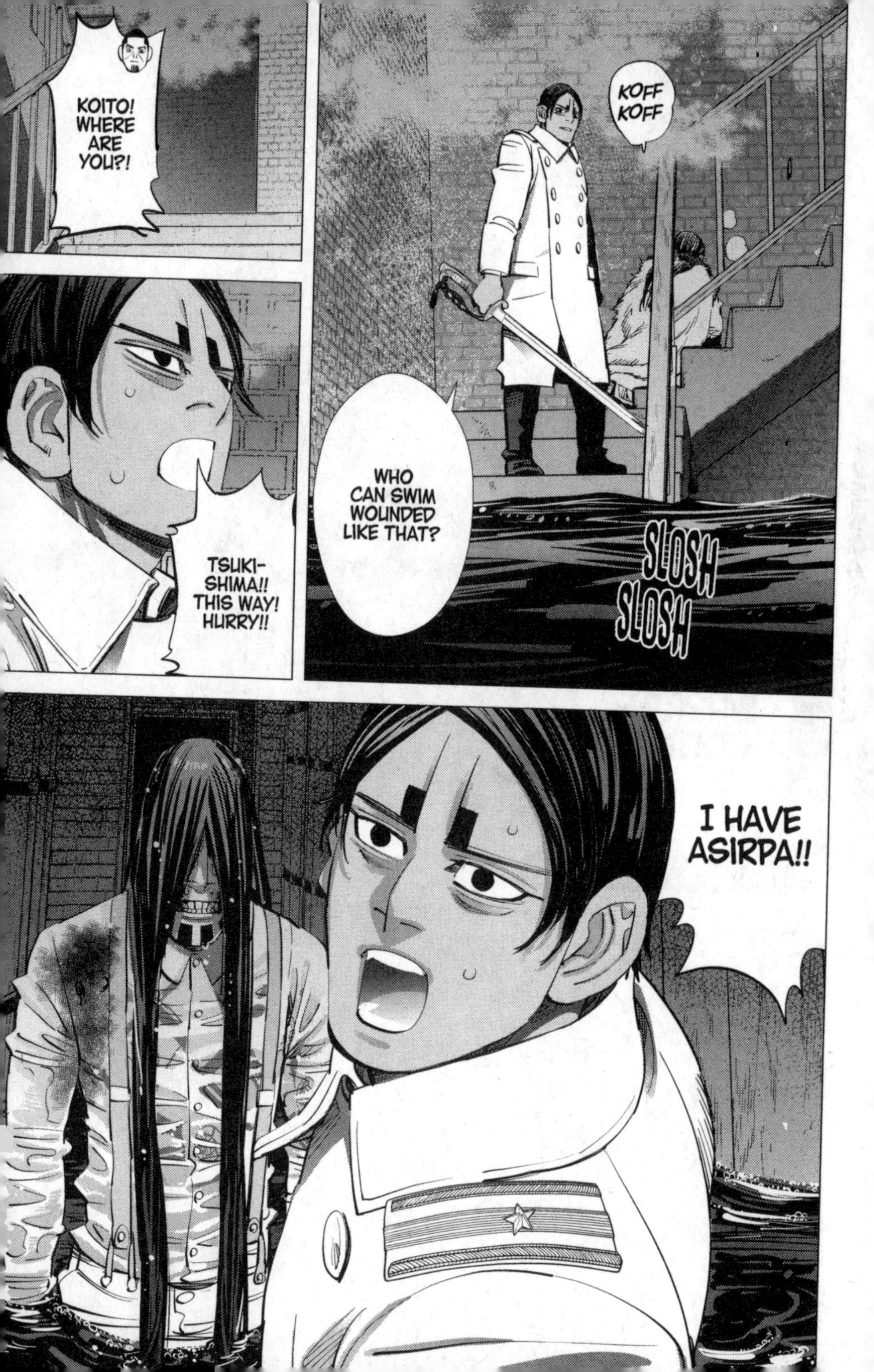
KOFF KOFF
WHO CAN SWIM WOUNDED LIKE THAT?
SLOSH SLOSH
KOITO! WHERE ARE YOU?!
TSUKI-SHIMA!! THIS WAY! HURRY!!
I HAVE ASIRPA!!

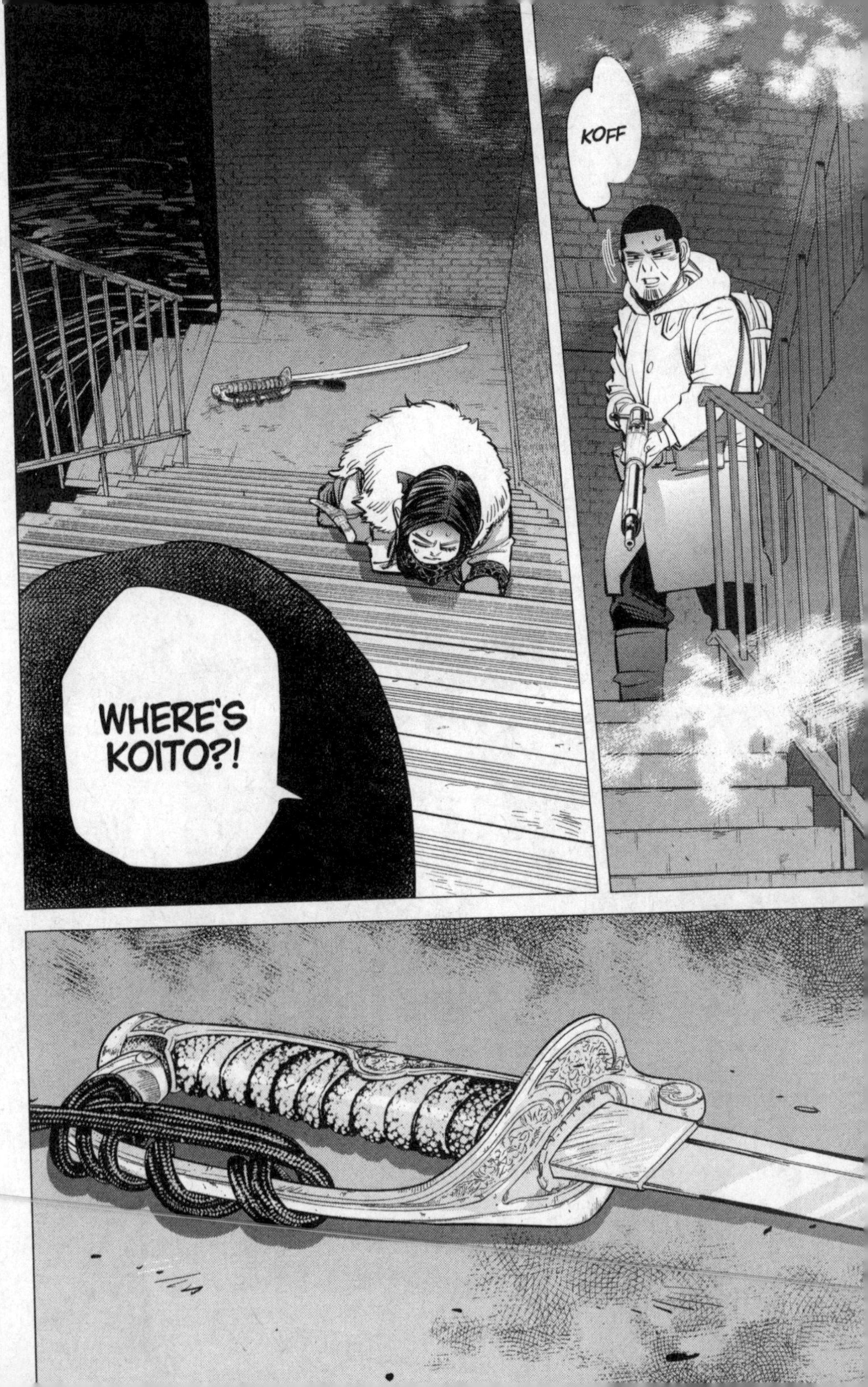
KOFF
WHERE'S KOITO?!

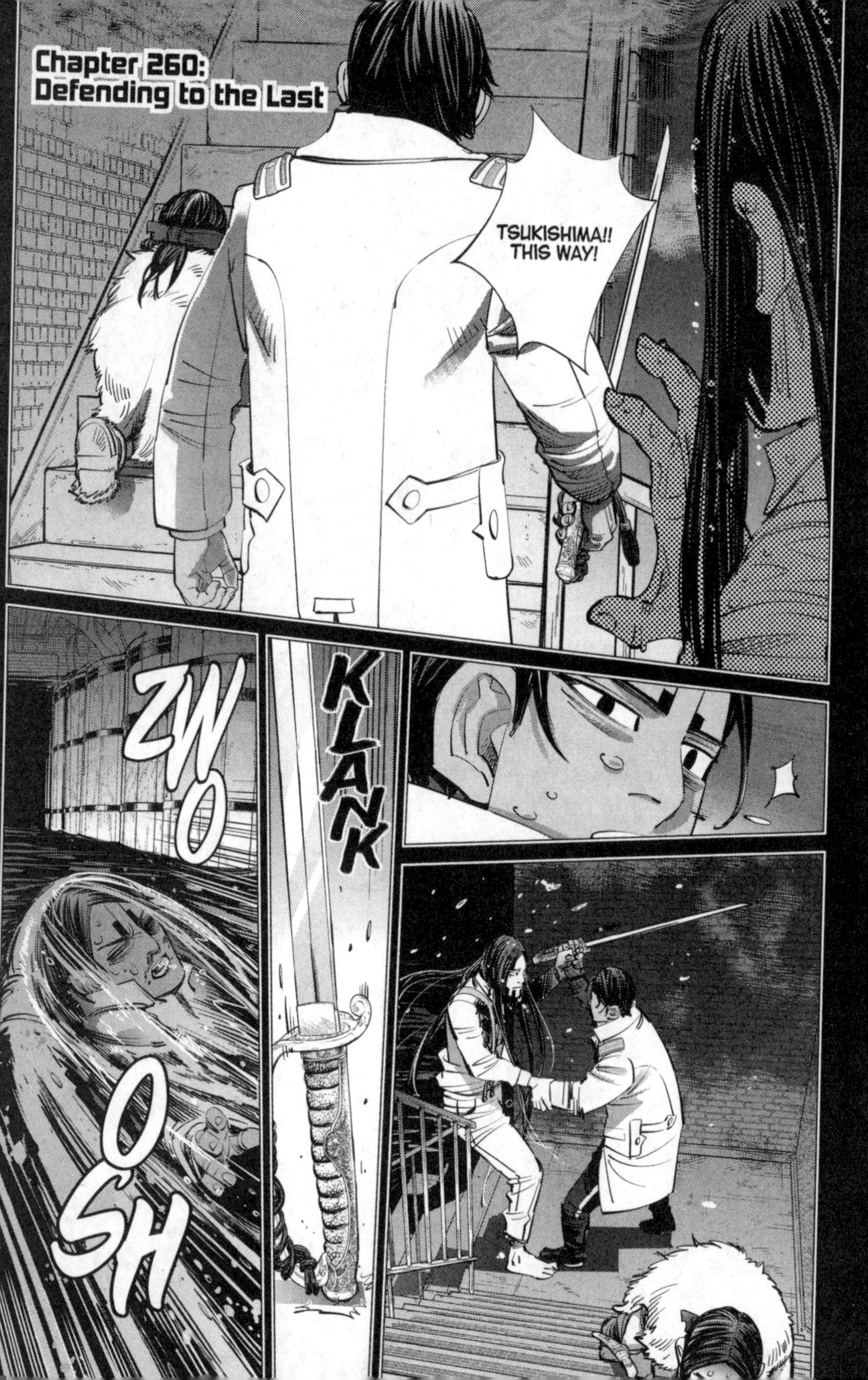
Chapter 260:
Defending to the Last
TSUKISHIMA!! THIS WAY!
KLANK
ZWOOSH

Chapter 260: Defending to the Last

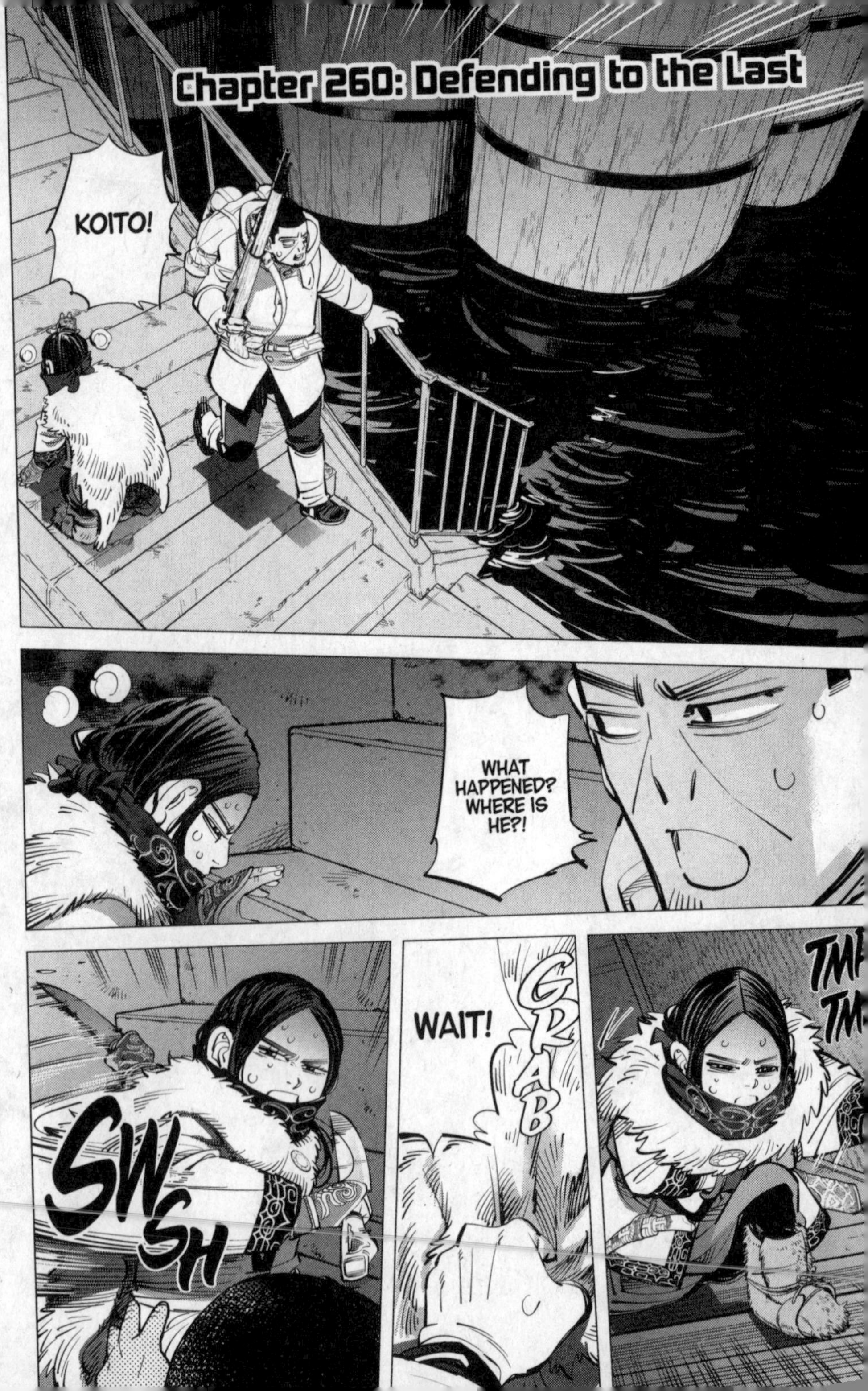
KOITO!
WHAT HAPPENED? WHERE IS HE?!
TM
TM
WAIT!
GRAB
SWSH

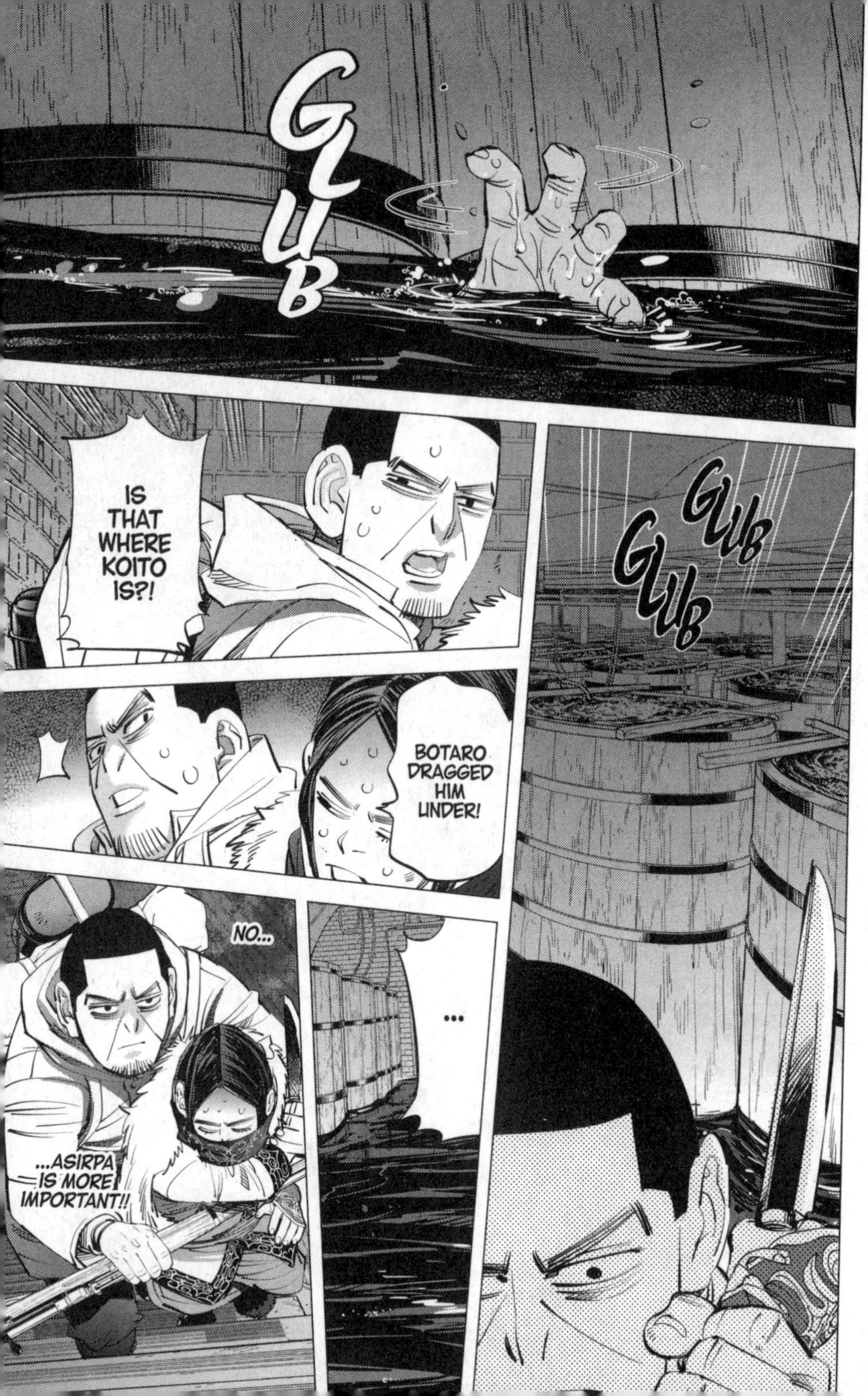
GLUB
GLUB GLUB
IS THAT WHERE KOITO IS?!
BOTARO DRAGGED HIM UNDER!
...
NO...
...ASIRPA IS MORE IMPORTANT!!

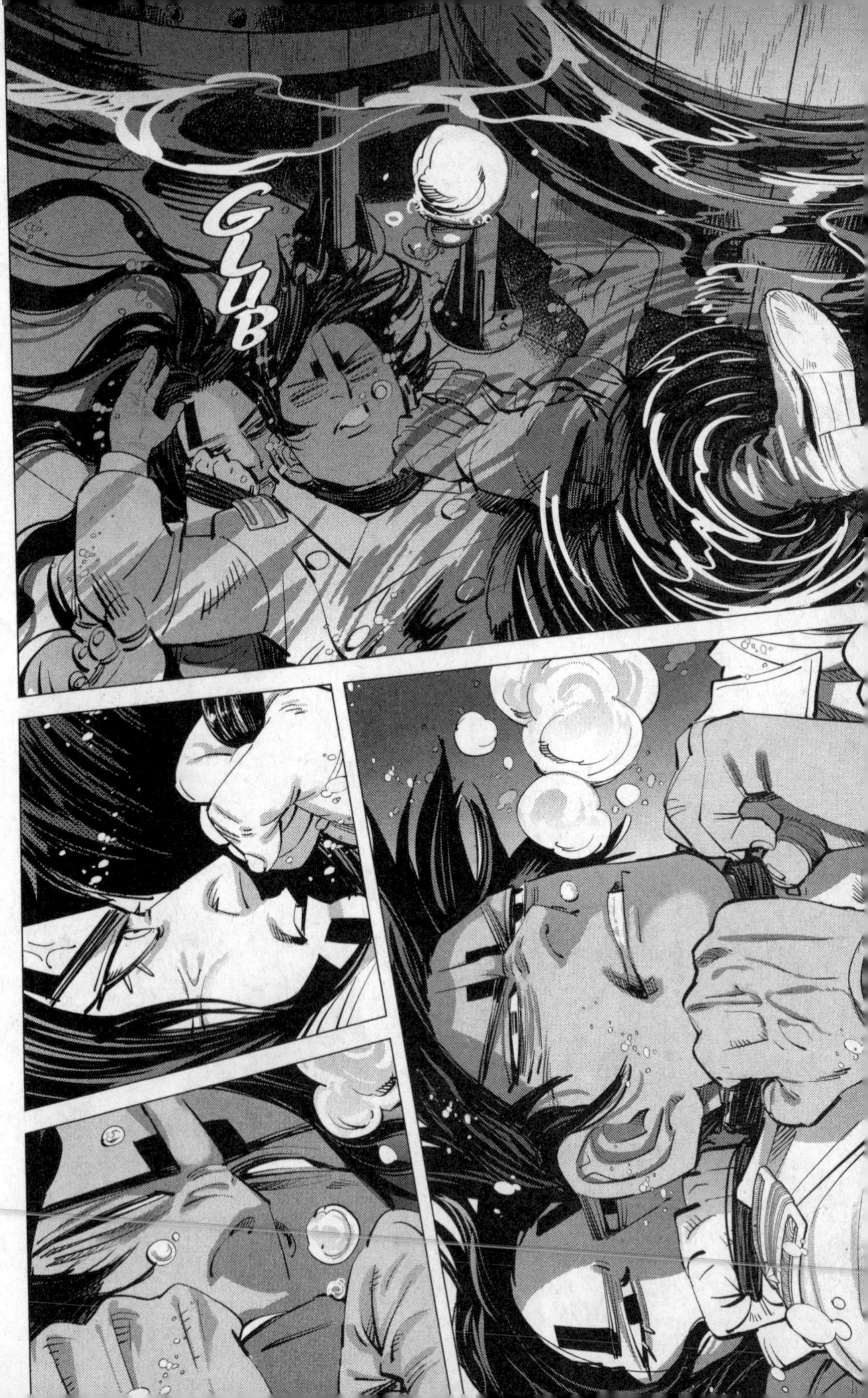
GLUB

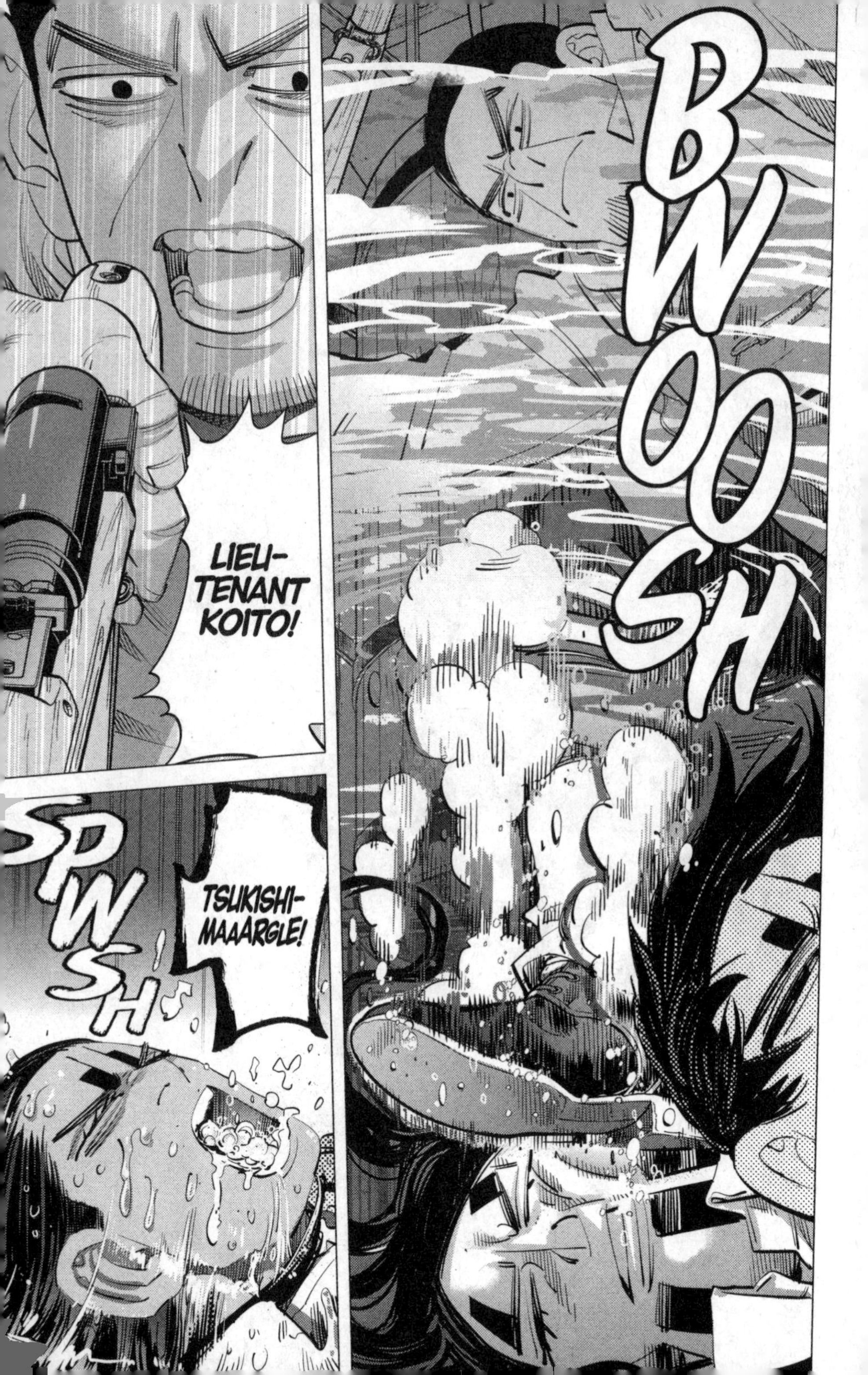
BWOOSH
LIEU-TENANT KOITO!
TSUKISHI-MAAARGLE!
SPWSH

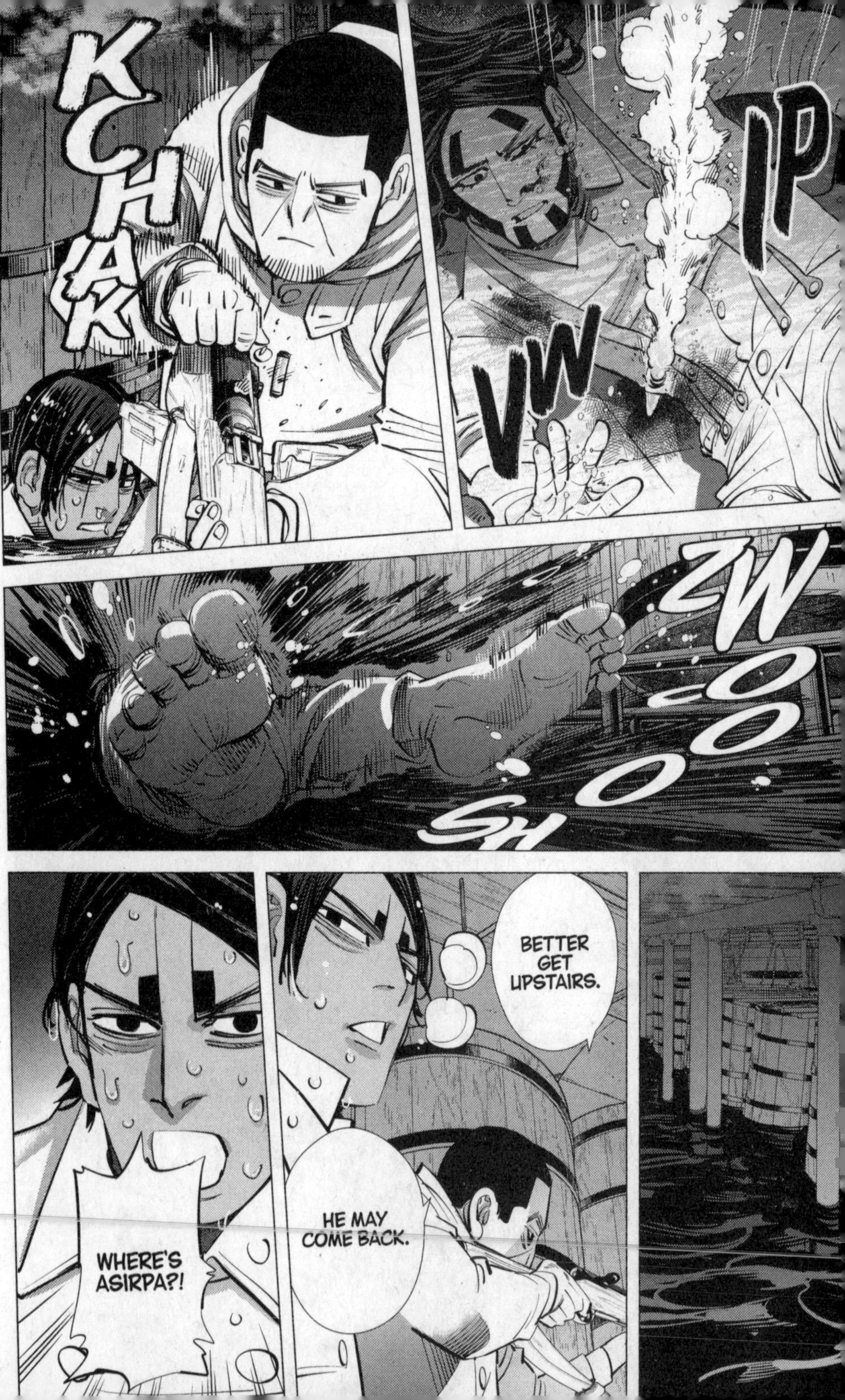
VWIP
KCHAK
ZWOOOOSH
BETTER GET UPSTAIRS.
HE MAY COME BACK.
WHERE'S ASIRPA?!

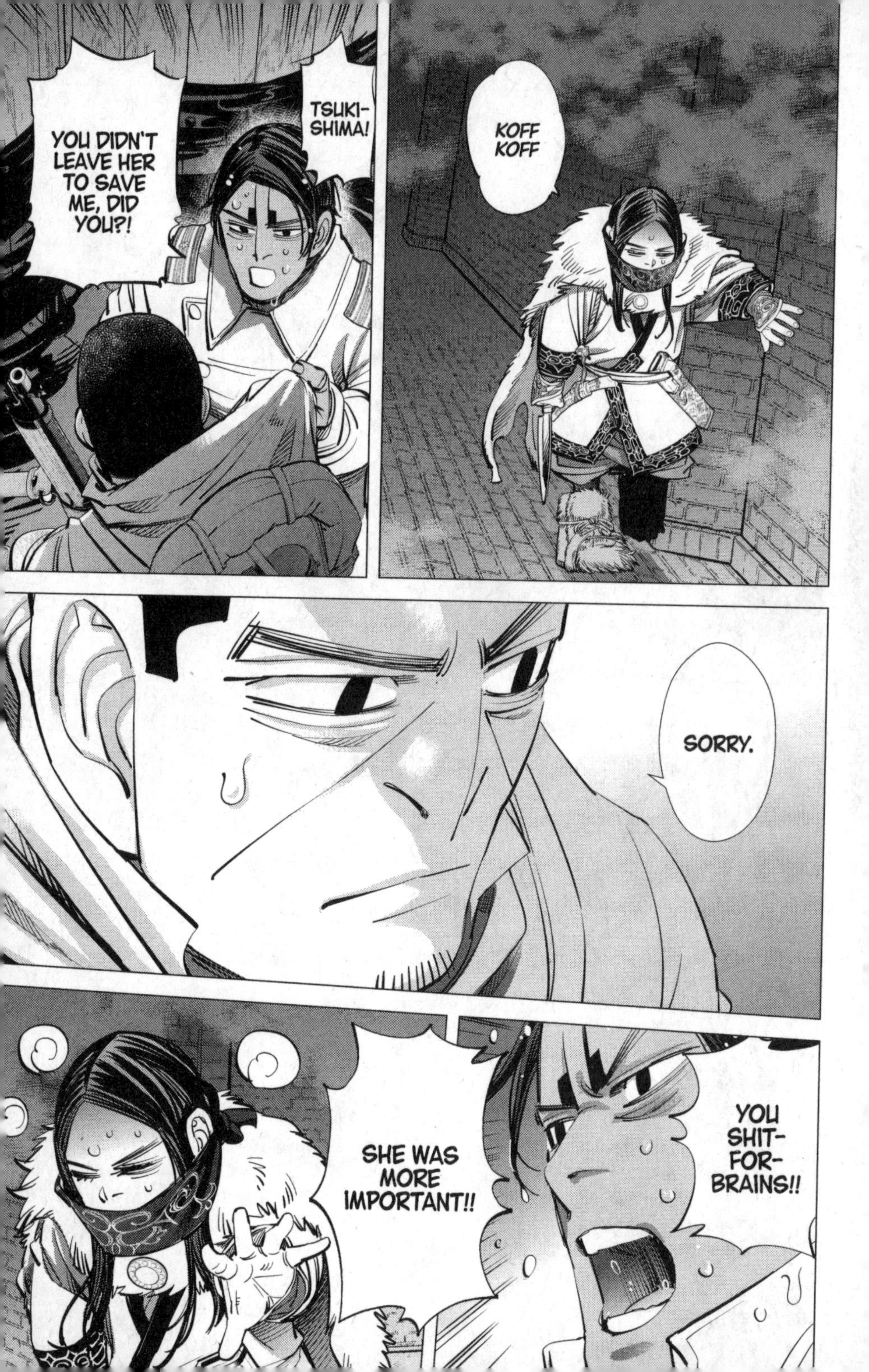
KOFF KOFF
TSUKI-SHIMA!
YOU DIDN'T LEAVE HER TO SAVE ME, DID YOU?!
SORRY.
YOU SHIT-FOR-BRAINS!!
SHE WAS MORE IMPORTANT!!

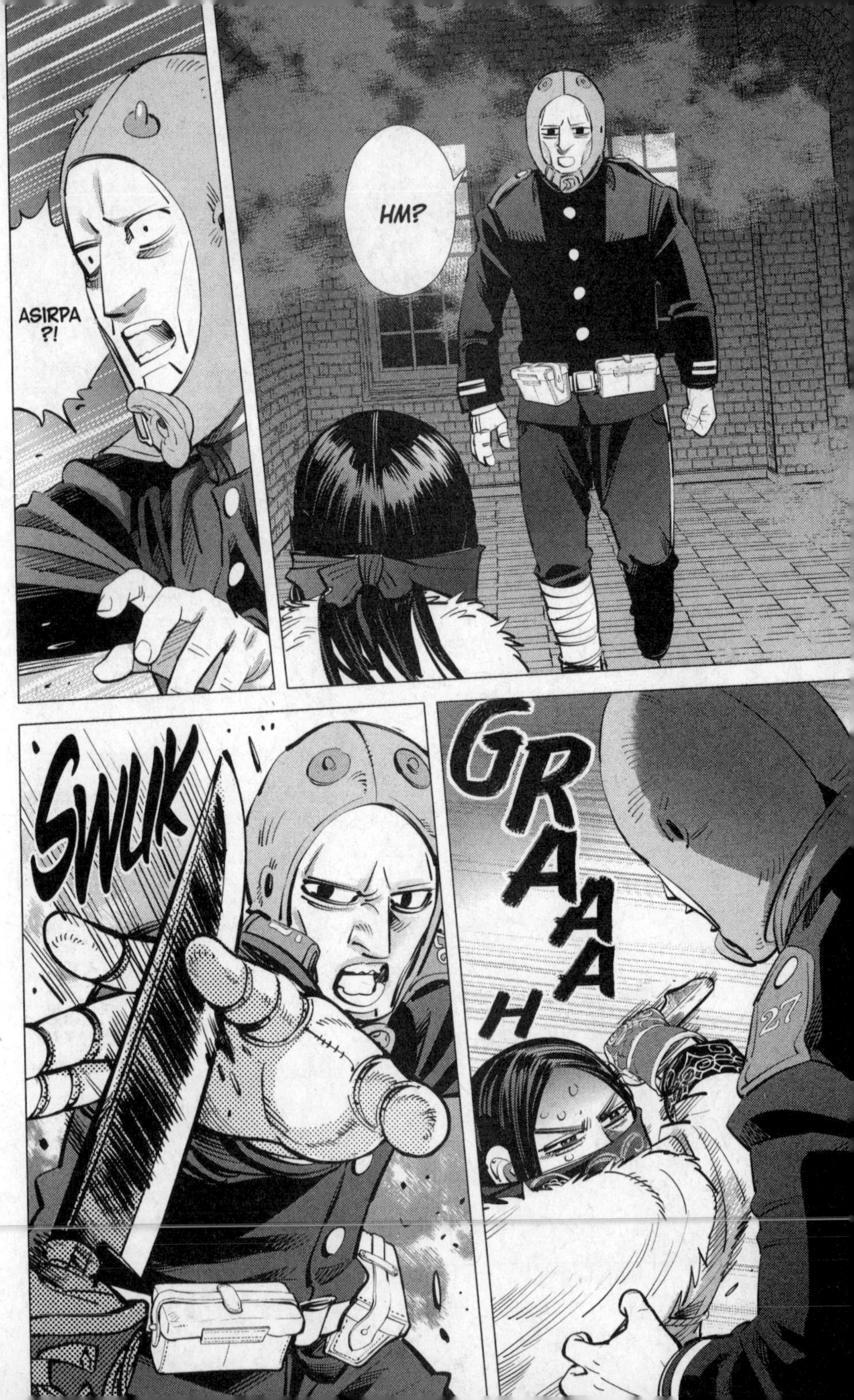
HM?
ASIRPA ?!
GRAAAAH
SWUK

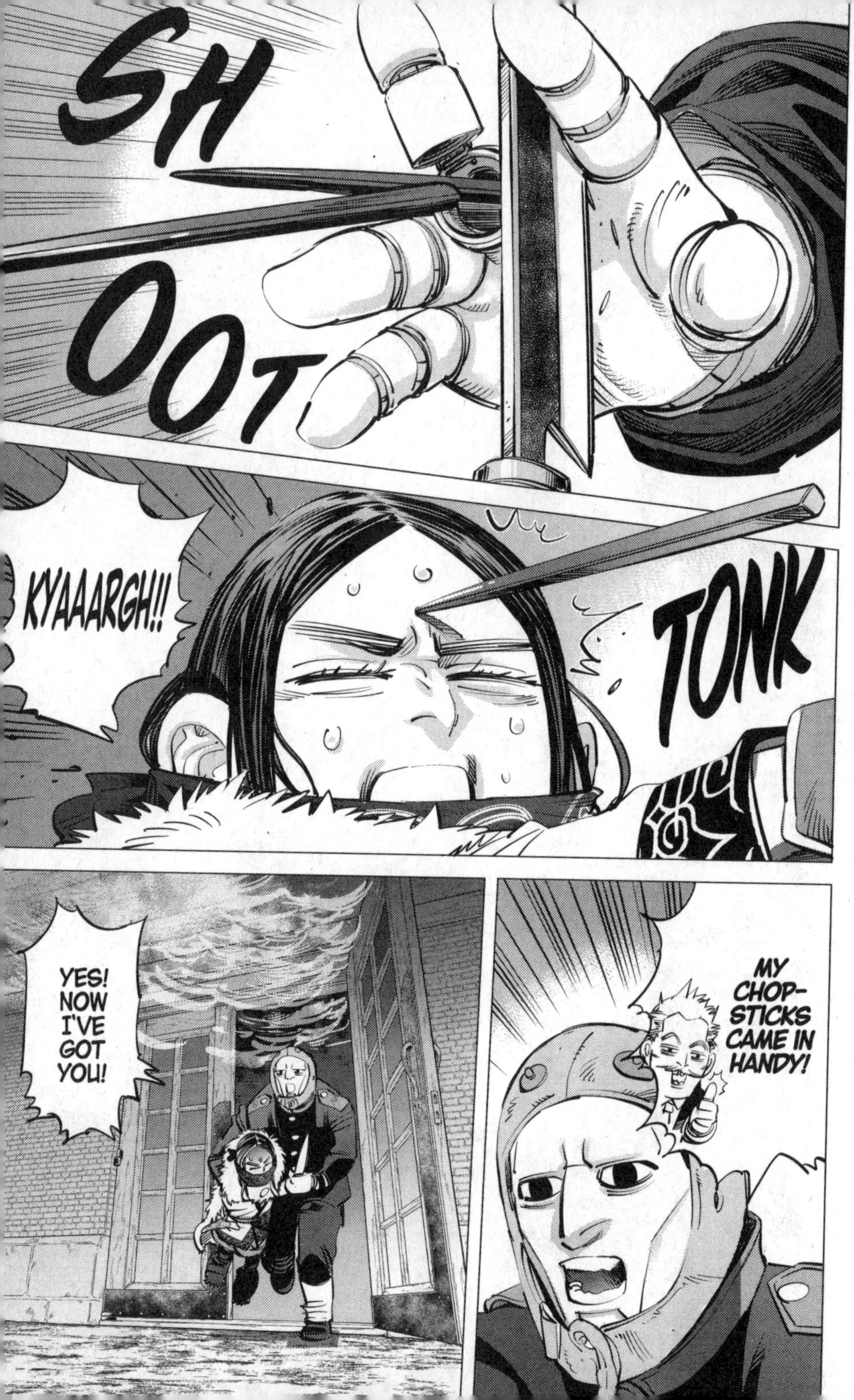
SHOOOT
TONK
KYAAARGH!!
MY CHOP-STICKS CAME IN HANDY!
YES! NOW I'VE GOT YOU!

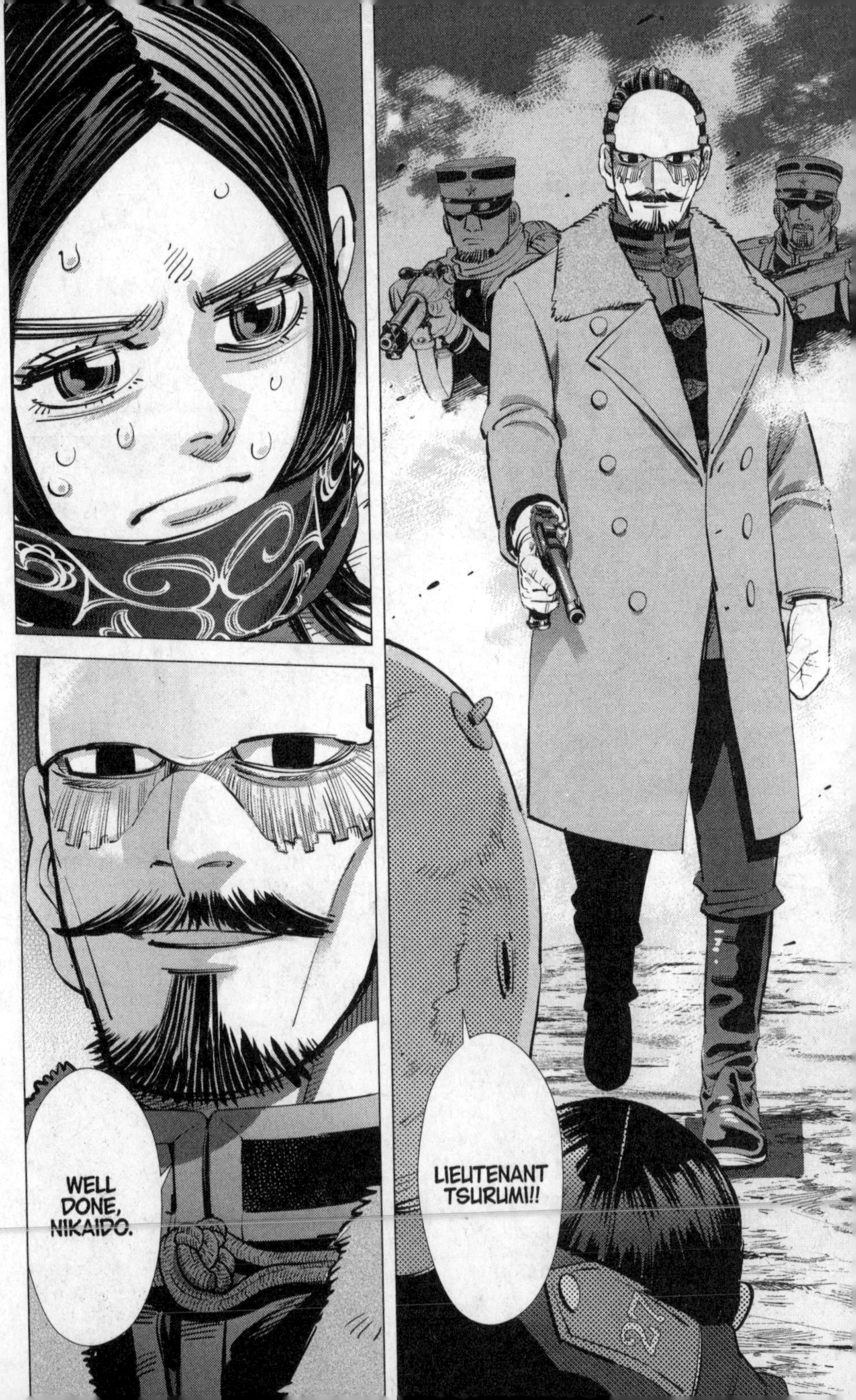
LIEUTENANT TSURUMI!!
WELL DONE, NIKAIDO.

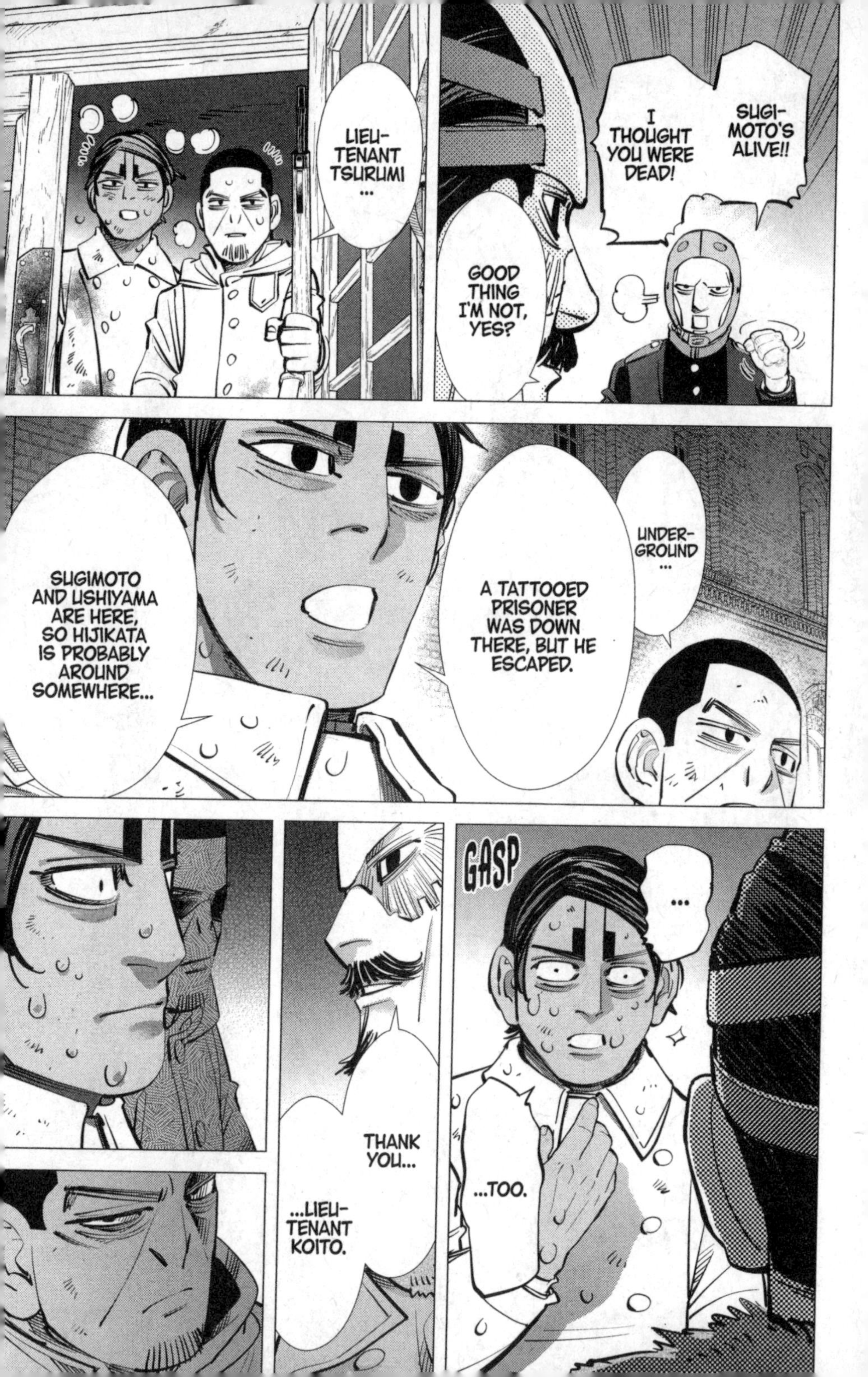
SUGI-MOTO'S ALIVE!!
I THOUGHT YOU WERE DEAD!
GOOD THING I'M NOT, YES?
LIEU-TENANT TSURUMI ...
UNDER-GROUND ...
A TATTOOED PRISONER WAS DOWN THERE, BUT HE ESCAPED.
SUGIMOTO AND USHIYAMA ARE HERE, SO HIJIKATA IS PROBABLY AROUND SOMEWHERE...
GASP
...
...TOO.
THANK YOU...
...LIEU-TENANT KOITO.

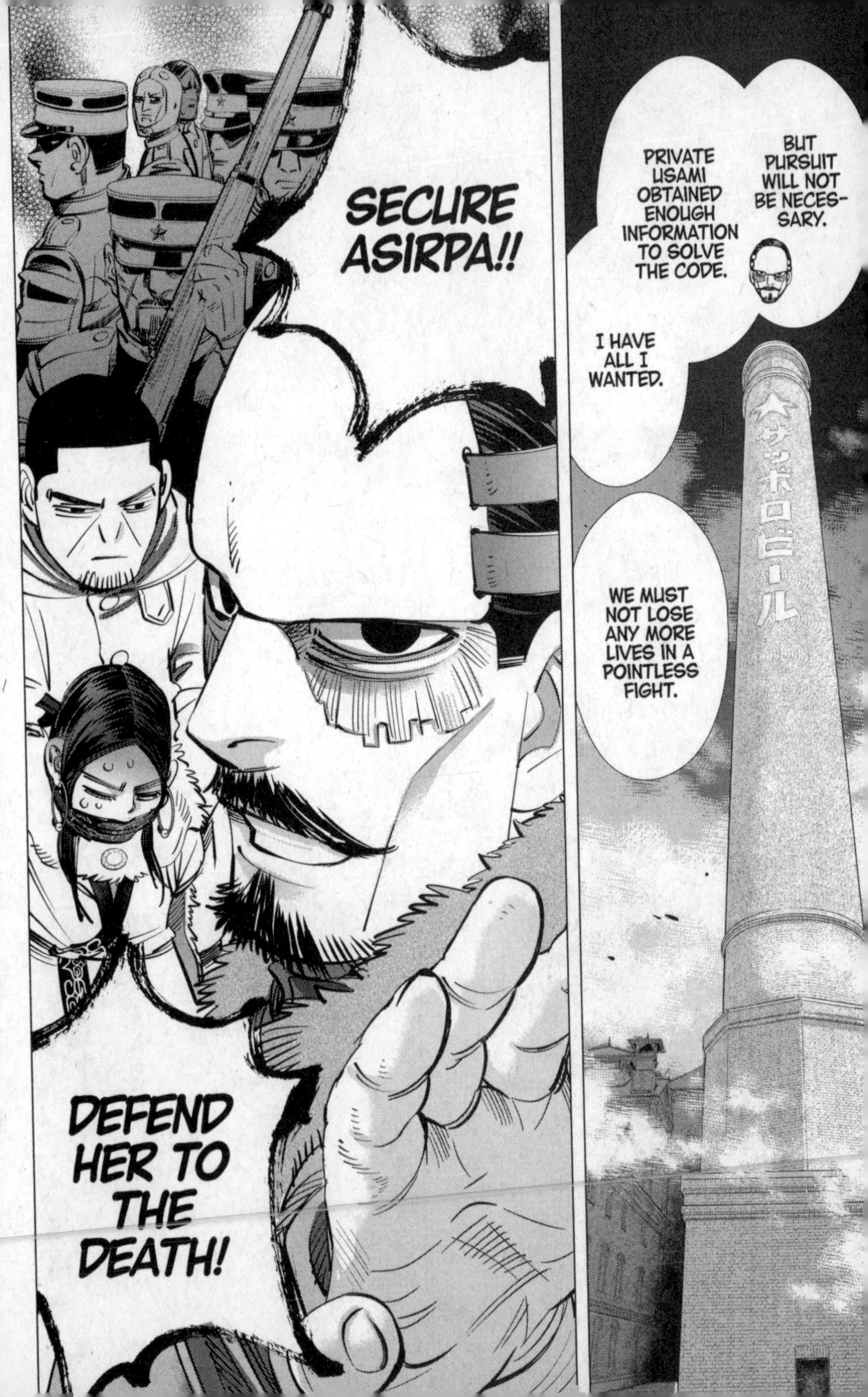
BUT PURSUIT WILL NOT BE NECES-SARY.
PRIVATE USAMI OBTAINED ENOUGH INFORMATION TO SOLVE THE CODE.
I HAVE ALL I WANTED.
サッポロビール
WE MUST NOT LOSE ANY MORE LIVES IN A POINTLESS FIGHT.
SECURE ASIRPA!!
DEFEND HER TO THE DEATH!

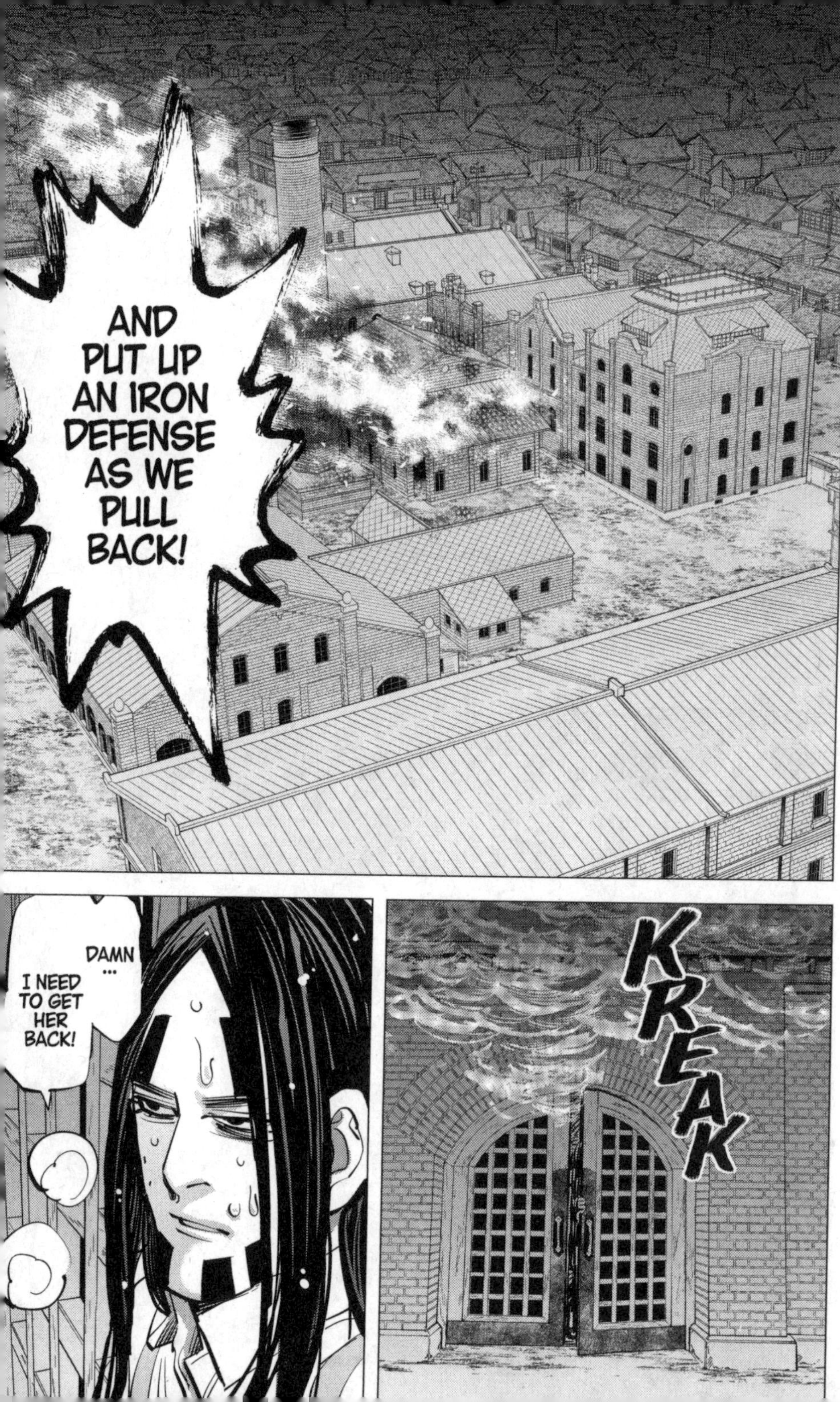
AND PUT UP AN IRON DEFENSE AS WE PULL BACK!
KREAK
DAMN...
I NEED TO GET HER BACK!

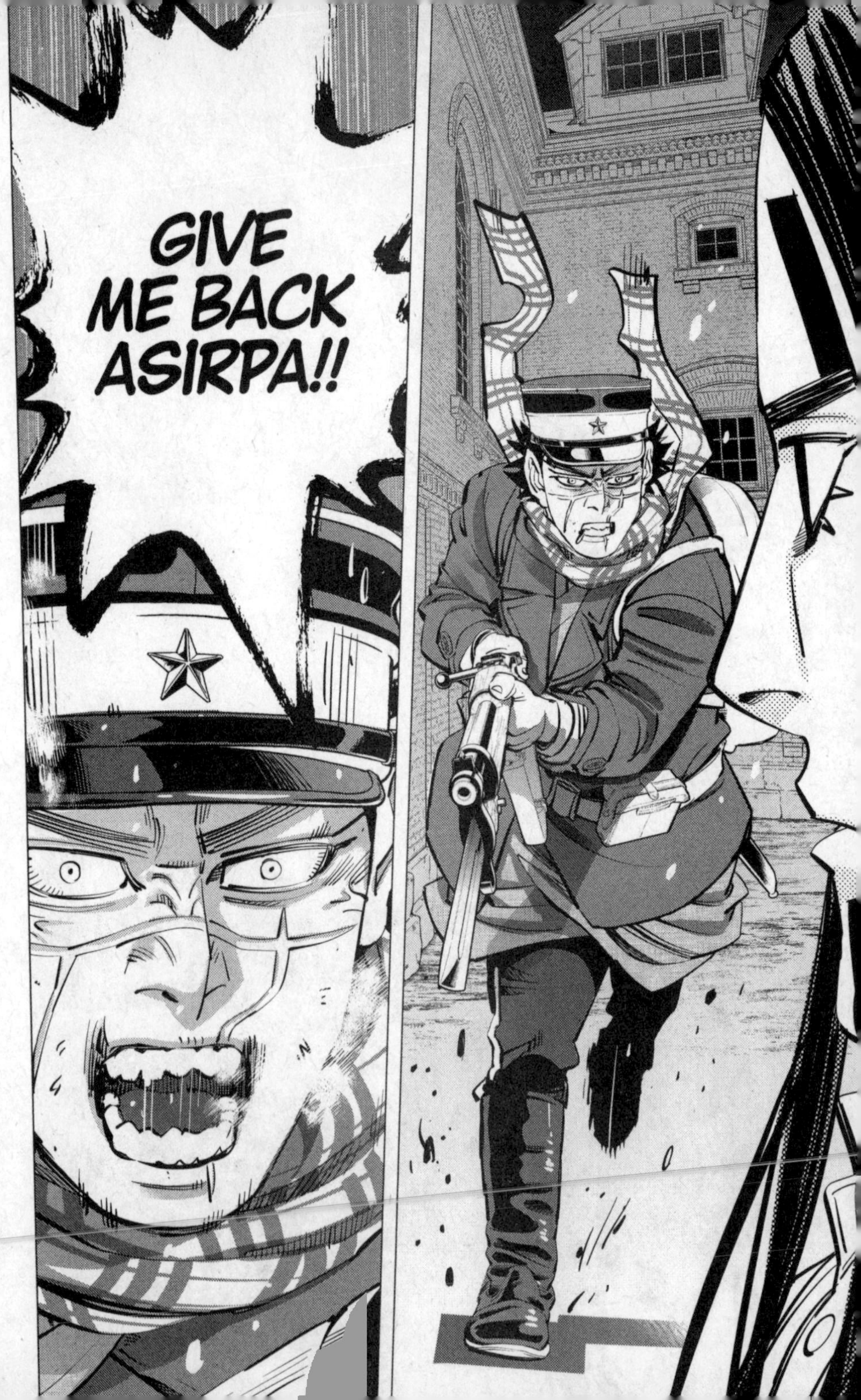
GIVE ME BACK ASIRPA!!

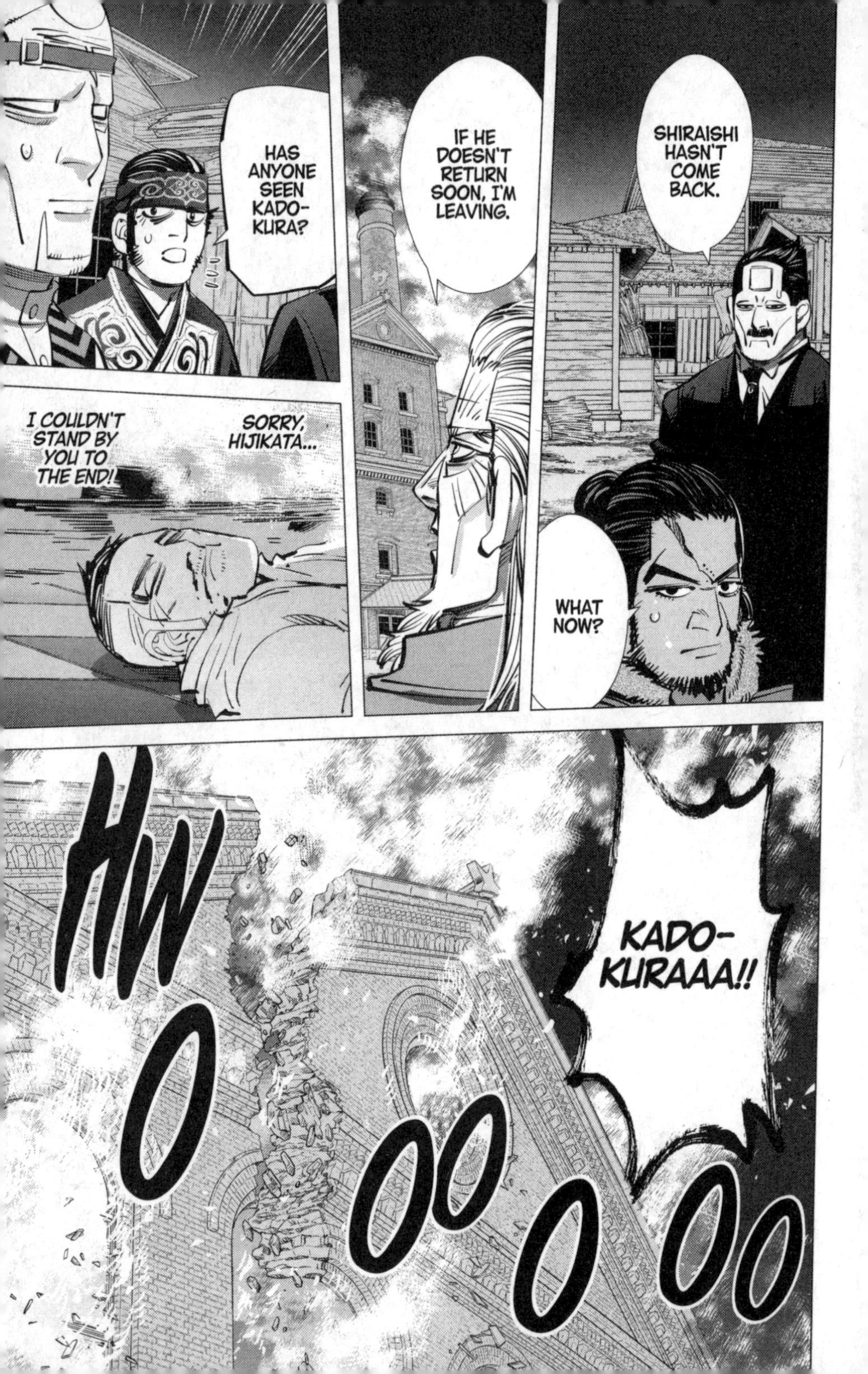
SHIRAISHI HASN'T COME BACK.
WHAT NOW?
IF HE DOESN'T RETURN SOON, I'M LEAVING.
HAS ANYONE SEEN KADO-KURA?
SORRY, HIJIKATA...
I COULDN'T STAND BY YOU TO THE END!
KADO-KURAAA!!
HWOOOOOOOO

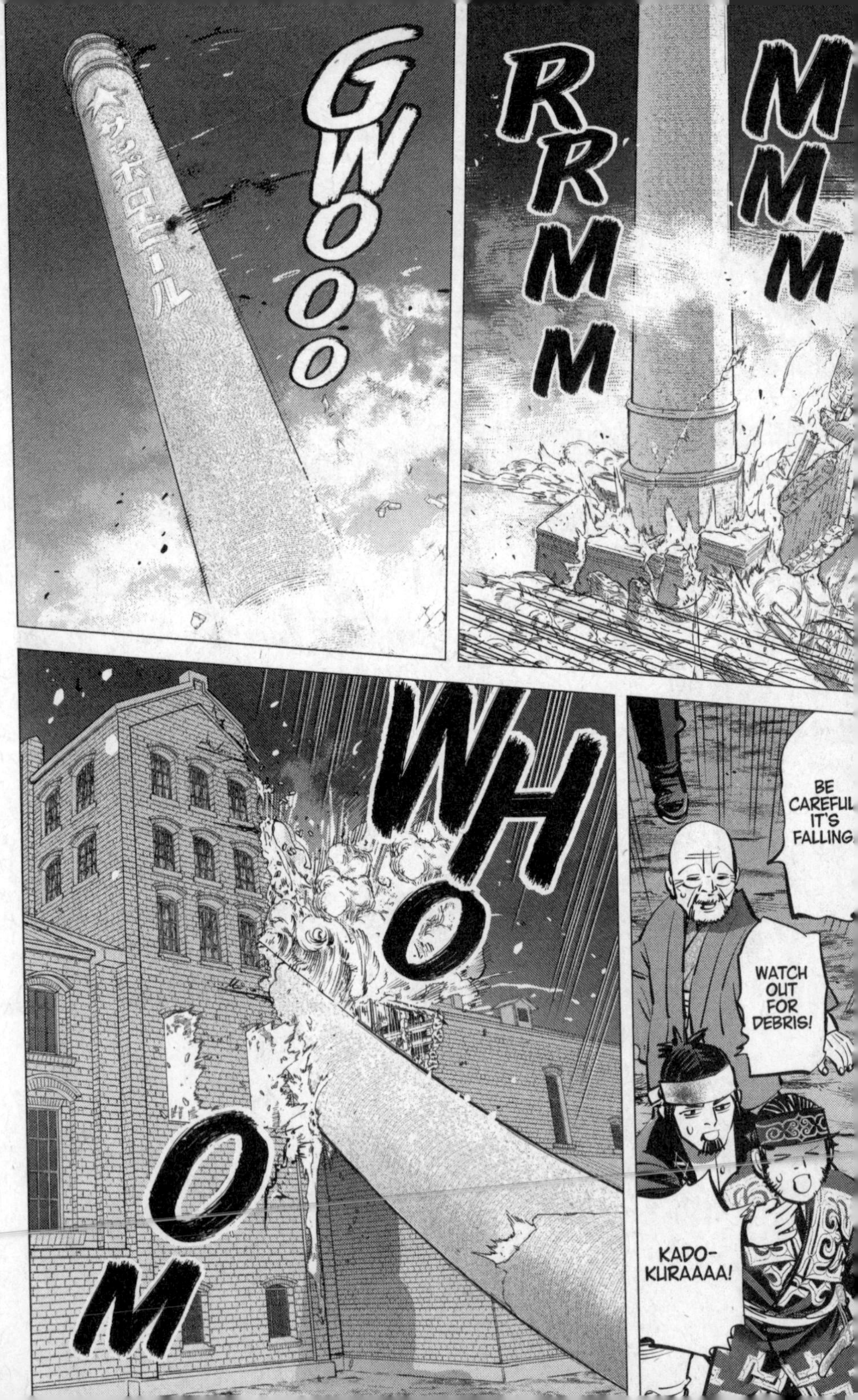
RRMM
MMM
★サッポロビール
GWOOOO
BE CAREFUL IT'S FALLING
WATCH OUT FOR DEBRIS!
KADO-KURAAAA!
WHOOOM

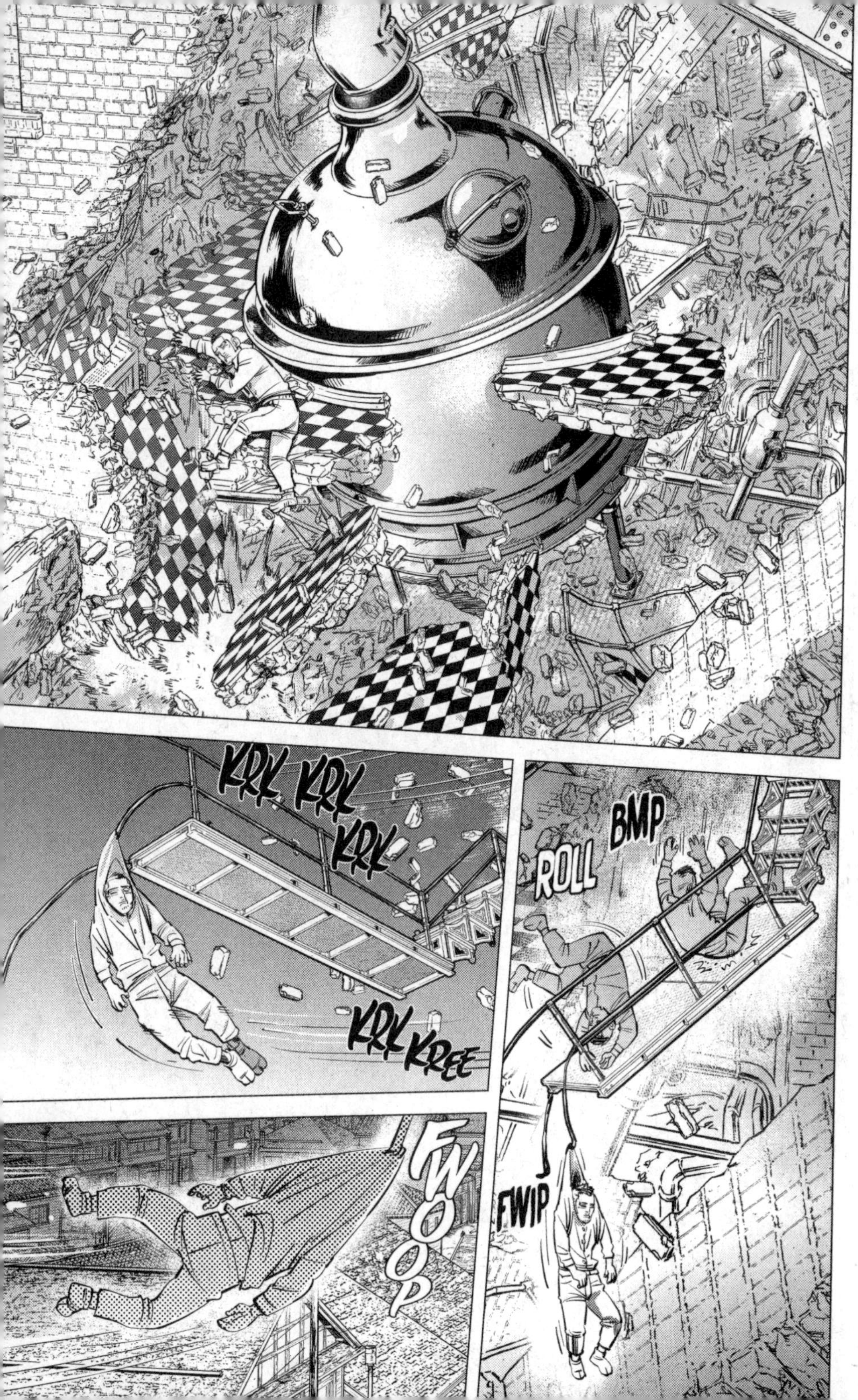
BMP
ROLL
FWIP
KRK KRK KRK
KRK KREE
FWOOP

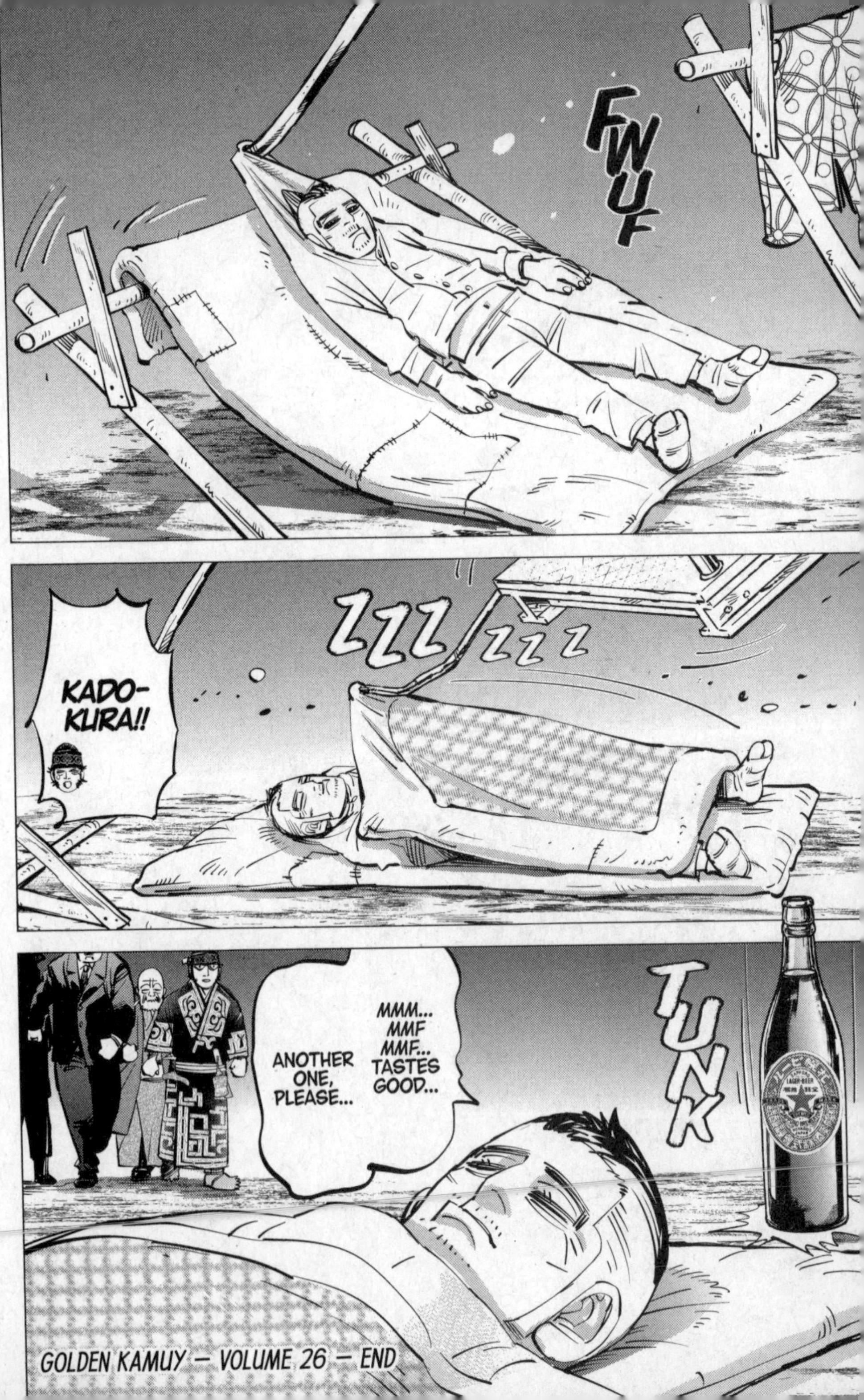
FWUF
ZZZ ZZZ
KADO-KURA!!
TUNK
MMM... MMF MMF... TASTES GOOD...
ANOTHER ONE, PLEASE...
GOLDEN KAMUY — VOLUME 26 — END

Ainu Language Supervision • Hiroshi Nakagawa •
Russian Language Supervision • Eugenio Uzhinin •
Uilta Language Supervision • Yoshiko Yamada • Satsuma Dialect Supervision •
Shogo Nakamura • Niigata Dialect Supervision • Fumiya Ito

Cooperation from • Hokkaido Ainu Association and the Abashiri Prison Museum • Otaru City General Museum • Waseda University
Aizu Museum • Kazunobu Goto, • Botanic Garden and Museum, Hokkaido University • National Museum of Ethnology •
Nibutani Ainu Culture Museum • The Ainu Museum • Moon Kabato Museum • Kushiro City Museum • Atsuyo Hisai •
Tatsuhiro Tokuda • Shigeharu Terui • All Japan Federation of Karafuto • Tokyo National Museum • Sakhalin Regional Museum •
Shiraishi Hidetoshi • Masato Tamura • Historical Village of Hokkaido • Asahikawa City Museum • Hokuchin Museum •
Tomakomai City Museum • Museum Meijimura • Sapporo Breweries Ltd.

Photo Credits • Takayuki Monma, Takanori Matsuda, Kozo Ishikawa, Shigekazu Kizu, Minoru Noda

Ainu Culture References

Chiri, Takanaka and Yokoyama, Takao. *Ainugo Eiri Jiten* (Ainu Language Illustrated Dictionary). Tokyo: Kagyusha, 1994

Kayano, Shigeru. *Ainu no Mingu* (Ainu Folkcrafts). Kawagoe: Suzusawa Book Store, 1978

Kayano, Shigeru. *Kayano Shigeru no Ainugo Jiten* (KayanoShigeru's Ainu Language Dictionary). Tokyo: Sanseido, 1996

Musashino Art University – The Research Institute for Culture and Cultural History. *Ainu no Mingu Jissoku Zushu* (Ainu Folkcrafts – Collection of Drawing and Figures). Biratori: Biratori-cho Council for Promoting Ainu Culture, 2014

Satouchi, Ai. *Ainu-shiki ekoroji-seikatsu: Haruzo Ekashi ni manabu shizen no chie* (Ainu Style Ecological Living: Haruzo Ekashi Teaches the Wisdom of Nature). Tokyo: Kabushiki gaisha Shogakukan, 2008

Chiri, Yukie. *Ainu Shin'yoshu* (Chiri Yukie's Ainu Epic Tales). Tokyo: Iwanami Shoten, 1978

Namikawa, Kenji. *Ainu Minzoku no Kiseki* (The Path of the Ainu People). Tokyo: Yamakawa Publishing, 2004

Mook. *Senjuumin Ainu Minzoku* (Bessatsu Taiyo) (The Ainu People (Extra Issue Taiyo). Tokyo: Heibonsha, 2004

Kinoshita, Seizo. *Shiraoikotan Kinoshita Seizo Isaku Shashin Shu* (Shiraoikotan: Kinoshita Seizo's Posthumous Photography Collection). Hokkaido Shiraoi-gun Shiraoi-cho: Shiraoi Heritage Conservation Foundation, 1988

The Ainu Museum. *Ainu no Ifuku Bunka* (The Culture of Ainu Clothing). Hokkaido Shiraoi-gun Shiraoi-cho: Shiraoi Ainu Museum, 1991

Keira, Tomoko and Kaji, Sayaka. *Ainu no Shiki* (Ainu's Four Seasons). Tokyo: Akashi Shoten, 1995

Fukuoka, Itoko and Sato, Kazuko. *Ainu Shokubutsushi* (Ainu Botanical Journal). Chiba Urayasu-Shi: Sofukan, 1995

Hayakawa, Noboru. *Ainu no Minzoku* (Ainu Folklore). Iwasaki Bijutsusha, 1983

Sunazawa, Kura. *Ku Sukuppu Orushibe* (The Memories of My Generation). Hokkaido, Sapporo-shi: Miyama Shobo, 1983

Haginaka, Miki et al. *Kikigaki Ainu no Shokuji* (Oral History of Ainu Diet). Tokyo: Rural Culture Association Japan, 1992

Nakagawa, Hiroshi. *New Express Ainu Go*. Tokyo: Hakusuisha, 2013

Nakagawa, Hiroshi. *Ainugo Chitose Hogen Jiten* (The Ainu-Japanese dictionary). Chiba Urayasu-Shi: Sofukan, 1995

Nakagawa, Hiroshi and Nakamoto, Mutsuko. *Kamuy Yukara de Ainu Go wo Manabu* (Learning Ainu with Kamuy Yukar). Tokyo: Hakusuisha, 2007

Nakagawa, Hiroshi. *Katari au Kotoba no Chikara – Kamuy tachi to Ikiru Sekai* (The Power of Spoken Words – Living in a World with Kamuy). Tokyo: Iwanami Shoten, 2010

Sarashina, Genzo and Sarashina, Hikari. *Kotan Seibutsu Ki <1 Juki / Zassou hen>* (Kotan Wildlife Vol. 1 – Trees and Weeds). Hosei University Publishing, 1992/2007

Sarashina, Genzo and Sarashina, Hikari. *Kotan Seibutsu Ki <2 Yacho / Kaijuu / Gyozoku hen>* (Kotan Wildlife Vol. 2 – Birds, Sea Creatures, and Fish). Hosei University Publishing, 1992/2007

Sarashina, Genzo and Sarashina, Hikari. *Kotan Seibutsu Ki <3 Yachou / Mizudori / Konchu hen>* (Kotan Wildlife Vol. 3 – Shorebirds, Seabirds, and Insects). Hosei University Publishing, 1992/2007

Sarashina, Genzo. *Ainu Minwashu* (Collection of Ainu Folktales). Kita Shobou, 1963

Sarashina, Genzo. *Ainu Rekishi to Minzoku* (Ainu History and Folklore). Shakai Shisousha, 1968

Kawakami Yuji. *Sarunkur Ainu Monogatari* (The Tale of Sarunkur Ainu). Kawagoe: Suzusawa Book Store, 2003/2005

Kawakami, Yuji. *Ekashi to Fuchi wo Tazunete* (Visiting Ekashi and Fuchi). Kawagoe: Suzusawa Book Store, 1991

Council for the Conservation of Ainu Culture. *Ainu Minzokushi* (Ainu People Magazine). Dai-ichi Hoki, 1970

Okamura, Kichiemon and Clancy, Judith A. *Ainu no Ishou* (The Clothes of the Ainu People). Kyoto Shoin, 1993

Hokkaido Cultural Property Protection Association. *Ainu Ifuku Chousa Houkokusho <1 Ainu Josei ga Denshou Suru Ibunka>* (The Ainu Clothing Research Report Vol. 1 – Traditional Clothing Passed Down Through Generations of Ainu Women). 1986

Yotsuji, Ichiro. Photos by Mizutani, Morio. *Ainu no Monyo* (Decorative Arts of the Ainu). Kasakura Publishing, 1981

Yoshida, Iwao. *Ainushi Shiryoshu* (Collection of Ainu Historical Documents). Hokkaido Publication Project Center, 1983

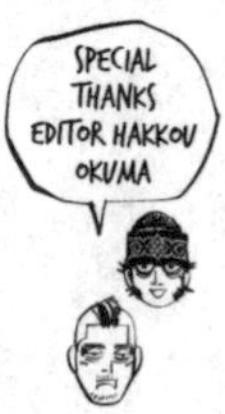
SPECIAL THANKS EDITOR HAKKOU OKUMA

Kubodera, Itsuhiko. *Ainu no Mukashibanashi* (Old Stories of the Ainu). Miyaishoten, 1972

Kubodera, Itsuhiko (trans.). *Ainu Minzokushi* (Ainu People Magazine). Dai-ichi Hoki

Inoue, Koichi and Latyshev, Vladislav M. (coed.). *Karafuto Ainu no Mingu* (Karafuto Ainu Folkcraft). Hokkaido Publication Project Center, 2002

Russia ga Mita Ainu Bunka (Ainu Culture as Seen by Russia). The Foundation for Research and Promotion of Ainu Culture, 2013

Russia Minzokugaku Hakubutsukan Ainu Shiryoten—Russia ga Mita Shimaguni no Hitobito (Russia Museum of Ethnology Ainu Materials Exhibition—Island Peoples as Seen by Russia). The Foundation for Research and Promotion of Ainu Culture, 2005

The Foundation for Research and Promotion of Ainu Culture (ed.). *Senjima, Karafuto, Hokkaido—Ainu no Kurashi* (Ainu Life on the Kuril Islands, Karafuto and Hokkaido). The Senri Foundation, 2011

SPb-Ainu Project Group (ed.). *Russia Kagaku Academy Jinruigaku Minzokugaku Hakubutsukan Shozo Ainu Shiryo Mokuroku* (Ainu Collections of Peter the Great Museum of Anthropology and Ethnography Russian Academy of Sciences Catalogue). Sofukan, 1998

Yamamoto, Yuko. *Karafuto Ainu—Jukyo to Mingu* (Residences and Folkcraft of the Karafuto Ainu). Sagami Shobo, 1970

Yamamoto, Yuko (author and ed.). Chiri, Mashiho and Onuki, Emiko co-authors). *Karafuto Shizen Minzoku no Seikatsu* (Lifestyles of Karafuto Natural Peoples). Sagami Shobo, 1979

Chiri, Mashiho. *Chiri Mashiho Chosakushu 3 Seikatsu-shi / Minzokugaku-hen* (Mashiho Chiri Collected Works, Vol. 3: Lifestyles and Ethnology). Heibonsha, 1973

Yamamoto, Yuko. *Hoppo Shizen Minzoku Minwa Shusei* (Northern Natural Peoples Folk Tales Compilation). Sagami Shobo, 1968

Yamamoto, Yuko. *Karafuto Genshi Minzoku no Seikatsu* (Lifestyles of Karafuto Primitive Peoples). ARS, 1943

Nishitsuru, Sadaka. *Karafuto Ainu*. Miyama Shobo, 1974

Kasai, Takechiyo. *Karafuto Ainu no Minzoku* (Folklore of the Karafuto Ainu). Miyama Shobo, 1975

Tanigawa, Kenichi. Kita no Minzokushi-Sakhalin / Chishima no Minzoku (Northern Ethnography—Sakhalin / People of the Kuril Islands). San-Ichi Shobo Publishing Inc., 1997

Takabeya, Fukuhei. *Hoppoken no Ie* (Houses of the Northern Regions). Shokokusha Publishing Co., Ltd., 1943

Abashiri City Northern Folkore Cultural Preservation Society. *Uiruta no Kurashi to Mingu* (Uilta Lifestyles and Folkcraft). 1982

The Foundation for Research and Promotion of Ainu Culture (ed.). *Zaidan Hojin Ainu Bunka Fukko / Kenkyu Suishin Kiko Shuzo Mokuroku 7 (Ishida Shuzo Kyuzo Shashin)* (The Foundation for Research and Promotion of Ainu Culture Collection Catalog 7 (Ishida Collection Old Collection Photograph). The Foundation for Research and Promotion of Ainu Culture, 2012

Uilta Society Museum Steering Committee (ed.). *Shiryokan Jakka Duxuni Tenji Sakuhinshu* (Museum Jakka Duxuni Exhibition Works Collection). 2002

Bird, Isabella L. (author), Kobari, Kosai (trans.) *Meiji Shoki no Emishi Tanboki* (Report on Emishi in the Early Meiji Era). Sarorun Shobo, 1977

Munro, N.G. (author), Seligman, B.Z. (ed.), Tetsuro, Komatsu (trans.). *Ainu no Shinko to Sono Gishiki* (Ainu Creed and Cult). Kokushokankokai, 2002

Batchelor, John (author), Tetsuro, Komatsu (trans.). *Ainu no Kurashi to Densho* (Ainu Life and Lore). Hokkaido Publication Project Center, 1999

Shinmyo, Hidehito. *Ainu Fuzokuga no Kenkyu: Kinsei Hokkaido ni Okeru Ainu to Bijutsu* (Study of Ainu Genre Painting: Ainu and Art in Modern Hokkaido). Nakanishi Publishing, 2011

Aoki, Aiko (teller). Nagai, Hiroshi (recorder). Ainu O-san Baa-chan no Upashikuma Densho no Chie no Kiroku (Ainu Midwife Upaskuma: A Record of Traditional Wisdom). Jushinsha, 1998

Segawa, Kiyoko. *Ainu no Konin* (Married Ainu). Miraisha, 1998

Hitchcock, R. (author) Kitakamae, Yasuo (trans.). *Ainujin to Sono Bunka—Meiji Chuki no Ainu no Mura Kara—* (The Ainu People and Their Culture: From the Ainu Villages of the Mid-Meiji Era). Rokko Shuppan, 1990

Landor, A.S. (author). Toda, Sachiko (trans.). *Ezo-chi Isshu Hitori Tabi: Omoide no Ainu Country* (Traveling Alone Around Ezo: Ainu Country as I Remember It). Miraisha, 1985

Kanto or wa yaku sak no arankep sinep ka isam.

Nothing comes from heaven without purpose. —Ainu proverb

ATTUS
(BARK CLOTHING)

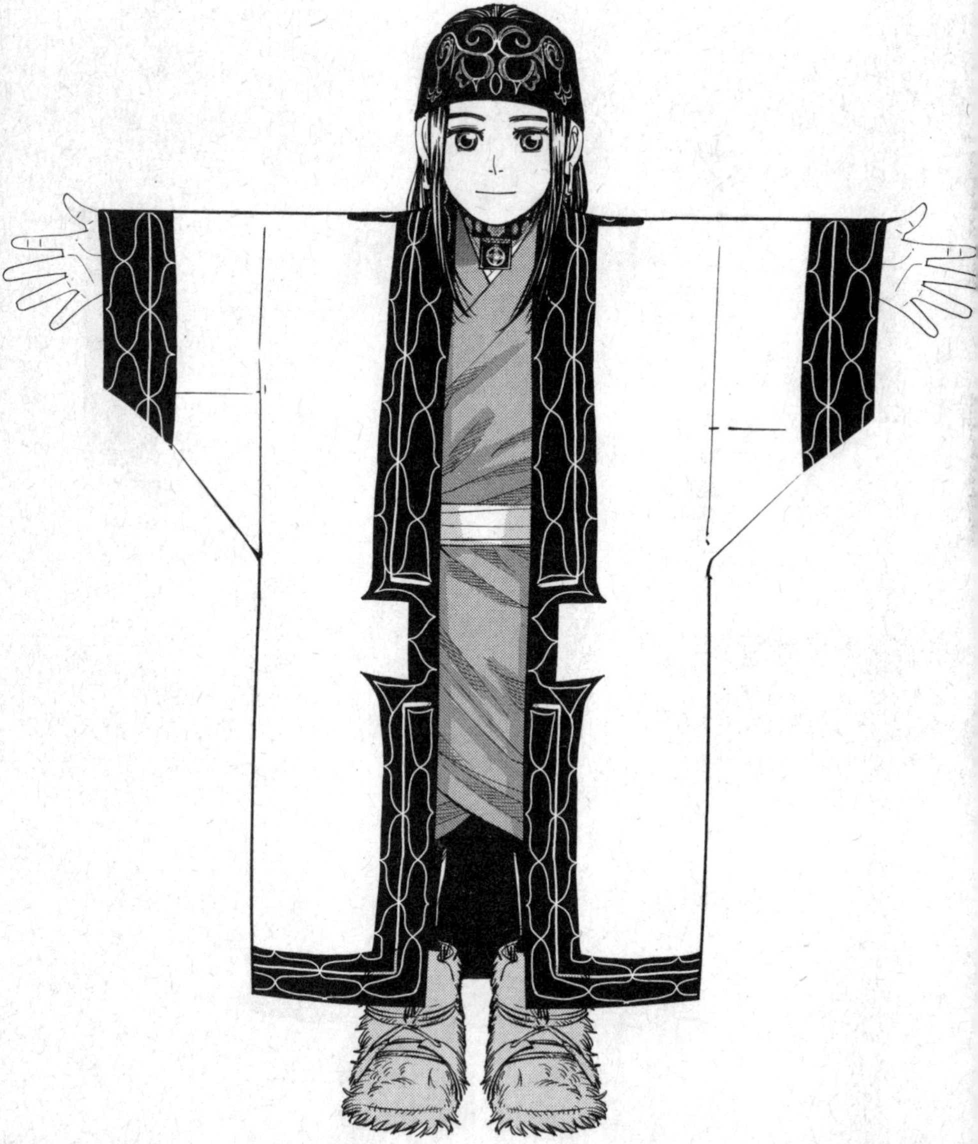

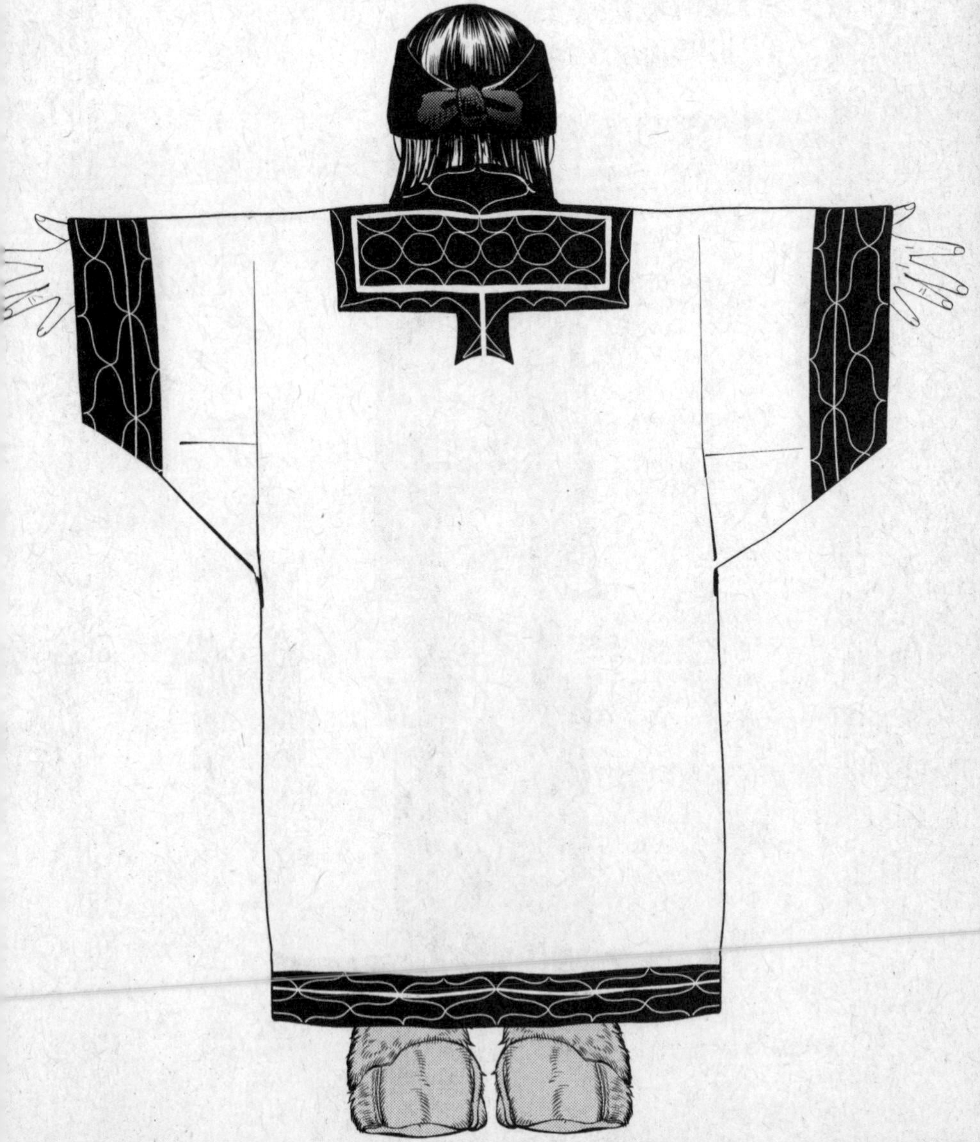

GOLDEN KAMUY

Volume 26
VIZ Signature Edition

Story/Art by Satoru Noda

GOLDEN KAMUY © 2014 by Satoru Noda
All rights reserved.
First published in Japan in 2014 by SHUEISHA Inc., Tokyo.
English translation rights arranged by SHUEISHA Inc.

Translation/John Werry
Touch-Up Art & Lettering/Steve Dutro
Design/Shawn Carrico
Editor/Mike Montesa

Printed in Canada

Published by VIZ Media, LLC
P.O. Box 77010
San Francisco, CA 94107

10 9 8 7 6 5 4 3 2 1
First printing, May 2022

VIZ SIGNATURE

VIZ MEDIA

viz.com

THIS IS THE LAST PAGE.

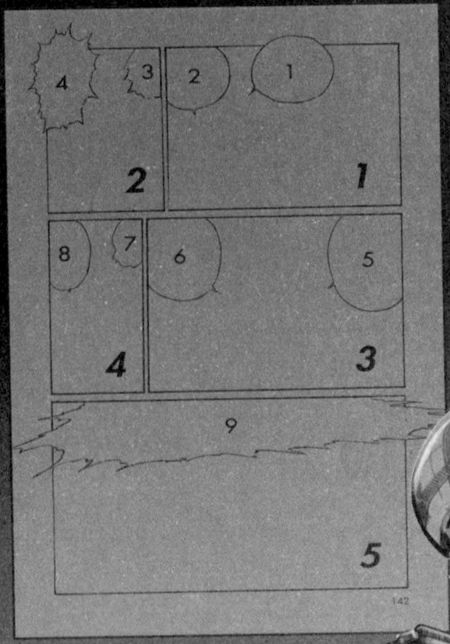
1
1
2
2
3
4
3
5
6
4
7
8
5
9
142

←Follow the action this way.

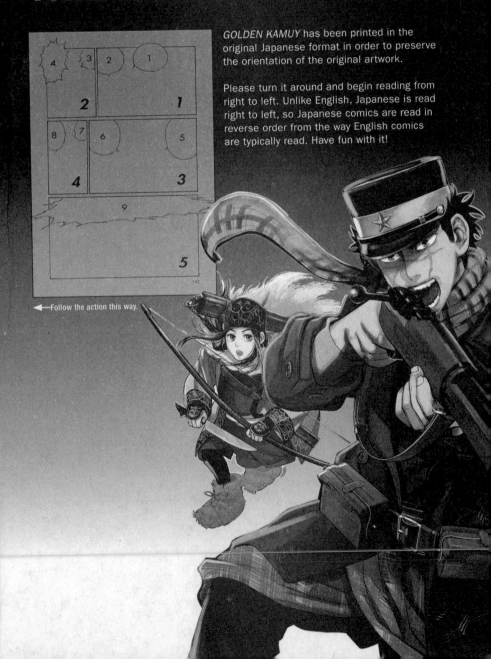

GOLDEN KAMUY has been printed in the original Japanese format in order to preserve the orientation of the original artwork.

Please turn it around and begin reading from right to left. Unlike English, Japanese is read right to left, so Japanese comics are read in reverse order from the way English comics are typically read. Have fun with it!

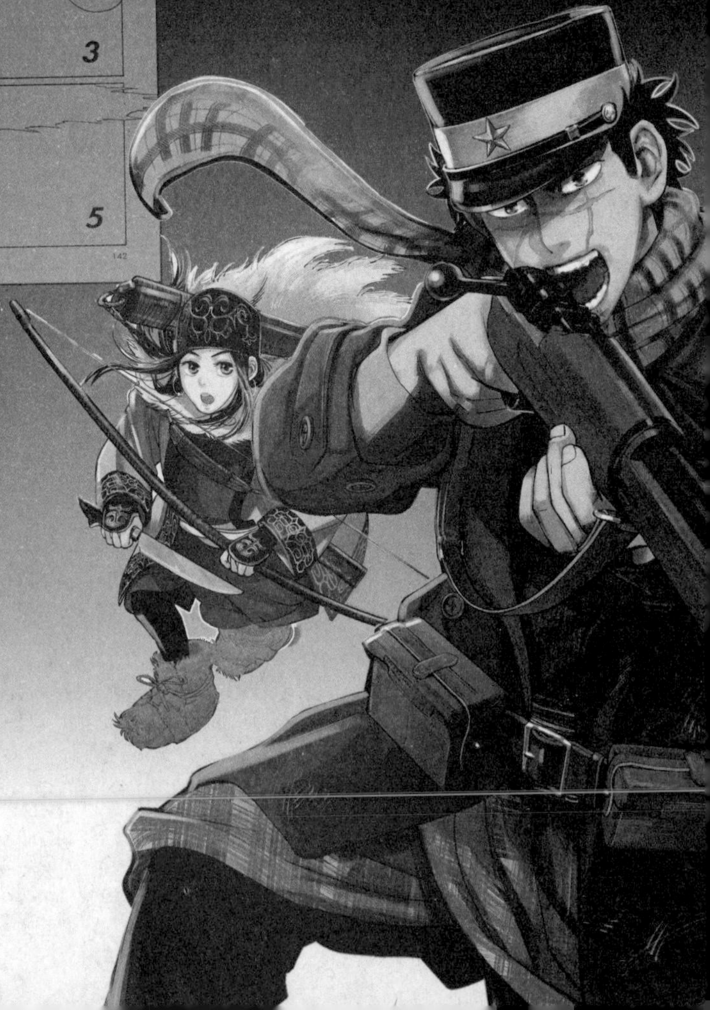